"This anthology asks us to join in the work of reconciliation—not simply the 'restoration of friendly relations' but rather the wrenching, cruciform work of holding together our lives and experience with the largely dehumanizing systems that churn all around us while we summon God to end the oppression of avoidance and fear. It also reintroduces us to the meaning of regeneration—*not* merely a 'radically renewed creation' but rather our God-given ability to self-heal, grow, and recover after violence." —Malinda Elizabeth Berry, PhD, associate professor of theology and ethics, Anabaptist Mennonite Biblical Seminary

"*Resistance* is a magnificently woven book with stories of courage, love, pain and suffering that lifted me up and took me down. If you care about Church and healing the broken places especially caused by clericalism, patriarchy, power, sexual abuse, and exclusion, read *Resistance*. It won't disappoint; it will take your breath away." —Mary Dispenza, international speaker, national representative of Survivors Network of those Abused by Priests (SNAP), and author of *SPLIT: A Child, A Priest, and the Catholic Church*

"This collection of varied voices is an important resource for understanding the nature of power and how to apply Anabaptist peace theology to more effectively confront abusive power and resist evil. Those interested in learning how to stand in solidarity and mutuality with people who experience violence, injustice, abuse, and oppression will be grateful for this significant work." —Carolyn Holderread Heggen, PhD, author of *Sexual Abuse in Christian Homes and Churches* and co-leader of Sister Care International

"Sexual abuse casts a long shadow. Victims struggle with the lasting effects of trauma, often only coming forward to confront their abusers after many years have passed. Where do they find the courage? It may be the wrong question. When the burden

of suffering in silence outweighs the risk of confrontation, there is often no other choice. In this groundbreaking book, Cameron Altaras and Carol Penner have assembled a plurality of voices to speak truth about one of the most pernicious and intractable forms of sexual violence—abuse by clergy within sacred settings, where victims don't just find themselves in conflict with their abusers but may also have to confront institutions that have no interest in justice but wish only to protect their own."
—Clark Strand, co-author of *The Way of the Rose* and author of *Waking Up to the Dark*

Resistance

Resistance

Confronting Violence, Power,
and Abuse within Peace Churches

Edited by Cameron Altaras and Carol Penner

AMBS
INSTITUTE OF MENNONITE STUDIES

Copyright © 2022 by Institute of Mennonite Studies

Anabaptist Mennonite Biblical Seminary
3003 Benham Avenue, Elkhart, IN 46517

To order copies or request information, please call 1-574-296-6239, email ims@ambs.edu, or visit www.ambs.edu/ims.

Library of Congress Cataloging-in-Publication Data

Names: Altaras, Cameron, 1963- editor. | Penner, Carol, 1960- editor.
Title: Resistance : confronting violence, power, and abuse within peace
   churches / edited by Cameron Altaras and Carol Penner.
Description: Elkhart, IN : AMBS, Institute of Mennonite Studies, 2022. |
   Includes bibliographical references. | Summary: "If it's not safe in the
   church, where is it safe? Are churches complicit in supporting racism,
   colonialism, and heterosexism? How do churches excuse sexual violence?
   How are abuses of power justified to protect church institutions? In
   Resistance, storytellers, academics, poets, administrators, students,
   activists, and pastors bring these questions to life through stories of
   personal and systemic violence and betrayals when theology is
   weaponized. Each story is connected to the Anabaptist religious context,
   but the harms suffered and responses to those harms are universally
   applicable. This collection directly confronts violence within historic
   peace churches, providing strategies for using power to resist violence
   and promote transformation"-- Provided by publisher.
Identifiers: LCCN 2022026102 | ISBN 9780936273587 (paperback)
Subjects: LCSH: Peace--Religious aspects--Christianity. |
   Anabaptists--Doctrines. | Historic peace churches--Doctrines.
Classification: LCC BT736.4 .R46 2022 | DDC 261.8/73--dc23/eng/20220711
LC record available at https://lccn.loc.gov/2022026102

International Standard Book Number: 9780936273587

Book design by Mary E. Klassen.

Unless otherwise noted, all Scripture references are from the NRSV.

Contents

Preface

It matters who wrote the words you are reading. Who we are shapes the words on the page.

We, Cameron and Carol, grew up in different branches of the same denomination; we met at graduate school in the 1990s. Our identities are similar, but our experiences and career paths were different. We are both white, middle-class, North American, able-bodied, heterosexual mothers and theologically educated women.

I, Cameron, was born into an Amish Mennonite family. Focusing on abuse of power in my doctoral dissertation made sense when I consider that intellectualizing allowed me distance from emotional injury. My work in the field of business ethics brought me concrete examples of lives affected by systemic and individual abuses. In the throes of a marriage breakup, I came to understand how childhood sexual abuse by my uncle had set me on a path of painful self-discovery. To reclaim the emotional voice, I now write poetry and prose.

I, Carol, grew up in a Mennonite family where abuse was present. I studied theology, eventually doing a doctoral dissertation on Mennonite responses to violence against women. For several years I pastored a church that included a number of men recently released from prison who had sexually offended against children. My later pastoral work included advocacy for survivors of pastoral sexual misconduct. I now teach practical theology at Conrad Grebel University College.

In the era of #MeToo, we reconnected to share our passion for spirituality, for abuse issues, and for theological inquiry. We decided the times called for a book. The book we present now is different than it would have been if we had written or edited it when we first met. It is shaped by hard-won wisdom, long years of study, personal betrayals and abuses, and many stories of people we have supported.

As we planned this book, we came to the conclusion that it would have more integrity if we did not just write about various issues but had the people most affected write for themselves. Neither of us could write in a way that would reveal the truth about what it means to endure and live through all the experiences in this book.

Our desire for integrity in the book led us to seek voices from many different walks of life. We encouraged all the writers to write about their relationship to their topic and through the lens of their experience to tell us why their chapter matters to them and what difference engaging with this topic makes in their lives.

The personal is the political, to borrow from Virginia Woolf. Our individual experiences reflect the larger systems within which we live. The writers here have articulated some of the whys and whats and hows of the truth at the core of their lives. Writing is a courageous act because, in so doing, an author dares to give form to the ambiguity and anguish of their truth.

We recognize that even as we have attempted to be inclusive, we have inevitably excluded. There are more experiences we would have liked to include. Some of the people we invited were unable to commit to the project. Others, who initially committed, had to drop out, causing delays as we sought someone else to speak on their topic. We appreciate the patience of our writers who have waited to see this book in print.

Significantly, two writers wrote excellent chapters, but in the end, fear caused them to withdraw. One person wrote about how difficult it is for women to find their identity in a Conservative Mennonite church. We agreed she could use a pseudonym, but she was afraid her writing would still identify her and lead to the excommunication of her and her family. Another writer was overcome by the pain they had experienced growing up in the Amish church and decided they could have nothing to do with any project addressed to the church. While our book includes many painful stories, we realize that it lacks the stories that are not yet safe to tell.

We hope this book helps to creatively push the edges of current discussions on violence and abuse in the church. We hope that in not only detailing destructive power but also highlighting redemptive power, we can together create communities where differences are honored.

The writers who contributed to this book form a type of community where we stand together, powerfully, against destructive abuses of power. We can testify to the fact that speaking up against abuses of power is personally costly and at times dangerous. We, and our writers, have experienced attacks upon our character, have been bullied, stonewalled, ignored, shamed, ridiculed, threatened, and shunned by family and by those who were once friends— simply because we have spoken up. Nevertheless, we persisted, we resisted, we insisted that the truth be told. Knowing the cost, we are so grateful for everyone who was willing to contribute. And we thank you for reading this.

Thank you to the Institute of Mennonite Studies who believed in this project and worked to create the book you have in your hands and for their diligence in all the fine details.

A final word of thanks to the many teachers who shaped us and helped us think critically about our own experiences. A special thank you to Ruth E. Krall, who mentors us. Ruth was one of the first to break open the topic of abuse in the Mennonite church, and her clear and incisive writing continues to inspire. We acknowledge with gratitude that she is one upon whose shoulders we stand, and without her courage to expose wolves in sheep's clothing, this book would not exist.

Cameron Altaras, Washington, USA
Carol Penner, Ontario, Canada

Introduction

Cameron Altaras and Carol Penner

If it is not safe in the church, where is it safe? Christian churches, founded on the teachings of Jesus and the promise of a loving God, ironically house all types of violence. In this book, we name and address particular examples of how power in the church has been used to hurt others. We also provide strategies for how power can be used to heal and protect people from violence in the church.

It matters that this book is being written at this time and in this place in history. The recent #BlackLivesMatter and #MeToo movements are reverberating through religious communities, provoking self-reflective questions within broader sections of the church: How are churches complicit in racism? How is the church using theology to support patriarchy and excuse violence against women, children, and men with less power? How is the church sanctioning abuses of power in protection of its own institutions? The era in which this book is published is replete with complex situations demanding answers that are not easy to reach.

Even as we write this introduction, the church is watching the weaponization of the Christian faith by insurrectionists unleashing violence on the Capitol of the United States. How does the church respond when white supremacists bow in prayer to a white, blond-haired, blue-eyed Christ figure just prior to committing acts of terrorism? Two chapters speak to the roots of such terrorism in the Doctrine of Discovery, and other chapters build on these insights by pointing to the church's complicity in racist ideology. What current events show us is that our shifting and changing contexts require profound personal and communal inquiry and critique, as together we seek truth-telling throughout society and its many churches.

This book is grounded in real church settings, examining both personal and systemic violence in the lives of the authors. Why reach out to potential contributors and invite them to make themselves vulnerable by putting a piece of themselves on the page? The short answer is because we believe that giving voice to pain and putting experiences into words unmasks what was hidden. It brings truth into our shared space, our commons. When betrayal occurs in the commons, healing must likewise occur in the commons. Each chapter of this book brings an individual component forward, which, when set one next to the other, composes the long answer.

We believe that, just as it is in great art, the more particular, the more universal. We hope that the particulars of the stories shared by our contributors will reach deep truths within readers, no matter what their context is. We take to heart the words of Elisabeth Schüssler Fiorenza, one of the mothers of feminist theology, who declared that feminist critique "must come from within a particular religion" if one hopes to "engender the transformation of . . . societies and religions."[1]

From nonresistance to resistance

This book is situated within the particular religious context of the Anabaptist tradition, which is a Historic Peace Church. Originating in the Radical Reformation of the 1500s, Anabaptists emphasized, among other things, *nonresistance* to violence. Biblical literalists, they took to heart Jesus's words in Matthew 5:39[2]: "But I say to you, Do not resist an evildoer. But if anyone strikes you on the right cheek, turn the other also."

Based upon this biblical precept of not resisting evil, the Anabaptists cultivated the qualities of defenselessness and

---

1 Fiorenza, *Congress of Wo/men*, 5.

2 Unless otherwise noted, Scriptural references throughout this volume are from the New Revised Standard Version (NRSV).

"yieldedness."[3] They are sometimes characterized as pacifists, but, according to Mennonite theologian J. Lawrence Burkholder, "pacifism designates to the modern mind a general attitude toward war as an instrument of national policy. [. . .] With the Anabaptists, nonresistance was a comprehensive Christian ethical attitude [. . .] conceived as a personal approach to the problem of evil."[4] Anabaptists emphasized "the grace to suffer" and "the complete renunciation of defense, whether for one's self, for one's children, or for one's possessions."[5] Faith in God, for the Anabaptists, "enables the Christian to absorb evil and even to lose everything for the sake of Christ."[6] This "peace principle," writes Burkholder, "is absolute nonresistance."[7]

Such an absolute understanding of not resisting evil in its many forms has enormous implications for those under the Anabaptist umbrella on the receiving end of violence, whether personal or systemic, especially since this principle applies "to all areas in which coercion is the dominating principle."[8] We understand the use of the term coercion to refer to any instance where one imposes one's will upon another, whether that be via force, a threat, manipulation, or a passive-aggressive word or act.

We use *resistance* in our title to pay tribute to the power of survivors of evil and immoral acts of violence, abuse, and betrayal. It is not a rejection of nonresistance but a hope of creative interaction with the tradition. *Nonresistance* often conjures up an image of an absence of power. According to Burkholder, the use of the word in its "negative form is somewhat unfortunate since it fails

---

3   The term *yieldedness* is a translation of the German word *Gelassenheit*, which for early Anabaptists signified "an inner conquest of the will to power and existence. It is what it means to 'lose one's life' for Christ." J. L. Burkholder, *Mennonite Ethics*, 274.

4   J. L. Burkholder, *Mennonite Ethics*, 273.

5   J. L. Burkholder, *Mennonite Ethics*, 274, 271.

6   J. L. Burkholder, *Mennonite Ethics*, 271.

7   J. L. Burkholder, *Mennonite Ethics*, 176.

8   J. L. Burkholder, *Mennonite Ethics*, 177.

to convey the concept of the dynamic positive outpouring of love, which certainly must be regarded as the motivating power of the practice of nonresistance."[9] What might it mean, therefore, to practice love for one's enemy and at the same time resist evil and seek healing for those affected by the resultant harm?

To get at possible answers, we set for ourselves the task of bringing to the Anabaptist commons examples of ways in which the many forms of evil and violence have caused, sanctioned, and justified harm. We want to begin to imagine ways in which resistance could occur and at the same time honor the Anabaptist theology that has shaped us. The task of doing so in the spirit of being truthful to possible ways of transforming and healing hearts and lives of real people underlined for us as editors that we needed to engage in what Schüssler Fiorenza describes as "a much closer collaboration among scholars and ministers or religious leaders and community builders."[10]

This book is the product of such a collaboration, and the resultant theological project is the richer for it. Diverse voices with diverse experiences bring to light understandings that none of us could reach on our own. The authors of this book are storytellers, academics, poets, survivors, administrators, students, activists, and pastors, each connected to the Anabaptist religious context. We invited them to write about the violence they have experienced in the Anabaptist tradition of which they are a part. Several branches of the Anabaptist family are represented: Mennonite, Conservative Mennonite, and Amish, mostly from Canada and the United States, with a few international voices (the Netherlands, Germany, and Congo).

We acknowledge that all of our North American writers are situated on the traditional territories of the Indigenous Peoples who lived on this land for thousands of years. We decided to place the voices that address colonialism and racism at the beginning of

9 J. L. Burkholder, *Mennonite Ethics*, 153.

10 Fiorenza, *Congress of Wo/men*, 26.

our book to signify the foundational injustices on which so much North American Mennonite theology is based.

Kelly Brown Douglas, in her book *Stand Your Ground: Black Bodies and the Justice of God*, talks about "sacred canopies" or narratives that both legitimize social-cultural violence against black bodies and shelter it from view. These narratives are expressed in ideological, theological, legal, and political terms.[11] The early chapters in our book describe how Anabaptists create and support these colonial and racist sacred canopies, causing so much harm to Indigenous Peoples, Black People, and all people of color.

Violence against the LGBTQ+ community is also fronted in part 1 to point to the foundational discrimination and oppression they face. Sacred canopies of heterosexism are woven in the Anabaptist community.

Anabaptist theology has also created sacred canopies that support and legitimize patriarchy. Our writers in part 2 address how Anabaptist theology supported the sexual violence and abuse they faced in their homes, on the streets, and in churches. It is ironic that a movement that began by challenging the established church developed a theology that encouraged unquestioning submission to male authority. It is no coincidence that so many Anabaptists in North America (the Amish and Conservative Mennonites) cling to patriarchal ecclesiastical and social organizations long after much of the rest of the Christian church has embraced the egalitarian insights of twentieth-century feminism. Submission to God-given authority and suffering silently are values imbedded deep in the Anabaptist psyche shaped by a "doctrine of nonresistance";[12] such qualities are not conducive to changing the social order.

One corner of the Anabaptist sacred canopy is woven of martyr stories. Early Anabaptists faced persecution, and rather than fight back, they practiced nonresistance, even if it led to death. Remarkably, four different authors in this collection independent-

---

11 Douglas, *Stand Your Ground*, 4.

12 J. L. Burkholder, *Mennonite Ethics*, 154.

ly brought up the story of Dirk Willems—an Anabaptist martyr whose story is celebrated as an example of nonresistance. Yet, for women who have suffered patriarchal violence, this martyrology is a canopy that legitimizes suffering and conceals the option of faithful resistance to violence.

Chapter summaries

Throughout the book, the chapters illustrate how different systems of violence overlap, with some people suffering under multiple webs of oppression. This intersectionality points to the oppression found in the church today. The betrayals collected in this volume all have roots in personal experiences in the Anabaptist church. In ways particular to each story, the theology of a historical peace church was weaponized in the hands of the perpetrators of betrayal.

The first four chapters show how Anabaptists have used their power in the service of colonialism and the attempted destruction of Indigenous Peoples. They offer reinterpretations of our history, both personal and institutional.

We begin with a chapter by Sarah Augustine that reveals the power of the ideology of the Doctrine of Discovery and the cost to Indigenous lives as governments and the church have implemented their programs of colonization, displacement, and eradication of Indigenous Peoples. Augustine explains how these practices of domination and greed are not only a matter of history but continue to be implemented in the twenty-first century. The World Council of Churches (WCC) called for member churches to repudiate this doctrine; Augustine helped to draft the WCC's statement and mobilize an Anabaptist response. Her chapter shows parallels between the ways power is shared and mobilized in Anabaptist and Indigenous communities.

Amanda K Gross next outlines how reference to martyrdom stories have clouded the Anabaptist connection to American Exceptionalism. Abusive power dynamics are an integral part of the Mennonite story, through agricultural colonization of native land in the Americas. Gross uses the framework of collective trauma healing to reinterpret the Mennonite story, looking for redemptive theological directions where we use our power for justice rather than exploitation.

Lydia Neufeld Harder, with Ingrid Bettina Wolfear, tells the story of adoption of an Indigenous toddler by a white Mennonite family in the context of the Canadian government sponsored "Sixties Scoop." The daughter talks about blood memory, racism, and discovering her Indigenous roots. The mother talks about her gradual realization of how her family was implicated in a racist agenda. Their intermingled stories present a testament to the pain of abuse of power and the strength of Indigenous identity.

Jennifer Delanty describes the actions her congregation has taken against racism and the history of colonialism. She recounts how this largely white congregation unpacked its power and privilege and reputed the Doctrine of Discovery in their effort to be truer to their Anabaptist values. Delanty acknowledges the complexities and uncertainties of coming to terms with their perceptions of history shaped by white supremacy. Among their concrete efforts, this congregation has found ways to stand alongside the marginalized in their neighborhood and an Indigenous tribe in Suriname, exploited by mining companies.

The next two chapters deepen the discussion of racism and the church. Regina Shands Stoltzfus unveils how white supremacy pervades America, including the segregation of neighborhoods and schools. She discusses the socialization process which undergirds how society shapes itself around racist practices and how powerful mythologies are perpetuated by those who benefit from them. Racism continues because histories are hidden or not believed. Shands Stolzfus calls on churches to deconstruct how their own institutions have and continue to perpetuate and support systemic racism against Black and brown communities.

Jenny Castro shares the challenges organizations in the church face when confronting systemic racism. The Women in Leadership project, which Castro directed in her position as its coordinator in the Mennonite Church USA, was structured so that women of color had the balance of power and could plan conferences that did not center white women. Even here, the racism of white women made it difficult for women of color. Castro outlines strategies taken to confront this and create safer spaces for marginalized groups, including LGBTQ+ people.

The next four chapters highlight the power of heterosexism in the church. Pieter Niemeyer outlines how dominant cultures have used their power to erase LGBTQ+ people. Niemeyer, a former Mennonite pastor, claims his place as a gay Christian man, discussing his personal coming out story in a non-affirming church and how it cost him personally and professionally. While Scripture has been weaponized to erase and punish queer people, Niemeyer describes the hope he sees for caring communities that address injustice.

Steph Chandler Burns reflects on how difficult it is for an LGBTQ+ person on the margins of the church to find their voice in the church. Themes of power surface repeatedly throughout her prose and poetry, both the power congregations use to silence and marginalize and the power of queer people to create safer spaces.

Part 1 concludes with two reflections on Mennonite Church USA conventions. Jennifer Delanty's poem "Phoenix 2013" is a pointed meditation on power, how the church wields it, who benefits, and who is harmed. Bradley Siebert then explores the power dynamics of discernment practices in the church regarding inclusion of LGBTQ+ people. Analyzing the 2015 convention in Kansas City, Siebert reveals practices in the church that are not egalitarian and peaceful and how even the singing of hymns has been weaponized. In spite of ongoing opposition, the queer community within the Mennonite Church continues their advocacy and support of each other.

In part 2, we look at abuses that coexist and overlap with the systemic abuse of colonialism, racism, and heterosexism. Cameron Altaras opens this part by discussing the binary lens of either/or and how the patriarchal view of the world shaped Scripture, its interpretation, and the Christian tradition. She describes how such a worldview affected her life and the lives of her female

Amish ancestors. Altaras concludes with a discussion of the power of language to shatter the binaries we inherit and move patriarchal tectonic plates.

Torah Bontrager writes of her own harrowing escape from a tortured childhood of abuse. Bontrager focuses on how Amish children are deprived of the same education as other children in the United States, and how this makes them vulnerable to sexual assault. Narratives about the Amish hold power in society, which perpetuates abuses of children while abusers face few consequences.

The author of the poem "What Is Abused Authority?" uses the pseudonym Keturah C. Martin. Writing about escape from a life of abuse in a Conservative Mennonite context, Martin vividly portrays how authority is abused.

Jeanette Harder is a Mennonite social worker and professor who works with the Amish. In her chapter, she acknowledges that lack of education (especially about sexuality), the patriarchy of the community, and the isolation of children from outsiders leave children vulnerable to abuse. Indicating that a wide diversity exists among the Amish communities across North America, she suggests that among them there are strong and loving communities who are slowly addressing the problem of child abuse.

In her poem "Artemis Patiently Waits," Cameron Altaras imagines how women can take the reins to empower themselves in Amish communities.

Ruth Krall next offers an analysis of authority and power in the Mennonite church. She outlines the effects of affinity violence (violence by someone you know) not just on the individual but also on the community. Mennonite communities too often ignore or excuse affinity violence and the trust that it shatters. Indeed, asserts Krall, their theology leaves them ill equipped to handle it. This leads to a second and often more severe institutional revictimization. Krall concludes with hopeful directions using the term "bearing witness."

Sylvia Klauser continues the discussion of affinity violence by describing her own experiences of abuse growing up in a

Mennonite family in what she refers to as "the tail-end of" post-World War II–era Germany. Patriarchal structures and repressed pain characterize many Anabaptist communities. She offers four themes for future research and action.

Sarah Bixler next describes the history and ideology behind the relatively recent mandate of headcoverings for women in the Mennonite context. She charts the rise of this late nineteenth-century patriarchal practice from a custom to an ordinance and its eventual demise in some Anabaptist communities. The traumatic effects of the headcovering linger on, however, and affect even subsequent generations of women no longer required to wear it.

Kimberly Schmidt takes on Dirk Willems, the most popular Mennonite martyr, outlining his importance to Mennonite ideology and setting the story in the context of her own abusive marital relationship. In a culture where men have the power to abuse women, she describes how the narrative of Willems serves to perpetuate abuse. Schmidt provides an alternate early Anabaptist story of Helene Von Freyburg as a much healthier model.

Lisa Schirch next outlines the triple threat that women who are abused in Mennonites institutions face: they are harmed by their abuser, they are told to be silent by church authorities, and, if they speak out, they are shunned by their community. Schirch identifies common patterns in this patriarchal theology and culture and argues that these must be addressed in order for us to find paths for restitution, accountability and healing.

Cameron Altaras then recounts the dynamics of pastoral abuse. She relates the impact of this type of abuse on every aspect of life. The chapter discusses moral injury, the power of anger, and the strength of community as a healing environment.

Drawing on the work of philosopher Hannah Arendt and using practical examples, Catherine Thiel Lee provides an analysis of power, illuminating the power of survivors and the community. She concludes that when we speak and act together, there is so much we can do to change the tides of power among us.

Julia Spicher Kasdorf tells a story of abuse and recounts the cost of surviving in her poem "A Pass."

David Martin gives an insider look at how abuse is adjudicated in institutional settings. Drawing on his experiences as a denominational leader, Martin details lessons he learned dealing with issues of pastoral sexual misconduct. Challenged by the prevailing culture of denial of clergy sexual abuse even as survivors of such abuse stood before him, Martin came to understand how the healing paths of those victimized would either be helped or hindered depending on how he wielded the power of his position. The actions taken by Martin, his staff, and his board have brought forward a model of a survivor-affirming church.

Bryan Born provides a case study of how to deal transparently with historical sexual misconduct. He offers the challenge of a survivor who came forward decades after she had been abused by a professor and the response of the church-affiliated college of which Born was the President as yet another healing model for how professional sexual misconduct can be addressed in church institutions.

From the experiences of those who addressed sexual abuse in institutional settings, we turn to several chapters featuring survivors' stories of sexual abuse and those who have walked along beside them. We begin with personal experience of sexual abuse as related in five poems by Elizabeth Wenger.

Sylvia Shirk and Rev. SWANA then present an intercontinental dialogue about sexual misconduct in the church. The writers examine the roots and consequences of misconduct in their settings and cultures, finding similarities and differences between churches in Africa and North America. Power abuse can be confronted, they conclude. By dismantling structures that oppress, healing is possible.

Brenda Gerber presents a view into another survivor's story. Gerber's visceral words expose the power of fear and pain, with abusers, families, and institutions all closing in against the survivor. She also speaks of the power of faith in God and how healing comes inch by inch in spite of all the forces arrayed against it.

Elsie Goerzen tells two harrowing stories of intimate partner abuse. She offers a first-hand account of how faith communities put the survivor in danger by siding with the abuser. As one who has walked with and supported many caught in spirals of abuse, Goerzen provides practical advice for churches that want to support survivors on their healing journey. Church programs can unmask abusive power and model new ways of living.

Joanne Gallardo shares her personal story of assault, fear, anger, and empowerment, grappling with Anabaptist theology, love of enemies, and love of self. The concept of forgiveness becomes real in the lived reality of her story.

Johannes van der Meer reflects on how forgiveness works in community. Drawing on the resource of Jewish rabbinical writing and his experience as a pastor in the Netherlands, van der Meer looks at the abuse of power and the relationship between repentance, forgiveness, and reconciliation. He calls for solidarity with victims and a victim-centered approach to forgiveness.

Carol Penner provides a short history of why we do or do not talk about abuse in church. Addressing head on the nefarious power of silence, she gives practical examples of how mentioning abuse in worship settings can be transformative for both survivors and those who abuse. The words we choose to use in worship can bring healing and hope to those caught in webs of abuse.

When institutions are silent in the face of abuse, it is an abuse of their power. In his poem and reflection "My Tradition," Jerry Holsopple expands the theme of silence to include silencing. With the succinct imagery poetry affords, he offers observations about Anabaptist history and theology and the treatment of people who are abused.

Kimberly Penner pulls together several themes around which this book is built. This final chapter explains how Mennonite theology has too often sanctioned patriarchal power and viewed the human body in negative terms. Drawing on the work of Mennonite feminist theologians, she discusses commitments to obedience and submission and advocates a theology of shared power. Commitment to nonviolence needs to take into account the nuances of unequal power relationships, she argues. Otherwise there is a risk of perpetuating the abusive status quo.

Conclusion

As editors, we honor—and are in awe of—the risks our contributors have dared to take in entrusting us with their words, which we now bring to the community of readers. Because each of the chapters in this book speaks to an injury that occurred in the context of the Anabaptist church—a community shaped by a theology of peace—we, in turn, must dare to look at how our theology and interpretations of it have sanctioned violence and betrayal. We invite readers to join with us as we address this need head on and face the reality of the destructive power of violence and abuse in the concrete and particular stories of individuals and groups in the church. We hope that the paths forward proposed in this book can move us beyond the assumed ways we are in relationship to a place of safety, where differences are honored.

That there is violence in Anabaptist churches and communities does not make Anabaptists unique. There is violence in every religious organization. What is notable is the irony that Anabaptists claim to be peaceful people, who worship in a religious tradition that is part of the Historic Peace Church. We have faith that directly addressing examples that are not peaceful in this particular corner of the church will help in the larger project of addressing violence in the church universal.

Part 1

1

The Doctrine of Discovery and the Anabaptist Coalition to Dismantle It

Sarah Augustine

My grandmother was a Tewa woman, from a small Pueblo in what is now called Northern New Mexico. When I talk about myself and where I am from, I orient myself in relation to her. I never lived on the Pueblo where she lived, and I never knew my grandmother. Her son, my father, grew up in Denver; I grew up in Albuquerque. Like generations of Indigenous Peoples in the United States, we were separated from our homeland and our people as a matter of US policy toward Native Americans. But like my grandmother, I am an Indigenous Woman.

Many ask what motivated me to involve myself with the Doctrine of Discovery and the movement to dismantle it. I think the short answer is that it directly impacts me—it is a major force that has shaped, and continues to shape, my life. The longer answer is that I believe it is my responsibility to care for other Indigenous Peoples, on behalf of a grandmother I never knew, who was separated from her baby son more than seventy-five years ago. In this chapter I explain what the Doctrine of Discovery is using my own experiences of the places and people that are hurt by it now.

The Doctrine of Discovery and the World Council of Churches

In February 2012, in response to a request from the World Council of Churches (WCC) Indigenous Desk, I co-authored with Robert Miller, Steven Newcomb, and John Diefenbaker-Krall the "Statement on the Doctrine of Discovery and its Enduring Impact on Indigenous Peoples."[1] Thus began a long journey of discovery for me, discovery of a body of law and policy that would set the pattern for how the European explorers were to claim new lands for European empires by conquering those who already lived there. This pattern of empire domination continues to shape policies even in the twenty-first century.

Fifteenth century church documents—the *Dum Diversas* (1452) and *Romanus Pontifex* (1455)—"called for non-Christian peoples to be invaded, captured, vanquished, subdued, reduced to perpetual slavery and to have their possessions and property seized by Christian monarchs."[2] These documents are at the root of a principle of international law which has come to be known as The Doctrine of Discovery and has guided hundreds of years of legal decisions and laws that invalidate and ignore the rights, sovereignty, and humanity of Indigenous Peoples around the world. Thus, the Doctrine of Discovery is not just an abstract idea. It is very plainly a system of laws and policies that advantage some people and disadvantage others.

Our 2012 Statement brought to the attention of the WCC Executive Council the fact that "the ways of life, identities, well-being and very existence of Indigenous People are threatened by the continuing effects of colonization and national policies, regulations and laws that attempt to force them to assimilate into the cultures of majoritarian societies. A fundamental historical basis and legal precedent for these policies and laws is the Doctrine of Discovery, the idea that Christians enjoy a moral and legal right based solely on their religious identity to invade and seize indigenous lands and to dominate Indigenous Peoples."

---

1 Augustine, Diefenbaker-Krall, Miller, et al, "Statement."
2 Augustine, Diefenbaker-Krall, Miller, et al, "Statement."

We pointed out that the "patterns of domination and oppression that continue to afflict Indigenous Peoples today throughout the world are found in numerous historical documents such as Papal Bulls, Royal Charters and court rulings. . . . Collectively, these and other concepts form a paradigm or pattern of domination that is still being used against Indigenous Peoples."[3]

Christopher Columbus, for example, under the direction of the Spanish Crown, was instructed to "discover and conquer," "subdue," and "acquire" distant lands, and John Cabot was given similar direction by the British Crown. North and South America were colonized according to this pattern, as were Australia and New Zealand. Indigenous Peoples were given a bleak choice: either submit to the Crown and Christianity or suffer attack, enslavement, and death. Although these documents directing European explorers were written more than 500 years ago, in the 2012 statement we articulated that "the current situation of Indigenous Peoples around the world is the result of a linear programme of 'legal' precedent, originating with the Doctrine of Discovery and codified in contemporary national laws and policies. . . . The Doctrine remains the law in various ways in almost all settler societies around the world today."[4]

Our Statement spelled out specifically that the WCC Executive Committee:

A. Expresses solidarity with the Indigenous Peoples of the world and supports the rights of Indigenous Peoples
. . .;

B. Denounces the Doctrine of Discovery as fundamentally opposed to the gospel of Jesus Christ and as a violation of the inherent human rights . . .;

C. Urges various governments in the world to dismantle the legal structures and policies based on the Doctrine of Discovery and dominance . . .;

---

3 Augustine, Diefenbaker-Krall, Miller, et al, "Statement.

4 Augustine, Diefenbaker-Krall, Miller, et al, "Statement.

D. Affirms its conviction and commitment that Indigenous Peoples be assisted in their struggle to ... exercise their right to self-determination and self-governance;

E. Requests the governments and states of the world to ensure that their policies, regulations and laws that affect Indigenous Peoples comply with international conventions ... ;

F. Calls on each WCC member church to reflect upon its own national and church history and to encourage all member[s] ... to seek a greater understanding of the issues facing Indigenous Peoples, to support Indigenous Peoples in their ongoing efforts to exercise their inherent sovereignty and fundamental human rights ... ;

G. Encourages WCC member churches to support the continued development of theological reflections by Indigenous Peoples which promote indigenous visions of full, good and abundant life and which strengthen their own spiritual and theological reflections."[5]

Maria Chavez, the Indigenous Bolivian theologian and organizer who staffed the Indigenous Desk at the WCC in 2011, sent out a plea to member churches, asking them to encourage the WCC to repudiate the Doctrine of Discovery. Her plea was forwarded to me by a colleague, Doug Hostetter, then the Mennonite Central Committee representative to the United Nations. I reached out to Maria, offering to help. In our first skype conversation, she told me I was the only person of the 350 WCC member churches who responded. She urged me to draft a statement and bring it to the WCC. I wrote to theologians and called others, asking for help. When no help was forthcoming, I reached out to Robert Miller, a Native legal scholar and expert on the Doctrine of Discovery. Shortly after he published *Native America, Discovered and Conquered*, I met him at a book signing on the reservation where I live. He in turn recruited John Diefenbaker-Krall, who had written the

5 Augustine, Diefenbaker-Krall, Miller, et al, "Statement."

first repudiation statement on behalf the Episcopal Church, and Steve Newcomb, a Native history scholar and expert on the Doctrine of Discovery. The statement took many months of work for each of the authors. Each of us engaged in extensive research and met via teleconference every few weeks. Each member of the team brought specific expertise to our bi-monthly conference calls for often hours-long discussion and revision. In addition to the writing, I also spent many months lobbying and organizing to bring it to the attention of the WCC Executive Committee. Maria encouraged me all the way. I often felt I was not qualified to convene the calls, author the statement, or call the largest Protestant church body on earth to change course. Maria urged me, "If not you, then who? You answered the call. You can do it." Ultimately, it took the collaboration of Indigenous people around the world to write the statement and get it before the executive committee. I met many amazing people. One Indigenous man I knew by phone but had never met even flew to a nearby city to get the statement in the hands of an executive committee member. In the end we were successful; they adopted the statement with no significant changes. Sadly, Maria, my stalwart friend and support, died of cancer before the statement was adopted.

The question then was how to get action to be taken: action that would bring about the changes we articulated were necessary; action that, in short, would dismantle the Doctrine of Discovery. I was then to learn that the adoption of this statement would result only in the following action: the WCC would post the statement on their website. I worked on the statement because I was asked to and because I was appealing to the largest body of Christians I could find, petitioning them to stand with Indigenous Peoples globally in resistance to the oppression that binds us, that dehumanizes us. What I had hoped for was an institutional commitment to stand up to the powers that continue to violate our rights as human beings. Posting a statement on the website meant only that the most representative church body on earth understands what the Doctrine of Discovery is and what it does, and it is choosing to remain silent with full knowledge. It felt like a slap in the face—this institution understands what is happening to us and is choosing to do nothing about it.

For those of us who claim to be Christian, there is an irony to the fact that it is on a three-legged Christian theological stool which the Doctrine of Discovery stands:

1. The covenant between God and Israel regarding the Promised Land. The Israelites were an oppressed people, whom God brought out of Egypt and instructed to conquer and slaughter the Canaanites who were living in what was to be the land promised to the children of Israel. With the coming of Christ, Christians believe that God's covenant is now with the Church. Thus, the church of the fifteenth century believed it was their God-given right to go to all lands and conquer those who were there and claim the land as Christian land.

2. The Divine Mandate and Divine Right of Kings of Romans 13. Here Paul instructs Christians to submit to authorities because all authorities have been established by God.

3. The Great Commission of Matthew 28: 19–20. Here Jesus instructs Christians to go into all the world and make disciples of all nations.

Passages from the Bible have thus been used to establish and justify these documents for discovery of new land. However, to conquer and kill and completely ignore the human rights of those who are Indigenous to that land flies completely in the face of the teachings of Jesus, who called us to love our neighbor as ourselves, to care for the meek and the sick, the orphan and the widow. And for those who are in the Anabaptist tradition, the Doctrine of Discovery is completely contrary to the theological stance of our peace church tradition.

Taking action

I began working on behalf of the Indigenous Peoples of the Guyana Shield (Suriname, French Guyana, and northern Brazil) in 2004. The gold mining industry in this small region dumps 200 tons of mercury into the food web each year. This is the mercury that is reported; it is likely that much more is released in practice. Gold mining is taking place on the traditional lands of Indigenous Peoples. The impact on them is profound. Mercury impacts the nervous system and has the greatest impact on fetuses in-utero and on small children. It results in still births and profound birth defects since mercury attacks the developing brain and spinal column. In the very least, it diminishes the neurological potential of developing fetuses and small children. It has impacts on older children and adults as well, which include neurological impacts of every kind—blindness, inability to walk, tremors, depression, and all types of neurological disturbances.

I have been working among communities in this region for fifteen years and I have seen up close the impact of the Doctrine of Discovery: Indigenous people in this region have no land rights since the title to their lands "belonged" to the European states that "discovered" them and was duly passed to national states where independence was eventually achieved; the exception is French Guyana, which remains a colony of France.

Development programs have been devised and executed during my time in relationship with the Indigenous Peoples of this region, and the Suriname Land Management Program is the one I know the most about. Like the allotment act in the United States, it was devised to ensure all lands would be owned by someone and to sort out who owned what. This economic development program, which is now enshrined in Suriname's national policy and which was devised to build the infrastructure for mining, is detrimental to the Indigenous Peoples who live in Suriname. The Indigenous Peoples I represent have no agency over what occurs on their lands, and mining is displacing and killing them.

As an Indigenous woman, it is clear to me that the program of colonization and displacement is current and ongoing. What I often hear from the descendants of settlers is: "That was so long ago; what can we do about it now?" The global policy of domination and displacement, the targeting and displacement and wholesale eradication of Indigenous Peoples is ongoing and legal. It is ongoing in North America as we see with the pipelines being built across the Midwest; with coal, gas, and uranium mining on Indigenous lands; in the removal of the rights of Indigenous Peoples to their economies and traditional hunting and fishing lands; and in removal of environmental protection for lands and waters they depend on for food and shelter. In the United States, there is an effort now to remove the Indian Child Welfare Act that was put in place in 1975 to cease the removal of Indigenous Children from their lands and Peoples.

The plight of Indigenous Peoples globally is urgent. There are no reservations or reserves, treaties or rights for most Indigenous Peoples in the world. As I have allied with Indigenous Peoples in Central and South America, Asia, and the Pacific, I have seen wholesale removal of communities from their lands in service to extractive industry for wealthy nations. As someone who has felt the impact of the Doctrine of Discovery personally in my life, it is my responsibility to stand with my brothers and sisters globally who suffer from the same structures of domination and greed.

Economic development programs

The purpose of economic development from the perspective of powerful nations—what we broadly term international aid—is (1) to extract resources cheaply and efficiently, at a profit, from less developed nations and (2) to ensure national security for the nations providing aid. Simply, the purpose of international development is to protect the interests of powerful nations providing this "aid."

"Aid" is provided with strings attached, most often in the form of loans. When the International Monetary Fund (IMF), the World Bank, and regional development banks devise an aid package, they lend money backed by securities—that is, they strive to protect their investments with collateral of value the borrowing country has to offer: most often land and raw materials. Development programs are most often geared toward monetizing these raw resources—that is, making them commodities that can be bought and sold. Development programs provide infrastructure to extract raw resources and get them to market; most often these resources are processed in facilities that add value elsewhere. For example, if the country receiving aid has minerals as a raw resource of interest, the ore will be exported on ships and refined somewhere else so that the countries making the investment benefit most from the ore's extraction. If the resource being extracted is labor, then the investing agency will develop tax-free international zones, or free trade zones, where workers can provide labor without having to comply with the labor laws of the country receiving "aid." Often in order for aid to be administered, the country borrowing money must revise national policies, such as undermining or weakening environmental, labor, and other laws that are viewed by the lender as barriers to free trade.

Economic development programs are detrimental to Indigenous and vulnerable peoples. It is often their land that is offered as security against development loans. Development programs do not reduce poverty for the bottom 20 percent of the population in the country being aided but rather reduce well-being and result in displacement, disease, and death for the most vulnerable.

The consequences of globalization that converts land and resources held in common by people living subsistence lifestyles into private ownership reduces poverty when measured in terms of per capita GDP. But it creates a crisis for people in communities that become disassociated, impoverished, and alienated and whose health status is reduced to unacceptable lows when measured in terms of death, disease, disability, and a burgeoning rate of suicide. Life expectancy in affected communities is a result of the assimilation process inherent to economic development.

The development agencies know this. They have mountains of data and internal reports that explain that development programs damage the most vulnerable people. They have determined that this is an acceptable cost of doing business.

What results is a slow-moving crisis of death by attrition among marginalized communities living in extreme poverty. This, in turn, creates a fast-moving crisis on a global scale. The reason: physical security and political security go together.

The health of minority populations is a requisite for sustained human development and national security. Those who feel insecure about their survival needs have a fundamentally different outlook and political behavior from those who feel secure. A key task in choosing a solution to these paired crises is defining causes and discerning the difference between the crisis and its aftermath. The health crisis among vulnerable and marginalized people is the aftermath of economic development. At the same time, it is the cause of serious social and political problems. This is the link between economic development programs and violence. Addressing the health crisis as a factor that contributes to political unrest is an essential requirement not only for improving health and sustaining human development but also for enhancing national security.

The health and human rights issues caused by projects like the *Integration of the Regional Infrastructure in South America* (IIRSA) or the *Suriname Land Management Project* (SLMP) demand immediate action. The release of sixty tons of mercury from small-scale gold mines in the Guiana region annually will eventually be recognized as an environmental disaster comparable to other global disasters such as the Minamata disaster in Japan (mercury contamination in Japan in the 1950s), the Bhopal tragedy (gas leak in India in 1984), Thalidomide scandal (pharmaceutical birth defects in the 1960's), and the Fukushima Daiichi disaster (nuclear meltdown in 2011).

An Anabaptist response to the Doctrine of Discovery

As an Anabaptist, I value three core traditions: responding to the spirit, discipleship (*Nachfolge*), and co-discernment (*Gelassenheit*). I have found that Indigenous spirituality shares these three primary features with Anabaptist theology.[6]

First, both traditions affirm the importance of spirit in discernment, or forming an understanding of how we must live. The oral tradition of Indigenous Peoples is shared over and over again,

---

6 For a more complete explanation of how I integrate both my Indigenous tradition and my Anabaptist faith, see Augustine, "Negotiating," 105–115.

where all members of a community are free to interpret sacred stories from their point of view. The opportunity to experience spirit is available to all. Stories are interpreted and reinterpreted according to life stage and context, not necessarily according to one's status or expertise. Likewise, Anabaptists have proclaimed that anyone who has received the Holy Spirit is qualified to interpret Scripture, regardless of rank or education.

Responding to the Spirit means that I will go where I am sent, I will carry the message that is my charge, no matter how difficult it is for me to say it or how difficult it may be to hear it. I experience the movement of the Spirit in two ways: the first is in the voices of those who ask me for help. When I come in contact with a person in severe need, who calls on me directly, I receive this as a direct call from the Creator. In my understanding, this is what Jesus teaches in Matthew 25.[7] I experience the movement of the Spirit secondly as an energy inside me that does not desist and will not let me go. It persists in my body, in my mind, and I can't let it go. I wake up thinking about it. It is the last thought in my mind as I drift off to sleep. This is the voice of the Creator, telling me to go. In Anabaptism, the voice of even the smallest in the assembly can provide wisdom to the group. We are all moved by the Spirit, to reveal the steps of our days.

Second, Anabaptist tradition prioritizes internal spiritual discernment expressed in outward action. Discipleship, or *Nachfolge*, broadly means forsaking one's own desires and self-interest in order to live out Christ's teachings.[8] Indigenous spirituality likewise values living in harmony with the Spirit of life, prioritizing wholeness over fractured self-interest.

Discipleship in my experience is denying my own interests in favor of the interests of the Spirit of Life. Discipleship is adhering to the Kingdom of God that Jesus reveals in his ministry and the values he reiterates first spoken by the prophets: justice for the poor and meek, justice in the courts, an end to oppression. This

---

7 I have written about this fully in Augustine, "My commissioning."

8 Bender and Huebner, "Discipleship."

is the peace tradition in Anabaptism I so revere: I can be a peace-maker when I seek justice. Peace is not the avoidance of conflict; rather, it is the necessary engagement in conflict to resolve injustice. This goes beyond simply bearing witness to injustice, which is not enough. It is an engagement with those who seek to harm, to dispossess, to enslave, regardless of the cost. And it can be costly to pursue justice on behalf of the dispossessed. It can mean a lot of work with small reward and rejection by the values and narratives of the mainstream. It can be being branded as irresponsible by those who value legitimacy and comfort or material security. It can also mean putting my life in danger. My husband has been detained, and my life has been threatened. Yet I find comfort in the Anabaptist tradition to adhere to a Spirit more powerful than violence or oppression—a Spirit of Peace.

Finally, both traditions emphasize and revere community. Many Indigenous spiritualities acknowledge the systematic integration of all living things. In this system of thought, survival among all living things is co-mingled, and harm or destruction for one means destruction for all. Based on this spiritual understanding, Indigenous communities are group-centric, where group identity is mutually reinforced and individualism is discouraged. Anabaptist theology historically emphasized self-surrender or yieldedness, where God's will is made manifest only to those who have surrendered their individual will. The German term for this concept is *Gelassenheit*,[9] or submission. Although this is a concept found primarily in Amish writings, I have found it to be relevant to my experience as a Mennonite. Discernment takes place in the workings of community, where those in the body discern the will of God together, yielding to each other in the process. Humility and yieldedness are interpreted as outward signs of discipleship.

Because working in community is such a strong force in who I am, I felt compelled to bring together Anabaptists to work together to respond to and take action regarding what I have come to understand is the destructive history of the Doctrine of Discovery. Out of this was formed the Dismantling the Doctrine of

---

9 Friedman, "Gelassenheit."

Discovery Coalition, where we discern our collective work each year in a pragmatic way.[10] We gather once every twelve to eighteen months to determine together what we will focus on in the coming months. We work together to define our priorities in conversation, followed by aligning ourselves around the work we all affirm. We define work groups we believe are vital to our priorities, and then we volunteer to be on work groups. If there are no volunteers for a work group, we acknowledge there is no energy for that work. In this way, we discern together what we will do and affirm our commitment to it. We affirm our leadership at each gathering in the same way. The Spirit moves within us and among us, animating us toward action. In my mind, this is an Anabaptist way to relate. We acknowledge our mutual inter-dependence, rely on each other's gifts, and assist each other in our labor. We seek the movement of the Spirit collectively and work to submit to that leading. Because we are a national coalition and cannot meet face to face often, we meet by phone according to a schedule devised by each group. Our working committees then meet by phone quarterly to work together in advancing our collective work.

A historical obligation

Historian John Roth explains that Mennonite history is tied to land.[11] This topic is addressed by multiple figures in the Mennonite Church in the documentary *Doctrine of Discovery: In the Name of Christ.*[12] Anabaptists were historically invited into harsh territories in order to gentle or better harsh lands. This history means Anabaptists have a legacy of settlement on the lands of Indigenous and vulnerable peoples. Anabaptists have individually and collectively benefitted from this settlement. This is not a process of the past but is ongoing. In a recent article for *National*

---

10 For more information on the Dismantling the Doctrine of Discovery Coalition, see https://dofdmenno.org.

11 Roth, "Mennonites and Land."

12 Hartman, *Doctrine of Discovery.*

Geographic magazine, Nina Strochil describes current conflict between Indigenous bee keepers and Mennonite farms growing genetically modified crops that threaten the existence of Indigenous People.[13] The economic security for many Anabaptists is rooted in the acquisition and betterment of land that was taken from Indigenous Peoples. We are thus responsible for righting this wrong, for seeking shalom, or right relationship, with Indigenous Peoples.

In this respect, we must take seriously three questions as articulated by Rich Meyer of Christian Peacemaker Teams: "Where do I live? Whose land did this used to be and how did they lose it? And where are their descendants today?"[14] In the words of the prophet Amos, we must seek good and not evil, that we may live. Then the Lord, the God of hosts, will be with us, just as we have said.

---

13 Nina Strochlic, "Unlikely Feud."

14 This statement was made by Rich Meyer in Hartman, *Doctrine of Discovery*.

2

Ploughshares
Recovering from the Myth of Mennonite Exceptionalism

Amanda K Gross

When I was a child, my Mennonite congregation broke in two because the transformation of conflict we are so known for throughout the world was not a skill brought back home. At the end of the day, the strong men could not bear what vulnerabilities would be exposed if women took the pulpit and divorcees sat in the pews. From then on, there was my aunt's church and my parents' church. One loved gay people; the other pretended they did not exist. The silent cloud that permeated my home church community hovered immediate: a "don't ask, don't tell" policy shrouded in fear. It was our mothers' tactic for making space for difference without causing waves. We were loved for who we were as long as who we really were did not make it to the father's ears. We were protected in the best way they knew how, which they learned from their mothers before: to be private in their fears, in their questioning of church doctrine, in their disbelief. In the North American Mennonite way of silence and power and its petri dish for abuse, I learned to look out for myself while keeping the waters still. This cultural message still rings true across many Mennonite communities: don't tell your truth if it implicates others, but especially don't tell your truth if it implicates yourself.

I have always known that Mennonites were not only white. My home congregation, surrounded by honeysuckle, poison ivy, and Georgia pine, was begun as an intentionally multiracial congregation when segregation was still barely legal. Much like the history of my European Anabaptist ancestors, Southerners were dying for the opportunity to worship together. By the time my white girlhood came along, their deaths and the congregation's half-white, half-Black balance were a near-distant memory. Instead, the global Mennonite church helped fill the pews, and although there were still several Black congregants, there were many more white ones.

Like others before them, my parents migrated to Atlanta from places further north. Their migration pattern was consistent with generations of white North American Mennonites leaving their rural Mennonite home communities to be of service in a broken world. For some, like my parents, this meant a permanent move to the big city. For others, it meant a temporary stay abroad.

Those who leave home for such God-inspired reasons continue to occupy a special place in Mennonite hearts and on church walls. The bulletin boards of Mennonite fellowship halls peacefully request prayer for those doing the will of God away and apart from us. We send them a carefully allotted portion of our tithes. We warmly welcome their slideshows with curiosity, interest, and an eclectic potluck. Depending on their presentations, we may learn about war, conflict, and famine. They may share about the political power dynamics of their host country and perhaps even about the impact of the US government and military on the local people. But they will not speak of imperialism in a way that implicates us, at least not the North American Mennonite *us*. What you will not hear in such a slideshow presentation is the way their very service contributes to these imperialist dynamics. What you will most likely not hear is how our lives do too.

The myth of (North) American Exceptionalism is a useful touchstone for understanding Mennonite abuse of power. Influenced by thinkers and leaders over time, the dogma of American Exceptionalism uplifts the United States as unlike any other nation on earth, positioning the United States as superior. American Exceptionalism is surprisingly inclusive in its philosophical foundation. Just as many roads lead to Rome, there are many ideological pedestals of American Exceptionalism to choose from depending on your particular entry point into nation-state politics. For those committed to God-ordained political greatness, American Exceptionalism proclaims that because "In God We Trust," God has entrusted us with the best interest of others. For those who worship democratic electoral politics, American Exceptionalism assures us that, even if the founding fathers did not exactly get it right the first time (after all, white men are imperfect too), their well-meaning democratic intent has ultimately leant itself to an equitable process. For those with more financially focused interests, American Exceptionalism preaches the faith of the US dollar. Economic strength, it turns out, proves a helpful stand-in if God is absent. And for those who are aroused by patriarchal military might, American Exceptionalism anoints US imperialist success with the blood and oil of people, cultures, and places who dare threaten our exceptional way of life.

With a few exceptions, North American Mennonites are loathe to identify with this brand of American Exceptionalism. Our pacifist theology rejects, at the very least, an association with military might. Our history of suffering at the hands of political power has instilled a suspicion of authoritarian governmental politics. Our separatist calling *to be in the world but not of it* suggests distance from American Exceptionalism, forming quite ironically a sort of Mennonite Exceptionalism that offers us godliness in spite of our North American context. I offer that this myth of Mennonite Exceptionalism (particularly for white North American Mennonites) comes out of deep-seated unhealed historical multigenerational trauma, has perpetuated abusive power dynamics by rendering invisible structural and cultural violence, and continues to obstruct the healing and transformative justice that would lead to the peace theology we so vocally seek.

Suffering as far as the mind can see

There are many stories that get passed down from one generation to the next. Certain tales get told more often than others. Usually there are larger themes at play. In church, the main themes centered tales of the martyrs. When I was the age of four, sixteenth-century Dutch martyr Dirk Willems's commitment to enemy-loving (at the expense of his life) entered my vocabulary, along with the stories of other gruesome deaths as highlighted in the *Martyrs Mirror*.[1] These martyr narratives that were told during congregational children's time emphasized the Jesus-centered righteousness of our victimhood. This narrative lens has been used to explain the plight of Mennonites of later generations long after the European colonization of the Americas. Martyrdom explained American animosity towards Mennonites' refusal to fight in the Revolutionary and Civil Wars, the World Wars, and in Korea and Vietnam. It gave context and explanation to the outsider status felt both by conservative apolitical Mennonite communities and by politically engaged liberal ones who abstained from voting and refused to prop up state violence by withholding taxes for war. This martyr narrative grounded in five hundred years of history continues to have a tremendous hold on North American Mennonite culture, power structures, and self-perception today. At the crux of this powerful narrative lies a deep-seated and unhealed collective trauma.

In the popular imagination of dominant culture, the concept of trauma calls to mind individual incidents that are usually one-time events happening in the past and now over and done with. Survivors of rape or childhood abuse, soldiers suffering from post-traumatic stress disorder, and victims of natural disasters or mass shootings may be navigating the impact of those time-bound traumatic experiences for a lifetime. Less accessible to dominant culture is knowing, acknowledging, and grappling with societal trauma, which occurs across people groups, may be continually recurring, and spans centuries or even millennia. The *Strategies*

---

1 For more on the Dirk Willem's story, see the chapter by Kimberly D. Schmidt in this volume.

for Trauma Awareness and Resilience manual describes large-scale trauma in the following ways:

Collective or Societal Trauma—traumatic events that affect specific groups or entire societies.

Historical Trauma—the cumulative emotional and psychological wounding over the lifespan and across generations emanating from massive group trauma. Transfer through generations.

Cultural Trauma—the effect created when attempts are made to eradicate part or all of a culture or people.

Structurally-Induced Traumas—trauma created by policies that result in unjust, abusive, racist, or unsafe systems that cause hardship often on a long-term, continuous basis. These include situations of conflict and/or poverty that result in the inability to meet basic needs such as adequate food or health care.[2]

While there are several historically traumatic events that Mennonites of European descent have participated in—the colonization of Indigenous land in what is now the United States and Canada,[3] the ownership of humans during the antebellum chattel slave system,[4] imperialist efforts to spread Christianity across the globe via missions and service work, and the Holocaust in twentieth-century Europe[5]—the traumatic influence that has stood the test of time and still determines a strong sense of collective identity centers on the persecution of Anabaptist ancestors as part of the heretic movements five hundred years ago. To quote Franciscan friar Richard Rohr, "Pain that is not transformed is

---

2 *STAR Level I Participant Manual*, 4.

3 For more on this colonization, see the chapters by Sarah Augustine and Jennifer Delanty in this volume.

4 Cranford and Roth, *Kinship Concealed*.

5 B. Goossen, "Mennonite Fascism."

transferred."[6] This unhealed collective trauma based in religious persecution is precisely what has led Mennonites to directly and indirectly participate in the aforementioned acts of violence. I will only briefly touch on the first example here.

1763[7]

Recently I visited my twice alma mater to find a newly installed sixteen-foot sculpture tilling the campus grounds. *Guns into Ploughshares* is Esther and Michael Augsburger's late–twentieth-century artistic interpretation of a biblical scripture oft-cited in pacifist circles: "they shall beat their swords into plowshares, and their spears into pruning hooks; nation shall not lift up sword against nation, neither shall they learn war any more" (Isaiah 2:4). Making news in the *Washington Post* for its recent relocation, this sculpture is made with "thousands of actual guns taken off city streets during a no-questions-asked gun-buyback program."[8] *Guns into Ploughshares* takes firearms—symbols of violence consistent with the Mennonite Peace Church narrative—and transforms them into a gigantic plough, a symbol of violence less recognizable to Mennonite eyes. The gun violence epidemic in urban centers symbolically referenced in the Augsburgers' work is a phenomenon from which white Mennonite communities are largely personally removed. By contrast, the attempted genocide of Indigenous people and the illegal, immoral, and ongoing occupation of their land have directly resulted from the agrarian settlements of Mennonites of European descent. In this case as in many others, the looking glass of Mennonite Exceptionalism positions us as external critics of the violence of the world. It desensitizes us to the ways we have perpetuated violence to the extent that we can collectively erect and celebrate a blatant sym-

---

6 Yoder, *Trauma Healing*, 30.

7 The year 1763 marked the end of a Native American presence in Lancaster County, except for one elderly couple. Martin, *Clash*, 29.

8 Kelly, "'Guns' Running."

bol of Indigenous trauma on the grounds of a Mennonite institution in the name of God's peace.

While the martyred tales of my ancestors were offered to me at the age of four, now in my thirties I am only beginning to access my family's histories of colonization. I am learning that just as the early Anabaptists were key players in threatening the power hierarchies of their day, their descendants were pivotal in the establishment and maintenance of white dominance.

The story I was told about how my ancestors ended up in what is now called the United States went something like this: *Mennonites were persecuted for our faith in Europe, and because we were following Jesus's way of nonviolence, we were brutally massacred and burned at the stake. We justifiably fled persecution and ended up in Pennsylvania or Russia, eventually making it to the other regions across North America as well.*

If there is even a recognition of Indigenous people on early colonial arrival, it goes something like this: *William Penn was a Quaker who was tolerant of religious freedom, which is why Mennonites settled in Pennsylvania. He also was fair in his dealings with Native Americans, but his sons were not.*

And in Virginia: *In search of land, Mennonites migrated south to the Shenandoah Valley, where there were not many Native Americans—probably because they had died of disease due to other earlier (non-Mennonite) settlers.*

These vague summaries leave out the political context of seventeenth- and eighteenth-century colonization in which European Mennonite settlers were actively engaged. Regardless of William Penn's religious pluralism, pacifist views, or reputation as fair in negotiating with the Lenape, his original acquisition of a large swath of land by King Charles II in payment for debts owed to his father was based off of both the ideology and practice of stealing land. Penn's vision for a religiously tolerant utopia was predicated on a Eurocentric relationship to land use, one that centered the idea of ownership and a worship of written documents (often falsified) to disenfranchise native people of their lands. This paved the way for the Lenape to be exploited through the infamous Walking Purchase and, after successive push outs, be forcibly relocated to Oklahoma.[9] In addition to land theft and sneaky treaties, the use of agriculture proved a strategic colonizing tactic.

Enter the Mennonites. Known for agricultural abilities, looking for arable land, and eager to get out of Europe, Mennonites were perfectly positioned to aid in colonial occupation and expansion. Besides, in contrast to other farmers living on the edges of European settlements, we were unlikely to take up arms when dissatisfied with the colonial government as had been the case in 1676 with Bacon's Rebellion.[10]

In the Shenandoah Valley, Mennonites also farmed the violence of colonization. Unlike myths of recent depopulation, the valley was abundantly used and inhabited by Indigenous people. In his essay "'From the Ground Up': Space, Place, and Diversity in Frontier Studies," Robert D. Mitchell describes the early eighteenth-century Shenandoah Valley as "one of several north-south conduits containing trails for long-distance contacts between Iroquois groups in northern New York, Virginia's tributary groups on the Piedmont, and Catawba, Creeks, and Cherokees in the southern Piedmont and Appalachians."[11] The Monacan Indian Nation traces its roots back ten thousand years in the adjacent Blue Ridge.[12] As native tribes faced displacement, and French fur traders were increasingly grouchy about British westward expansion, an explicit strategy of "buffer settlements" was developed in 1716 by Virginian Governor Spotswood (and later adopted by his successor Governor Gooch) to protect the "colony's Tidewater settlements from Amerindian or French attack since neither tributary tribal groups nor frontier militia units seemed reliable

---

9 "The Walking Purchase."

10 Bacon's Rebellion first rallied against Native Americans and then later against the British colonial government and united both European indentured servants and enslaved Africans as a major threat to the ruling elite, prompting anti-miscegenation legislation, the first appearance of the racial category white in colonial law, and the Virginia Slave Codes of 1705.

11 Mitchell, "'From the Ground Up,'" 27.

12 Wood, *Virginia Indian Heritage Trail*, 30.

for such purposes."[13] Spotswood was looking for "Loyal Foreign Protestants" and Mennonites fit the part.

The stories we tell ourselves matter. The myth of Mennonite Exceptionalism keeps us from seeing truth. Our unhealed chosen traumas warp our lenses due to our pain. In the STAR manual, a *chosen trauma* is:

> When an individual or group is victimized and the resulting hurt, powerlessness, shame, and humiliation prevent complete mourning. Groups then:
>
> - do not move on in healthy ways and so experience complicated grief
>
> - become obsessive about the trauma
>
> - develop an unchanging narrative and can come to have a sense of entitlement about what they are owed
>
> - Use the unhealed trauma to justify acts of aggression/ violence against others, acts that are seen as helping to regain what was lost
>
> - make the chosen trauma an important part of group identity

On the other hand, a chosen glory is marked by:

> High points, often victories in a group's history and story that are a source of pride for a group, often but not always won at the expense of another group. A chosen trauma and chosen glory may be the same event(s).[14]

Following initial settlement in Pennsylvania and Virginia, Mennonite communities experienced a number of attacks by various native groups, sometimes in coordination with French and

---

13 Mitchell, "'From the Ground Up,'", 27.

14 *STAR Level I Participant Manual*, 11.

Scotts-Irish settlers.[15] In both the eighteenth century massacre stories and in later depictions by early twenty century historians, Mennonites are not exceptional in our racist language, referring to native people as "savage,"[16] "tyrannical," and "barbarous."[17] These tales depict the innocence of Mennonite male-headed families, faithfully obedient to God by not succumbing to the temptation to take up arms for self-defense. Victims once again who were—as in one case of Virginian Mennonites—forced to flee their land due to violence, even to the point of referring to themselves as "refugees."

I make these observations not to minimize the fear and uncertainty that early Mennonite settlers must have felt, nor to ignore the experience of collective trauma that was most certainly triggered and re-lived, but rather to explore a historical explanation for the cognitive dissonance white North American Mennonites experience today. To put it in the framework of trauma healing, I want to know this: How did we get stuck in a narrative of heroic victimhood? How has that created a sense of entitlement to the lands we have come to occupy? How does our repressed pride in five hundred years of martyr identity block us from healing? How have we used chosen trauma and chosen glory to justify acts of structural and cultural violence against others in order to gain back the safety in our homelands that was once lost?

My heart wants to know how a community so committed to God's peace could participate in such wide-scale, far-reaching violence. My head wants to know how we can operate from a place of such deep denial about our complicacy in violence. My soul wants a way forward out of this hypocritical mess.

---

15 Some examples include the 1755 Jacob King Family Raid, 1757 Hochstetler Massacre, 1758 Jemison Raid in Pennsylvania, and the Road's Massacre in 1764 in Virginia.

16 Mast, *Family History*, 18.

17 Brunk, *Mennonites in Virginia*, 33.

To untie a knot, you must first go back through[18]

Whitewashed through the past hundred years of cultural white supremacy, at this point our chosen trauma and chosen glory do little to educate us as to the real potency of early Anabaptist organizing, and it does little to keep us from further abuse. The martyr tales that trickled down through church sermons and children's time consistently mention adult baptism, traumatic consequences, and a pacifist response. But why were Anabaptists so dangerous to the powers that were? The answer I received claimed them as a theological threat to the state church's hierarchical power but did not really explain what made them so threatening. The answer I did *not* receive is the one outlined by Silvia Federici's *Caliban and the Witch*:

> It was through the prism of the Peasant War and Anabaptism that the European governments, through the 16th and 17th centuries, interpreted and repressed every form of social protest. The echoes of the Anabaptist revolution were felt in Elizabethan England and in France, inspiring utmost vigilance and severity with regard to any challenge to the constituted authority. "Anabaptist" became a cursed word, a sign of opprobrium and criminal intent, as "communist" was in the United States in the 1950s, and "terrorist" is today.[19]

Anabaptists challenged the religious, political, and economic order of the day. They "condemned economic individualism"[20] and were revolutionaries. Their movement's defeat led to the defeat of greater resistance to economic oppression in Europe, paving the way for a resurgence of misogyny and ultimately the racist colonization of the globe.

---

18 I owe my understanding of this phrase to my yoga teacher Felicia Savage Friedman, founder and director of YogaRoots on Location.

19 Federici, *Caliban*, 119.

20 Federici, *Caliban*, 116.

The stories that we do not tell ourselves matter too, and what tales of Mennonite Exceptionalism leaves out is that the witch hunts are also a part of our collective trauma. Anabaptist betrayal of women emerged almost as soon as its attempt to establish God's kingdom on earth began. Women in the Anabaptist movement enjoyed a degree of freedom unparalleled to most European communities in the 1500s. But that changed with their final large-scale attempt to take over the town of Münster in 1535. Leaders imposed a patriarchal practice of polygamy, causing women among them to revolt. After the defeat of Münster, the political potency of the Anabaptist movement waned, and church and state power were free to hunt down the ruling class's next biggest threat, women—wise women, to be exact, who were often revolutionary strategists and the keepers of community memory. These untold narratives erase the gender-based violence that came fast on the heels of Anabaptist martyrdom. Several historians make direct connections between the Anabaptist persecution and the witch hunts.[21] In places with high incidences of violence like Augsburg, the stakes that were constructed to first burn Anabaptist heretics were quickly refueled with alleged witches.

The scars of the witch hunts survive in us alongside our religious martyrdom, even if unacknowledged. They are present in our sanctuaries and in our bedrooms. They are evident in the rampant sexual abuse in our Mennonite institutions and in our male-dominated church leadership. They are visible in our fear of queerness and in our internalization of misogynistic racism. They appear in our mothers' silences and fearful self-effacement. Alongside traumatic religious persecution, the violence of European patriarchy has been passed down in our hips, from generation to generation. As with all these examples, it becomes ablutionary to abuse power when we are attached to our victimhood; it becomes righteously justified.

The martyr narrative of Mennonite Exceptionalism exempts us from participation in other forms of oppression. It draws on a dualistic understanding that offers us exclusive categories of vic-

---

21 Waite, *Eradicating*, 4.

tim or villain, oppressed or oppressor, godly or sinful. As people *in the world but not of it,* we have preemptively asserted our innocence, rendering it illogical to have cultivated a legacy of sexual abuse and gender-based violence. As purely victims of historical persecution, we built a narrative that does not allow for us to have been active participants in racist, state-sanctioned attempted genocide. And while our identification with victimhood rejects our responsibility in oppressing others, this specific narrative of European martyrdom excludes Mennonites from being the victims of other forms of oppression. We could not have been impacted by the historical gender-based violence of the witch hunts because we were too busy being persecuted by the state for our faith. We could not possibly be victims of colonization, enslavement, and racist discrimination because our all-consuming narrative of trauma in Europe portrays us as exclusively white.

Clearly this binary victim/offender arrangement does not serve the global Mennonite *us.* It also does not serve even the much smaller number of North American Mennonites who have direct ancestry to European martyrs. The problem with this chosen trauma and chosen glory is that we willingly give up our power. As victims, we are unable to see ourselves as powerful. We are passive in our pacifism. We are disenfranchised by the state. Our power lies in death, not in life—certainly not in resurrection. Victim identity diverts our attention away from the ways we have been complicit in abuse, the way our mothers remained silent in the fellowship halls, the way our fathers used their ploughs to cover up native blood. But our mothers commanded their own tongues and our fathers wielded their own ploughs. We too have power in how we position the trajectory of our lives. Drawing on the wisdom of our ancestors: it is best not to go it alone.

In recognizing the folly of our ancestors, how then *do* we go about it? As Eve Tuck and K. Wayne Yang boldly assert in their article "Decolonization Is Not a Metaphor," "When metaphor invades decolonization, it kills the very possibility of decolonization; it recenters whiteness, it resettles theory, it extends innocence to the settler, it entertains a settler future."[22] Tuck and Yang's insistence on a concrete rather than a theoretical practice of decolonization consequently disrupts the myth of Mennonite Exceptionalism. It interrupts our theories of martyred righteousness. It refuses to center European Mennonite histories of persecution and flight as justification for colonization. It confronts the physical impact of our ploughshares. It challenges the origin stories of our contributions, even and especially when those contributions are in the name of justice.

North American Mennonite Exceptionalism favors a particular origin story for the field of restorative justice, sometimes referred to as the "Kitchener Experiment." It is 1974 in Kitchener–Waterloo, Ontario. The offenders: a couple of drunk teenagers gone on a vandalizing spree. Their victims: neighborhood residents and homeowners at the site of the crimes. The heroes: two white North American Mennonite men working for Mennonite Central Committee (MCC), who through this particular case lobby the judge to allow direct contact between the offenders and their victims in the form of apology and compensation for damages. The result: MCCers, Mark Yantzi and Dave Worth, along with the emergent Victim-Offender Reconciliation Program, are oft cited as the origins of the modern Restorative Justice movement (or RJ for short).[23]

However, several notable scholar-practitioners take a slightly wider view, acknowledging (both vaguely and historically) RJ's roots in Indigenous cultures and practices and sometimes explicitly accrediting the communities who nurtured their learning, including Kay Pranis's apprenticeship under Yukon guidance and Howard Zehr's acknowledgment of the influence of First Nations People and the Māori.[24] Taking a more horizontal approach, Carolyn Boyes-Watson parses RJ into four main areas, each with distinct origins (criminal justice reform, youth behavior manage-

---

22 Tuck and Yang, "Decolonization," 3.

23 London, "Paradigm," 1–6.

24 Zehr, *Restorative Justice*, 7; Pranis, "Peacemaking Circles."

ment, democratic peace movements in post-conflict zones, and movements for Indigenous cultural and political self-determination[25]).

Yet despite the breadth and depth of connections between a diversity of Indigenous influences and the modern-day packaging of RJ, the Kitchener Experiment is still widely cited throughout Mennonite communities as well as "in the field"—even though the Kitchener Experiment in its ahistorical identification of victim and offender neglects to calculate how the neighborhood residents had come to acquire their homes in the first place, from whom, and at what cost.

North American Mennonite Exceptionalism lays claim to the territory of RJ. It assumes a protagonist role in the history of RJ. It allows for metaphorical decolonization without application. It encourages our theoretical liberation rather than a liberation as practice.

The time has come to practice. Those of us who are Mennonites of European descent have spent centuries considering the weight of our oppression. What now does it mean to consider the weight of being the oppressor? What now are the movements we need to make to stop and repair the abuse? How do we tell our truths in ways that intentionally implicate ourselves? What are the daily practices that decenter our future existence as colonizers on this land?

Perhaps as challenging as Tuck and Yang's call to decenter settler futurity is the call to dismantle our narratives of innocence, to adopt an ethic of incommensurability that prevents making false equivalences between one oppression and another:

To fully enact an ethic of incommensurability means relinquishing settler futurity, abandoning the hope that settlers may one day be commensurable to Native peoples. It means removing the asterisks, periods, commas, apostrophes, the whereas's, buts, and conditional clauses that punctuate decolonization and underwrite settler innocence. The Native futures, the lives to be lived

---

25 Boyes-Watson, "Looking."

once the settler nation is gone - these are the unwritten possibilities made possible by an ethic of incommensurability.[26]

Healing from five hundred years of multigenerational inherited trauma means releasing ourselves from the fixed identity of martyr. It means accepting the historical impact we have had on the world and moving forward with humility. Just as decolonization is not a metaphor, healing too means reclaiming our relationship to justice as no longer an abstract concept but once again a physical, life-changing organized act. This call to decolonize is one that my Mennonite upbringing has particularly prepared me for by cultivating an unattachment to worldly property, a courageous faith in the possibility of things unseen, a collective struggle co-created in relationship and community, and a love for enemy even when that enemy resides in me.

26 Tuck and Yang, "Decolonization," 36.

3

Remembering Rightly
Our Experience of the Sixties Scoop

Lydia Neufeld Harder with Ingrid Bettina Wolfear

We want to tell the story of how our mother/daughter relationship was affected by the Sixties Scoop of Indigenous children in Canada.[1] We will each speak in our own unique voice, Ingrid's words written in italics and Lydia's in roman.[2] Our memories are colored by the present and the past, by what we are learning now and what we knew then. In all of this we are attempting to "remember rightly" what happened then and what is happening now.[3]

The term "Sixties Scoop" was coined by Patrick Johnson, author of the 1983 report *Native Children and the Child Welfare*

---

1 I use *Indigenous, Aboriginal,* and *First Nations* interchangeably to refer to the descendants of the inhabitants of Canada before it was settled by Europeans.

2 Ingrid's words are excerpted from an interview recorded by Michele Rizoli for the purpose of this paper. Her words have been lightly edited for clarity.

3 Miroslav Volf uses the term "Remembering Rightly" in the subtitle for his book *The End of Memory*. His book is helpful but concentrates on how a victim should remember. Much more needs to be said about what it means for a perpetrator or someone involved in systems that perpetrate violence to remember rightly.

System.[4] It refers to the practice in Canada of removing primarily Métis and Aboriginal children from their families in the 1960s to 80s and placing them in foster homes or adopting them into white middle-class homes. Social workers, often untrained and unfamiliar with the culture and history of Aboriginal communities, evaluated the proper care of children according to Euro-Canadian values. For example, a diet of dried game, fish, and berries was not considered adequate, though this had sustained Indigenous people on the prairies for many years. In many cases children were unexpectedly and forcefully apprehended because parents were living in poverty or because children were being raised by relatives, even though otherwise the children were receiving loving care. According to one report by a social worker in British Columbia, almost all the newly born babies were removed from their homes on the reserves during some of those years.[5]

Mennonites, as a faith community, were involved in this process as well, both as social workers and as adoptive or foster parents. A resolution passed in 1966 by the Conference of Mennonites in Canada, on the theme of Indian-Métis relationships, testifies to this involvement. It reads in part:

> WHEREAS our country is increasingly facing race problems related to Indian and Métis, and
>
> WHEREAS we are largely responsible for the problem, and
>
> WHEREAS the solution also depends largely on us, and
>
> WHEREAS various governmental (i.e. Indian Affairs) and non-governmental organizations (i.e. Children's Aid) are making strong efforts to give first Canadians a better future . . .
>
> BE IT RESOLVED: . . .

---

4 Johnston, *Native Children.*
5 Hanson, "Sixties Scoop."

3. That we encourage more Mennonite families to adopt and foster homeless Indian and Metis children. . .[6]

What does remembering rightly mean for each of us in this context?

See, my body remembers, and my body reacts, and I don't remember. The research that has been done recently about blood memory is totally correct. . . . What the body retains and how far back it goes. . . . I was born Aboriginal, First Nations. All the pain and suffering that my people carried are part of my blood memory. I was born in Calgary as part of the Siksika Nation, who are Blackfoot, of the Plains Indian part of the Confederation, Treaty Seven. I have a ten-digit status card recognized by the Canadian government. But I did not know that until I was in my twenties. I grew up confused, with a loss of identity. . . . The question of why this was so was never answered until now when there has been more research done on how the connection between the physical, mental, emotional, and spiritual is carried in the body. So, for myself, though I don't remember consciously with my mind, I now know there is a good reason for that loss of memory.

I want to remember the story rightly of our adoption of Ingrid, whom we named Kristen, by recalling the larger political context and the systemic injustice that affected us deeply as a family. I was unaware of the power I carried as a Canadian citizen with the privileges and rights that I assumed were mine and as a Mennonite with a strong sense of identity as a Christian. I wonder how to tell my story when my memories are shaped by my own biases and prejudgments. I want to explore the power dynamics and injustices involved in this story; however, I also want to leave room for the joyful and reconciling moments that continue to nourish our relationship.

The adoption process

What I recall about the interviews with the social worker were her probing questions. "What are the prejudices you carry? Is there

---

6 "Minutes of the 64th Session," 1.

a child that you would find difficult to bring into your family circle?" She was most afraid, I think, that we were "do-gooders" who would soon tire of the challenges that came with adoption.

At the time we were happily settled in Edmonton after several years of seminary training. My husband, Gary, was pastor of a Mennonite church. I was a homemaker, parenting our two boys, ages six and four, and very involved in volunteer activities in our congregation and community. Why were we considering adoption when we already had two children?

First, we were hoping for a daughter since we had two sons. Both sides of our family tree seem to specialize in boys. Adoption would be a sure way to ensure the right sex for our next child. Second, we felt family planning was an ethical choice. During the 1960s, in our Mennonite theological circles, there was a great concern with the over-population of the world and the lack of resources for that population explosion. In addition, we were convinced that all life needed to be in service to God, including the shape of our family. Since successful methods of birth control were now available, we needed to make a choice about the size and type of family we wanted to be. And third, we naively thought we had something we could offer a child without a parent—a stable, loving home environment.

I knew I was not ready for another round of diapers and baby food and talk about babies and home-making with other mothers. I was yearning to go back to my career of teaching, to rational discussion of theology and politics, to move away from the physical labor of housework. We decided we were open to a somewhat older child and that racial background was not a barrier.

It was the Friday before Thanksgiving in 1973, nine months after we had received the approval for adoption. All day I had a premonition that the social worker would call. I remember feeling disappointed and discouraged when I glanced at the clock and realized that the social work offices would soon close. And then we received the call. An Aboriginal girl, age two years and four months, was waiting for us in Calgary. We could meet her on the Tuesday after the holiday weekend, and if everything went well, take her home the day after that. There was jubilation within our family. Our older son had been praying faithfully for a sister. Our prayers were going to be answered!

To our surprise, the social worker who met us was a friend and former pastor of our congregation. He was able to reassure us in our choice to adopt but gave us very little information as to the child's earlier life. That was all confidential and not available to us. We were more anxious to meet this little girl than probe into her background. Our sons, who felt privileged to meet her first, were playing with her in the playroom. As a child I had always envied other girls who had black hair and brown eyes but had never imagined I would have this beautiful girl as my daughter. We had no doubts that she belonged in our family. I remember going down the elevator on the day we took her home, overwhelmed with joy.

At the time of adoption, I knew that other Mennonites were adopting Indigenous children and that Mennonite social workers were involved in that process. But I did not reflect deeply on the birth parents and their pain or on the Indigenous community and its values, nor did I ask many questions about how these children came to be in the welfare system. I naively assumed that social workers knew what they were doing.

Yet I do remember that niggling feeling I had when the questions I did ask were so quickly and superficially answered. I was told that the mother was unable to parent the child and had given her up. The father was unknown. I asked about whether it was wise to rename the child or whether we should keep her name. The social worker told me she had been called "baby" for most of her life thus far and so changing the name would not be problematic. I asked about her somewhat delayed physical development and was told that in her first foster home, she had not developed well because she had spent too much time in her crib. I asked about getting some photos from her first two years but was told these were not available for adoptive parents.

Our daughter came to us with a large paper grocery bag filled with a few clothes and two stuffed toys. It was as if her first two important years of life were wiped away. But we thought our love and embrace would wipe away all neglect that she may have experienced. We did not recognize our middle-class white privilege or the class distinctions that were subtly affecting the adoption process. We now confess that our eyes needed to be opened.

As an infant who was handed off to various people for short periods of time, I never learned the right tools to protect myself. I have been labelled with Post Traumatic Stress Disorder, which helped me make sense of why I have been in survival mode all my life. . . . I grew up being uncomfortable, feeling different, yet not seeing myself as an Aboriginal person. Yet when people looked at me, that is what they saw. When I look at the family photos, I can see the discomfort in my face, not really believing that "OK, I am happy." Right from the first two and a half years, I knew how-to-put-on masks and how to build walls of protection around myself. I did not have the bonds with others that I should have learned as an infant. I missed out on life because I dissociated from my feelings and so was not linked with another human being. I became numb so did not know what it was like to feel. . . . I didn't know how to walk until after two. I didn't know my name, so that's messed up. For this newborn child to go through trauma immediately after birth, having that systemic bloodline of trauma (including parents in residential schools) and then also not getting the early tools to manage the trauma—that means I was already behind in so many ways. The "system" failed me from birth and did not allow me to develop and flourish.

Becoming a "family"

As I look at the photos and mementos of Kristen's childhood, I smile. Balloons and popcorn symbolize for me the celebrations and ordinary, everyday happiness that were part of our experience with our new daughter. Hiding in closets and jumping out to surprise us never failed to bring forth laughter. Kristen was certainly a unique personality with strong likes and dislikes. Yet she fit into our family patterns quickly. I remember our five-year old Kendall looking at a family picture only months after the adoption and wondering why Kristen wasn't in the picture.

A few months after the adoption, Gary's mother came to see us and to become acquainted with her new granddaughter. She arrived after our children had been put to bed. But I decided to wake Kristen, so she could meet her new grandmother. It took only one moment before Kristen ran to her for a hug. We wondered if this grandmother reminded Kristen of her last foster mother. A connection was established that only became stronger throughout that grandmother's life. Whenever Kristen had a difficult time falling asleep as a young child, I would suggest: "Think of a safe warm place where you can snuggle in and fall asleep." The place was always Grandma's lap.

I also remember that Kristen easily accepted anyone as a caregiver. Although she called us Mom and Dad, she did not demonstrate that there was a special bond between us for quite some time. She would give anyone a hug and stay willingly with any babysitter. It wasn't until the year we spent in Paraguay when she was six years old that our family relationships became stronger. In a foreign country where everyone speaks a different language, we had to learn to depend on each other. I do remember Kristen being excited to meet so many people with brown skin and black hair. She even expressed this to us: "Now you are the different ones and I am the same!"

One incident in Kristen's childhood demonstrates the cracks that were beginning to appear in our approach to Kristen. We were on a family outing and came to a park featuring a large teepee. I asked Kristen to stand in front of it for a photo. She steadfastly refused to do it. Was this her stance against being objectified as an "Indian"? Was this her intuitive grasp that I was placing her outside of our family circle because of her Indigenous roots? Was this her response to not having any exposure to the culture of the people to whom she belonged? I still cringe when I think about that day.

We were glad that we lived in a multicultural neighborhood, but our important church context was quite mono-cultural. I now recognize that I was trying hard to impart my values to our daughter without an equal effort to help her connect with her own Aboriginal community and its values. We had no Indigenous friends during those years and only read about "Indians" in books—not many of them accurate portrayals. Our efforts in parenting focused on Mennonite and Christian values subtly influenced by what we now understand as more generally Euro-Canadian values. We did not value the deep spiritual and cultural roots of the Aboriginal nations. We assumed that the differences in our blood heritage did not matter. No wonder that Kristen responded differently to situations and experiences than our other two children.

When I was around six years old, this girl in my Sunday school class said to me, "God doesn't love you because you're brown." I visually remember exactly where in the church she said it to me. She was younger than I was, also had an adopted sister my age. I was blown away that this little kid could say something so powerful, so terrible. And in church! So that stuck with me for the rest of my life.

When I was a child, my hair was kept very short and that made me uncomfortable. I was a girl, but I had a boy haircut. Oh, yeah, my dad pulled out the masking tape for the bangs so that they could be cut straight. I remember in kindergarten there was another Aboriginal boy and he was a big boy and I avoided him. And then in grade 7 I met an Aboriginal girl. When the Aboriginal dancers came to the school she would say, "This is who we are." And I said, "Okay?"

I remember my grandma as being gentle and accepting. But so often I was stepping into situations that I was not prepared for and was hurt in the process. Bonding is the key to relationships, but I was just receiving and not knowing what the boundaries were.

Moving throughout the country was another dislocation; there was no connection to the land, which is a major part of identity, especially for Aboriginals. It was during the move to South America that I started to see myself as a brown person after seven years of not knowing what people were seeing and not knowing how I'm feeling and just feeling displaced—not in the right spot because I'm brown and they're white with blond hair and blue eyes.

In Paraguay the ladies on the bus would take care of me because they saw me as indigenous. The care. I felt the care! And then I was put into a Mennonite private school (with its blond-hair, blue-eyed students) learning two totally different languages (German and Spanish). The Paraguay experience was a major turning point in my sense of identity.

A fragile identity

As Kristen grew older, she began to ask more and more questions, which revealed some of the struggles she was having. I wrote down some of her questions at age twelve: *How come it is so hard to live the right way? How come we have to live? Why are there words like love and care? Why is it so hard to not use God's name in vain? Why does Mark [older brother] have it so easy?*

The teen years were difficult. I became afraid for Kristen's safety when I realized how vulnerable she was to abuse as an Indigenous girl. Kristen began to seek her independence and try to find her identity in various peer groups. She was often angry, and at times she was quite depressed. I was losing patience with her and was discouraged when I realized how I so often reacted in anger. We took Kristen to a counselor, but she refused to say a word. I remember a conversation in our front yard when she told me that she often felt like running away and would do so if I forced her into counseling. We made a deal that she would not run away and that we would try to trust her more to make good decisions.

This was difficult for me to do as I watched her making choices that did not express our values and that put her in danger. I spent many nights waiting and worrying about her. When she did experience abuse and mistreatment, we tried to be there for her. I soon realized that I needed to create some space for nourishing my own spirit, so I entered a program of studies that led our family to Toronto, a difficult move for Kristen just before high school.

One day Kristen came home from high school and told me, "Now I can tell everyone I am a Mennonite!" This was a big surprise to me. She informed me that she had taken a course at school about Mennonites, describing them as conservative, Swiss background people, who used horses and buggies to drive to church, who refused to use electricity, and who lived in rural areas of Ontario. "Now I can tell everyone that I am a Mennonite! No one will believe me anyway!" she said.

Kristen was sure of one thing. She needed to get back to the western provinces where she felt more at home. For her last two years of high school she decided to go to Rosthern Junior College (RJC), a small Mennonite boarding school in Saskatchewan that some of her Edmonton friends were also attending. Though we were reluctant to send her so far away, we also realized that the independence she would have from us could be helpful in our relationship. She made some good friends and had some positive experiences. But she also found the rules and regulations restrictive and often felt misunderstood and even betrayed when she shared feelings that were not kept confidential by the staff. I began to sense how difficult it was to be one of only a few Indigenous students, all of whom had been adopted, in a town where the barriers between Mennonites and Indigenous folk were huge.

Now we see that we too were part of the larger system that was trying to destroy the culture and unique identity of First Nations people by assimilating them through the fostering and adoption process. As Fournier and Grey explain, "The impossibility of emulating the genetic characteristics of their Caucasian caretakers results in an identity crisis unresolvable in this environment. . . . The Aboriginal child simply cannot live up to the assimilationist expectations of the non-Aboriginal caretakers."[7] The harm that was done is summed up in a decision by Superior Court Justice Edward Belbaba who ruled in favor of the plaintiffs in an Ontario Sixties Scoop class action lawsuit. He stated that Canada had breached its common law duty of care to take reasonable steps to prevent adopted children from losing their Aboriginal identity. This left these children as "fundamentally disoriented, with a reduced ability to lead healthy and fulfilling lives. The loss

---

7 Fournier and Crey, *Stolen*, 30.

of Aboriginal identity resulted in psychiatric disorders, substance abuse, unemployment, violence and numerous suicides."[8]

Our vested interests as parents, as school administrators and teachers, as social workers and as guidance counselors were often disguised and hidden as we talked about doing what was best for the Aboriginal children in our midst. We did not understand that the choices available to Aboriginal teens were fewer and different because of the disorientation and loss of identity that came with adoption into a dominant culture that had oppressed their peoples for centuries. At the time I had little idea how deeply this affected not only individuals but also the larger Indigenous community.

I was asking questions as a teenager because I did not know what it means to love. There's a difference between the dictionary meaning of love and knowing what it means when people say, "I love you." I know I love popcorn, but do I know I love another human being? I can say to my kids, "I love you," but do I really? And for me to say I love myself; I don't know what that means. So I put on a mask of pretending to know what it actually means.

Before RJC I was confused with no answer to the question of why this was so. The world didn't make sense, society didn't make sense. I observed hypocrites within the church and community, seeing their actions and hearing the words but also seeing the disconnect. Rosthern is a small town in Cree territory where Mennonites had settled as immigrants. While at RJC I was connecting with Indigenous people who lived on the reserve. The poverty on the reserve was a reality that was ignored by the Mennonite people. Many of these Indigenous people had gone to residential schools and had lost their identity.[9]

When I went to the Truth and Reconciliation Commission[10] meetings in Toronto in 2011 with my brother Mark, I sat in on a session where somebody was speaking of their experience in resi-

---

8   Brown v. Canada (Attorney General).

9   I resonate deeply with the experiences and feelings of the main character in the novel Daniels, *Bearskin Diary*.

10   For more information on these meetings throughout Canada, see Truth and Reconciliation Commission of Canada (https://www.trc-ca).

dential schools. This triggered a strong response in me. I realized that the experience of the residential schools and my own experience as an adoptee were very similar. The adoption of Indigenous children was another version of the same thing—to take the Indian out of the human being. To lose the Indigenous part of us. To forget the unique role that we as Indigenous were given by the Creator.

Discovering roots

After successfully finishing high school, Kristen felt ready to begin the search for her birth mother. Together we looked through the adoption papers and especially her health records for clues to her birth family. It was not difficult to hold the papers up to the light and discover traces of Kristen's birth name that they had tried to erase. The name "Wolfear" led us to the Blackfoot reserve beside Gleichen, a reservation on which the Siksika nation had been placed only a few miles away from Rosemary, Alberta, where my husband, Gary, grew up. Over the next few months, both Mennonite and Aboriginal networks were enlisted to find her family. A call from a sister surprised Kristen one day, and they talked for hours as she discovered a family she knew nothing about. The experience of meeting her mother for the first time was traumatic. Kristen writes about her feelings in *Intotemak*, a Mennonite periodical for Native Affairs.[11]

> I get a lump in my throat
> Tears in my eyes
> When I think of that time
> The moment of fear
> "I would not survive"
> Every feeling known
> Jumping frantically
> In my heart and soul
> Feeling confused and alone

---

11 Special thanks to Mennonite Church Canada, the publisher of the periodical *Intotemak*, for permission to republish this poem, which originally appeared in *Intotemak* 22, no. 2 (March–April, 1993): 6–7.

Laughing on the outside
Crying on the inside
Patience and time
Proved I could survive
And I will the next time too.

This marked the beginning of Kristen's formal search for her Aboriginal roots. In 1992 she went to Guatemala with a Mennonite Central Committee (MCC) Youth Discovery Team to acknowledge and affirm the resilience and survival of native people of America during the last 500 years. Perhaps this could counter the recognition of the "discovery" of North America by Christopher Columbus (who had lost his way in the trip to India!). She was disappointed to discover that MCC was unable to enlist any other Indigenous person for what she had understood was to be a four-member Indigenous team from North America. The other three young people who were now part of the team were not nearly as engaged in the larger purpose of the group as she was. She then worked as an MCC volunteer at the Walnut Receiving Home for helping Indigenous mothers in Winnipeg. She also traveled across Canada with a Peace Bus tour that visited various reserves to encounter Aboriginal peoples. They caught a glimpse of the rich culture and spirituality but also noted how much was taken away. In an interview after these varied experiences she speaks about how churches should respond to adopted native children in their midst: *Churches should support whichever decision that person would make, whether it is to never look into their blood heritage or stay with the Mennonite system or . . . try to make them match.*[12] She has continued her search for roots as she meets more of her relatives, as she visits reserves and hears the stories, as she participates in the ceremonies and rituals of native spirituality and as she meets Aboriginal folk in a variety of other settings.

The words of my mother to Kristen when she told her she was going to Calgary to meet her birth mother encouraged me

---

12 Reimer, "Kristen," 5.

during those years. "Kristen," she said, "you know you can always love *more* people." My mother recognized that we need not fear that finding a birth family would necessarily erase the experiences and love that we had shared over the years. I have held that truth tightly through the many ups and downs in the years that followed.

Kristen's search for her roots also began our search for greater understanding of the relationship between the First Nations of Canada and the settlers who came later. What we discovered was a trail of oppression by government, churches, and ordinary citizens like us—residential schools, physical and psychological abuse, broken treaties and promises, and much deception. For example, the government took reserve land (Kristen's home reserve) without permission to build a dam that brought prosperity to the Mennonite community in which Gary grew up. Kristen's parents and her husband's parents spent time in residential schools and have told us stories about the abuse suffered there. Stereotypes of Indigenous people and distorted historical facts continue to be taught in our schools. As settlers we benefitted from these abusive situations.

Emotionally we also needed to come to terms with the fact that not only was Kristen searching for her family; her family was also searching for her. We cannot imagine the pain of families who were separated without having the knowledge and power to find out where and why this was happening to their family. A CBC podcast titled "Finding Cleo" tells a heart-wrenching story from the point of view of those searching for the truth about their lost family member.[13] We are only beginning to hear how these forced separations of family members have affected not only individuals but the larger communal identity of our First Nations people.

So much of our own thinking was influenced by the settler mentality which assumed that the Doctrine of Discovery with its "fabric of lies" gave us the power to decide what happened to

---

13 Connie Walker, *Missing and Murdered: Finding Cleo.*

Indigenous folk who had lived in the land for centuries.[14] This false sense of privilege has permeated every aspect of the relationship between settlers and Indigenous peoples by legitimating untold violence and injustice. We need to consciously repudiate and reject and dismantle this Doctrine of Discovery in order to be open to transformation. As Christians who settled on Indigenous land, we need to look again at the biblical and theological justifications that were used and point out how they benefitted us as settlers.

Why did I look for my parents? It was all Lydia's influence. She wanted me to find out what my last name was. . . . To meet my mother was devastating because I saw the poverty and the distrust. . . . I also met my younger sister. She's messed up too. Going from a middle-class family into what I assume was social housing, experiencing the difference in lifestyle was traumatic. . . . To be with bloodline family but they were strangers—perfect strangers.

One of the commonalities was humor, so there was a lot of laughter and joking to avoid the opposite feelings. It is more natural for Indigenous people to resort to humor.

I had a relationship with my mother, Heather, for ten years before she died. Meeting her, meeting my family, that in itself was traumatic. Finding out the traumas that my family have gone through (and of course not talked about) and seeing the effects as the aunties and uncles and my mother were trying to numb themselves, and then seeing their kids who were also trying to numb themselves and I too for various reasons . . . It's the body that remembers.

The first teaching that I remember came straight from the Creator. . . . I saw a white owl on my cedar tree in my back yard. . . . Several different elders explained to me its meaning: "It is a messenger of death." That is when I was called to the hospital because my mother was dying. . . . I was put as next of kin but did not know

---

14 The Doctrine of Discovery is the "ostensibly legal justification for European claim to, and sovereignty over, indigenous lands and peoples." Woelk and Heinrichs, *Yours, Mine, Ours*, 7n1. See also Russell, "Still Questioning," 28–31. See as well the chapters by Sarah Augustine and Jennifer Delanty in this volume.

what this meant, who to ask, and what part of culture should be involved. . . . I was at her bedside when she passed. . . . This was all confusion, not knowing the power of the Sprit and the connection with the Creator; it was all foreign ground.

The funeral was traditional, a new teaching for me. My instinct was to do the traditional thing, but I didn't really know what that was. That's when my gut instincts guided me. . . . I had my head shaved and put the hair into the coffin. . . . At the funeral everyone else began taking small strands and braids from their own hair to also put into the coffin. It was instinctively the right thing to do.

Small pieces toward reconciliation

Through the counseling and being part of the Aboriginal elder wisdom and really observing what is in front of me and going with the flow brought me to where I am today. It has been a gift, having my eyes opened. There are many blessings, but at the same time, it has been extreme. . . . So I was brought into this world in trauma, in pain. My question is, Why? What is the larger teaching in that? There is still some anger; there is a lot of confusion; there are communication barriers. . . . The physical element (the body memories) is what is holding me back. But I had the inner strength to go through all that! The "intuitive vibe" is an amazing thing that I was given. I know that with everything, there is a time and place, plus everything happens for a reason. . . . Patience is the way to live.

As for the adoption, that's been one of the strong poles that has allowed me to connect back to my Indigenous side. Because my parents were open-minded, they were supportive. They were able to take things in. Having a father who has the teachings on how to manage trauma is a blessing. And him being an introvert as well because he can listen. (That has been a challenge, having an introvert as one parent and an extrovert as the other. It's quite a dynamic.)

I have to accept what has happened for what it is. It is not something that as a human being I can overcome, but spiritually I have trust in the Creator and in time.

Kristen has blessed us in so many ways. We took many trips to British Columbia where she had settled and were able to hold each of Kristen's babies in our arms soon after their birth. When she moved to Toronto, after she became a single mom, we could support her and participate more in the daily and weekly life of her family. We have also shared pain—when there was abuse, when relationships were broken. Sometimes our relationship was tenuous; however, gradually we were able to reconnect in more healthy ways, giving each other space when needed.

There were many birthday parties for grandchildren and trips to the zoo or the lake. Watching our grandson dancing at a pow wow, attending school graduations, camping with the larger family circle all hold precious memories for us. We have experienced many joyous times together and have met some of Kristen's Indigenous family and friends. Most important to me was meeting Kristen's mother and sharing a Christmas meal with her at our home. We thanked each other for the part we each played in Kristen's life. Kristen gave us each a similar candle holder. I cherish the photos of that Christmas. Another highlight was the wedding of our daughter a few years ago—celebrated by a Mennonite ceremony attended by the two families, Aboriginal and Mennonite, followed several months later by an Aboriginal ceremony also attended by both extended families.

Yet the question of what reconciliation looks like on a personal and a systemic level still haunts me. Healing is often elusive for Aboriginal people who continue to bear the wounds of injustice because injustice continues in a variety of ways. But I know that we, who adopted children during the Sixties Scoop, also need healing and forgiveness. Remembering rightly is part of that process for me.

A few weeks ago, Kristen came to me and asked my help in applying to change her name officially to Ingrid Bettina Wolfear, the name given to her at birth. Intellectually I was ready for this; what surprised me was that I wholeheartedly could support this emotionally as well. Ingrid has moved north to live with her husband on First Nations land and is appreciating the presence of the lake and trees and sky all around her. She has a young daughter named Charlotte Marlene, the "Marlene" chosen because my second name is Marlene. We continue to keep in close touch with each other.

Our grandchild, Mitchell, when he was around six years old, asked us, "When did God and the Great Spirit become friends?" Somehow, he had caught a glimpse of a reconciliation "made in heaven." I pray that this kind of reconciliation may come on earth as it is in heaven. Remembering rightly may be the first step.

4

Dismantling the Doctrine of Discovery
One Congregation's Response
Jennifer Delanty

> We are all newcomers on this land, the unceded land of the
> Duwamish people, a tribe still living and thriving in this
> city. Neighbors with whom we seek, in small and faltering
> ways, to be in repaired relationship.

This acknowledgement leads off each worship service of Seattle Mennonite Church, whether in our sanctuary or online in the days of the COVID-19 epidemic. Mentioning our
Indigenous neighbors and the truth that the rest of our population is living on land originally in their domain is a grounding
that helps us be thoughtful and intentional in our relationships
with our neighbors and each other. We consider this vital since
the Duwamish people have been repeatedly denied federal recognition of their existence by the United States government,
despite our city (and church) being named after one of their
members, Chief Sealth.

It is true that our ways of living in repaired relationship with
the Duwamish are too often faltering; we are not being humble
when we state this. Finding our way out of white supremacy is
complex, unwieldy, fraught with error, and full of uncertainty. As
believers in Jesus Christ, we are subject to the wild, unpredictable

movement of the Holy Spirit, and we are learning there is so very much we still need to learn. Our nearly all-white congregation has the best of intentions and a collective phobia against making mistakes, yet at times we find ourselves messing up royally. Perhaps that means we are learning. God help us if we don't.

In the 1990s, our congregation was gifted a substantial stock portfolio by a grateful recipient of care arranged by an anonymous Mennonite woman on the Russian front during World War II. In the early years there was some shareholder activism on some of the stocks in the portfolio, including a gold mining company with operations in Indonesia and East Timor. Little did we know at the time that these efforts would help prepare us to dig into the complexity of human rights and land sovereignty.

Prophets also entered our Lake City neighborhood sanctuary in the guises of addicted military veterans, starving and cold people without homes—the dispossessed who also kept our attention immediate and local. Community ministers were hired. A drop-in hygiene center named God's Lil Acre was one of many services and advocacies to respond to the trauma of homelessness, evolving into the formation of a non-profit organization to coordinate winter shelter operations, Lake City Partners Ending Homelessness.

Members of our congregation began sharing about their work with Indigenous people in Suriname dispossessed of citizenship and access to governmental services. Multinational corporations involved in gold mining were poisoning their streams with mercury, a watershed that had sustained and nourished the Wayana People for millennia. Growing increasingly sick, they implored Dan Peplow, a visiting epidemiologist contracted by the Suriname government, to assist them in their desire for access to test results as well as the rights of citizenship.

The Suriname Indigenous Health Fund (SIHF) was formed out of this request by Dan and his wife, Sarah Augustine, members of Seattle Mennonite Church. They invited their congregation to learn about and engage their work, which was set up on a "power with" model of engagement. This model mainly involves listening and supporting a constituency's effort for self-empowerment in lieu of a more typical "power over" stance taken in Western or white engagement with non-white peoples.

A congregational discernment process was undertaken in 2013 to consider repudiating a historical doctrine sanctioned in the name of Christ. In seeking to understand how a group of people like the Wayana in Suriname came to be excluded from citizenship and land sovereignty, further research revealed the historic and legal underpinnings from a series of papal bulls issued by the Catholic Church in the age of purported "discovery" of the "New World" beyond Europe and Asia. This series of documents issued by the Church and granting credence for laying claim to land on distant continents became collectively referred to as the Doctrine of Discovery. By claiming land for distant European Christian princes, and setting up legal structures to claim sovereignty, the Doctrine of Discovery was claimed as justification and eventually codified into law by new nations establishing themselves. Like churches in other denominations, Seattle Mennonite Church discerned this doctrine as antithetical to our Anabaptist values of justice, mercy and humility. We issued the following repudiation.

SEATTLE MENNONITE CHURCH STATEMENT
REGARDING INDIGENOUS PEOPLES

December 2013

Seattle Mennonite Church seeks to live in a just peace with our fellow human beings, both as individuals and as peoples. Throughout the world, within the United States, and within Washington State, indigenous peoples have suffered from historic injustices. Many times, they have been dispossessed of their lands, territories and resources via colonization, treaties, and governmental and corporate exploitation. We confess that we, as individuals and as a congregation, have benefited from the historical and institutional actions and policies carried out against indigenous peoples both here and abroad. In response, the Seattle Mennonite Church endorses and supports the United Nations Declaration on the Rights of Indigenous Peoples adopted September 13, 2007.

We honor the inalienable rights that sustain the existence of indigenous peoples. Indigenous people have rights to their homeland, water, spiritual practices, language, cultural practices and self-government. Indigenous people have the right to make decisions and conduct international relations on their own behalf.

Catholic church documents such as *Dum Diversas* (1452) and *Romanus Pontifex* (1455) were designed to award sovereignty of discovered lands and indigenous peoples; to exclude other European nations from claiming such lands; to call for non-Christian peoples to be invaded, captured, vanquished, subdued, and reduced to perpetual slavery; and to have their possessions and property seized by Christian monarchs. Subsequent European monarchs likewise granted commissions for the right of discovery to "undiscovered" land, notwithstanding their occupancy by indigenous peoples. Collectively, these and other concepts form a paradigm or pattern of domination that is still being used against indigenous peoples by governments and corporations throughout the world. We condemn and reject this so-called "Doctrine of Discovery."

We commit ourselves

- to recognize our own participation in the structures of power at the expense of indigenous rights;

- to work with indigenous peoples to carry out the UN Declaration on the Rights of Indigenous Peoples;

- to speak to governments and corporations whose policies undermine indigenous rights; and

- to bring these concerns to the denominational family for future action by Mennonite Church USA.

Seattle Mennonite next entertained an opportunity to fund SIHF's work with congregational monies in 2014. Our consensus model of deliberation prevented this due to one person blocking the affirmation to release funding. Many mourned this as a repudiation of the repudiation we had so recently issued. The opportunity to have a "power with" relationship with SIHF was thwarted.

A coalition formed in 2014 by Mennonites primarily from the West Coast to educate and advocate about the far-reaching and current impacts of the Doctrine of Discovery. Some members of Seattle Mennonite Church were involved in its formation and further expansion beyond the initial group who began working together.

******

> And you shall hallow the fiftieth year and you shall proclaim liberty throughout the land to all its inhabitants. It shall be a jubilee for you: you shall return, every one of you, to your property and every one of you to your family. –Leviticus 25:10 (NRSV)

As our congregation approached its fiftieth year of existence from its 1968 beginnings as a house church in South Seattle, the Spiritual Leadership Team of the congregation discerned naming our anniversary as Jubilee. A two-year process was undertaken to review the land, labor, and capital assets of the church. As we learned about the traumatic effect of our national history riddled with genocide, enslavement, and domination, our privileged inheritance sat heavily, feeling less like blessing and more like something we received because the welcome table was so heavily tilted in our direction.

This disorganizing presence, learning an alternate narrative to the histories we were educated with, calls us into a deeper engagement that requires setting aside the lenses that have formed our individual and collective perceptions. Standing down on our privilege and power as local settlers of European descent has led us to ask our local Indigenous neighbors how to stand *with* rather than stand *by* (and *over*) as witness to their ongoing denial of existence by our federal government structure, a structure whose creation is rooted in the Doctrine of Discovery.

We are willing to try. We are ever slowly learning, over many years, how the complex history of racial prerogative and oppression has shackled us too as inheritors of privilege and wealth. We stand discomfited in the face of the long reach of oppression's affect. We recognize we are complicit too—inheritors of a legacy as American as baseball and apple pie. What is God's will for a fifty-year old congregation of descendants of European settlers planted in one of America's wealthiest cities?

Small groups have formed in the congregation, studying together writings on the topic of White Privilege and Reparative Justice. Other members are showing up in meetings and activities of the Seattle chapter of European Dissent, a national network of self-identifying White folks committed to doing their own anti-racist and white privilege or white supremacist disentanglement so they might show up in support of communities of color and not be a disorganizing presence. The Coalition of Anti-Racist Whites has also organized a Duwamish Solidarity Team that encourages local residents to pay "Real Rent" to the first peoples of this land, which many individuals from our congregation do as a household commitment, in addition to our congregational financial commitment as a "Real Renter." Real Renters are also invited to lend their time and talents to support Duwamish fundraising projects and educational programs, like documentary film nights and the Princess Angeline Annual Tea. Our youth recently painted a mural on the church exterior wall, with input from Duwamish Elders, that publicly acknowledges that our church gathers on the traditional lands of the Duwamish people, who are still here. Church leadership undergoes anti-racism training. We actively participate in local interfaith and national Anabaptist Coalitions that seek out ways to disrupt systemic oppression. We host neighborhood movie nights on topics related to Indigenous Solidarity and education. We have also begun releasing funds to organizations run by non-whites that support their communities, and releasing our non-profit tenants on our campus from paying rent during some months of the COVID-19 pandemic.

We are walking an uncertain and unknown road. We don't know what direction the Holy Spirit will breathe us toward. We have consented to listen deeply, connect with our Indigenous siblings in our watershed, and loosen our grip on what appears—in the context of all we have learned—to be ill-gotten gain. We hope to show up when and where we can, with humility and sincerity, and be open to what is unfolding before us.

May God's will be done.

5

The Everyday Power of White Supremacy and Casual Racism

Regina Shands Stoltzfus

When I was nine years old, I went away to an overnight camp, which was, for the most part, wonderful. Our camp counselors kept us busy with crafts and activities. I had never been away from home with people who were not related to me, and there was something thrilling about that. I was also the only Black child in my cabin—perhaps even at the whole camp. My memory is fuzzy there. But there is a moment I remember quite well. At one point during the week we paired off and were instructed to hold hands with our partners. My partner announced that she could not hold hands with me because I was brown. I don't remember what happened immediately after that; I'm assuming some adult intervened and made it "right" in some fashion. My body memory of that moment—someone didn't want to touch me because of my skin color—has never left me. It is a combination of nine-year-old shame, with a touch of anger and confusion.

I was not naïve or uninformed. I was, after all, a Black child in America, and it was the 1960s. But I was raised in a predominately African American context; my neighborhood and the kids I went to school with were Black. My lived experience with white people was primarily at church, which was racially integrated, and there I had close friends who were white, Black, and multiracial. I had never had a white person recoil at the sight of me or the thought of touching me.

All these years later, I am struck by the assumed "of course-ness" of that long-ago encounter. That little white girl was not a bit hesitant in her declaration. Whatever her life lessons had been thus far, she knew that there was a limit to the ways in which she could interact with me. That encounter was miniscule—nay, hardly existent—compared to what other Black children experienced at the hands of white racists: the four little girls killed in a Birmingham church three years earlier or fourteen-year-old Emmett Till, lynched ten years earlier. I understand fully that I walked away from this encounter able to go about my day. Yet adult hindsight also helps me understand how this and other acts of casual racism uphold white supremacy that allowed those other acts to happen and continue to allow the policing and punishment of Black bodies.

My formation as a peace studies educator is grounded in the church that raised me—an urban congregation that taught Anabaptist theology in a primarily Black church context. I learned peace and justice by watching my elders embody Jesus's teachings, in large part as they committed to being church in an integrated context, which was nearly unheard of during the middle of the twentieth century. Their commitment to God, to each other, and to the church meant confronting institutions that sought to diminish Black life. My understanding of what it means to wage peace and foster justice is built on a foundation of understanding and addressing structural injustices like racism and sexism. It is the underpinning of my teaching in the college classroom and the peace education work I did for a number of Mennonite organizations. A foundational element in understanding how structural oppression persists, and is carried down from generation to generation, is understanding *power*. I believe understanding the power of what I'm calling *casual racism* is critical.

What is casual racism?

Casual racism is a socialization process that teaches there is something essentially different and wrong about people of color and that Black people are potential contaminants that must be avoided. This notion fueled decades of segregation and fostered the creation of Black codes. For instance, the first Fugitive Slave Law of the United States was signed by President George Washington in 1793. This legislation provided for the return of suspected fugitive slaves (i.e., any Black person) from any state or territory in the Union. By 1824, other states—including Indiana, the state in which I currently live—passed their own laws that required white citizens to detain suspected fugitives (again, any Black person). Whites and Blacks who participated in abolitionist activity were subject to trial and conviction. The federal Fugitive Slave Law of 1850 subjected every free Black person in the North to capture by slave hunters; under the terms of the law, a person simply had to swear to a justice of the peace that their captives were fugitive slaves. Private citizens could be deputized in order to do the hunting, and anyone who resisted or helped supposed fugitives could be fined. Some states, like Indiana and Oregon, enacted legislation to keep Black people from settling in the state.

Divided by race

In a racialized society, it may be difficult to remember that classification by race is a recent development in human history. Because societies construct the language and the meaning around racial difference, the meaning of race and how people navigate it are highly contextualized. The United States has a unique racialized history that may be baffling to people who come from different historical and societal contexts, and especially for monocultural contexts. There is evidence that indicates children begin to notice race as a category of difference as early as three months old. However, they only begin to attach meaning to this difference when they see that the world around them attaches meaning to it.

The first census in 1790 had a grand total of three racial categories: free whites, all other free persons, and slaves. These categories echoed the newly adopted (in 1787) Constitution's way of identifying people groups: "free persons," "Indians not taxed," and "three fifths of all other persons" (enslaved Blacks).

The census categories held for the next hundred years. By 1850, other categories were added, included the terms "mulatto," "quadroon," and "octoroon" in deference to the "one drop" rule. This rule, known sociologically as the rule of hypodescent, designated persons with "one drop" of Black blood as Black. The significance of such quantification is clear; it was (is) critically important to know who is Black, even if visual identification of Blackness is not possible.

In the early days of American nation building, citizenship was attached to race: only "free white persons" could be naturalized. While the question of who was white was yet to be settled, the concept of a racial category called *white* was inscribed with privilege and power. In a racial hierarchy, whiteness was something to be desired, which immigrants quickly learned. Whiteness also needed to be protected.

In 1790, Congress enacted "that all free white persons who, have or shall migrate into the United States, and shall give satisfactory proof, before a magistrate, by oath, that they intend to reside therein, and shall take an oath of allegiance, and shall have resided in the United States for one whole year, shall be entitled to the rights of citizenship."[1] As a racial designation written into a large body of laws, whiteness is tied to distinct and clear privileges, advantages, and power. To not be in the category of "white" meant a denial of citizenship and all of its accompanying rights. The rights of citizenship and freedom of movement were racialized right from the beginning.

When tested, the courts found again and again that framers of these laws were deliberate in their intent, and later courts intended to honor the intent. Immigrants who sought to become naturalized citizens faced naturalization acts that only allowed "free white persons" and "persons of African descent" to naturalize (in deference to the fourteenth amendment—previously per-

---

1 Jacobson, *Whiteness of a Different Color*, 22.

sons of African descent who were born in the United States were denied citizenship).[2]

Whose lives matter?

Events characterized by many journalists as "racially charged" or "racially insensitive" marked the summer of 2018 in a way that was eye opening for some and business as usual for others: what had been dubbed as "driving while Black" (DWB) several years earlier to call attention to racial profiling that resulted in a disparate number of Black drivers being pulled over by police, events that sometimes resulted in the death of said drivers at the hands of police.

While today the term *white supremacy* might bring to mind violent extremists clad in white robes and hoods, the reality is much more mundane. White supremacist notions undergirded the ways in which US society shaped itself from the earliest years of nation building. This strongly held belief is what allowed the system of chattel slavery to be kept in place for over two hundred years and what orchestrated the subsequent Black codes that were introduced after the brief period of reconstruction. Black codes were laws enacted to govern the movement and conduct of African Americans. Most of them were enacted after the 1865 emancipation of enslaved persons and were a way of re-inscribing the country's racial hierarchy in a visceral, embodied manner. Common examples were the segregation of public places and transportation and requiring Black people to enter white homes or establishments through the back door. In some places, Black people were required to step into the street to allow whites to pass on the sidewalk or were forbidden to look a white person in the eyes or call them by name.

The notion of white supremacy's longevity and persistence depends on its incredible seductiveness; people of all races need to buy into it in order to support and sustain it. Whiteness is the preferred standard for humanity. Whiteness is valued above all, it is rewarded. The rewards are powerful enough for people to support

---

2   See Takao Ozawa v. United States, 260 U.S. 178 (1922).

the notion, even when they disagree with it. It builds such powerful mythologies about things like violence and crime, for instance, that even a casual observer can safely predict which violent acts will be attributed to a violent nature and which are attributed to mental illness, bullying, or other reasons that do not involve the person's character.

Citizens were socialized to participate in this system whether they agreed with it or not.

Whiteness was the standard for humanity; because white men were the ones who could be property owners, voters, and legislators, their rulership was considered *natural*.

Soul murder

Historian Nell Irwin Painter illustrates the importance of this socialization in compelling people to participate in the system. Slaveholding families socialized their children to understand themselves as part of the owning class. If, for instance, a child demonstrated sympathy for an enslaved person, the child would be reprimanded and reminded of their role in the system.[3] Painter calls the effects of this "soul murder," a phenomenon with deep psychological impact in which both white and Black children learned inequality as normal.[4] Such teaching did not end with slavery but re-inscribed itself generation after generation. Within such scenarios, identity is shaped in the face of trauma.[5]

If white racism is understood solely as slavery and legalized segregation, then it follows that, since slavery and segregation are over, racism must be over. Because systems of oppression are shape shifters, rearranging themselves with the times, racism is not over; it simply looks different. Additionally, the resurgence of racist acts and the normalization of racism support and teach it to new generations. It is perpetuated by the benefits it affords to some people in the system—the people with the most power or

---

3 Painter, "Nell Irvin Painter on Soul Murder and Slavery."

4 Painter, "Nell Irvin Painter on Soul Murder and Slavery."

5 Painter, "Soul Murder and Slavery," 9.

the people who have access to white skin power—so even if people within the system are poor or have other aspects of marginalization, the system of white supremacy still works on some level for them.

In the twentieth century, Black people whose families had lived in the South for generations began to migrate north and west. While industries competed for Black workers and used various strategies to entice them to move north, white society at large was not ready to live with African Americans. While the history of racial conflict and violence in the North has not been given as much attention as events in the South, in city after city, Northern and Southern white homeowners and white-owned institutions colluded with one another to preserve all-white neighborhoods.[6]

In 1910, Baltimore was one of the cities that saw a growing population of African Americans. This was called a "Negro invasion," and the legislative solution to it was the creation of separate white and Black neighborhoods. Other cities across the nation similarly enacted policies that were intended to preserve white spaces.[7] This legal enforcement did not last long but was followed by years of other forms of segregation that emerged in a number of municipal institutions. These were not uniquely Southern responses; as African Americans migrated, so did opposition to Black bodies in previously white spaces across the nation.

Two decades later, the containment of Black people to exclusively Black neighborhoods increased. The machinery of segregation continued to evolve, becoming more sophisticated and normalized. Restrictive covenants sought to ensure the preservation of white neighborhoods for generations. The covenants, established to maintain neighborhood stability, outlined what residents could and could not do with their property. In many areas restrictive covenants perpetuated the practice of segregation by restricting property owners from selling, leasing, or renting their property to Black families for a specific period of time, usually

6 Sugrue, *Sweet Land of Liberty*, Kindle edition location 61.
7 Power, "Apartheid Baltimore Style," 299.

ninety-nine years.[8] By the 1940s, residential segregation practices were also aided by mortgage companies, banks, and developers and justified by the language of the free market, citing the rights of white homeowners to protect the value of their property by keeping their neighborhoods white.[9]

This system of segregation was held in place by custom, policies, and procedures; the threat of violence against African Americans also enforced it. Riots along the East Coast and throughout the Midwest accelerated the push of Black people out of white neighborhoods and helped Black neighborhoods become firmly entrenched ghettos by World War II.[10]

Entrenching the hierarchy

From the beginning, the formal education system in the United States functioned as a way of supporting a hierarchy of owners and workers. Education was a commodity that was withheld from enslaved people—it was illegal to teach enslaved persons to read and write. The slave narrative genre attests to this in two aspects of its formula: the accounting was vouched for by a white person in the introduction or foreword, and the slave's own accounting of their life chronicled the attaining of literacy, often by subterfuge.

In the twenty-first century, many schools in the United States remain racially segregated, even though Brown v. Board of Education ended racialized segregation. According to one study of twenty-first-century segregation in schools, white parents tend to support neighborhood schools *if* the neighborhood school is white; if the school is Black, white parents then support school choice. This phenomenon is called "curated diversity": diversity that still holds white students in the majority. "White Americans, in general, are willing to accept about the ratio of Black Americans at large: 10 to 15 percent."[11]

---

8   Meyer, *As Long as They Don't Move Next Door*, 36.

9   Meyer, *As Long as They Don't Move Next Door*, 14.

10   Meyer, *As Long as They Don't Move Next Door*, 31.

11   Douglas, "Are Private Schools Immoral?"

While schools teach literacy, skills, and critical thinking, schools are also an important factor in the development of a citizenry. In addition to knowledge and skills, educational institutions teach the norms and values of a society—they socialize individuals into an important fact of their identity as part of a people group.

In the early years of US history, most children in the colonies were taught at home. Formal education in schools was reserved for wealthy families. After the Revolutionary War, schooling became more institutionalized due to the production and distribution of textbooks. Books standardized the curriculum; they also promulgated patriotism and religion.

These textbooks perpetuated the racial hierarchy that was already in play. It was not uncommon to see illustrations that showed the hierarchy in graphic form—either a linear progression of "primitive" to civilized "man" with Indigenous and Africans on the far left and Europeans on the far right, or an up/down hierarchy with white men at the top, or "the races of man" with a white man in the center and other racial groups in a circle around him. All-in-all they gave a visual representation that mirrored society's attitudes. Further, these books included negative stereotypes of Native Americans and other non-European groups or the European groups that had not assimilated into whiteness yet, such as Italians and other southern European groups.

Free, required education began in the 1800s and was widespread by the end of the century. It was still illegal to teach enslaved persons to read and write. The penalty for a white person was a fine of not less than one hundred dollars and possible imprisonment. The fee for a free person of color was fining, imprisonment, and or a whipping of no less than twenty lashes.[12]

Eventually the country needed more people with the ability to read, write, and do math, and so school became available and required for children of all classes. Additionally, streams of immigration made it necessary to teach "American" values. Until

---

12 General Assembly of the State of North Carolina and the Session of 1830–1831 (Raleigh: 1831).

the mid-twentieth century, most people did not go to college, and those who did were generally wealthy men. Recent studies show that class, race, and ethnicity continue to be major factors in tracking. Schools were segregated by law until 1954. Northern schools were segregated by residential patterns instead of law.

Schools are funded through tax dollars; an economically disadvantaged city will correspondingly have schools that lack resources like books and experienced teachers. Even something as basic as temperature can affect a student's experience and ability to learn; a recent working paper has noted children from schools that lack sufficient air conditioning in the warmer months fare poorly on standardized tests.

Telling the truth

Many people are surprised to learn the depth and breadth of official policies that legislated white supremacy in the United States. In large part, this dearth of information is due to the lack of including this history in our schools. We may learn the broad strokes and the big stories. We might be able to recall the names of the "heroes," particularly the ones whose actions seem out of reach for the average person. We may learn vastly oversimplified versions: slavery happened, and then it ended; segregation happened, and then it ended. Missing are the stories of the generations of everyday people whose lives were orchestrated by the practices of segregation.

Those of us who were impacted by this history—the specific policies, practices, and procedures that disenfranchised our communities—do have our stories, like my parents' migration from the South to the North. As many did, they fashioned a life—and a good life for the most part—within the confines of this system. In many ways families like mine seem to belie the truth that racism and segregation are detrimental to the life chances of entire groups of people. In my many years of doing anti-racism work, I and others are faced with a common argument in the form of the myths of the self-made person, of rugged individualism, of "you can make it if you work hard enough; this is the land of opportunity, and if you don't take advantage of it, then it's your fault that you failed." These myths play a powerful role in the machinery of systemic oppression.

They are the "truths" that make sense if you don't have any other truth to fall back on, if there is no foundational knowledge base to tell the long, ugly history of racist oppression. This is why systemic oppression persists from generation to generation; our histories are not told or are not believed.

The work ahead

I don't know what happened to the nine-year-old girl who refused to take my hand at summer camp that day so many years ago—what kind of person she became, what kind of community she lives in now. But I do know that the beliefs and practices that taught her that she should not hold my brown hand still exist. I hear them from my college students. I hear them from my colleagues. I hear them from people across the church and in neighborhoods when they tell stories about their families and their communities. I see them in the disparity of resources that are apportioned to poor Black and brown communities. I see them in the persistence of mass incarceration. I see them in the growing visibility and boldness of white supremacist groups as they attack religious leaders, educators, and activists who continue to work to dismantle racism.

I am not saying that nothing has changed. Progress of some sort is seemingly inevitable, and I am grateful for it. I know that my children's experiences in the world are different than mine because of progress that has been made. But I also know that my children's life chances still suffer because of the stronghold white supremacist attitudes still have on many policies, practices, and procedures.

In June 2019, my extended family gathered in Washington, DC, where my parents live. We visited the National Museum of African American History and Culture, a Smithsonian museum. The museum itself is a wonderment, a testimony to the past. It presents, in its many exhibits, an unflinching look at the history of race in the United States. It also tells many hard truths about the complicity of religion, particularly Christianity, in that history.

For my young adult children, being faced with the degree to which the biblical text had been used to justify slavery and segregation, cruel and vicious separation of families, and the controlling of Black bodies with violence was devastating. The cognitive dissonance of Jesus's teachings juxtaposed with the historic evidence of slave ships with names like Jesus, Hope, and La Amistad (Friendship) was real. Faced with the artifacts of this history, my children, as with generations before them, found it impossible to understand how Christians could support, participate in, and defend this system to the death.

And yet they did. And our systems and structures remain capable of upholding racist practices that go beyond personal prejudices. I deeply believe that people of faith are called to understand how the oppressive power of racism (and other -isms) permeates our communities through the processes of socialization. At many times in our collective histories, racism's power is overwhelmingly blatant. It makes sense that people compare, for example, the era of enslavement in the United States to the present day and determine that things are really different now. But because things are different does not mean racism and its death-dealing properties have ended. They have merely adjusted to the times. We need to learn our history. We need to believe people's stories. And we need to examine the ways in which our institutions and our own actions perpetuate systems of oppression so that we may develop new ways of being.

6

Women Doing Theology
A Journey toward Widening the Circle
Jenny Castro

Who determines what theology is or what doing theology means? At its core, this question is rooted in power. When it comes to religious institutions, where systems of faith and practice are developed and defined, it is my sincere belief that shared power—a wider circle to speak into these matters— is not just beneficial but also necessary. Unfortunately, this has not historically been the case. As a Mexican American woman, raised Catholic and then evangelical, I chose as an adult to worship with Mennonites for reasons rooted in Anabaptist-Mennonite theology. In 2014, I was invited to coordinate Mennonite Church USA's program called Women in Leadership. In this chapter, I tell the story of a process of widening the circle, confronting racial discrimination, and opening space for historically marginalized voices (specifically women of color but also LGBTQ people) to speak into our shared understanding of Anabaptist-Mennonite theology.

A place for women in theology

Over the last two thousand years of Christian theological formation, powerful, white men have determined the accepted canon for the Christian scriptures, interpreted the meaning of these scriptures for the masses, and weaponized these scriptures to justify oppression, silencing, slavery, sexual violence, and genocide. These powerful men, with limited capacity to imagine an experience outside their own, have spent hundreds of years determining who God is and interpreting right Christian faith and practice for millions of people whose daily lives would be incomprehensible to these same men. Women's stories were diminished little by little as the biblical canon was created and the biblical narrative took shape. And even as we were (and, to some extent, still are) excluded from academia, church leadership, and the circles of power and influence, women still did (and do) theology, passing on testimonies, wisdom, learning, and experiences of God and God's work in the world, in and through them. Women, forced to the margins of our Christian faith and practice, did theology in our kitchens, in our homes, around dinner tables, with our children, and with one another. Meanwhile, Christian theology up to the twenty-first century has been shaped primarily by men who assume their own objectivity in elaborating true theology and right Christian faith practice, unaware of all they are missing. They do not perceive the reality that the lenses through which each of us understands and articulates theology are informed by our own personal experiences with God, in our communities and in the world.

As denominational coordinator of Mennonite Church USA's Women in Leadership (WIL), my goal was to create resources and spaces that empower women to live into the fullness of who God created them to be and offer their gifts in their contexts. A large portion of my work involved planning and organizing Women Doing Theology (WDT) conferences every two years. These conferences created opportunities for Anabaptist-Mennonite women, and others, to offer their insight, study, and scholarship to what we say we believe about God—to bring to the center of our discourse the ongoing, flourishing work of women already, always, still doing theology. WDT conferences historically and in recent years have centered the voices of women to inform and shape our understanding of God and faith.

It has been my experience that Anabaptist theology is most fully realized in community—sharing and learning from one another, discerning together what God is saying through scriptures with the help of the Spirit. This community discernment is what first attracted me to Anabaptist Christianity—the idea that each of us is vital in understanding and interpreting scriptures together. As we each bring specific wisdom, perspective, and insight, we offer depth and diversity to our collective understandings of God and our faith. The process of understanding and articulating theology, then, is no longer reserved solely for church leaders and academics. It becomes something more alive, in motion, active.

Background to Women in Leadership

I began working as coordinator of WIL for Mennonite Church USA in November of 2014. But the program existed for about five years before I began in my role. WIL grew out of a noticeable absence of intentional resourcing and support for Anabaptist-Mennonite women in leadership across the United States. Mennonite Central Committee US had dissolved their Women's Concerns desk in 2011. And Mennonite Women USA, the official denominational women's organization, focused on international missions and world relief as well as healing circles for women within the United States and abroad. Leadership development for women within the United States was not part of their project portfolio. In 2009, Joanna Shenk conducted an audit of women in leadership across Mennonite Church USA, its agencies, educational institutions, and organizations and found a downward trend of women in leadership positions. As a result of this audit, with the support of a few key Mennonite Church USA leaders, Shenk began organizing what was then called the Women in Leadership Project. But from the beginning, the project lacked full institutional support and even faced regular threats of dissolution. This has continued to be a reality for Women in Leadership—to be required to constantly justify our work and legitimacy within the Mennonite Church USA structure, to self-fund our work through appeals and grants, to defend the necessity of our work to church leadership. Shenk and Hilary Scarsella, who later led this work together with Shenk, developed a strategy to involve as many women as possible with Women in Leadership so that termination of the project would trigger a public outcry. One step in this effort was the formation of a steering committee. As a white, dominant culture Mennonite woman, Shenk must have understood her limits in leading a truly inclusive empowerment movement within Mennonite Church USA, and so in 2012 she gathered a diverse group of women from across the United States. Original members of the steering committee were Moniqua Acosta of Lititz, Pennsylvania, Erica Littlewolf of Albuquerque, New Mexico, Aveani Moeljono of Azusa, California, Linda Gehman Peachey of Lancaster, Pennsylvania, Sandra Perez of New York City, and Regina Shands Stoltzfus of Goshen, Indiana. These women served as guides for WIL, speaking into the overarching vision of the program. It was clear from the beginning that it was a priority for Shenk and Scarsella that the experiences of Mennonite women of color inform and shape the work. This reflects a marked shift in the way Mennonite leaders have used and still use power.

All you need is love: Honoring the diversity of women's voices in theology—Women Doing Theology 2014

Under the leadership of Shenk and Scarsella along with this steering committee, a new iteration of WDT took shape. Anabaptist-Mennonite WDT conferences had been held in the United States and Canada beginning in the early 90s through the early 2000s. The planning committee for the 2014 conference included Moniqua Acosta, Michelle Armster, Sarah Augustine, Hannah Heinzekehr, Gayle Gerber Koontz, Chantelle Todman Moore, and Scarsella. Again, it is important to note that the majority of these women are women of color. At the 2014 conference, women of color were being centered in a way they hadn't been before, at least not in Mennonite Church USA spaces. Six of the eleven plenary presenters were women of color, 20 percent of the breakout presenters were women of color, and nearly 15 percent of participants were women of color. These statistics reflect significant change.[1]

Creating spaces for women of color to lead and shape conversations at WDT is worth noting. It means that the experiences of women of color were informing our collective understandings about God and our Anabaptist-Mennonite faith. It also represented movement in the way planners began thinking about what women doing theology means, not just as a conference but also that act of doing theology itself. Both womanist and mujerista theologies elevate the lived experiences of women of color in articulating our understandings of who God is and how God works in the world.[2] At the 2014 conference, women's stories informed the conversations every bit as much as interpretations and responses to Scripture. The insights provided through storytelling were as significant as exegesis. And women of color played a significant role in that—but not without cost.

As an Anabaptist Latina working with and among Mennonites, I've learned that at Mennonite gatherings, you begin by finding your people—other people of color—so you feel less alone, less invisible. At the very least you need someone to listen and maybe help you process what you're experiencing. You quickly learn that the worship services, the agenda, the programs aren't designed with you in mind because among Mennonites, although you're welcome to become *one of us*, there is a specific way to be Mennonite among US Mennonites—a right way. And the way you look, the way you worship, the way you speak, the

---

1 For a history and demographics of earlier versions of WDT conferences in Mennonite Church Canada and Mennonite Church USA, see C. Penner, "Mennonite Women Doing Theology," 53–76.

2 Alice Walker coined the term *womanist* in her book *In Search of Our Mothers' Gardens: Womanist Prose*. Delores S. Williams was the first to use the phrase *womanist theology*, describing a theology rooted in the experiences of Black women since neither Black theology nor feminist theology had taken Black women into account. See Williams, "Womanist Theology," 66–70. In *Mujerista Theology*, Isasi-Díaz says that mujerista theology is born in the daily struggle of Latinas for justice, peace, and liberation not only for ourselves but also for our whole community.

way you pray don't quite fit. This happens within congregations and at meetings, conferences, and conventions. There is a sense that *this is the way we do things*. This is not because it works best or is more efficacious but because *we've always done it this way* or, put another way, *it's comfortable for us*. And so people of color have learned that in white Mennonite spaces, if we are going to have room for bringing all that we are, being honest and processing together, seeking and offering support, we'll need to create those spaces for ourselves.

At the 2014 conference, planners began challenging some of the traditional Mennonite norms by creating opportunities for women of color to contribute substantially. At the same time, women of color named that worship felt mono-cultural and expressed a need for autonomous women of color space—to support one another and process with each other. That wasn't provided at the conference. And although many of the dominant culture participants named on evaluations that they valued what they experienced at the 2014 conference, it was clear from evaluations from women of color that they experienced a range of discrimination or othering—from micro-aggressions to blatant racism and a general sense of not belonging.

The theme for the 2014 conference was *All you need is love: Honoring the diversity of women's voices in theology*. Conference planners envisioned that women would come together to learn from one another about God, sharing their insights and experience, loving each other, and honoring one another's perspectives even when they disagreed. Conference planners were intentional about setting expectations as participants encountered disagreement—which was expected and inevitable. Regina Shands Stoltzfus wrote a statement titled "Creating safe(r) spaces together." In it she names that leaders and planners will "commit ourselves to not doing violence by our words or deeds." And she asks participants to commit to that as well. With this commitment in mind, conference participants engaged themes of love in the midst of struggle. But it was clear that women of color carried the emotional burden of the struggle. This laid the groundwork for what would come in 2016 and 2018.

I've got the power! Naming and reclaiming power as a force for good—Women Doing Theology 2016

The theme for the 2016 conference built on the work of the 2014 conference. In 2014, we laid a foundation, a commitment to love through struggle. In 2015, the WIL steering committee met in person and brainstormed our next steps for WDT. Several members of the committee (through the process that I named above—creating their own women of color autonomous space at the 2014 conference and processing their experience together) named that women of color still experienced a sense of *this wasn't meant for me* at the 2014 conference. And this led to questions of power: Who gets to decide what worship looks like? Who gets to lead the group in prayer? Who decides how the conference is organized and how we move through the time together? How do we create safe(r) spaces for women of color? How do we create more space for LGBTQ people?[3] How do we shift the demographics of the conference and bridge access barriers so that more women of color can participate? How can we be intentional about naming these power dynamics honestly and openly, creating a space that feels more like home to us as women of color and challenging our

---

3   Part III of Mennonite Church USA's membership guidelines states, "We hold the Confession of Faith in a Mennonite Perspective (1995) to be the teaching position of Mennonite Church USA: 'We believe that God intends marriage to be a covenant between one man and one woman for life' (Article 19). We hold the Saskatoon (1986) and Purdue (1987) statements describing homosexual, extramarital and premarital sexual activity as sin to be the teaching position of Mennonite Church USA." WIL, as a program of Mennonite Church USA, cannot take a clear and unequivocal stance that we are open and affirming of LGBTQ inclusion, nor could I as a Mennonite Church USA employee officially say that out loud, even if it was the consensus of our steering committee. So, we worked within those limitations and practiced radical inclusivity, honoring and welcoming our LGBTQ siblings through our actions, in our programs, in our conversations, and in all our work.

white, dominant-culture sisters to sit with the discomfort when their ways of doing and being are not necessarily reflected in the norms we create together at WDT? We carried these questions forward together.

This was the first conference I'd organized as coordinator of WIL. This was the first Mennonite Church USA Women Doing Theology conference whose primary organizer was a woman of color—a Latina, a Mexican American. In many ways I had no idea what I was getting myself into. I took the lead in conference planning with some fear and some naiveté. The entire WIL steering committee participated in different facets of planning and organizing.

To help mitigate access barriers, I wrote a grant to fund scholarships specifically for women of color. We sought to open the space to more women of color, as a reflection of women doing theology across Mennonite Church USA and not just women who would or could prioritize a conference like this in their personal budgets. This created opportunities for women of color to influence the norms we established and the way we did theology together. Thirteen women took advantage of this scholarship—women of color from south Texas, San Francisco, Miami, and many places in between.

We organized panels for the plenary sessions using the *kitchen table* model for discussion. We invited three panelists to each give a short presentation that was then followed by a discussion. In each of the panels, two of the three panelists were women of color, connected in some way to Mennonite Church USA or Mennonites. This was an incredible challenge, and we spent a good many months securing our plenary presentation panelists. But the time and energy were worth it to us—our priority was to center the voices and experiences of Anabaptist-Mennonite women of color, creating meaningful dialogue with our white, dominant-culture sisters and digging into real and difficult conversations about power in the systems and structures in which we operate, where we encounter each other and where we are in relationship with one another.

It was important to me personally to create opportunities for different and diverse women to lead worship and singing at the conference. The act of worship is so very personal. And in the context of large Christian gatherings, worship establishes norms and communicates power. It identifies whose ways of being are centered and whose are not. It communicates who is at home and who will be a bit uncomfortable. I've personally experienced exclusion and othering through worship at Mennonite gatherings, and at the 2016 conference, I wanted to create opportunities for all the women present to feel a connection to God through singing, prayer, and worship. I remember a specific conversation during the worship planning process, where one worship planner suggested we invite just one woman (who happened to be a white, dominant-culture Mennonite) to lead the singing the entire conference—she said it would give continuity to our overarching worship plan. And she said we could sprinkle in a "special song" or two outside of traditional Mennonite hymns throughout the weekend. I explained that tokenism in worship wasn't what I was hoping for. I believe it is important for white, dominant-culture Mennonites to feel a little less at home—a little more discomfort in worship. People of color who have chosen to participate in work and worship with Mennonites because of Anabaptist-Mennonite theology experience this discomfort all the time. I wanted to normalize discomfort in the work of widening the circle and making space for one another. In the end, we invited four different worship leaders to organize and plan each of the worship services, inviting their own song leaders and readers, creating rituals and prayers in ways that felt authentic. On evaluations, several white, dominant-culture women named that this approach to worship was indeed discomforting. At the same time, several women of color participants named that this was the most at home they'd ever felt at a Mennonite gathering.

Our theme, *I've got the power! Naming and claiming power as a force for good*, gave us a vehicle through which to name and explore power with honesty and intentionality. Women of color were naming some hard things about racism and power, both from the plenary stage and in breakout sessions. And as planners, we began to notice what some have described as "a reaction" from white, dominant-culture women in response to their discomfort—things like interrupting women of color presenters during their presentations, talking over women of color during discussions, and correcting women of color presenters from the audience, among other things. At this conference, Erica Littlewolf, a member of the WIL steering committee, together with Chantelle Todman Moore, one of the plenary panelists, organized an autonomous space for women of color during the breakout sessions. This space was built into the conference schedule and listed during the breakout offerings. During this session, women of color came together and named the realities and the tensions they were carrying. We wondered together if the foundation of love we had built (2014) and the ideas of power we had explored together (2016) could hold naming these realities to the larger group. Could we as women of color stand in power and invite our sisters to increased self-awareness? Could we name for them that these reactions were not okay? Before her plenary presentation, Todman Moore did just that. She named instances where women of color had been hurt or mistreated at the conference that weekend. She didn't name names, but she named situations and invited white, dominant-culture women to reflect on their own actions, their own discomfort, and to sit with it.

One of the most difficult takeaways from the 2016 conference was recognizing the burden of emotional labor women of color were forced to carry because we as planners didn't build in clear expectations or create spaces for reflection as we invited white, dominant-culture Mennonite women to widen the circle.

Talkin' bout a revolution: Dialogue, practice and the work of liberation—Women Doing Theology 2018

After the 2016 conference, there was a transition in the WIL steering committee. Aveani Moeljono, Sandra Perez, and Moniqua Acosta transitioned off the committee, and we added Chantelle Todman Moore, Melissa Florer-Bixler, and Maribel Ramirez

Hinojosa. We gathered with this new group in September of 2017 to brainstorm, among other things, the next WDT conference. As we reflected on where we had been with WDT, we realized that we needed to move beyond discussing abstract ideas about widening the circle and creating space for the most marginalized among us. We wanted practice, which for us meant action. We wanted WDT participants to move beyond happy, aspirational, someday thoughts about what widening the circle and making space for one another could look like. We wanted to create a real-life, moving, and active model for space-making and circle-widening.

We landed on the theme *Talkin' Bout a Revolution: Dialogue, Practice and the Work of Liberation*. We hoped participants would engage in both the theory and practice involved in the work of liberation, not just for themselves but especially for the most marginalized among us, being mindful of the space we take up and intentional about sharing it. From among the steering committee, Melissa Florer-Bixler and Chantelle Todman Moore volunteered to be my primary partners in organizing and planning the 2018 conference.

In our preliminary planning, we identified several growing edges for WDT: creating safe(r) spaces, inequity in carrying the load of emotional labor, accountability, making more room for people who identify as LGBTQ, and partnering with people who don't identify as women (in this case, men). We also committed to continuing to build on the movement that had begun at the 2016 conference, centering the voices and experiences of women of color through representation—in worship, plenary presentations, and breakouts.

Shands Stoltzfus's "Creating Safe(r) Spaces" document had been used as a reference point at both the 2014 and 2016 conferences. But we realized that we needed some concrete expectations that would inform how we would be together in the WDT space. So, in addition to "Creating Safe(r) Spaces," at the 2018 conference, we came up with what we would come to call our WDT Community Commitments:

- **Centering the margins.** We will create and hold space at the center of our shared experience, discussion, worship and action for those whose voices have been historically on the margins in our country, in our denomination and in conference settings.

- **Comfort with discomfort.** We will come to this shared space expecting to be challenged and uncomfortable, pushed out of our comfort zones, letting go of business as usual or what feels normal to us in conference and/or church gatherings.

- **Bringing our whole selves.** We will create a place together where we each can feel safe enough to be authentic, sharing the gift of ourselves with one another.

- **Naming hard things.** We will not always get it right. We will make mistakes. We enter this space expecting to encounter difficult situations. We commit to naming and engaging with one another when things get hard. We commit to speaking truth with love.

- **Practicing grace and space.** We will extend grace to each other. And we'll set boundaries recognizing that sometimes the most loving thing we can do is create healthy space between us.

We published these commitments on the conference webpage and in the program book. In addition, five weeks before the conference, we sent out weekly emails with reflection questions inviting registered participants to reflect on each of the five Community Commitments as they prepared to come to WDT. And finally, on the first night of the conference, five conference participants each reflected on one of the commitments, framing it through their own personal perspective and experience—highlighting, again, the importance of these commitments for how we would be together at WDT, creating a common set of norms.

In an effort to share the emotional labor load and challenge white, dominant-culture Mennonites to reflect on their WDT experience—tensions or discomfort with new ways of being—

we created both autonomous and accountability spaces. Autonomous spaces created safe(r) space where women of color, Spanish speakers, LGBTQ people, and folks with disabilities, who might be experiencing similar things, could meet together—to process, to not feel so alone, to not have to create those spaces on their own. We also offered accountability spaces for men and for those who identify as white or part of the culture of whiteness. These spaces challenged both these groups to reflect on the tensions they carried, to name where their discomfort caused harm, and to hold one another accountable. All these groups met during the breakout sessions: there were two offerings each for autonomous spaces and whiteness accountability space and one offering for men's accountability. Themes that arose or situations that needed naming were collected in the notes for each of these groups, and their reports were compiled and read aloud at the closing session of the conference. This created opportunities for public accountability—to acknowledge areas of both growth and tension, for people to sit with their mistakes, and for us to collectively commit to doing our work to be whole people and authentic community.

This was the second WDT conference organized by Mennonite Church USA where men were invited. They had been invited to the 2014 conference "as listeners," without many guidelines. Three men attended, and a few women named through feedback that they had experienced harm as a result. This kind of harm happens because men (especially white men) are socialized and accustomed to the privilege of experiencing a world created for them. They walk into a room expecting to be respected and acknowledged, that others will assume the best about them, to feel a certain degree of comfort. If they aren't able to recognize this privilege, if they are not self-aware, they tend to assume everyone experiences the world the way they do, free from the daily trauma of oppression and discrimination. And, without intentional inner work, it is difficult for these men to co-create a space that honors the voices of women. This manifests in a context like WDT with interruptions to presenters, denying or negating women's experiences, keeping women after presentations to argue, or questioning the truth in women's stories. And when women come expecting a safe(r) place to share ideas, create and do theology together, these kinds of interactions can feel like betrayal. So, in 2016, we elected not to invite men. Increasingly though, WIL recognized the advantages in building bridges with allies and began seeking to create partnerships in our work. We saw WDT as one way to build those connections, offering men an opportunity to participate. We partnered with Isaac Villegas, a Mennonite pastor from North Carolina, who the planning team recognized as an ally already, and together we created an application form for men who wanted to participate in WDT. Men could register only after they had submitted an application and had received an email invitation from Isaac and the planning team. Nine men participated in the conference. They were given some clear guidelines beforehand about their participation—their primary purpose to listen and learn, they were urged to save comments and questions for after presentations—creating space for women to be the primary guides for shaping conversations. As I mention above, they were also invited to accountability space to process together and hold one another accountable. Participants in the men's cohort expressed gratitude for the new and different ways of being they were able to experience as a result.

We let go of the kitchen table model for discussion at this conference and invited three women of color, two who were not Mennonite, to present during the plenary sessions. We invited a womanist pastor, an Anabaptist-Mennonite professor, and a Tejana poet to reflect on our theme and offer insight from an even broader perspective.[4] There can exist among Mennonites a tendency toward insularity. We begin to believe that truth and enlightenment can only come through "one of us." Which leads to the question: Who is "one of us"? Who decides where enlight-

---

4 The word *Tejanos/as* refers to Latinos/as of Mexican decent whose families have inhabited this land since before it was called Mexico. It is sometimes easy to forget (if you aren't from here) that a quarter of the United States used to be Mexico. Texas is one of those places, and Mexican people were living in Texas, on this land, when it became part of the United States.

enment comes from and through whom? Is it possible that the Spirit of God can move through a womanist non-Mennonite pastor, a Tejana poet exploring theopoetics? As planners, we hoped that this stretching of boundaries of the definition of "us" would also help widen the circle. We hoped to break down more barriers so that even more people, people who might not even consider themselves Mennonite, would catch a glimpse of a new liberative way of doing theology. And WDT did indeed attract a broader demographic in 2018—9 percent of conference participants self-identified as non-Mennonite.

My mantra in organizing all the elements for this conference—worship planning, presenters, special music, workshops and papers, autonomous and accountability space leaders—was *representation matters.* I urged us not to choose or invite out of convenience or based on who we know but to be intentional about inviting women of color and LGBTQ folks to participate actively from the stage and the podium. It matters who is there. It is important for all participants to be able to see a reflection of themselves at the center of our action and activity.

Conclusion

Over the course of five years, Mennonite Church USA's WIL has organized three WDT conferences—each one a step in widening the circle, each one an invitation to share more and own more power. Every conference taught us a bit more about what it means and what it costs to create spaces where we can all, tentatively and tenderly, bring our authentic selves and contribute our perspectives and experiences to a broader conversation about theology. Leading this work has felt vulnerable, sacred, and so important—using the power of my position to create space for more women of color to stand confidently in their own power and—together with all who are willing—building something new. I have been so grateful for the honor of ushering this movement further into being.

7

Attempted Erasure

Pieter Niemeyer

A peculiar people are we.
    Our history not lived in plain sight.
    Apparently, we're not supposed to be.
    Abomination! They declare with brutal might.
    Unnatural! Abhorrent! Can't you see?
    "Go invisible, into the shadow of night."
    "Disappear," my whisper says to me.
    But, it's not done without a fight.
    I refuse to leave,
    To hide out of sight.
    Peculiar I will be.

Many marginalized people often speak of their experience of erasure, especially as it relates to the intersectionality of marginalized identities. For example, erasure can be compounded by the intersection of multiple marginal identities such as someone who is Black, a transwoman, and an immigrant. Erasure is experienced when people who have power and privilege within a society control whose voices are heard or whose stories or histories are told. They control who has access to addressing matters of justice, well-being, and self-determination. Erasure is feeling as if you don't exist within the very society within which you live—your stories are not reflected back to you, your voice is not heard, and access to power and self-determination are denied you.

In the spirit of resisting erasure, allow me to introduce myself. My name is Pieter Niemeyer, and I am gay, and I am Christian. I know in many church circles this is considered a contradiction of terms—a point not lost on me when I came out to a family member several years ago. To them I was either gay or I was Christian but not both. To be Christian, I would need to erase being gay. To be gay, I would need to erase being Christian. The intersectionality of them both was something that could not be recognized. This family member could not reconcile these two realities because the church had taught them that these were irreconcilable. Hence, the experience of erasure. Those with power in the Church were erasing the current and past realities of lesbian, gay, bisexual, trans, or queer (LGBTQ+) people in the Church.[1] I can't erase being gay. I know. I tried. And, I don't want to erase being Christian. I have grown up hearing that being gay is an abomination, a perversion, unnatural, a sin. It's an exercise of power by the church in messaging that leaves a deep negative imprint within the spiritual, emotional, psychological, physical, and social well-being of us who are LGBTQ+ in the church.

Over the past several years, a growing number of Christian communities have developed more nuanced ways of framing it, but in the end, the heart of the matter is that LGBTQ+ people within the church have been perceived, by straight, cis-gender Christians, particularly those in positions of power, as a "problem" to resolve.[2] History reveals the many and varied ways in which both church and state sought to resolve the persistent presence of LGBTQ+ people through doctrine, teaching, moralization,

---

1 I use the terms *queer* or *LGBTQ+* for simplicity sake. I add a + sign to indicate those who are intersex, two spirited, questioning, asexual, genderqueer, gender fluid, or allies, acknowledging an evolving company of people as we come to better understand the complexity of gender and sexual identity. I understand there is complexity in using labels that can oversimplify complex matters and engender polarization.

2 I use the terms *straight* and *cis-gender* to refer to those who do not identify as gay and who identify with the gender assigned to them at birth, respectively.

criminalization, and pathologization. LGBTQ+ people have been incarcerated, burned at the stake, murdered, shunned, persecuted, silenced, and subjected to drug therapy, castrations of various kinds, electric shock therapy, and conversion or reparative therapies.[3] Others have tried to be more compassionate by allowing a gradation of "acceptance-with-restrictions" approach—a position that accepts that sexual orientation cannot be changed and therefore should not be punished but requires LGBTQ+ people to not be "practicing."[4] This, for example, is the current official teaching of the denomination to which I belong, Mennonite Church Canada. LGBTQ+ people who are "practicing" are officially identified by the denomination as being at variance to church teaching. Whether a "practicing" (or non-practicing for that matter) LGBTQ+ person within Mennonite Church Canada denominational bodies are subjected to punitive measures is entirely dependent on individual congregations and denominational area church leadership. This makes navigating the uncertainties of the various levels (local, regional, national) of denominational life difficult for LGBTQ+ persons. Some churches make it clear what their stance is, either supportive or not, while a significant segment leave the matter ambiguous, placing LGBTQ+ persons in a state of uncertainty at every turn. Employing uncertainty is a power tool because those with the power will always be the ones to "clarify" the meaning. Some churches have also employed passive means to isolate and discourage LGBTQ+ persons from being active in congregational life or pastoral ministry or leadership positions within congregations or the denomination. Speaking from personal experience, to "come out" and remain in ministry within Mennonite circles is costly. It cost me professionally and personally.

Within the broader church over the past couple decades, a minority of churches and a handful of denominations have reached

---

3 "UN Issues First Report on Human Rights of Gay and Lesbian People."

4 The term *practicing* is used as a euphemism that refers to being sexually active within a same sex relationship. It is a term that strikes many LGBTQ+ people as being humorous and revealing of its homophobic source. Such a term would never be used to describe heterosexual relationships.

resolutions of full acceptance of LGBTQ+ persons. However, such resolutions have been obtained only after intense, divisive, painful processes that demand of LGBTQ+ people extensive emotional, physical, spiritual, and mental stamina to endure. People of faith who do not fit into the heteronormative framework—a worldview that promotes heterosexuality and its associated binary gender roles as the normal or preferred sexual orientation—require deep resolve to persist in faith. Many of these denominational processes, including within my own denomination, excluded the voices of LGBTQ+ persons from the very decision-making processes affecting LGTBQ+ people most directly—a powerful example of erasure and abuse of power by the majority. Even though I value my faith, the church has not made it easy to stay. The deep resolve of many LGBTQ+ people to persist in faith is a gift to the larger church but, unfortunately, one often overlooked or even trampled underfoot. I am grateful for my current congregational home that has done significant work to reach a place of full acceptance, though it came at a significant price for those LGTBQ+ people who used to or currently call it their church home.

I came to embrace faith as a teenager—a stage of life when I was also being infused with life-altering hormones. Like most other teenagers, I experience this time of life as awkward and unsettling for me. However, unlike most other teenagers, I wasn't fitting into the larger powerful social script. It's a script so powerful that most people don't even notice it exists, unless you don't fit, and then it's impossible to ignore. The script, ritualized by the larger society, is that you grow up, fall in love, get married, and have a family. It assumes that one identifies with the sex assigned at birth and that one will fall in love with someone of the opposite sex, or that one's biological make-up is clearly identified as male or female. Go to any gift card store, and you will see how this powerful narrative is told, celebrated, and honored. The rituals are well known and are reinforced through family rituals, stories, and traditions. As a gay teen, all of this terrified me because the way I was instinctively wired didn't fit those overarching life narratives. There simply weren't positive role models or rituals known to me of men who fell in love with each other, married, established families, and attended church. It just didn't exist.

Such people existed, and such relationships were there, but they were erased, hidden out of sight. This felt isolating, and I knew from all the social cues that to reveal my being gay would be dangerous, so it was better to just keep it to myself and hope and pray that it would just go away—be erased. I have since discovered that this is such a common experience for queer people when facing these powerful social narratives that there is even a phrase for this: praying the gay away. Unfortunately, this form of prayer also leads to another common experience for LGBTQ+ kids and adults alike: compartmentalisation—separating one's life into various compartments because of the apparent impossibility for the various parts to exist in an integrated, holistic, healthy way. Being in the closet is compartmentalising, which is unhealthy for psycho-social development. It is physically, spiritually, emotionally, relationally, and sexually exhausting and abusive.

"Do you not see me?"
God, what's the matter with you?
Do you not see me?
Have you not heard the stifled sobs and inward groans?
God, what's the matter with you,
That you have not seen what's the matter with me?
Were it just me, maybe I could understand the oversight,
But there's been a river of queer tears,
A chorus of inward groans.
Do you not have eyes to see or ears to hear?
God, what's the matter with you
not seeing what's the matter with me?
Has their erasure of us
made us invisible to you?

How is it that you stay?

There came a time when I couldn't sustain being in the closet anymore, and the draw to become integrated became overwhelm-

ing. So I began the process of moving toward integration, complicated by the fact that I was in a straight marriage and employed
as a pastor in a non-affirming church. This reflects the situation
of numerous mixed-orientation marriages—a marriage with one
straight partner and the other either bisexual or gay—that exist
but are rendered invisible in both church and society. It was not
uncommon in years past for pastoral—and even secular clinical—
counselors to encourage those struggling with their sexual orientation to pursue heterosexual relationships and marriages as a
way to resolve their struggle. Many of these marriages represent
deep pain and reflect a history of a deeply abusive approach for all
involved. This upholds heteronormativity and employs again a
use of power for the purposes of queer erasure.

How is it that you stay in the church? The question, and
underlying challenge, came from a friend, also in a mixed orientation marriage, as we were walking along the banks of a river one
day. We were catching up with each other and sharing about our
journeys of faith and being gay. I was out, and he was not. I knew
from his story that he left the church some time ago; however, his
employment was still church affiliated and being "out" would cost
him his job. In his personal faith journey, he was no longer able,
or willing, to put up with the ongoing brutality that came from
many sectors of the church—official church teaching, leadership,
clergy, and laypeople alike. The church has been and remains one
of the most pernicious contributors to homophobia.

How is it that you stay? It was a fair question to ask. As a pastor, I had always counseled those in abusive relationships to seek
safety first—to remove themselves from the situation—and then,
from a position of safety, to evaluate whether the relationship can
be salvaged and, if so, how to re-establish it on healthier grounds.
Yet, here was I staying in relationship with church. The decision
my friend took made perfect sense to me. My friend is no longer a
believer. His pedigree was thoroughly conservative and evangelical, but now he was agnostic at best—on his good days. The pain
of holding onto the faith is costly, and I don't blame any LGBTQ+
person for laying faith aside. I have often struggled with God as to

why God allowed the Bible to be so easily weaponized by people. Religiously encoded discrimination can take on some of the most intense expressions of disdain, hatred, and abuse.

Why were Jews subjected to such vicious attacks by Christians who read Scripture through such an anti-Semitic lens, which in turn laid the foundations for the Holocaust? Why were women subjugated by men who read Scripture, from their positions of power and privilege, through a misogynistic lens that argued for women's subordination and inferiority? Why was slavery permitted to be sanctioned as part of the law of Israel and then later sanctioned by the church for over eighteen hundred years? Furthermore, why was this institution of slavery allowed to be racialized through a racist reading of Scripture? This racist reading of Scripture, paired with European Imperial Colonialism and its economy of the slave trade, devastated the people of Africa and the African diaspora in the Americas.[5] Why were Indigenous peoples torn from their families and denied their culture and language under the direction of both church and state? Such unimaginable horrors. Why have people experienced, and why do they continue to experience, such life threatening, religiously encoded, "righteously held" discrimination?

The scriptures are clear! is a phrase that I am all too familiar with. It's a silencing tool, an instrument used to ensure that I know my place and to cut off any kind of meaningful conversation. It is a response that works on an erroneous assumption that Scripture speaks with a unified voice on all matters, and all that is required is unbridled obedience. The problem is that it doesn't work that way. For example, Moses, married to a Midianite, declared prohibitions against Israel marrying foreign women. In Deuteronomy 23:3, the Law states, "No Ammonite or Moabite shall be admit-

---

5 See the chapters in this volume by Augustine and Delanty, which discuss the Doctrine of Discovery, encoded in documents written in the fifteenth century and still influential today, which gave religious justification for the subjugation and exploitation of Indigenous and non-Christian peoples. The United Nations DESA has also produced a helpful report: "Impact of the 'Doctrine of Discovery' on Indigenous Peoples."

ted to the assembly of the Lord. Even to the tenth generation." It sounds straightforward. But, like a lot of verses in the Bible, it wasn't as clear as that. Israelites married foreign people anyway, as evidenced in the genealogy of Jesus, several times over. One of the most treasured stories of Jesus's ancestral heritage is that of Ruth and Boaz. Ruth was a Moabite. Her husband had been an Israelite seeking refuge in the land of Moab during a famine. They married. Ruth's mother-in-law, Naomi, had two other sons who did the same. As fate would have it, Naomi's husband and sons all die in Moab, and Naomi decides to return to Israel. Ruth refuses to remain behind and boldly states her love and loyalty: "Wherever you go, I will go with you." To make an intriguing story short, Ruth ends up marrying the Israelite, Boaz. Ruth was the great grandmother of David, the celebrated King of Israel— just barely two generations out from this mixed marriage, much less ten.

The story of Ruth was recorded and told during a time of Israel's history in which Ezra extended the intermarriage prohibition even beyond the nations listed in Deuteronomy. The story of Ruth, however, was an interruption to Ezra's call. It stands as a testament over and against Ezra. Ruth, and her inclusion into the genealogy of Jesus, along with Bathsheba and Rahab the sex worker, all give evidence that the Bible is not at all clear regarding rules and who keeps them, including God.

The world is not a clear place, nor is the Bible in its reflection of us, yet God seems comfortable to work with it, even if we are not. The genealogy of Jesus introduces us to the strangest story of them all. We might even call it a queer story. God gets Mary— a young, unmarried woman—pregnant. God then encourages Joseph to step up and take the heat for the situation. Jesus grows up with one mother and two fathers. The Christian confession is that Jesus himself is part and parcel of the Godhead, three in one! Talk about blended family and queer, non-binary identity! If my telling of this story sounds offensive, that is because we have become used to a sanitized, domesticated telling of the story. This is a story that tears open great possibilities in a messy world that isn't remotely clear. So, the next time I hear *The scriptures are clear*, I will take it as a cue to offer God a quiet prayer of gratitude for its messiness.

I wrote a prayer that arose from my wrestling with God regarding Scripture. I wrote it while contemplating two stories from Scripture that gave me hope. The first is a relatively obscure story of the daughters of Zelophehad, found in Numbers 27:1–11. In this story, Zelophehad dies, leaving his five unmarried daughters to face destitution because they are not entitled, according to God's law, to inherit their father's land because they are female. In the face of this stark reality, they bring their complaint to Moses and implore him to ask God to change the law. God hears their complaint and agrees with them that the law needs to change.

The second story is the story of the Syrophoenician woman from Mark 7:24–30. She is a gentile woman who asks Jesus to heal her child. Jesus refuses her initial request by saying he came for his fellow Jews and not for "dogs." The woman replies, "Even the dogs get to eat the crumbs that fall from the table." This response softens Jesus, and he responds to her act of faith by healing her child.

In these two stories, the women refuse to be silenced or rendered invisible and call out God in a manner of faith that changes God's mind. These are scriptures that affirm hope and faith in a God committed to transformation aligned with mercy, justice, and love—from which the courage arose to pray this prayer for myself.

Prayer for courage to find my voice for change

God, I lack the courage to find my voice. It's like I cannot breathe. My body seems to sabotage me. The knees feel like buckling from under me, should I give voice to what I need to say.

My stomach is in turmoil and what would come forth, I fear, would not be words. My tongue is tied, and what

words that could come,
would only be stammered.

God, grant me courage.

I will remember Mahlah, Noah, Hoglah, Milcah, and Tirzah. The five daughters of Zelophehad, who in the face of the law that denied them, found their voice of protest.

What courage was summoned to call you out, God.

How easy it would have been to remain silenced and just endure, and yet they found their voice to say your law was unjust—not fair!

I will remember the nameless woman, an outsider, a Syrophoenician.
She, whom even Jesus called a dog, was up against the wall, denied.

Desperate.

Yet, it was there that she found her voice, and quipped back,
"But even the dogs eat the crumbs that fall from the children's table."

God, you heard the complaint of the daughters and changed your law to accommodate mercy and justice.

God, you heard the complaint of the Syrophoenician woman, whom you knew by name, and responded with healing and wholeness.

God, hear my voice, and those of my queer siblings.

We too have been silenced and treated like dogs by your people and your word.

It's not fair. It's not just.

God, we are calling you, and your people, out.

In the tradition of these brave women, I too will raise my voice for change.

A change of heart.
A body set free.
A voice of your breath,
received in grace.

Amen.

Why I stay

I stay because I believe that God is one who acts toward justice and always calls the people of God to interpret Scripture through the lens of love, mercy, compassion, and justice. I believe the Bible is a beautifully complex collection of writings that requires us to hold generous space in the task of interpretation, not only because of the abusive and deadly history of poor hermeneutical readings of Scripture but also because the communities from which the writings emerged are themselves filled with tensions that refuse to allow only one interpretation. We queer Christians have a phrase for those passages of Scripture used by the church to discriminate against us. We call them the *clobber passages* because of their history of weaponization to do us harm. I stay because I want to unarm the use of Scripture to discriminate against anyone. I stay because I believe the original intent of God is for the unfolding of love and that the witness of Scripture is that those who have experienced erasure—the stranger, the foreigner, the widow, the outcast—have been the vehicle of this love revealed.

Susie, my queerly covenanted family partner (another story to be told), has called me a "coming out tank." Why? Because I came out to well over two hundred people, mostly face to face, in a rather short period of time. What seemed to be the path was to have one on one and small group conversations or correspondence. We would ask people to guard our conversations by holding confidentiality to allow this to unfold until our faith community was fully informed. When I relay this process to others, there is an overwhelming sense of gratitude for the remarkable gift of confidentiality offered to allow this process to unfold.

Over the course of sharing my story, I have heard words of encouragement—often expressed through comments as *It doesn't matter, It makes no difference, It's not my business,* or *It doesn't change anything.* What I understood by these comments is that the relationship isn't negatively affected in any way with this disclosure. Recognizing that people have often ended relationships over the sharing of such information, I am grateful for affirmations of relationship. As I heard these comments many times over, however, I began to think to myself, *It does matter, and it does make a difference, and it is your business.* I began to feel that these phrases needed to be unpacked more for all our sakes.

My goal is to explore the faith reasons for why it matters, and why it makes a difference, and why it is other people's business. Right now, it matters. Relationally, theologically, spiritually, and sexually—it all matters. A time will come when we can say, *It doesn't matter, It makes no difference,* or *It's not my business,* and that will be fine. But that time is not now.

It matters now because of the power imbalance and the abuse suffered by LGBTQ+ people. As Christians, we believe we are the body of Christ. Therefore, we are interconnected. Paul's argument is that when one part of the body suffers—or, conversely, when one part is honored—it affects the whole body. I, as a member of the body of Christ, suffered as a gay person because of the church's abuse of power. We, together as LGBTQ+ Christians, have experienced pain and suffered invisibility and open discrimination as members of the body.

It matters because we are members of the body of Christ, and we are to care for each other. *It makes a difference* because there is a difference. I am not the same as one who is straight. Growing up straight in a straight person's world is no struggle for many. Growing up gay in a straight person's world is all about struggle because of the power imbalance that exists. It makes a difference because there is a difference. The church has always celebrated straight relationships and offered rituals and positive role modeling and encouragement. Virtually none of this was offered to its LGBTQ+ children. I look forward to a time when it doesn't matter. But we are not there yet.

It makes a difference because we are members of the body of Christ and in our difference, we are to care for each other. My story, our stories, as LGBTQ+ Christians, *are all Christians' business.* Business as usual only benefits straight people, as power within church systems and rituals and blessings of milestones and relationships benefit them. The status quo doesn't allow for generous space for LGBTQ+ Christians to be who they are without being at variance to our various confessions of faith and church doctrine. Because we are members of the body of Christ, it is everyone's business as we care for each other.

Caring for one another means listening and hearing each other's story and not assuming matters of honesty or dishonesty regarding being in the closet. My oldest brother didn't congratulate me about "finally being honest" about myself. No. Instead, what he offered me was an apology, saying he was sorry our family had not been a safe place for me to come out. He understood. I didn't always know how to hold my truth, but I held it. The larger world wouldn't hear it. For those courageous enough to come out, or who were forced out, or who had no option of ever being in a closet in the first place, the larger world often punished them. Therefore, the wisest thing was not necessarily to come out, but rather to stay safe. The lack of safety did not come from LGBTQ+ people.

As I shared my story, many people were concerned and afraid for me and my family. I was often told that I was being very courageous. Why? It isn't an issue of dishonesty, as some have made it out to be. It's an issue of safety. That's why people are in the closet. So, *it does matter. It does make a difference. And it is your business.* I was afraid. There are others who are afraid within the body of Christ. I stay because I am resisting erasure. I refuse to disappear. Despite the church's attempt to erase us, there is a legacy of LGBTQ+ people within the history of the church, and I want to be a part of that peculiar story. My coming out story and those of my fellow LGBTQ+ siblings matter to the church because together we make up the body of Christ, and it matters that the abuse stops and those with power learn what it means to care for one another.

Caring requires creating safe communities.
Caring requires educating ourselves
and re-evaluating assumptions.
Caring requires honest reflection regarding
use of power and privilege.
Caring requires taking responsibility for harm done and
seeking reconciliation.
Caring doesn't require agreement;
it requires generous and gracious space.
Caring doesn't ignore the wounds in the body;
rather it pays careful attention.
Caring requires us to model the radical hospitality of Jesus.
Caring requires seeing.
Seeing those who have been erased.
Learning their stories, celebrating their gifts.
This matters, and it will make a difference in our
business of being church.

8

Poetic Reflections on Being Queer and Mennonite

Steph Chandler Burns

Identifying as queer and Mennonite is both gift and difficulty. These dual, sometimes at-odds identities often clash or confuse one another. They can create wedges in how I find I can interact with the wider church or other people and even in my own healthy interactions with myself. But do not be mistaken: these difficulties do not come from being queer. Knowing God to have created me with love and seeing that even in the parts of myself that the church would reject have long brought me closer to God. Self-exploration, reflection, and discernment on these two, often competing, parts of identity have been a beautiful and fruitful piece of my life and my relationship to a God of love, compassion, and justice.

Over recent years I've come to realize the ways that pieces of our identities can show us parts of who God is. My lived experience as a white, middle-class, bisexual, queer, Mennonite, Christian woman has influenced my understanding of the divine. I have begun writing intentionally to include both themes of faith and sexuality in the same work. My poetry explores topics of faith, sexuality, belonging, lament, pain, and exclusion and reflects my journey to find my place of belonging within the body of Christ. Given that LGBTQ+ folks still have fewer spots at the proverbial table in faith discussions, power ends up being a key theme throughout these works. What does it mean to seek power as someone on the margins of the church? Whose voices are heard, and who needs others to advocate for them? What does it mean to find a voice in the church? This work is not meant to get into the weeds of making an argument for LGBTQ+ inclusion. It is not meant to prove that the church is not yet a safe place for LGBTQ+ voices, or even to explain queer theory or theology, as these things are handled in more detail elsewhere.[1] Instead, this work shares a few glimpses of my own experiences with being queer and Christian.

Grandmother God

My first poem is about my grandparents, who were active in the early days of LGBTQ+ advocacy in the Mennonite Church. They and other advocates in the mid-to-late 1980s began the work of trying to make room for LGBTQ+ people in the Mennonite Church.[2] I am deeply grateful for the previous generations of advocates and justice workers who began paving the way for the level of acceptance and welcome that I do get to experience today. My own grandparents have taught me something of God: God is a grandmother. She is fiercely loving of her grandchildren and stands up to anyone who would exclude them. More than anything, she wants her beloved grandchildren to thrive in a church that loves them as much as she does.

Grandmother God

I remember the day I learned
my grandma was a feminist
how much less alone I felt knowing
this really is in my blood

---

1 See, for example, Chandler Burns, "Nonbinary Identity," 95–106, and my other works delving into queer and Mennonite identity in more depth.

2 For more information on this history, see Rogalsky, "Voice from Outside the Gate," 19.

and grandma,
   in fighting by resisting
   the norms placed on her and her children
   in quietly, in her way
   standing up to the world, proclaiming:
     "this is not okay"

made room
     for queer little me at the table
     for me to own my voice
     in echoing her lament:
"this is not okay"

and in so doing
     ushering, birthing

Her kingdom come
   On earth as in heaven

An Attempt at Shaking Off the Dust

This past year has been a painful one in my relationship with the church. I love God deeply, and I feel called to share this love with the church. I have gifts in preaching, worship leading, and group facilitation that have been affirmed in my faith community. Nothing else brings me the same joy or fulfilment as reflecting on God's Word and joining with others in discussions about where we see God together. Yet in the past year, I was not selected to speak and serve in a number of contexts specifically because of my sexuality. These are painful moments, which make me question whether the church is a place where I should stay involved. There is a violence present in being told my gifts are not welcome in God's family. Yet my love of God and my love of the church keep me coming back. In this second work, I grapple with my interconnectedness with even those who might reject me.

An Attempt at Shaking Off the Dust

That you would have
  me stand before you
  to share my own fear
  my learnings or my struggles
  to feed only your agenda

This is violence

That you would see
  me only by one label
  one term of many descriptors
  that rises to the top
  and thus assume my agenda

This is violence

That you might meet
  me on the street
  and care enough to give me food—
  physical nutrition
  but refuse me spiritual sustenance

This too is violence

That you would read
  the story of my struggles
  with how the church has pushed me away
  and use it as a reason to refuse me space

This is traumatic, physical, spiritual, and sexual violence

This is wielding of a lord's power
  in a way that is not
  God-ordained

This makes an idol of your comfort
  an altar of your traditions where you
  worship your own fears

A dear friend told me
  "wherever they will not receive you
  shake the dust off your shoes
  and move on to the next church"

But it's hard to shake the dust off
  when we are made of dust
  and it's hard to write you off as other
  when we breathe the same Spirit of God

And as much as I'd love to
  move on to the next church

You and I remain intimately connected

Claiming Voice

When I was completing my Masters of Theological Studies at Conrad Grebel University College in Waterloo, Ontario, my last course was on preaching. Allan Rudy-Froese, our professor, focused on preaching as performance, teaching us to pay attention to our bodies, energy, and voices as we deliver a message.[3] Throughout the class, he encouraged us to be intentional about voices and invited us into deeper self-knowledge in order to do our best work when delivering a spoken message. I was deeply uncomfortable with the exercises on the topic of voice and on later reflection realized that this was because one of my major triggers is feeling voiceless. There are many times, as someone occupying marginal spaces of the church, that I feel voiceless. Such voicelessness feels like powerlessness. This poem describes one of our class exercises: naming our voice. A few weeks following the class, my voice found a name. Now, when I am feeling like I lack power or voice, I remember the story of Vashti from the Book of Esther, chapter 1.

---

3 Rudy-Froese, "Preaching."

Claiming Voice

"Think about your voice,"
  he said, "and name it."
And I thought, "What a cheesy idea."

But, tired of being
  pushed down
  ignored
  silenced
  she answered,
  "My name is Vashti."

Vashti, for an ancient,
  slighted queen
  who, refusing to be made
    an object
  refusing to have her
    needs ignored
  refusing to be silenced
  told her king,
  "HELL NO."

And that is where her story ends.

Except now, my voice
  refusing to be made an object,
  refusing to have my needs ignored,
  refusing to be silenced
  responds,
  "HELL NO."

Early Sunday Morning

My final two poems are from a writing exercise I did one Easter season, when I reflected each day on queerness. What is the message of Easter in queer lives? Easter Sunday was particularly beautiful. Just as Mary's eyes were opened to God in her midst even through grief and pain, I need the reminder that God is with me. Even in church dialogue when I disagree, or have a hard time seeing Christ in another's point of view, I need to remember that God is not far from me. In the church, in a time of debate over queer lives, LGBTQ+ welcome, and affirming processes, those of us with stakes in the conversation must remember that God goes with us there. We all do well, on any side (of any topic), to remember that we all have a limited understanding of who God is and what God is doing. Just like Mary turned to understand Christ anew at the tomb, so too must we.

Early Sunday Morning

Remember that time
   the time at the tomb
   when Mary saw angels
   she saw Jesus
   but still kept seeking her Lord?
   "Why are you crying?"
   "They've taken my Lord, and
   I do not know to where."
   Until finally she recognized
   he hadn't been so far after all.

And this reminds me
   of the times when I've broken down
   when confronted by pictures of God
   which differ from mine
   when God seems distant
      or different
      or too small
   and I cry
   "They've taken my Lord, and
   I do not know to where"
   only to turn around and realize
   God maybe wasn't too far from me after all.

Death into Life

We remember Christ's death and resurrection through ritual on Easter Sunday. In the congregation in which I grew up, they have recently begun covering the cross with flowers as an act of communal worship on Easter Sunday. This time becomes a holy time of remembering together that death has no grip. My queer reflections on Easter had me asking what it means to similarly transform today's instruments of death. In reflecting on this, I realized that, far too often for queer and LGBTQ+ folks, the church and Christianity remain such instruments of death. What would it mean to cover the church in new symbols of life that thrives in the face of the loss of queer lives?

Death into Life

We covered the cross with flowers
　　A defiant act
　　of turning an ancient instrument of torture
　　into a symbol of life

How I long for queer new life
　　and I wonder:
　　if we could turn our own instruments of torture
　　into symbols of new life

How would Christianity change?

Conclusion

My most difficult times with the church are when I feel my voice or agency is denied to me by those who can wield power over me. My deepest grief has come when I have been uninvited from preaching or denied work specifically because of my sexuality. These are times when I was not given a voice, both literally and metaphorically. My agency in speaking the word of God as a preacher or in discerning my call to ministry was denied.

While too often I feel like power is denied to me, and my voice is weak and unheard, Isaiah 35 offers a vision of God's people redeemed. This new vision promises water in the wilderness and streams in the desert. In the new creation, Isaiah tells us that "the eyes of the blind shall be opened, and the ears of the deaf unstopped; [. . . those who cannot walk] shall leap like a deer, and the tongue of the speechless sing for joy" (vv. 5–6). Indeed, in my life, this is where I get a glimpse of the new heaven and earth: when my voice is affirmed and I can sing praise to my God as a queer person.

I see God working for the new creation in people making space for my voice and the voices of others like me. I see God working for the new creation in allies using their power to share power with me. I see God when I'm able to claim my own voice. I see God when I learn I need to share the power I do have. And I see God as I'm able to build relationships with others who see the world differently than I do, and we come to understand each other better. These moments of shared and claimed power point toward the new creation, one that is coming and, sometimes, is already here.

9

Phoenix 2013
A Poem
Jennifer Delanty

Mennonite Church USA's Executive Board voted to convene their 2013 national convention in Phoenix, Arizona. (These conventions occur every two years at the start of July.) This was a controversial decision that aggrieved many across the denomination, as it meant Hispanic pastors and church members who were undocumented would be at risk of arrest or deportation due to Arizona's draconian immigration laws. The installation of our denomination's first Latina moderator on the Executive Board, Elizabeth Soto Albrecht, was slated to occur at this convention. En route to Phoenix, she visited Hispanic congregations across the United States—many of whom elected to stay home for safety reasons or in protest of the decision to meet in Arizona. This poem gives voice to what I experienced at the delegate tables with my fellow white brethren while attending my first national convention.

Phoenix 2013

We claim the Prince of Peace as our Savior
Yet have not a cup of cold water for those
Crossing the blistering desert.

We worship the same Lord
But do not wish to learn Spanish
Nor give serious thought about why
Lives are risked over a border
Drawn through this inferno.

We claim each other as brother and sister
Yet seem unable to appreciate the portent
Of our incoming Latina moderator.
Instead "we" fret about whether "they" will assimilate—
After all, "The Blacks have never assimilated,"
An Iowa delegate declares.

We listen to stories of sacrifice
And sermons of radical hospitality
Then turn to each other at delegate tables
With unrepentant hearts, drained of compassion.

As I think of my pioneer ancestors
Emigrating on the Oregon Trail
Sweeping life as they knew it
From Native Americans all along the way,
It strikes me that "they" were not accommodated
In an air-conditioned convention center
To mull over their misgivings about "us."

10

Silencing Sacrificial Lambs
The Use of Power in a Mennonite Church Convention

Bradley Siebert

I study religious rhetoric, particularly that of American Mennonites. I'm interested in the communication practices we use to develop our understandings of things and, in turn, get things done. Like many other religious people, we Mennonites call this process *discernment*. Mennonites prioritize doing discernment as communities: in our local congregations and, through delegates that congregations authorize to do the broader church's collective business, in the conventions of our area conferences and our denomination—which are more abstract communities but still communities that lend us cherished facets of our spiritual identities. We like to believe that our communication practices are egalitarian and peaceful, which they can be. However, as people set an agenda and run a meeting, power is inevitably exercised—we trust—benevolently. But even so, well-intentioned people have their biases, and harm may be done.

In 2015, I attended the national convention of Mennonite Church USA (MCUSA) not as a delegate but simply as a convention-goer without official responsibilities. In part, I went to observe delegates and other officials of the church do their business, particularly the business surrounding two resolutions for addressing the denomination's intensifying conflict over the inclusion and ministry of LGBTQ+ believers. Strongly inclined to inclusion and affirmation, I also planned to attend presentations and discussions and other activities organized by LGBTQ+ believers and their allies. What follows is my account of my observations, rooted in a moment of wordless communication, interspersed with some historical background to the convention.

Disappointment

My sister, Joleen, and I emerged from the delegate session hall at the Kaufman Center, downtown Kansas City, Thursday, July 2, 2015. Mennonite Church USA convention delegates had just passed the resolution reaffirming and even fortifying MCUSA's divisive Membership Guidelines. It passed by a relatively narrow margin—relative, that is, compared to that morning's passing margin for the resolution affirming forbearance as the denomination's guiding principle amid "differences," specifically, differences over the membership and ministry of faithful people who identify as LGBTQ+. In 2001, the Mennonite groups merging to become MCUSA instituted these differences, through their Membership Guidelines, as their defining conflict.

Aimee, my oldest daughter, was still inside the hall, beside herself with disappointment, sobbing, though less violently now. Her husband, Michael, was comforting her, as were others, startled by her powerful show of sorrow. (She feels so strongly.) However, that she felt strongly at that moment was hardly startling. She represented First Mennonite Church, Denver, the congregation that some currently misplaced at the center of the conflict that motivated denominational discernment about forbearance and about its Membership Guidelines. FMC Denver was in the process of ordaining for ministry a woman who identifies as lesbian.[1]

Passage of the forbearance resolution that morning with a nearly 72 percent approval had encouraged Aimee, Michael, Joleen, me, and many others.[2] And, naturally, Aimee and Michael

---

1 Huber, "Conference to License Gay Pastor," 1, 14. Schrag, "MC USA Won't Recognize Colorado Pastor's Licensing," 1, 13.

2 Schrag, "What Works for Denominations Now?," 12.

felt especially good at that moment because their congregation seemed about to emerge from beneath the shadow of possible denominational discipline, perhaps excommunication. Because the two resolutions were at odds in significant ways, we were hopeful that the Membership Guidelines resolution would fail. But its 60 percent passage had yanked the "welcome mat" out from under our feet—but even more from under the feet of the faithful who identify as LGBTQ+.[3]

Background: Membership Guidelines

MCUSA's Membership Guidelines had bedeviled the denomination since its pre-history amid the work of integrating the former Mennonite Church (MC) and General Conference Mennonite Church (GCMC). As originally conceived, the Membership Guidelines had two parts: one part summarizing spiritual principles guiding integration, the other delineating the mechanisms for congregational membership via area-conference membership. On the one hand, these had been satisfactory for those churches becoming Mennonite Church Canada. On the other hand, in 1999, on the US side, they were approved by the former GCMC but not by the former MC, holding the integration process hostage, just two and a half years before its anticipated conclusion.[4]

The disapproving parties were consulted concerning their reservations. In response to these, a third part, "Clarification on some issues related to homosexuality and membership," was added to MCUSA's Membership Guidelines. In a nutshell, it allowed challenges to the membership of congregations that had previously held dual-membership in conferences from both former denominations but had been excommunicated by one for having the boldness (misperceived as sinfulness) to welcome into membership faithful people who identify as LGBTQ+. Further, it made the act of performing a same-sex covenant ceremony grounds for reviewing and, perhaps, withdrawing a pastor's ministerial

3 Schrag, "What Works for Denominations Now?," 12.
4 Schrag, "Membership Rules Divide Delegates," 1–2.

credentials—his or her license and ordination.[5] By overwhelmingly approving these modified Membership Guidelines, MCUSA chose reluctant heterosexual members over LGBTQ+ believers and their allies.[6]

In 2015, the resolution "Forbearance in the Midst of Differences" was brought before the Delegate Assembly in Kansas City, six days after the United States Supreme Court decided the case called Obergefell v. Hodges in a way that legalized same-sex marriage, not just the covenants the resolution refers to. The text of the resolution first contextualizes the resolution in a "decades-long conflict over issues related to human sexuality" before proposing this: "We call on all those in Mennonite Church USA to offer grace, love and forbearance toward conferences, congregations and pastors in our body who, in different ways, seek to be faithful to our Lord Jesus Christ on matters related to same-sex covenanted unions."[7] Passing the resolution was a step in the right direction, although mere *forbearance*—or tolerance—seems "right" particularly from a position of heteronormative privilege and less so from a marginalized position, one of people seeking affirmation, appreciation, and equality.

The resolution "On the Status of the Membership Guidelines" not only upheld the controversial third part; it doubled-down on it, proposing formal mechanisms for mediating challenges to congregational and pastoral departures from the principles condemning same-sex relations as inscribed in such documents as the Membership Guidelines, *Confession of Faith in a Mennonite Perspective*, and *A Shared Understanding of Church Leadership.* Passing this resolution made it possible for area conferences to call each other into "mutual accountability" through the Constituency Leaders Council, which it admonished "to exercise mutual accountability by engaging in conference-to-conference peer

---

5   "Membership Guidelines."
6   Schrag, "Mennonite Church USA Formed," 1–2.
7   "Forbearance in the Midst of Differences."

review when area conferences make decisions that are not aligned with the documents named above ...."[8]

Silent witness

Joleen and I turned left, heading toward the convention-center hub. I looked ahead and didn't know what I was seeing at first. The foot-traffic was weaving around strangely.

For a moment, I thought a small crowd was walking against the general flow, toward the delegate hall. After a few more steps, I recognized that the people facing my direction were *not* moving. They were just standing there, distributed across the 20-to-25-foot-wide corridor and some distance down it. What was this?

As I neared, I saw that they weren't quite *obstructing* the way. Unavoidable, they acted more like a *maze* or, perhaps, a *sculpture garden* for others to find paths through.

They stood there, silently. When I reached them, I saw that some were crying. Some had duct-tape over their mouths. Then, I recognized some of them and *where* they stood. Meaning took shape.

We were in the corridor outside the meeting room adjacent to the delegate hall, the room assigned to Pink Menno for the group's activities during the conference. Many were people I had met inside when I had participated in these activities. But there were more, others I hadn't met before. They all were standing for themselves and for all the other LGBTQ+ Mennonites and allies who would possibly be intimidated to silence by the reaffirmation of the Membership Guidelines.

Background: Pink Menno

As their website describes, Pink Menno is a group that aims to "celebrate the goodness of LGBTQ people in the Mennonite Church, focusing on visible presence at each biannual conference." This presence was first felt at the 2009 convention of MCUSA in Columbus, Ohio. Not officially recognized by MCUSA, Pink Menno has had to secure meeting spaces on its own, near MCUSA

---

8 "On the Status of the Membership Guidelines."

convention centers. Its activities are not listed in the convention program. Most visible through the hymn-sings where people— many wearing pink—gather before or after major convention meetings and worship services, Pink Menno offers presentations on and discussions of conditions for LGBTQ+ people in MCUSA and its agencies. In addition to organizing a presence at MCUSA's national conventions, Pink Menno also maintains a website, Facebook page, and Twitter account.[9]

Silent solidarity

As I made my way into their midst, I met their eyes and nodded sympathetically. Internally reaffirming my allegiance, I leaned toward Joleen and whispered, "I want to be part of this." She whispered back, "Me too." We found places at the back and stood in silent solidarity with the rest—for ourselves, for others who couldn't be there, and for others who had been made to believe that they *shouldn't* be there or simply wouldn't dream of it, perhaps having found other, more affirming places to be than MCUSA.

Others followed behind me and Joleen. Some made eye-contact and nodded sympathetically and even whispered words of encouragement. A number of these, Aimee and Michael included, found places and joined the silence. The group eventually swelled to around seventy people.

Some passed through, looking preoccupied or confused. Others passed through, wearing expressions of uneasy opposition. Still others passed through with expressions I read (in an ungenerous spirit) as smug, self-righteous, dismissive.

I stood there, gladly adding mass to the message, weighing its possible implications. Nurtured to be "the quiet in the land," as Mennonites sometimes say, I appreciated the silent protest, as opposed to chanting or shouting. At first, I was uneasy with the duct-taped mouths, possibly a symbolic over-statement. But not presuming to better understand their experience, I tried to further sympathize, imagine their perspective, and grasp their meaning.

---

9 "History & Vision."

It didn't take me long to remember more of what had happened that morning. Not a delegate myself, I was in the hall to observe the proceedings. During the lead-up to the discussion of the forbearance resolution, well before the time for comments from delegates, the speaker on the dais was suddenly interrupted by people speaking loudly through an open microphone on the delegate floor. I think they were saying something about divorce and remarriage. (I couldn't hear well.) But I soon heard the dais ask for that floor mic to be cut off. After a moment, it was. Realizing that the public address system no longer broadcast what they were saying, those involved in the "disturbance" raised their voices in a greater effort to be heard by the delegates gathered there.

Almost as quickly, someone in another corner of the hall started singing a familiar hymn, and many others joined in, drowning out the interlopers' efforts to be heard.

In a way I had never been before, I felt deeply ashamed of our Mennonite hymn-singing tradition. The four-part harmony filling the hall, though skillful, was profoundly disturbing—sacred music weaponized and used as an instrument of oppression. The interruption was procedurally "out of order," but the responses seemed immoral.

By that afternoon, when we all stood silently there in that corridor, I had heard that Pink Menno had requested an opportunity to address the delegate assembly but had been denied any time at the microphone. Desperately, even defiantly, they apparently had tried to claim some on their own.

As I stood there, I recognized the considerable power wielded by those who "merely" control access to microphones or manage meeting agendas. This gathering of Anabaptists was supposedly doing egalitarian, communitarian discernment but, again, was demonstrating that "some people are more equal than others"— or at least are mistakenly thought to be. And although even having a meeting room at the convention site was a small victory for Pink Menno—let alone a room adjacent to the delegate hall— that didn't mean that their voices were equally welcome by some people right there during the delegate discernment, even those controlling it.

Moreover, the denial of Pink Menno's request screamed with irony (assuming the truth of what I had heard): the principle of forbearance under consideration hinged on LGBTQ-believers' desire to be affirmed by and to minister in MCUSA. Still, they would only be *talked about*, not *listened to*.

This irony would enlarge during "open-mic" time, when a representative of the Hispanic Caucus (a historically marginalized constituency) was allowed—with due sensitivity from the dais— to voice their concerns about the resolution and vaguely threaten the caucus's withdrawal from MCUSA if it passed. The comments took over five minutes, even though speakers from the floor were supposed to limit their comments to no more than two minutes.

The irony compounded further when, in the afternoon, the executive director of MCUSA, for over thirty minutes, pontificated in support of the resolution reaffirming the Membership Guidelines, with no one else on the dais calling for *his* mic to be cut off. When the forbearance resolution had come to the floor, he had limited its two co-sponsors to two minutes each.

While the executive director held forth on the Membership Guidelines, one of his main arguments was that reaffirmation of the Membership Guidelines would even the score between the progressive and conservative members of the denomination. This suggested that some delegates should perhaps *not* vote based on their congregation's (or constituency's) discernment, nor even based on their own consciences, but rather to appease those who so opposed forbearance that they threatened to lead a denominational exodus if the score were not evened somehow—reasoning that patently distorts the concept of communitarian discernment being rooted in conviction.

Two days after the Membership Guidelines' reaffirmation and our silent protest, the irony exploded. The day between, a group of delegates (including Joleen and Aimee) requested and was granted time at the microphone to lament the reaffirmation. There were ten in the group, and they were granted ten minutes. But this time was cut to five minutes that morning. Each speaker made cuts and spoke briefly but passionately about the loss they felt, about how reaffirming the Membership Guidelines reopened wounds suffered when loved ones, over the years, had been marginalized or outcast by the Membership Guidelines and the inhospitable spirit they empowered.

When the second speaker asked for all those in the hall who felt so wounded to stand with them, a couple hundred people— maybe more—stood. Speakers from the group continued, voicing pain for many others. But despite the pains each had taken to be brief, they overran their time. They had planned for a minute each.

It had been nearly seven minutes when the seventh delegate started speaking. He spoke briefly, then stepped aside to let the person with him, a young woman who identifies as lesbian, have the rest of his time. The young woman described her plan to struggle to forgive her church for rejecting her and discrediting her faith. She feared she would fail.

When she finished, the dais interrupted to announce that only one more person in the group would be allowed to speak. A murmur arose, then quieted when the next speaker began. When she finished, the microphone was cut off. Calling for respect of other's time, the dais tried to quiet the rising murmur and several objections shouted by delegates. One voice called out, "Let them speak!" Failing to quickly restore "order," the dais resorted to prayer (another shameful rhetorical ploy). Her prayer took about as long as the other speakers may have.

When the dais pushed the agenda forward, the delegates and observers who were already on their feet remained standing in solidarity with the silenced speakers. I stood there too for ten or fifteen minutes before I left the hall, disgusted.

I wonder whether I should have stayed and stood. I wonder whether others should have also walked out. Clearly, the dais was stubbornly moving on, disregarding the protest. The rest of the official agenda had lost its appeal.

Adding insult to injury, the dais shortly thereafter called for a thirty-minute break. It could easily have been only twenty or twenty-five minutes. Only two speakers' laments remained, but the dais never asked. They may have taken less time than the prayer or only the time originally promised.

Perhaps those keeping the time so miserly were unintentionally thoughtless, but there seems no better time to be intentionally thoughtful than when people are expressing their pain. Using power to cut the power allowing others to be heard distorts the dialogue in favor of the already powerful, belying any claim of egalitarianism.

I couldn't bring myself to re-enter the hall after the break. Michael told me later that he and many others continued standing. I regret not being part of *that*.

Michael and I had planned already to participate in Pink Menno's final worship service, scheduled for that afternoon on the grounds outside the convention center and outside MCUSA's control. In the meantime, I tried to reconcile myself to all that had happened.

I failed.

Deflated, I was only able to resign myself to events. How would MCUSA go on from here, having consigned ourselves again to internal conflict? Only time would tell.

Refusing to be silenced

As it turned out, our denominational "progress" was not graceful. Within several months, many conservative congregations and some entire area conferences withdrew from MCUSA, shrinking our already small denomination by almost a fifth. Apparently evened scores couldn't appease some peoples' felt-need to distance themselves from others whose sexuality, in their vision of things, supposedly invalidates faith and compromises God's grace toward anyone who associates with them.

During those same months, an inclusive minister performed a same-sex wedding ceremony and made his action known to, among others wielding power, the Constituency Leaders Council

(CLC), of which he was a member. Some on the CLC made him feel so uncomfortable about continuing his service there that he submitted his resignation. Making no effort to model forbearance, the Executive Committee accepted his resignation—rather than refusing to do so and perhaps censuring the CLC members who failed to forbear, as supposedly the denomination had resolved.

Clearly, in the balance between the conflicting resolutions, the scales were tipped threateningly away from forbearance, authorizing efforts to silence inclusion and affirmation.

But on that last day of the 2015 convention, the Pink Menno service reflected a more graceful way in which many of us would go on. In the face of explicit institutional threat again empowered through the Membership Guidelines resolution, we could simply remain present and resolve *not* to be silent.

Around two hundred LGBTQ and allied conventioneers gathered. And though many of those gathered seemed, like me, somewhat deflated, they were not entirely discouraged. I suppose they had been there before and, for the most part, seemed braced to carry on as before.

We listened to speakers expressing courageous conviction. We sang together, soothed by the beauty of our combined voices and energized in our determination to use them. To my ears, these sounded like voices that deserve time at the microphone—attention and amplification.

Finally, though worn, we were blessed for the ongoing journey—anointed and offered words of benediction by long-suffering servants who, though rejected by the builders, would not be silenced and would continue to build themselves into their beloved, if not-always-loving, church.

Part 2

11

Cracking Binaries, Shifting Plates
Becoming Aware of the Power of Language

Cameron Altaras

The only time I ever heard my Amish grandma raise her voice was to call to Grandpa: *"Pop! Komm 'rein zu essen!"* (Pop! Come in to eat!) Otherwise, I knew her as quiet or soft spoken. I have concluded that even though she never went beyond the eighth grade—because the bishops declared education dangerous—Grandma was a smart woman. She had an uncanny ability to observe any situation and quickly decipher if it was appropriate for a woman to speak and whether what she was thinking was worthwhile (and, for goodness' sake, what would other people think?). That takes a certain level of intelligence.

I grew up knowing that as a female, there were certain rules that applied to me because of my gender. The deep collective psychic history of being a woman of Amish and Mennonite roots was transmitted as much without words as with words.[1] Sometimes they were the hesitantly spoken words of my grandma, sometimes they were stories in sermons and Sunday School or overheard between the women around me; each of these stories was in some way shaped by the story of Adam and Eve, an original story

---

1 My background is Beachy Amish Mennonite from Ontario, Canada.

that views the world through a binary lens. In this chapter, I interweave aspects of my personal and ancestral histories and suggest the value of both questioning and expressing dissatisfaction with the assumed status quo, while examining how theology based on a patriarchal world view shapes how we understand God and each other, how we view power, and how the abuses of that power transmit psychological and spiritual wounding through generations. And I ask readers to consider becoming aware of the language we use to tell our stories, articulate our theology, and talk about power. I believe in the inherent power of language itself: power to perpetuate abuses that divide us into binaries and power to open us up to more affirmative and expansive ways of relating to one another and to God.

The binary world of Adam and Eve

Although there are two versions of how Adam and Eve were created, in my world, one of the versions received more airtime. The Genesis 1 story has male and female, in the persons of Adam and Eve, created at the same time in the image of God. In Genesis 2, by contrast, God causes a deep sleep to fall on Adam, takes a rib from Adam's side, and then creates Eve. In this story, man is first and woman is second. Although this is the second story, this is the one that has been emphasized. It's been puzzling to me how easily glossed over are the inherent discrepancies in the two versions, and it's interesting that much of the biblical record continues along the line where women are portrayed as subordinate to men. There are, for example, accounts of kings such as David and Solomon who had harems even as they had wives, and they are seldom reproached by prophets for doing so.

The Christian New Testament continues in this vein, with the apostle Paul as one strong influence. In 1 Timothy 2:11–14, he is credited with stating: "For Adam was formed first, then Eve." Paul adds to this the gravity of the first sin: "Adam was not deceived; but the woman was deceived and became a transgressor." Because of this, a woman "is to learn in silence with full submission." And Paul "permit[s] no woman to teach or to have authority over a man; she is to keep silent." In 1 Corinthians 14:34–35, he sets out similar instructions: "Women should be silent in the churches. For they are not permitted to speak, but should be subordinate, as the law also says. If there is anything they desire to know, let them ask their husbands at home. For it is shameful for a woman to speak in church."

There are contradictions between the two stories of how humans were created, and there are contradictions in the words of the apostle Paul. For example, in Galatians 3:27–28, Paul attempts to move his readers beyond a binary way of seeing one another: "As many of you as were baptized into Christ have clothed yourselves with Christ. There is no longer Jew or Greek, there is no longer slave or free, there is no longer male or female; for you are all one in Christ Jesus." What is one to do with this?

The language we use to tell our stories about God and how God created us shapes the lens through which we view God, the world, and each other and influences who we allow ourselves to become in this world. Early twentieth-century sociologist of religion Émile Durkheim proposed that the way humans relate to their god shapes the way they view their god, and the god they worship comes to reflect those who are worshipping.[2] Contemporary author Anne Lamott puts it another way: "You can safely assume you've created God in your own image when it turns out that God hates all the same people you do."[3] The words we use—and the images we build with those words in the stories we tell—make a difference.

The tectonic plates of patriarchy

According to Carol Gilligan and David Richards, *patriarchy* can be understood as "an anthropological term denoting families or societies ruled by fathers." They explain that patriarchy "sets up a hierarchy—a rule of priests—in which the priest, the *hieros*, is a father, *pater*. As an order of living, it elevates some men over oth-

---

2 Durkheim, *Elementary Forms*.

3 Lamott, *Bird by Bird*, 22.

er men and all men over women; within the family, it separates fathers from sons (the men from the boys) and places both women and children under a father's authority."[4] The Christian religion developed in the context of Jewish and Hellenistic societies, societies that were socially constructed according to the principles of patriarchy. This particular way of viewing the world, which has inherent within it an order and a hierarchy based on assumed gender categories, continues to reverberate through Christianity centuries later. As I discuss below, this perspective ignores any way of being human that does not neatly fit into one or the other gender category of male or female. Any shift in that order is akin to shifting tectonic plates along a fault line in the earth; such a shift can cause our assumptions about our world to crack beneath our feet, shattering the way we see ourselves in the world.

Viewing the world through the binary lens of masculine or feminine provides the "DNA: the building blocks of a patriarchal order"[5] where some have more power and others have less. Those with more power and positions of authority at the top of a hierarchy have powers by virtue of the position they hold in that socially organized structure. In their hands is "a capacity which *enables or empowers* some agents to make decisions, pursue ends or realize interests; it empowers them in such a way, that without this institutionally endowed capacity, they would not have been able to carry out the relevant course."[6] The ways this power is used or abused, and the language used to talk about it, have ramifications that outlast the individuals with the power.

The book *Jesus Wars*, for example, outlines how decisions made by a few people at the top of the Christian Church hierarchy in the first to fifth centuries CE determined what Christians still believe.[7] These were human decisions that were often politically motivated (as indicated by the subtitle of the book: *How Four*

4 Gilligan and Richards, *Darkness*, 10.
5 Gilligan and Richards, *Darkness*, 2.
6 Thompson, *Ideology*, 129.
7 Jenkins, *Jesus Wars*.

Patriarchs, Three Queens, and Two Emperors Decided What Christians Would Believe for the Next 1,500 Years). Doctrinal wording was voted on, and the books of the Bible were chosen by the early church fathers (and, yes, three queens were involved in some of the doctrinal questions). The process of choosing which books made it is called *canonization.* Many books, written at the same time on the same subject, were not placed in the biblical canon because they didn't fit the theological or political schema those with the power had in mind.

A theology built on the foundation of a hierarchical worldview has been weaponized to both justify and perpetuate the power and abuses of power in the hands of the powerful. And while binary gender categories may indeed be "a linchpin that holds structures of oppression in place,"[8] such hierarchical structures also oppress in cases where some males have more power than other males. The experience of the division of power in the world of the early church extended its influence even centuries later. For instance, a series of fifteenth-century papal bulls, referred to as The Doctrine of Discovery, favored European Christian colonialists over the Indigenous inhabitants whose land the colonialists "discovered" and claimed for the crown and the church. The hierarchical understanding that "elevates some men over other men"[9] worked hand-in-glove with the words of the Great Commission from Matthew 28:19 attributed to Jesus: "Go therefore and make disciples of all nations." This command became a rationale for capturing, enslaving, forcefully converting, and massacring millions of people around the world because those who were not Christian were deemed less human than those who were.

I am among the descendants of those who benefitted from the claims of the Doctrine of Discovery. I, and others like me, must figure out how to come to terms with the fact that a theology that we claim is one of peace was so easily twisted and used to kill

---

8 Gilligan and Richards, *Darkness,* 4.

9 Gilligan and Richards, *Darkness,* 10. See chapters by Sarah Augustine and Jennifer Delanty in this volume for further discussion of the Doctrine of Discovery.

millions so we could live on their land—all because our ancestors held a place higher on the socially and economically structured hierarchy.

Oppressive structures using theological language to justify power abuse are not limited to fifteenth-century papal bulls. Another example crops up two centuries later within Anabaptist history. Although at the roots of Anabaptism is the desire to break away from the power structures created by the Roman Catholic Church and the ways in which that power was being abused, nevertheless there arose within one wing of Anabaptism a movement where the leaders fell into the same pattern of abusing the power they claimed was theirs due to their position at the top of a hierarchy they constructed within their church community.

Oppressive rigidity in the Amish hierarchy

My other grandma also grew up Amish. One time she proudly dug out her Ontario Elementary School graduation diploma and told me how she won the county Spelling Bee. She got all As in school and had so wished to go beyond the one-room school house to high school. Her parents wouldn't allow it because the bishops insisted education was forbidden—no matter how many As she had attained. Throughout her life, she resented declarative directions from bishops and ministers. "They're all men, preaching at us women, telling us what we can wear and so everywhere I go," she told me. "I stick out like a sore thumb! Why do the men get to make all the decisions anyway, and why do they get to tell us women what to wear?" When she and Grandpa joined the Mennonite Church, it was better for Grandpa because he didn't have to wear a beard, and he blended in with the world, but Grandma still had to cover her head and dress plain. She complained and then succumbed, saying she did what she had to do.

The lives of both my grandmothers were limited by the religious descendants of Jakob Ammann, one of the ordained men commissioned by seventeenth-century Alsatian Mennonite congregations to ensure clarity and agreement between them and their brethren in Switzerland on issues of church discipline, or

Ordnung. Ammann and his colleagues determined that Mennonites had lost "the true Christian discipline," so they resolved "to rebuild the temple of God on the old foundations."[10] In their opinion too many compromises had been allowed—sometimes concessions to avoid persecution—and instead of holding each other accountable, they had let their ethical rigor become lax. Ammann, from whom the Amish derive their name, insisted it was not his intention to "start a new faith"; rather his "highest desire [was] to maintain order according to the Word of God and Christian discipline."[11] His desire begat new rules and stricter discipline, to retain a distinct identity from the world around them: no fashionable clothing or grooming styles. Anyone who broke these rules was "justly punished."[12]

My grandmother was not the first to challenge this dress code. Gerhard Roosen, a prominent eighty-five-year-old Mennonite from northern Germany, wrote to Mennonite friends in the Alsace regarding Ammann:

I am deeply sorry that you have been so unsettled by people who hold or think highly of themselves and make

---

10   Roth, *Letters*, 49. For further information on Jakob Ammann and Amish beginnings, see especially Hostetler, *Amish Society*, chapter 2, "Birth of Amish Society." The German word *Ordnung* refers to order and rules. In the language of the Amish, the Old Order Mennonites, and other Swiss-German Mennonite communities, this word has the added weight of theological and church-sanctioned rules and traditions, with which one must abide if one is to remain a member of the church and community. For further elaboration, see the chapters in this volume by Bontrager and Harder about the Amish experience.

11   See Jakob Ammann, "Summary and Defense," in Roth, *Letters*. Peter Giger, a contemporary of Ammann's, wrote about how the Swiss ministers "pleaded with Jakob Ammann, for God's sake, that he should not create more confusion or a division, or cause such anguish and confusion. Then Jakob Ammann replied: We will not always travel about; I will not cause a division." However, in the end, that's exactly what happened: theological differences resulted in the Amish division. Giger, "Summary and Defense" (c. 1693), in Roth, *Letters*, 22.

12   Hostetler, *Amish Society*, 39.

laws about things that are not established for us in the
Gospel. If there were commandments in the writing of
the apostles regarding how and with what a believer
should be clothed [. . . ,] then the passage might have
something to say. But in my view, it is contrary to the
Gospel that one wants thus to bind the conscience to a
style of hat, dress or stocking, shoes, or the hair on your
head [. . .] and then punishes with the ban [. . .]. No,
inheritance of the heavenly kingdom or the kingdom of
God will not be accomplished through food or drink, nor
in this or that style or form of clothing. The loving Savior does not bind us to external things. From where then
does friend Jakob Ammann get that which he adopts as
the basis for giving commandments to those people and
expel from the fellowship those who do not want to obey
him? If he truly considers himself a minister of the gospel of Jesus Christ and wants to pursue the external law,
then he must not have two coats, nor money in his purse,
nor shoes on his feet. If he does not abide by the letter
of his master, how then can he impose on his neighbor
that which he has not received as commandment from
his lawgiver?[13]

Ammann was "astounded at the great blindness and ignorance"
of his opponents, "for if [they] would have heavenly wisdom and
a proper understanding of the holy Word of God," he insisted,
they would agree with him. Instead, Ammann writes, they "were
stubborn and did not want to confess the Christian faith with us
until we—Jakob Ammann with the judgment and counsel of the
ministers and elders—finally had to excommunicate them from
the fellowship of God [. .] and placed under the ban by us, especially by me, Jakob Ammann, [. . .] as apostate and heretical people
and unhealthy members."[14] Amish humility expected of people

13 Roth, *Letters*, 66–67.

14 See Ammann, "Summary and Defense," in Roth, *Letters*. With regards
to Ammann's lack of humility, see the letter written by five ministers from

such as both of my grandmothers seems not to have been a virtue required of the one who began the Amish church.

Seven years after the controversy started, Ammann, along with ten other ministers, wrote a letter acknowledging "that in this controversial matter and in the harsh ban which we have used against you in Switzerland we have grievously erred."[15] But the schism had already occurred; there was no going back.

Ammann subscribed to a theology with pacifism as one of its core tenets, but his tactics regarding how he used theological language to bolster his power position were no different from those of other power abusers. Because he was in a position with power, Ammann had the capacity to use his words and his interpretation of Scripture to influence fundamental change to the group. Ammann's rigidity far outlasted his lifetime and continues to this day to shape Amish theology. There was a deep rift for my grandma between the inner meaning of her faith and its oppressively rigid institutional form, which dictated how she must dress and whether she could go to high school. The lives of generations of women, like my grandmothers, have been objects shaped, reshaped, and crammed until they fit the mold that the men at the top of their particular patriarchal tradition deemed appropriate.

Female lineage and the need to know

Wisdom gathered early proved that I am but a fractal manifestation of all the Amish and Mennonite women who came before me. The spirit inherent in that female lineage taught me to painstakingly examine everything I wanted to do or say and weigh it on the scales prepared by my grandmothers. Rules of conduct: do what I have to do, judge what I have to say, and discern whether the time is appropriate for me to speak or be quiet—no matter

---

the Alsace to Hans Reist, a minister in Switzerland, wherein they speak of Jakob Ammann, "by whose order all the trees which happen not to please his proud eyes and do not bear the fruits of this unchristian shunning . . . must be chopped down, cut off and condemned." "Hans-Rudolg Nägeli, et al. to Hans Reist" (November 13, 1697), in Roth, *Letters*, 73.

15 Roth, *Letters*, 107.

what level of education I attain—and submit to the men who set the rules! I longed for the certainty that comes with understanding the essence of who I am as a female born into this male world and how to make of what I am into a woman and feel good about it. At times, it felt as if my gender taunted me like a cruel joke. Perhaps seeded by Grandma's grumbling, instead of just accepting the theological framework of what life is, I asked, *Why?*

As a teenager, I jumped at the chance to work at the public library. I surmised that someone had to have written the answers somewhere. Surely, I was not the only human with a ton of questions. The smell of books, combined with the unfulfilled desires of female ancestors, fueled my unquenchable yearning to figure it out.

My parents' choice to attend a more progressive Mennonite church and their desire that their children's education would not be limited meant that, unlike my grandparents and even my mother and my father, my siblings and I all went at least to college. My mom, a teenager during the 1950s, had not been allowed to go to high school because, again, the bishops said it was forbidden. She told a friend: "If it's at all in my power, my kids are going to high school. They're going to go as far as they can go." Her friend said that never mattered to her. Mom's single intention voiced over and over was that we would get an education.

My questioning led me to graduate school to study theology, philosophy, and religion. One male professor, who also grew up Amish Mennonite, warned me that the best way to lose my faith was to study theology. Examining anything under a microscope eventually turns it from something of mystery to just another specimen to be analyzed and categorized. My questions spiraled further, and sometimes, indeed, they dead ended me in existential angst.

I moved away from the faith of my childhood, and when I came upon the philosophical writings of Theodor Adorno, I knew I'd found a kindred spirit. He, too, doubted that what is is just fine the way it is and therefore ought not to be questioned. He assured me that there are often legitimate reasons to question that what is is all there is. Our feelings of despair are a clue that shows us that our questions do mean something. By use of an analogy, Adorno insisted that "grayness could not fill us with despair if our minds did not harbor the concept of different colors, scattered traces of which are not absent from the negative whole."[16] Along with Adorno, I came to understand that I (in the footsteps of my female ancestors) was not the only one dissatisfied with "playing along," and his words assured me that it is okay to "doubt that this could be all."[17] Through his writings, I found that the desire of my grandmothers and my mother for education was, in contrast to the dictates of the bishops, not dangerous but necessary to what it means to be human.

I believe that a lot of damage has been done to individuals and much has been lost to the world because of prohibitive theological codes put on women like my grandmothers. Who knows what wisdom may have issued forth from the lips of my Amish grandma had she felt free to speak her mind? And what accomplishments might any of my female ancestors have attained had they been allowed an education?

If "mental health," according to one psychiatrist, "can be described as having your head, mouth, and heart in a straight alignment [. . .] and when what you believe in your heart is the same as what you say with your mouth,"[18] then putting restrictions on a woman's ability to voice what she needs to say affects her mental health. How much damage to the mental health of women does theology do when that theology insists on keeping women quiet and uneducated just because they are on the non-male side of the socially constructed binary? And what about the damage to a woman's mental health when the language of Scrip-

---

16 Adorno, *Negative Dialectics*, 377–8.

17 Adorno, *Negative Dialectics*, 363.

18 "You are mentally healthy when what you feel is something you also believe. When the alignment isn't straight, when the mouth doesn't say what the heart feels or when the head knows something the heart doesn't choose to acknowledge, then sooner or later you will get sick." Hammerschlag, *Dancing Healers*, 45.

ture is used to tell her that the salvation of her soul depends on her clothing herself a certain way and covering her head a certain way, whether she wants to or not? Did my grandma, for example, believe in her heart she had to dress plain and cover her head, or did she give in out of fear of chastisement by her community, the bishop, or God? Certainly, what she said with her mouth did not match what she did—that alignment was definitely askew.

Did Grandma complain because she had some inkling that it didn't have to be that way? Did Grandma ever wonder, like Roosen, where Ammann got his ideas about "this or that style or form of clothing"?[19] Was she, as Adorno proposed, in despair because somewhere in the deepest reaches of her being she harbored a concept of another way of being that didn't include having to succumb to the words dictated by those with the power at the front of the church? And yet, that part of her that didn't want to play along still played along right until her dying day. In her ninety-ninth year, Grandma's voice was finally silenced; she was buried wearing a dress far plainer than the fashion of her day and with her white mesh covering on her head.

Cracking binaries and shifting plates

We humans have a habit of anthropomorphizing—putting our human qualities and characteristics on that which is not human. As both Durkheim and Lamott suggest, we've done this to our concept of the divine. Using masculine terms in reference to God has meant that female aspects and any aspects that do not fall under the rubric *male* have been understood as less than, subordinate to, and not as good as. Encoding our theological language and setting up our stories in this way provides a perfect way to silence the dissension of any who do not identify as male. Christian theology in many of its various iterations has done a good job of keeping those who don't fit this category under a "trance of unworthiness" (a phrase I borrow from Buddhist teacher Tara Brach), even when they show a great deal of intelligence, like my grandmothers.

19 Roth, *Letters*, 66–67.

Theologians remind us of the spokespersons of God—the prophets—whose words often called into question the assumed way of thinking and living and whose task it was to bring to light the lie of "the closed world of managed reality" that had been accepted as truth.[20] When those at the top of a socially constructed hierarchy—whether a first century apostle, an early church father, a fifteenth-century pope, a seventeenth-century Anabaptist, or anyone else—use the words of doctrine or Scripture to define their role as "stabilizing the existing social order and justifying its power structure," then, insists theologian Rosemary Radford Ruether, the prophetic voice must critique it.[21]

What if we emboldened our voices of critique, and transformed the language we use, to tell our stories of God? How would that shift the plates of the earth on which we stand? What if our story of creation, for example, was more like the story told by the Navajo, who refer to Rainbow Woman as their birthmother and for whom the presence of a woman representing "First Woman" is essential during ceremonial rituals? Without the blessings by "First Woman" on the food and water, or her prayers for the assembly gathered, the "night's ceremony would not be acceptable. . . . [And] words spoken to the Creator without First Woman's light of dawn blessing would not be heard. This part of the ceremony," according to one (male) author, "sort of reverses the story of Eve, the fruit-bearing temptress who brought about Adam's fall. Here, civilization is sustained by women."[22]

How would our understanding of our place in the world and our relationship to God and to one another be different if this was our creation story? Or, to make things simpler, what if we were just to focus on the first story of creation in Genesis 1, the one wherein male and female are each equally created in the image of God at the same time?

---

20 Brueggemann, *Prophetic Imagination*, 66.

21 Ruether, *Sexism and God-Talk*, 29–30.

22 Hammerschlag, *Dancing Healers*, 68.

To take the matter of our language even further and allow the tectonic plates of the earth on which we stand to shift even more, what about the ways we have not moved beyond the need to think in binaries that restrict everything we say to one category or another and promote exclusivist thinking? This dividing of life into binary categories is, according to Rabbi Tirzah Firestone, "the kind of thinking that professes easy ways to manage the world but butchers all sense of subtlety, the hallmark of true wisdom."[23] Not only does such thinking lack wisdom, but this butchering into restrictive categories also does tremendous harm to those among us who find themselves somewhere along the LGBTQ+ spectrum. Mennonite pastor Megan Ramer urges the use of "expansive language," not simply to be inclusive of all, for "'inclusion' implies an arrogant power imbalance: that one group [. . .] has the power and privilege to *include* or *exclude* deviant 'others.'"[24] Heeding Ramer's call to use "expansive language" shifts us to a place where we acknowledge both the arrogance and the limits of binary thinking.

Our arrogance in this respect knows no bounds. Not only are we arrogant when we insist on restricting our fellow humans to certain categories that fit the way we think, but even more so, we are arrogant to assume that we can overlay our human way of thinking on to the works of the Divine, a creator who is beyond what our human minds can fathom. How do we know we haven't misunderstood what that divine creator set out to do in the first place? If we believe we are created in the image of our creator, and if we are willing to entertain the idea that our creator is not limited to one side of a gender binary or the other, then might it be possible that we also have been created along a spectrum of possibilities? Why would we assume that we are correct when we restrict theological thinking to a simplistic division of male or female, when there is "an increasing recognition . . . that gender

---

23 Firestone, *Receiving*, 53.
24 Ramer, *Letter*.

sits on a spectrum"?[25] A theology that insists on gender binaries continues to do tremendous damage to anyone who deviates from these categories and flies in the face of anti-gender discrimination laws.

Not only is such a theology limited in terms of gendered thinking, but it also "represents a fundamental misunderstanding about the nature of biological sex."[26] Such a "hard-and-fast separation between the sexes" is not supported by scientific research, according to the bone research of anthropologist Alexandra Kralik. "Science keeps showing us that sex also doesn't fit in a binary, whether it be determined by genitals, chromosomes, hormones or bones."[27] With reference to studies that back up her data, Kralik explains that "about 1.7 percent of babies are born with intersex traits; that behavior, body shape, and size overlap significantly between the sexes, and both men and women have the same circulating hormones; and that there is nothing inherently female about the X chromosome. Biological realities are complicated. People living their lives as women can be found, even late in life, to be XXY or XY."[28]

If the research findings of scientists like Kralik is correct, then it is not only female voices that we need to hear as they critique and express anger or discontent with theological language that structures our world along hard-and-fast binary lines, but also the voices of anyone who is frustrated with the rules of a hierarchically structured order that would stick them on one side of a socially constructed gender or sex binary. It's all those whose "posture," says Adorno, "expresses doubt that this could be all."[29]

That we are now able to articulate that there is a socially constructed binary worldview that shapes the way we think is a sign of hope because it means we are aware of the way that we think.

---

25 Kralik, "We Finally Understand."

26 Kralik, "We Finally Understand."

27 Kralik, "We Finally Understand."

28 Kralik, "We Finally Understand."

29 Adorno, *Negative Dialectics*, 363.

And to know that there is this way of thinking means that there might also be other ways of thinking. Awareness of what is is the first and necessary step to propel us beyond it. We begin to sense dissatisfaction with assumptions about our world when we notice that reducing our world and the situations, people, things, and thoughts of our world to one side of a binary equation limits how we experience our world and the people in it—and, it follows, how we experience God. Jesus, as Ruether reminds us, "pressed beyond the critique of the present order to a more radical vision, a revolutionary transformative process that will bring all to a new mode of relationship."[30] Consider the possible shifts that could happen under our feet and before our eyes regarding how we might relate to each other if we were to embrace a spirit of "joyous affirmation that *all* are invited to full participation,"[31] as Ramer would have us do. What words might we use to speak with each other if we permitted ourselves to move beyond automatically fitting the person standing before us onto some rung or another of a hierarchy of power, either higher or lower than ourselves? Or instead of fitting that human into some assumed binary category, what if we cracked that binary for good and saw them in the wholeness of who they are as a unique individual? What if we approached one another in a spirit of reverence, always remembering that the one who stands before us has been created in the image of God? And what if we allowed ourselves to open to a God beyond our human ways of thinking and speaking? What new language might we begin to use?

---

30 Ruether, *Sexism and God-Talk*, 29–30.

31 Ramerm "Letter."

12

How the Right to Not Educate Enables Child Abuse among the Amish
One Woman's Response to the Crisis
Torah Bontrager

I escaped in the middle of the night. I was fifteen. I fled a childhood of abuse and dreamed of going to school beyond the Amish eighth grade. The Amish religion, an insular fundamentalist form of Anabaptism, forbids members from acquiring an education that would ease the transition away from the Church and into mainstream society. Educational deprivation is in the best interest of the Amish institution and is its most effective tool to keep children from questioning and challenging the authority of over three hundred years of male-only leadership. In the 1972 landmark case *Wisconsin v. Yoder*, the US Supreme Court ruled that the Amish religion's rights outweighed my individual right to be given an adequate education.[1] This ruling not only violates children's constitutional rights but also enables and fosters child abuse. Sexual assault runs rampant within many Amish communities; children and women don't know that they have rights as American citizens, and most individuals who make the leap to the outside suffer greatly due to

---

1 Linder, "Yoder v. Wisconsin."

a lack of culturally competent support. In this chapter, I share my path from my Amish home to graduating from Columbia University and then founding the Amish Heritage Foundation (AHF) to address these crises. It is my hope that a time will come when losing the only world one has ever known isn't the price one has to pay for safety and freedom.

The Amish revolution that led to *Wisconsin v. Yoder*

I was born traditional Amish in, at the time, a mostly farming community in Buchanan County, Iowa.[2] From birth to age three, I lived on my maternal grandparents' farm in the *Doddy haus*, the small house attached to the big farmhouse. At eleven years old, I consciously realized that practicing the Amish religion wasn't for me. That knowing crystalized when I asked my father to explain how airplanes could fly in the air. One corner of my father's lip curled up: "Don't ask dumb questions." He glared at me. I knew never to ask that question again, and I also knew he didn't know the answer. If he had, he would have told me. In that moment, I realized something was wrong with a religion that made it a sin for a child to learn how planes fly. For four years I tried to figure out a way to escape from my abusive parents and the only world I knew. None of my dreams were compatible with the Church's rules: I dreamed of higher education, driving a car, and traveling

---

2 I use the term *traditional Amish* instead of *Old Order Amish* to refer to those groups who prohibit electricity, cameras, and cars, among other modern conveniences. The *Old Order* label is not used by us in our language, nor did we invent that label. We refer to ourselves as just *Amish*. There are many groups who spun off from the Amish who include an adjective with the word *Amish* as part of their group's identity and to separate themselves from us traditional Amish. Such spin-off groups include Beachy Amish and New Order Amish, who are more materialistically modern than traditional Amish. To make things even more confusing, there are groups within the traditional Amish who also identify as "adjective" Amish—e.g., Swartzentruber Amish and Swiss Amish. They aren't more modern or liberal than the range of traditional Amish but want to be identified as other than just Amish.

around the world. These visions of a happier future were a coping mechanism to make it through an oppressive childhood.

To prepare for my escape, I started to read the local daily newspaper, my only source of information about the outside world. One day the paper ran a front-page story about a boy who became "emancipated."[3] The article explained that a sixteen-year-old could be given the rights of an eighteen-year-old if they were abused by their parents. The list of different forms of abuse included educational deprivation. "Ah!" I thought. "That's how I can leave and go to high school before I turn eighteen. They'll have to 'emancipate' me when I tell them about *Wisconsin v. Yoder*." Throughout my childhood, I endured a range of abuse— physical, verbal, emotional, psychological, religious, and sexual— from my parents and other members in the community, but I felt that expressing the desire to go to school would be the path of least resistance toward obtaining my freedom.

Not every Amish child is aware of the 1972 Supreme Court case *Wisconsin v. Yoder*, but I grew up hearing stories about it because the protests against state education laws started in the community in which I was born. My parents and several aunts and uncles were pupils when the 1965 "Amish revolution" made national headlines. These protests led to *Wisconsin v. Yoder* (hereafter, *Yoder*).

Yoder is what allowed the Amish to send their children to Amish-only schools, for only eight years, with an Amish-approved curriculum, taught by Amish teachers with no education beyond the eighth grade in an Amish school. It's ironic that both my prohibition to learn and my freedom to learn came about because of *Yoder*. After I escaped, one of my uncles who had left the Amish found me an attorney who secured a hearing with a judge as soon as I turned sixteen. The judge ruled in my favor, citing *Yoder* as evidence that I was educationally deprived. Even now, I don't understand how it's legal for me to have been granted emancipation because *Yoder* agrees with the Church that, simply

---

3 I don't know the article details for this story. I believe the story appeared in the *Ludington Daily News* in 1995 or 1996.

by virtue of my having been born Amish, my only future was to remain an Amish housewife. In the eyes of the federal government, as a child born Amish, I don't have the right to any other future: I shouldn't be sharing my story with you, wearing non-Amish clothes, having an Ivy League degree, and living a life forbidden by the Amish religion *and* by the federal courts. The right to life, liberty, and the pursuit of happiness is explicitly denied to the entire population of Amish children post-1972. This is among the many reasons that *Yoder* needs to be overturned.

Yoder was and still is hailed as a landmark victory for religious freedom, but it was wrongly decided. It violates children's human and constitutional rights and, furthermore, enables and fosters child abuse, not only among the Amish but also among all other religious groups that use *Yoder* as precedent for exemptions in the name of religious freedom. According to attorney and professor Marci Hamilton at the University of Pennsylvania, *Yoder* provides a landmark victory for *extreme* religious freedom and remains an anomaly in the history of the Supreme Court.[4] A special exemption, intended only for the Amish, consequently affects all children in the United States and on Indigenous lands. As a result, no American has the federal right to any education as long as *Yoder* remains standing. *Yoder* didn't make a ruling on education minimums but instead ruled that the Amish Church has autonomy over the education of the children. Because the federal court granted this exemption to the Amish religion, every other group can demand that same exemption in the name of religious freedom.[5]

---

4 Hamilton, *God vs. the Gavel.*

5 I had thought every American had a federal right to education through eighth grade and didn't realize that no American has a federal right to any education at all until I started talking with attorneys in education law. Michael Rebell, professor and attorney at Columbia University and a supporter of AHF's work, has written a wonderful book explaining the difference between state education laws (every state is different) and federal law. Federal law supersedes state law, so no American is federally required to educate their children. Rebell, *Flunking Democracy.*

Over the course of the ten years prior to *Yoder*, my community protested the public school system's attempt to transition Amish children out of rural one-room schools and into the consolidated local Independent School District.[6] The ongoing battles between the Amish and the Iowa Department of Education came to a head in 1965 when what's now an iconic photo made national news. The photo depicted Amish children fleeing to the cornfields to avoid being forced to board a school bus. One of the children in that photo is my uncle.[7]

Public school officials in Oelwein, Iowa, had sent the bus to an Amish-only school, Hickory Grove, expecting to pick up all the children and deliver them to the consolidated school. Having been notified about this plan by the school administrators the day before, some Amish parents stood waiting. When the bus arrived and the officials tried to load the children on to the bus, one of the parents screamed, "*Schpring! Schpring zu de velschken feldt!*" (Run! Run to the cornfields!) A photographer who had accompanied the delegation that day snapped the photo that later went viral. Outrage erupted from all parts of the United States from those sympathetic to the Amish. That national outcry worked in the Amish's favor. Local and state officials deemed the controversy a public relations nightmare and subsequently let the Amish Church educate their children without state-certified teachers.[8]

---

6 This paragraph and the following two are based on my memories from childhood stories and Clayworth and White, "1965 Amish School."

7 The Iowa Department of Education was known as the Department of Instruction in 1965. According to my uncle, he's in the photo, but I haven't spoken to anyone else who has confirmed that.

8 My mother and her siblings had attended an Amish-only school taught by a state-certified non-Amish teacher, Mrs. Nolan. Before and after 1965, the Amish in Buchanan County disagreed about whether their children should be taught by certified non-Amish or non-certified Amish teachers. My maternal aunts and uncles learned from the former, but my paternal grandparents sent their children to learn from the latter. The 1960s conflicts arose due to the issue of certification, not because the Amish children weren't educated past the eighth grade, which was the point of contention later in *Yoder*.

Educational deprivation: A tool for maintaining power and control

It is simply not true that there were no private religious schools before *Yoder* or that overturning *Yoder* will result in one's religious freedom being taken away. Both Iowa and Wisconsin frequently made reasonable religious accommodations for the Amish leading up to each state's pivotal events. In addition, Catholics, Protestants, and Quakers had their own schools. Schools in the United States were first started by religious organizations, not the government. Except for Cornell University and the University of Pennsylvania, the Ivy League universities were started by churches or individuals affiliated with a church for the purpose of religious instruction.[9] My alma mater, Columbia University, still uses its original motto, which is from a Bible verse: *In lumine Tuo videbimus lumen* ("In your light we see light," Psalms 36:9).[10]

During the unrest of the 1960s, some Amish families moved from Buchanan County to Green County, Wisconsin. The Amish in that Wisconsin community, including Jonas Yoder, the lead plaintiff in the *Yoder* case, sent their children to the public school, until it became clear that the state would enforce the compulsory education law. Yoder had no problem with his children being exposed to non-Amish values until it interfered with his access to free labor: he wanted his children to work for him full-time after the eighth grade.

The State of Wisconsin was not as willing as Iowa to compromise when it came to making exemptions for children from compulsory education after age fourteen. In 1968 the Wisconsin Amish opened their own school in an effort to slide under the radar. However, public school superintendent Kenneth Glewen discovered that several children should have been attending ninth and tenth grades.

---

9 Although the University of Pennsylvania wasn't formed for the primary purpose of teaching theology, its first Provost was a minister, Reverend William Smith. Friedman, "Brief History."

10 "Columbia University at a Glance."

Glewen was motivated to enforce Wisconsin's law because the more students who attended public school, the more state funding his district received.[11] While Glewen's self-serving actions seem to have had no regard for Amish children's educational welfare, that lack of regard was no different from Yoder's and the other Amish men who refused to send their children to school past the eighth grade. Although argued from a seemingly religious perspective, neither the Iowa nor the Wisconsin conflicts were driven by a genuine concern for the spiritual welfare of the children; the disputes were about retaining the ability to force a child to work for free—and thereby reduce payroll expenses—and to keep the child ignorant of their rights as a US citizen, rights that supersede Amish law. Making it about religion was a convenient cover.[12]

What outsiders don't understand, and what was never revealed in the court hearings, is that in most Amish families, children are not allowed to keep any of the money they earn until (depending on the family) the male child is eighteen to twenty-one years old and the female child is twenty to twenty-one years old. Every paycheck before that age goes to the father, and none of it is deposited in a trust for the child.[13] In most cases, a female

---

11 Linder, "Yoder v. Wisconsin."

12 Today, none of the plaintiffs (Jonas Yoder, Wallace Miller, and Adin Yutzy) in *Wisconsin v. Yoder* are members of the Amish Church. Yutzy was a member of the Beachy Amish, but the case was ruled based on the traditional Amish Church, not Beachy. For the National Committee for Amish Religious Freedom, a non-Amish special interest group that hired the attorneys and paid the legal bills for the Amish, Yoder was about using the Amish as a guinea pig to see how far they could push religious freedom provisions for the benefit of the committee's non-Amish purposes (Linder, "Yoder v. Wisconsin"). By Mennonite sociologist Donald Kraybill's own admission, his career came about as a direct result of being involved in *Yoder* as a research assistant for John A. Hostetler, an Amish-raised sociologist whose work in the 1950s and 1960s led to Kraybill's creation of the field of Amish Studies. Until his death, Hostetler was a member of the committee, and, to date, Kraybill is a member.

13 As early as age twelve, I worked ten-hour shifts picking asparagus for commercial growers in Michigan. By age fourteen, I worked twelve to four-

child is married before she's of the age allowed to keep what she earns, and, hence, the majority of Amish women have no idea how to manage money and be financially self-sufficient. Additionally, married women aren't allowed to have a paying job; the exception is if the job is a home-based business, in which case it is most often the husband who controls the money, even if he himself doesn't earn it.

This financial illiteracy and dependence on the male is designed to maintain control over girls and women and prevent them from upward mobility. This also means that they have no way out from abusive situations. Fathers, husbands, bishops, clergy members, and adult sons all enjoy a higher status than women and girls. How is a female to provide for herself if she doesn't have access to transportation, a roof over her head, and a job that pays enough for her to pay the rent? How is she to even begin if she doesn't have a social security number? Such challenges are difficult enough for a single female and next to impossible for a married woman with a dozen children. How is such a woman to exit an abusive marriage, when the Church forbids divorce, refuses to provide shelter and funding to battered wives and children, and punishes anyone who reports to law enforcement or outside agencies?

Similar to financial dependence, educational deprivation is ultimately for the purpose of making it next to impossible for any child to smoothly and successfully transition to a life and community outside the Church. *Yoder* explicitly acknowledges and sanctions this: "During [the adolescent] period, the children must acquire Amish attitudes favoring manual work . . . and the specific skills needed to perform the adult role of an Amish farmer or housewife. They must learn to enjoy physical labor. . . . And, at this time in life, the Amish child must also grow in [the Amish] faith and his relationship to the Amish community."[14]

---

teen hour shifts in an Amish bakery. I was forced to turn over every penny I earned to my father.

14   Linder, "Yoder v. Wisconsin."

Thanks to *Yoder*, those of us raised in traditional Amish communities have been stunted in our development. We're a nation of eighth graders, an ethnic minority that doesn't speak English fluently. A good percentage of us don't make it through the eighth grade or, even within the Amish educational system, barely perform above a C or D.[15] We're forbidden from learning about science, mental health, technology, world history, music, current affairs, law, civics, and sex education. We don't even have words in our Amish language for *vagina* or *penis*.

Yoder was justified on the premise that the *only* future for every Amish child is an Amish agrarian one inside the Amish church. However, we're no longer an agrarian people. The Amish family farm can't compete with Big Ag, Silicon Valley, and globalization. The Amish child of today doesn't have the same occupational path as the Amish child of 1972. Yet our children are stuck with an inadequate education and insufficient knowledge—or none at all—of climate change, artificial intelligence, the global economy, national and world affairs, health issues, human gene editing, GMOs, human trafficking, pedophilia, STDs, transhumanism, dangerous drugs, and so on. *Yoder* fantasized that we would remain frozen in time. The outside world would change, but we wouldn't.

This idea that we should remain frozen in time is perpetuated by self-proclaimed Amish experts, who neither are Amish nor have bothered to learn our language.[16] Furthermore, with minor

---

15 One of my classmates failed or barely passed most of his subjects every year; Joe Slabaugh, no longer practicing Amish, made it through the third grade only. In general, we learn only the "three Rs" (reading, writing, arithmetic) from 1950s–1970s textbooks taught by teachers who haven't advanced beyond the Amish eighth grade themselves. In my first year of high school, all my chemistry classmates laughed at me when I raised my hand and asked, "What does H2O mean?" And today many Amish children have never heard of 9/11.

16 Except for John Hostetler, I know of no one raised traditional Amish who is or was an academic. It's possible more academics exist, but I haven't found them or been informed about them. Hostetler doesn't accurately represent us traditional Amish and refused to fight for Amish children's rights

exceptions, their publications are based on interactions solely with Amish men. The women's and children's voices aren't represented. For example, the sociologist Donald Kraybill's entire body of thirty-plus years of Amish "literature" is based on responses from male-only eighth graders—men who speak English as a second language, don't know what H_2O means, and ignorantly agree with whatever narrative Kraybill wants. The story that academics like Kraybill tell *enables* the abuse of Amish children. It manufactures a rosy Amish myth that has devastating real life consequences. By claiming that there's no crime among us, or that we take care of our own issues, these narratives allow women and children to suffer and criminals to prey freely on victims.

What *Yoder* has resulted in fifty years later is a platform for all sorts of religious actors to get away with committing crimes against women and children in the name of religious freedom. These crimes include sexual assault, which runs rampant throughout much of the Amish Church and diaspora. Perpetrators thrive because our women and children don't understand what their rights and responsibilities are as US citizens or that they even have rights. The only adults who do understand their rights are the one percent of the patriarchy who control the Church and comprehend that their power lies in keeping the rest illiterate, dependent, and in fear of going to hell if we report them or break other rules. The Amish clergy and the self-proclaimed academic experts work together to keep sexual assault and other abuses of power covered up.

A vision for Amish evolution

Around the age of thirteen, I read *Uncle Tom's Cabin* by Harriet Beecher Stowe and learned about the Underground Railroad. Harriet Tubman became my first female role model. In our three-hundred-plus-year history, no female has held a leadership posi-

---

to a quality education; instead, he provided expert testimony in favor of the parents in *Wisconsin v. Yoder*. Of all people, he should have advocated for the children because he himself left the Church in pursuit of higher learning.

tion among the Amish. Tubman was the first strong, fierce woman I found for guidance. What she did for enslaved people inspired me to believe in myself and do whatever it took to set myself free too. Tubman helped me to see that I could take ownership of myself. I didn't have to continue obeying abusive masters. I wasn't someone else's property. I told myself that if I made it, after my escape, I'd help the ones left behind, like Tubman did.

More than twenty years later, after graduating from Columbia University and publishing a memoir, I founded the Amish Heritage Foundation (AHF).[17] According to my research, AHF is the first 501(c)(3) nonprofit organization to advocate for Amish people without a religious price tag, to promote compassionate secular values, and to empower those who leave the Amish Church. No other nonsectarian organization does what we strive to do on behalf of women and children, both inside and outside the Amish Church. My work through AHF addresses the crisis of Amish abuse by attempting to overturn *Yoder* and by providing cultural awareness training to sexual assault survivor advocates, law enforcement, mandated reporters, and other agencies working with Amish victims and cases. Most Amish children grow up without much knowledge about their body. I didn't even know what my period was the first time I bled. My mother physically beat me for not telling her that I menstruated when she found my panties in the bottom of the hamper. I'm not alone in this kind of experience among girls.[18]

Everything about sex is taboo in my culture. Not once did it occur to me that the two uncles, Harvey Bell and Enos Bontrager,

---

17 Bontrager, *Amish Girl in Manhattan*. For more information about the AHF, see https://www.amishheritage.org.

18 I was embarrassed when I saw the dark stain and thought something was wrong with me. My mother never told me that one day actual blood would spontaneously emit from my vagina. This refusal to educate children about sexuality persists within the first-generation non-practicing Amish population. More than one child of a first-generation non-practicing Amish parent has confided in me that they, too, had had no idea what their period was.

who helped me escape when I was fifteen years old, would not be safe to be around. Both had escaped when they were young, and I trusted them to give me shelter and help me transition to mainstream America. Within a month of my escape, Harv began to repeatedly rape me and held me hostage in a dilapidated house on the outskirts of a tiny, isolated Montana town. He threatened me with death if I ever told anyone, and ultimately that bought my silence for over thirteen years. When I figured out how to leave Harv with my life intact half a year later, his brother Enos also raped me repeatedly. I thought I would be safe with Enos, who lived in Wisconsin, because he was married and had three small kids. But he wasn't any different from his older divorced brother.

What happened to me as a child and adolescent sadly is not an anomaly. The adults pretend that sexual assault doesn't happen and refuse to educate their children about their bodies and boundaries. In the rare instances that a rape does get acknowledged by a bishop, the baptized female victim is required, in front of all the baptized church members, to ask the baptized male perpetrator for forgiveness for having tempted him.[19] Both parties are then excommunicated for six weeks, after which all members are to forget that this heinous crime ever occurred. Rarely is the rape reported to outside law enforcement and charges pressed.

This is no different from a criminal justice system that lets rapists off with a mere slap on the wrist. Several months ago, I sat in the courtroom for my uncle Enos Bontrager's hearing in a criminal case brought against him by another of his victims. I witnessed the district attorney agree with my uncle's attorney that the plea deal was fair and that my uncle was an upstanding citizen of the community. The court had found Enos guilty of repeated sexual assault of a child that carried with it up to forty years in prison. But the district attorney had agreed to a deal of

---

19 The female victim being required to ask the rapist's forgiveness is rooted in the belief that Eve tempted Adam in the Garden of Eden and therefore that all the sins and ills of the world are the woman's fault; this is also why, sub- or unconsciously, Amish men are almost never held accountable for their crimes.

no jail time and only probation for a few years. The judge added only nine months of county jail to that. Earlier in the year, the district attorney had agreed to drop another count completely, one that carried up to forty years of prison time as well. My uncle got away with felonies that should have kept him in prison for eighty years. Now no one will know that a lifelong serial child rapist is in their midst, unless concerned citizens keep speaking out about this.

When these are the results for reporting and going through the hell of a criminal justice system that seems to care more for the rapist than the victim, what's the point in reporting? Why should Amish women speak out, risk being punished by the Church and community, and go through re-traumatization for reporting when the only thing that comes out of it is seeing their abusers walk free?

The biggest challenge I run into when trying to raise funds for AHF is the belief that we Amish are perfect. *Why do you need money? What issues? There's nothing wrong with the Amish.* These questions are driven by the false "peaceful, gentle, crime-free folk" image advertised by Kraybill and others.[20] *Yoder* itself states that the Amish never broke the law, and Kraybill and others have run with that for the past fifty years. Sexual assault—and other violence—has been a plague for generations, but even if no assault cases were publicized in 1972, the reason the Amish were in court was because they broke the law. Outsiders willingly don blinders when it comes to anything Amish, and instead of protecting the vulnerable, the State allows predators and others in power to sacrifice children in the name of religion.

In an attempt to start correcting the narrative about us, the first thing AHF did was create a credible body of Amish work. We launched with a historic annual academic conference, *Disrupting History: Reclaiming Our Amish Story*, which took place in Lancaster, Pennsylvania, at Franklin & Marshall College. The conference

---

20 Billig, "Lessons." Conference presentations are available at www. amishheritage.org/podcast. For more information about future conferences, see www.amishheritage.org/events.

marked the beginning of raising awareness about what our issues are, so foundations, corporations, and individuals understood why we needed funding and the general public could become educated about the facts of our history, identity, and culture. Collectively, our speakers represented five out of the eight Ivy League schools (as alumni or professors) and a variety of fundamentalist backgrounds, who share challenges similar to those we Amish face.

What surprised me the most from the conference was the revelation that there was no LGBTQ+ support group on Facebook for Amish people and their loved ones who wanted a safe, nonjudgmental space but didn't want to necessarily out themselves. That led to the creation of the AHF Support Group, which, in keeping with our secular mission, doesn't allow any Bible quoting. We also realized that we needed to explicitly include a welcoming message for LGBTQ+ visitors on our website.[21]

Another thing I learned was how deeply impacted the members of other insular religions were by meeting each other. For example, I heard someone say, "I didn't know how much my Ultra-Orthodox Jewish upbringing had in common with the Amish." That cross-insular awareness led to developing strategic partnerships with organizations focused on creating acceptance and support for fundamentalist-raised individuals who want more than what their community of origin offers them. These individuals range from still practicing the religion to not practicing any religion, from backgrounds such as Ultra-Orthodox Jewish, Jehovah's Witness, Mormon, Catholic, evangelical Christian, Muslim, Anabaptist, and their variations. Most don't want to leave their family and culture just to be safe from abuse or lead personally meaning-

---

21 That was driven home by a conversation online by AHF's response to a homophobic proselytizing Amish organization's actions. A comment by one person revealed to me how isolated and marginalized LGBTQ+ individuals (Amish-raised or children of Amish-raised parents) felt, but in hindsight it's obvious. Children of Amish-raised parents were not accepted by their parents when they came out as LGBTQ+. Homophobia and racism don't stop when Amish-raised individuals leave the Church. Due to the lack of education and exposure to more accepting belief systems, the cycle of violence continues among descendants outside the Church.

ful lives inconsistent with the religion. But they are forced to exit completely or lead stressful double lives to keep from being cut off from their families. I strongly believe that women and girls hold the key to bring about local, national, and global transformations, and I find it heartening that several organizations tackling religious fundamentalist systems are helmed by women.[22]

---

22 Below is a list of some organizations and prominent female voices that AHF collaborates with by sharing knowledge and resources, publishing cross-cultural articles, producing events, and holding conferences. We share a common quest to create a more just society, one that includes extending the ideals of life, liberty, and the pursuit of happiness to individuals raised in our respective insular or fundamentalist religious communities—especially when outsiders aren't aware of our communities or what our challenges are. Together, we grapple with bridging the gap between the world with rights and responsibilities that apply to all US citizens and the world that plays out behind closed doors within and among disparate closed communities, who have their own laws and deny the constitutional rights that members of the community have.

- An-Nas: Humanists Rising from Muslim Communities—
  an ethics-based organization with the mission of providing opportunities for personal growth, promoting social justice, and contributing to an inclusive, multicultural humanism. Founded and run by Hannah Abbasi, Noura Embabi, and Ginan Rauf.

- YAFFED—committed to improving educational curricula within Ultra-Orthodox Jewish schools, this organization was founded by individuals raised within the Ultra-Orthodox communities of New York City. Miriam Moster, one of the co-founders, has since stepped down from the Executive director position.

- Formerly Fundamentalist—a home for anyone from any fundamentalist religious background who is looking for a community that understands first-hand the unique challenges we face when we challenge the status quo of our upbringing. Although not founded by women, this group is extremely inclusive—not only of gender but also of religion, from practicing to atheist—and includes among its members prominent women who are advocating for change within Mormon,

Increasingly I find women with Anabaptist connections reaching out to me to express their support and desire to collaborate. These women are committed to protecting children and vulnerable adults and refuse to back down even in the face of bullying, backlash, and death threats from men in authority. Many of the women have concealed weapon carry permits; that we are carrying guns might come as a shock, especially when the impression is that the Amish and Anabaptist are nonviolent. But the work we are doing involves encountering dangerous criminals and situations, which warrant security protocols. One of my investigations included being in the same room as two serial rapists, both members of the Amish Church, one of whom is regarded by the rest of the community as a terrorist. Even the bishop is so afraid that he won't issue any reprimands or punishments when the rapist breaks a rule of the Church.[23]

There are many good women *and* men inside the Amish Church who want things to change for the better. An adult or child shouldn't have to give up the only world they have ever

---

Jehovah's Witness, Anabaptist, evangelical Christian, and Ultra-Orthodox Jewish communities.

- Chrissy Stroop, raised evangelical Christian, is a prominent voice in the ex-vangelical community and movement. She's a freelance writer, public speaker, and commentator on religion and politics, the US Christian Right, and foreign policy, as well as Senior Researcher with the Postsecular Conflicts project, directed by Kristina Stöckl at the University of Innsbruck.

23 Despite the terror, several women are privately advocating for this rapist's arrest. I sat in a meeting with half a dozen women, practicing members of the Amish Church, and couldn't believe my ears. "Excommunication and sending them to Amish counseling isn't enough. It doesn't work." "This sexual abuse of children starts with bestiality." "We need to report them." "They need to go to jail." I didn't think I would ever hear Amish women speak out like this until *maybe* on my deathbed, if my life's work was successful. These are women in their sixties who were abused as children. After all these years, they are seeing the effects of their wounds. Post-traumatic stress disorder (PTSD) doesn't ever fully go away.

known just for a chance at realizing a life of their dreams.[24] Asking questions, learning, and self-actualization shouldn't come at the cost of shunning, excommunication, and losing access to and support from your family, community, and heritage. I want to keep the good parts of my culture and weed out the bad. Children deserve safety and love and a chance to make informed decisions about their future. I, as a fifteen-year-old, shouldn't have had to escape under cover of darkness just to claim my rights to life, liberty, and the pursuit of happiness. And I shouldn't have had to lose *everything* for that chance.

Most of us who leave the Amish community are punished for life unless we return and repent. We're stripped of home, family, and identity, left to wing it in a world that's full of both promises and dangers, of which we have no knowledge. We need a safe way to transition, and that is what AHF offers. Recently, I helped an eighteen-year-old escape. As I had to do nearly twenty-five years ago, so he had to do in 2020: sneak out of the house and wait for virtual strangers to rescue him at night. He's legally an adult, a US citizen, but he had to literally escape, like a refugee, without telling his parents and siblings goodbye. He had no birth certificate and social security number—no documents proving his identity so he could get a job and go to school.

What he has that I didn't have is a safe house and safe mentors to guide him in his new life. That there's even a safe option is something most Amish youth aren't aware of, and getting the word out to a world disconnected from social media, internet, and phone is a challenge. As AHF grows, we'll be able to help more Amish refugees get to safety—documented, enrolled in educa-

---

24 *Rumspringa* is a myth that does untold damage to those of us stuck inside who want a different future. We don't get a choice to leave the Church, and we're not allowed to party or break the rules. Just as in big cities, the more teens there are, the harder it is to control them. In smaller communities, the teens are so tightly controlled that experiencing the world outside is extremely difficult. No matter what community you come from, it's always understood that you are never to leave the religion. Your only "choice" is to get baptized and remain a member of the Amish Church for the rest of your life.

tional programs, employed, and informed about their rights and responsibilities as US citizens. Our goal is to provide the tools for people to get to the stage where they can provide for themselves financially and emotionally, while becoming more enlightened contributors to the global community.

I envision a world in which Amish children are safe, free to learn, and free to choose. We Amish or other Anabaptists need to stop enabling evil by looking the other way, which allows rape culture and child abuse to continue. We need a new understanding of the golden rule. Our Amish teaching of "do unto others as you would have them do unto you" includes the belief that we're obligated to help our enemies even if it costs us our own lives, and that's not ethical. This interpretation comes from the Dirk Willems story in the *Martyrs Mirror*.[25]

For us Amish, Dirk Willems is the most popular Anabaptist martyr. He exemplifies all the Church claims to stand for. The story is accompanied by an illustration of a man drowning in a frozen river, and instead of continuing his escape, Dirk turns around and helps the drowning guard get out. "And then they let him go free, right?" I said when my mother first read me the story. "Because he saved the guard's life?"

"No, he was burned alive," my mother said. "No matter what, you must always follow the golden rule and turn the other cheek. Even if it means that you die for our faith, like Dirk did."

The idea is that we'll be rewarded with heaven if we keep turning the other cheek, no matter at what personal expense. The fact that our doing so enables rapists and other abusers to keep destroying our children doesn't even enter our Amish consciousness. Where is the compassion toward our children? What about the biblical teaching to "take no part in the unfruitful works of darkness, but instead expose them" (Ephesians 5:11)? The safety of our children must override our religion's demand to harm our children. Refusing to report and prosecute rapists, refusing to

---

25 I don't know the details of the *Martyrs Mirror* version I saw as a child. For more information, see Zijpp, Bender, and Thiessen, "Martyrs' Mirror." See also the chapter in this volume by Kimberly Schmidt.

allow our children to learn about sex and science, and refusing to recognize that women are equal to men are all taking part in evil.

Our responsibility is to provide safety, shelter, and freedom. Freedom to choose, is, after all, the reason our Anabaptist forbearers broke away from the Catholic Church.[26] But hundreds of years later, the Amish Church is no different from the Catholic Church of the 1500s in this regard: our children are being forced to remain inside or punished if they leave. It's up to us women to initiate transformation in each of our communities; we want the men to help us with this effort, but nothing will change unless the women lead the change that needs to take place in each of our communities. We're not powerless. We're not alone. We're not worthless. We're good enough, and our children deserve our protection. They, and we, have rights: the right to be safe, the right to learn, the right to choose, and the right to be loved, no matter whether we remain inside or outside the Church.

---

26 I grew up hearing stories of martyred Anabaptist men but not women. Until recently, I wasn't aware that women played any role in the emergence of Anabaptism. The stories read or told to me from the *Martyrs Mirror* were never about women. See the essay based on an interview that Elam Zook and I gave: Stella, "Dark Side."

13

What Is Abused Authority?
A Poem
Keturah C. Martin

The below poem was written in the deadly throes of domestic violence, four months before my children and I were rescued by three Mennonite pastors in Ontario on September 11, 2004—one from the Conservative Mennonite church and the other two from the Beachy Amish Mennonite church. Two of these rescuing pastors were the only two I could trust to open up to about a bit of the agonizing marriage of constant abuse, control, and pending death. Other churches and leaders were more worried about how the church would look if they even acknowledged it than in saving us from imminent death. I was born and raised in the Conservative Mennonite church in British Columbia but was not a member of any church for twenty-five years due to a forced marriage and the horrific repercussions, abuses, and aftermath. Currently my children and I are safe from the second most violent abuser/husband in my life. It is due to the abuses and death attempts of my husband against us that I opted to use a pen name. Thanks to Jesus, he has retrieved the shatters of my broken heart from rubble and ruin and is now creating a vessel of honor for his glory.

What Is Abused Authority?

Just what is "authority"? Please, can you tell?
For I know not of it outside literal hell;
A dictatorship meant for robotic slaves,
Where soul, mind, and body are owned and depraved.
Here one dare not think, speak, or move without leave,
May not have emotions, dare not joy or grieve;
Is held at grim gunpoint amid dictating rage—
Face harsh verbal whippings—enslaved in a cage.

Be blamed and condemned by authority's head,
Encased by assumptions, presumptive and dead,
Until all reality's sealed in a tomb—
May not be a human amid robotic doom.
Be used on demand for authority's blast,
While fed on by lust, its defiled realms so vast;
Be blamed for the fantasy women around,
Who feed porno's death-grip, amid squalor profound.

To live in dread terror through each daily breath,
Suppressed beyond measure amid life's living death,
Restricted from owning a thought, deed, or smile,
Lest harsh verbal beatings descend down each mile.
Here those 'neath authority crouch in despair,
Permitted no friends and with no one to care,
But stumble in anguish through agonized days,
As "self-propelled headship" patrols robot's maze.

Is it really so that authority, true—
Designed by the Lord, can be something that's new?
Providing a haven that's safe and secure,
Where Jesus and his love is proven and sure.
Declare unto me this authority true,
Explaining the difference from what I've lived through:
For all that I've known is what herein is laid,
So thus of authority I'm sore afraid!

14

Protecting Amish Children through Understanding and Relationship

Jeanette Harder

Our greatest strength is our greatest weakness. Let's take that another step: For those of us who are non-Amish, what most fascinates us about the Amish is what we most judge about them.[1] We admire the Amish for their seemingly simple, uncomplicated life, their focus on community, their resolute rejection of modernity, their audacious refusal to blend in. But then our values of individual choice and freedom and progress kick in, and we critique the Amish for the ways we perceive their old-fashioned, patriarchal systems stifle individualism and education and demand obedience and self-denial from its members. Is it possible to simultaneously hold these seemingly contrary views?

In this chapter, I present aspects of Amish culture and faith from a strengths-based perspective and through a lens of cultural awareness. I acknowledge the positive and negative role of power in their communities. And I offer strategies for building relationships with the Amish to help them prevent abuse in their communities. Yes, abuse is perpetrated within their communities.

---

1 For purposes of brevity, *Amish* may include Old Order Mennonite or other similar Anabaptist groups, often referred to as Plain communities.

Power is also understood and demonstrated differently in their "traditional" communities than in non-Amish communities, but in many of their communities and families, children are loved and cherished, and women are valued and heard.

I approach this topic of power and abuse from the position of being a Mennonite both by ethnicity and by choice but not of being a Plain community member. I am also a social work professor and researcher. I became acquainted with the Plain communities through my work with Dove's Nest,[2] a nonprofit organization that equips faith communities to keep children and youth safe, and an invitation to provide cultural awareness trainings to child welfare, healthcare, and law enforcement professionals. While I have spent considerable time with Old Order Mennonite and Amish families and communities across the United States and Canada since 2015, I am and always will be considered an outsider by them. I approach this work, as I do all work, through a strengths-based lens; I look for what is going well and find ways to build on those things—all the while, serving as a fierce advocate for any who are being harmed.[3] I am finishing a qualitative study of the role of Plain communities in providing foster care and adoption and hope to conduct a quantitative study of the prevalence of reported child abuse in Plain communities.

---

2 See www.dovesnest.net.

3 See, for example, Hoover and Harder, *For the Sake of the Child*, written with Plain community members as the intended audience. The book's wide reception within Amish and Plain communities speaks to the internal awareness of sexual abuse in these communities and the desire to address it. While I approach my work through a strengths-based lens that works within the existing structures of the community to address problems internally, I acknowledge that many survivors have left these communities to seek safety and support outside these structures. While these survivor networks are beyond the purview of the present chapter, I acknowledge that the work of advocating for those who are being harmed is very important. See, for example, Torah Bontrager's chapter in the present volume.

Diversity among the Amish

To the undiscerning eye, the Amish might all seem the same: women in cape dresses with head coverings, men in black, riding in horse-drawn buggies. But a closer look shows the styles and colors of their clothing and buggies are different. On closer examination, there are many other differences between Amish groups. One difference that has significant impact is whether the men are farmers, small business owners, or factory workers. This difference in employment status provides the most significant evidence in discerning the group's openness to outsiders, members' mastery of English language, and, most important to this context on power and abuse, the role of women and children in the family. Thus, writing about "the Amish" as if they were one group is absurd and possibly offensive. Amish communities are so incredibly different from one another that having encountered one group does not mean understanding them all.

One Amish home I visited had a long, muddy approach, was surrounded by dirt and free-range animals, and, along with the barn, was light gray in color and in general disrepair. As I stepped up the rickety stairs and into the house, I first saw a black wood-burning stove, a dirt-swept floor, water pumps by the sink, and hard-back chairs and benches. A wash line strung across the room had diapers and other clothing items hanging on it. Light streamed in through the bare windows. Many children of a vast array of ages peeked up at me, curious and quiet, with no toys in sight.

Another Amish home I visited was vastly different. The driveway was graveled, and the house was surrounded by trees, grass, and carefully planted and tended shrubs and flowers. At first glance, the house looked like any one might find in my neighborhood: siding on the walls, drapes in the windows, in good repair. Inside the home, I sat on a cushioned couch, looking at a bookshelf full of books, with electric lights on overhead. Two young children peeked curiously at me as they sat in a soft chair reading books.

The first family was from one of the most conservative Amish groups. They are farmers and have very minimal contact with "the

English," or non-Amish. They typically have large families. Even though the woman I spoke with was noticeably pregnant, this was not something she was ready to acknowledge, let alone speak of. Child protection services had visited this family frequently after the death of a baby with a significant genetic condition. Now that she was pregnant with another child, I was eager to speak with her about her hopes and dreams and fears. That, however, was not a welcomed conversation. Nevertheless, the children appeared happy, healthy, and content. The house smelled delicious as bread and pies were cooling on the counter. When the father and another man walked into the home, the children looked up in interest and anticipation. The father shared some quick information, perhaps news from a neighbor, perhaps a change in plans due to weather, and the mother replied—the exchanges all in a language I did not understand. I was reminded that English is not their first language.

I met the father from the second family at the business he owns—other staff looking curiously at us as we drove up. After we took a quick tour of his business, he hopped on his bike, and we followed him to his nearby house. His wife was on the phone when we drove up. After they introduced me to their children, the children went to visit their grandmother who lived just a few yards from their house. The family spoke to one another in English, although their accent and some of their words were a bit curious to my ears. The parents sat together in the living room and talked with us about the joys and trials of parenting. In talking with me, they mentioned a call they made to child protection services over concern for the safety of an English girl who lived nearby.

Both families are Amish. Both families use horse-drawn buggies. Both families send their children to their own one-room schools up through eighth grade. Both families embrace separation from society and hold firm to their faith. But the differences between the families are nearly as distinct as their differences from their English neighbors.

If an Amish community, even the most conservative one, has a wise and loving bishop, the whole community is likely to thrive and live in harmony, which may bode well for its group members. However, I fear for any Amish community that has a harsh and angry bishop, especially for those community members who are vulnerable. The power of the bishop and other church leaders is significantly influential for any Amish community.

Bishops and other church leaders are chosen by lot, so their ability and even willingness to lead the community are not assessed in a way that is understandable to outsiders. Since education beyond eighth grade is not typically allowed, bishops do not have any more or different education than any community member (which is true for teachers as well). In addition, bishops are not typically accountable to anyone (other than God), so their power and influence over the community and its members is nearly unilateral. While communities follow their *Ordnung*, these rules do not likely include the child protection policies and procedures held as best practice outside Amish communities.

The Amish way of life

Amish homes and communities have a lot of structure to them, along with many rules and defined hierarchy. More than just a set of rules though, the Ordnung may hold the community together and protect the community from disruption. Many Amish will tell you that this structure helps them to feel safe and that it frees them from having to make decisions as individuals. They would say that by looking and living alike, they stand stronger against negative influences of the outside world. They are also resolute about these group decisions and traditions and will not change them without considerable time and processing. In the face of an outside mandate, they will more likely refuse to comply and even physically move away than change.

This acceptance of the leaders' rules and the community's tradition and refusal to change fly in the face of values of individualism and the desire to always have the biggest and best and fastest. It may seem contradictory when Amish have a phone or use machinery for their businesses but do not have a phone in their homes or use a car for transportation. Through their eyes, having a phone in their home would distract from family life, and owning a car would make it easier to leave and, again, distract from their time and work together as a family. Their conformity of dress shows they are part of a community. They do not use appearance to enhance their reputation, show off their bodies, or demonstrate their wealth.

A main pillar of the Amish faith is forgiveness. This is beautiful in many ways, including the letting go of petty differences and anger that may build up and breed bitterness. However, the expectation to "forgive and forget" can be a set-up for those who are experiencing abuse. The offender can hold out the cultural tradition of forgiveness, and the cycle of violence they perpetrate may not be interrupted or stopped. This not only makes identification of abuse more difficult but also makes holding offenders accountable, providing them with needed treatment, and protecting children from them virtually impossible. This leaves the victim suffering in silence and perhaps living a life of trauma that spawns depression and anxiety, and it exposes other children to a substantially greater risk for abuse.

Amish children

Amish families typically have a lot of children. In some communities, a family with twelve children is quite common. This means grandparents may have upwards of one hundred grandchildren. Having such large families not only propels the incredible growth in the number of Amish but also has helped to spread them to more and more states as they search for fertile land.

Having large families presents both a strength and risk for children. Large families provide a significant and strong social network for communities. The typical Amish child will not be short for intergenerational companionship or work duties. Older children care for younger siblings and cousins. Instead of screen time, children are carrying wood, tending to animals, weeding the garden, and cooking family meals. The social fabric of an Amish community will not allow a member of their community, able-bodied or not, to become homeless or unemployed.

Amish parents love their children, but they won't usually physically demonstrate this, especially when others are looking. They will mute their emotions, positive or negative, in the presence of outsiders. From the stories they tell me though, I believe many of them relate to their children in a firm yet loving and patient manner, as they include children in their everyday life. I imagine parents also display to their children the same sense of humor they have displayed to me, including the occasional use of playful jokes and pranks.

Having large families also presents risks to children, however, especially considering the means by which they farm, transport, and live. Far too many children are hurt through burns, runover accidents, and falling through hay holes. (At the same time, not as many of them are hurt in car accidents or are suffering the negative effects of obesity or mental and physical complications due to an excessive amount of screen time—or have parents that are distracted by their own electronic devices.) Large families may also contribute to parenting that expects older children to look after younger in ways that may not be safe.

Children are expected to respect their elders and to follow the rules. They are not allowed to question parents or other older family members, and independent thinking is not taught or modeled for them. This accepting stance of children puts them at unique risk of someone who chooses to misuse their power and victimize others.

The limits the Amish put on their children in terms of education and access to the outside world make those of us who are non-Amish uneasy, and we worry for the Amish children who desire for more and those who experience abuse. English children who are abused too often think it's their own fault and may not recognize that the abuse they experience is different from what their peers experience in their homes. To an even greater extent, Amish children may not recognize abuse, and even if they do, will not likely speak to someone about it or have adequate language to do so. And the person to whom they reach out may not have the tools to respond in a way that brings safety and wellbeing to them.

Although true in both Amish and English settings, sexuality is considered a more taboo subject in Amish communities, leading to further silence or at least uncomfortable feelings surrounding sexual abuse. Children may not be taught the names for their body parts, and the totality of their sexual education may happen through watching animals, especially in the most conservative communities. The power of an abuser is significant given the child's limited sexual education and access to anyone outside their immediate community.

The role of women in Amish families

Another main pillar of the Amish faith is *Gelassenheit*, or yieldedness. Amish value obedience, submission, and resignation to the will of God. Children obey parents, wives obey husbands, and young ministers obey and respect older ministers and bishops. They will say this brings order and structure to their community. To varying degrees, depending on the community, they do allow room for individual choice, creativity, and expression. While husbands and wives play different roles, they each have responsibilities and are mutually dependent on each other to various degrees, again depending on the community.

In farming families, the husband-wife relationship may be more like a partnership—the boundaries between them are permeable as fathers participate in childcare and mothers help in the barn and out in the fields. In families where the father is employed outside the home, the family has more access to cash, but, ironically, the wife may have less power as traditional gender lines are drawn more clearly. The father leaves home to go to work and participates less in childcare. Unless the mother has a garden and sells produce, or has a job or business, she may have less access to cash and less interactions with people outside her community. She may even be more isolated from families in her community as the family has more cash to purchase things and less of a need to participate in community events such as butchering, processing food, and quilting.

While men occupy all visible leadership roles, subordination of women does not necessarily mean lack of importance. In many communities, women are respected, affirmed, and operative. While the communities are still patriarchal (only men are given leadership roles in family and church), in some communities women participate in decision-making and attend business meetings. They may also vote and nominate men for positions. So, while women do not have formal power, they do have some influence, especially in less conservative communities.[4]

While still an outsider, I have sometimes been equally welcome at the men's end of the table as at the women's end of the table. In more conservative communities, though, I have been relegated to the women-only area. On one occasion, in a Hutterite community, I quickly realized that I had no power or standing. In attempting to have a conversation with a male leader of the community, I found him intentionally walking a few steps ahead of me, leaving me struggling to catch up. And then on reaching his house, he ignored me for the whole hour we sat in his living room, with him addressing another adult male in the room and ignoring me, even when I made comments and asked questions. I was left to imagine what his female family and community members must experience around him and perhaps because of him.

In another, fairly progressive Amish community, I visited a group of women while they cleaned their school at the end of the school year. They laughed as they told me about a particular school board meeting in which the male board members made a significant decision about the direction of the school. When these fathers got home and spoke to their wives, they learned they had made the wrong decision. Another board meeting was called, and their earlier decision was reversed. The mothers may not have had positions of power or even been present for the meeting, but they did have influence.

---

4 Much of the information in this paragraph is drawn from Johnson-Weiner, *Lives of Amish Women*.

Power

With the high value they place on humility and obedience, the Amish do not often speak of power. The power of church leaders, all male, seems evident to outsiders, but to them, this is just the way it is, always has been, and should be. The influence the church has over its members' everyday life is astonishing to outsiders. The trust they put in each other and the mistrust they put in outsiders are strong. Unfortunately, the trust they put in each other puts their children at risk for abuse when they cannot or will not acknowledge abuse, do not provide safety to children, and do not hold offenders accountable.

Likewise, the mistrust they put in outsiders is a significant barrier for reporting abuse. They acknowledge the power of governmental systems and will follow laws and policies when they do not interfere with how they understand God calling them to live. I know many Amish leaders accept their role as mandated reporters of child abuse and make reports to authorities, but not all are yet of this persuasion. Rather than reporting abuse themselves, Amish leaders who suspect child abuse sometimes find indirect ways for a report to be made, such as insisting that the child see a licensed therapist or mentioning the situation to a neighbor, a professional, or an English (non-Amish) friend.

Child abuse victims are not likely encouraged to report, and when victims speak of abuse they have endured, they are likely heard but, unfortunately, are also likely made to feel, at least to some degree, that the abuse was their fault, and they need to seek forgiveness and restoration. Given their values on community cohesion and forgiveness, family members or community leaders may not acknowledge that offenders' actions need to be addressed and that significant steps need to be taken to keep others safe from offenders. When someone does muster the courage to speak out against an offender, they may be met with ambivalence or even resistance, squelching their concern.[5] Whenever abuse is treated solely as a sin to be forgiven and not as a crime that demands

---

5 As the volume editors note in their preface, two potential writers for this volume withdrew their chapters for fear of retaliation from their com-

accountability, communities will not be able to adequately protect the vulnerable from offenders.

Just as in mainstream society, there are Amish communities awakening to the presence and tragedy of child abuse, and many are seriously grappling with eradicating abuse. For example, I have heard verified narratives of bishops putting offenders in their buggies and driving them to police stations so they can turn themselves in. I receive calls from Amish leaders and family members who readily acknowledge the presence of abuse in their communities and are looking for information on how to report, support victims, and prevent further incidents of abuse. Many communities now have Conservative Crisis Intervention (CCI) or Family Restoration teams who respond to difficult situations such as child abuse. These crisis teams are composed mostly of men, and these men are typically trained by other Amish crisis team members to understand their role as mandated reporters and to have relationships with English professionals such as child welfare and law enforcement professionals.[6]

I have also heard many compelling narratives of Amish families fostering and adopting English children who have been traumatized by abuse, giving these children love and stability until they can return to their families, and becoming "forever families" for children who are freed for adoption. The baggage many of these children come with is sometimes immense, and they often come with an array of disabilities. Many Amish families I know become licensed with the state, provide 24/7 care for children, and connect them to physical and behavioral treatment. I find this lev-

---

munity or because of the pain they experienced in their community. Their painful experiences must also be acknowledged.

6 Research on the efficacy of these crisis teams has not yet been conducted, but they are mentioned here simply to illustrate that some Amish are beginning to acknowledge that abuse is happening and are working to address it. Still, some survivors who have left Amish or Plain communities have indicated that crisis teams can also contribute to the problem when instead of following mandated reporting protocols, they cover up abuse or silence victims under the guise of forgiveness, reconciliation, and community cohesion.

el of commitment to the wellbeing of children to be a remarkable display of power for the sake of the vulnerable.

Building relationships that influence

There are some inroads for non-Amish into Amish communities. While most leaders and members of the less conservative communities will be cautious in engaging and dialoguing with outsiders, they won't all refuse if approached with respect and curiosity and desire to find common ground. I find them to be welcoming and friendly when I approach them with respectful questions and not ultimatums. Through face-to-face time, openness, and meeting them on their terms, I can build relationships with them.

Through positive, mutual relationships non-Amish can help foster safety for Amish women and children in their communities. I have had positive exchanges with Amish communities on sensitive topics such as domestic violence and even sexual abuse. I bring a strengths-based approach and a quiet demeanor to these conversations and meet them partway in building on things we have in common, like understanding God's love and care for children and those who are vulnerable.

For example, I built a trusting relationship with the Old Order Mennonites who run a residential home for women and couples with mental health concerns. Knowing I had a relationship with child welfare in their community, the Old Order Mennonite men asked me to set up and facilitate a meeting between them and child welfare staff. They wanted to clarify protocol for reporting and responding to child abuse and inquire into how the Old Order Mennonite families might provide foster care to English children.

On the day of the meeting, I arrived a few hours early for their morning devotions. As I had grown accustomed to, everyone and everything had its place, and the preparations and service were done in a quiet and orderly fashion. The children sat quietly and still next to their mothers. Although they motioned for me to sit outside the circle, they graciously handed me the hymnal and other materials during the service. It was clear that I was outside and they were inside. And it was clear that the women were to ask questions and the men were to answer them. I also observed the men's humbleness before God and the scripture, as they solemnly acknowledged the mystery of God.

When it came time for the child welfare staff to arrive, I noticed that the women and children were absent, and the room was even more grave and somber than before—Old Order Mennonite leaders on one side, child welfare on the other. I started the meeting with acknowledgment of what we all have in common: a highest concern for the safety of our children. We then went around the room with introductions, and we broke the ice by each sharing a favorite memory of a grandparent. From there, the stage was set for a straightforward, fruitful conversation on foster home needs and requirements and abuse response protocol. The meeting ended with many handshakes and mention of a follow-up meeting.

Power dynamics are complicated. While the quietness of the children and the subordinate role of women trouble me, I appreciate the humble, caring demeanor of the men. I enter their world as one who enters another culture—with curiosity and openness to what I might learn. I do not seek to radically change them, but I do know that through my presence and my questions, change does occur. By nature, I am an action-oriented change-maker, but when in their midst, I act as their guest and put on a cloak of patience.

Change comes slowly for any of us, in any culture, but among the Amish, it comes slower than for most others. I have found that if I go in with mandates and expectations, I won't get anywhere and may even do harm. But if I go in respectfully and quietly and meet them where they are, I just may have some influence. And I may also learn a few things myself.

Conclusion

I fully acknowledge that child abuse and other forms of violence are present in Amish communities, as in all communities. I lament the pain experienced by victims at the hands of their family members, church leaders, and other community members. Rather than judge the Amish from the outside, however, I seek to understand their culture, to get to know them beyond the superficiality of gawking at their "quaint" way of life and admiring their handiwork, and to help them prevent abuse.[7]

Since my strengths-based approach values diversity, I respect that Amish and Plain communities can be different from my own, and this isn't necessarily wrong. I also recognize the Amish are not all the same, nor do they claim to be perfect. This leads me to grapple with difficult questions: To what degree do people have the right to be different? What if their differences impact their health, how they raise their children, or even the safety of their children? To what degree should I accommodate a group's culture and faith?

These questions are challenging to answer. I call on those of us who are not a part of these communities to spend time in self-reflection and to refrain from grouping all Plain communities together, whether they be Amish or Mennonite. God's creation is beautiful and diverse, and God declared this as good. Let us also be open to difference. And may we be willing to invest time and work in building relationships with those who are different from us. Through relationship, we can learn about ourselves, and we can influence others.

---

7 As I mentioned above, there is also important work being done by survivors of abuse who have left their Amish or Plain communities to form survivor-support networks on the outside. Advocacy efforts such as these speak to the ways Amish and Plain communities have failed vulnerable children who face significant barriers to getting help outside these communities and provide important perspectives on how abuse continues to be tolerated and perpetuated within them. While beyond the scope of the present chapter, advocacy plays an important role in supporting survivors of abuse and advocating for change.

15

Artemis Patiently Waits
A Poem
Cameron Altaras

This poem brings together two very different worlds: the world of the Amish and Mennonites of Swiss-German roots, on the one hand, and the world of Artemis, an Olympian (Greek) goddess, on the other. In the cosmology of Greek myths, Artemis is referred to as the goddess of the hunt, the moon, and chastity. She is most often depicted as a young, beautiful, vigorous huntress, holding a bow and carrying a silver quiver filled with her arrows. The arrows of Artemis never miss their target. In the world of the Amish and Swiss-German Mennonites, there is a German word that is often used to refer to order and rules: *Ordnung*. For the Amish and Swiss-German Mennonites, this word has the added weight of theology and a couple of centuries of church-sanctioned rules and traditions, with which one must abide if one is to remain a member of the church and community. This poem focuses upon rules that women must obey. One rule of particular significance is that of wearing a head covering, which symbolizes a woman's need to remain submissive to men and to the church.

Artemis Patiently Waits

I

Scriptures shape-shift to
Rein in life and
Direct the horses to
Keep black buggies full of girlhood dreams
    to the side of the road.
Artemis patiently waits.
While the world evolves beyond
    their blinders and out past the reaches of their reins,
Artemis patiently waits.

Rules morph and cover
Never-cut-wound-tight hair
White head coverings tied just so under chins to
Keep female heads full of questions
    out of sight and in submission.
Artemis patiently waits.
While answers develop beyond
    Their grasp and farther than the reaches of their
        covering strings,
Artemis patiently waits,
    until one of them reaches for her hand.

II

Longings labeled "sin" drape
Plain capes over shoulders
Growing heavier one generation to the next to
Keep women from giving birth
    to forbidden strengths.
Artemis patiently waits.
While secret urges manifest new forms beyond
    their inbred obedience and the reaches of the last thread
of tradition's cape,
Artemis patiently waits,
    until one of them reaches for her hand and
Takes the arrow that she offers from her silver quiver
Shooting holes in every twisted scripture keeping
        women down
Wildly cutting every strand of hair bound up by
        Ordnung and the Bishop
Reclaiming words, rekindling longings,
Unleashing dreams and urging vibrant life
Teaching women now to
    Drop their blinders
    Ask their questions
    Use their strength
    Grab their reigns and drive their horses right down
        the center of the road.[1]

---

1 The author was invited to perform this poem at the Toronto Storytellers' online event, "Her Voice Returns: Stories of Forgotten Women," September 25, 2021. A recording is available at https://www.youtube.com/watch?v=oLvExfNL3bc&t=5s.

16

Bearing Witness

Ruth E. Krall

He, who does not prevent a crime, when he can, encourages it.
—Seneca[1]

How do churches respond when violence happens within the faith community? How are power and authority used in response to this violence? I begin this chapter with some reflections about power in the church community in which I grew up. I then describe how violence impacts communities and how safety must be a priority. I conclude with reflections on the quagmires that Anabaptist-Mennonite communities face and offer a model of "bearing witness" as a way forward.

Introductory comments

In the congregational church of my childhood, authority and power were embedded inside the soft velvet glove of community and communal conformity. Within this community, it was expected of children, adolescents, and adults that they would be obediently guided by adults in positions of power and authority—adults such as Bible teachers, ordained congregational ministers, and denominational bishops.

Once a confession of faith was made and baptism had occurred, the baptized individual was a full participant in the life of the

---

1 This quote is attributed to Seneca. See William Hermans quoting Albert Einstein who is quoting Seneca in Hermans, *Einstein*, 93.

community. She or he was expected to voluntarily and respectfully abide by the social and spiritual norms of that community.

Periodically there would be a paroxysm of evangelism: sin, as defined by the community, was exorcised, or at least corralled and brought under control. The only open public confessions of sin that I witnessed in my childhood were for smoking and premarital sexual relationships. The only excommunication I personally witnessed happened during the Korean War when a baptized young man from the congregation enlisted in Uncle Sam's armed forces. On the Sunday morning this young man was excommunicated, his family was in attendance, and the minister announcing the excommunication cried openly. Something in the community contract had broken, and it needed to be openly addressed and repaired. Everyone in the community needed the communal accounting to be public so that rumors were checked.

Behavioral faithfulness was monitored by bishops of the regional church. I didn't know it then, but theological correctness and personal behaviors of ministers were also monitored by the bishops. Not only did members of the congregation need to be accountably faithful to the community's norms, so too did the congregation's ordained spiritual leaders need to be impeccably faithful.

Inside this community adults were to be respected by children and adolescents. I was taught by my parents to call adults by their last names: Mr. and Mrs. Smith, for example. To this day, I do not know the first names of the parents of my childhood friends—in whose homes I played almost weekly.

In the small world of my childhood, I was taught, therefore, to recognize, accept, and accommodate to adult authority. But there were ground rules for that authority. There needed to be mutual respect and courtesy between adults and children. Adult cruelty and its concomitant violence were no more acceptable than childhood rudeness and disobedience.

The custom of my religious congregation in formal church settings was to call all adults by the title of Brother or Sister. Children and adolescents were called by their first names. While in my parents' home, my parents might call ministers by their first name—as in *Henry preached a good sermon this morning*—children and adolescents in the public sphere were expected to use adults' formal titles as a sign of deference and respect.

There was no mystical sense that human ministers spoke God's word firsthand. Their authority was not absolute. All religious and spiritual teaching needed to be tested inside the community. Only as the baptized community accepted the rightness or properness of the minister's spoken words, would they become part of the community's daily life.

Biannual communions were held, and they were serious affairs. Members of the congregation cleaned the church during the week before communion. Windows were washed, ceilings and walls were dusted, and the stern wooden pews were cleaned and oiled. Men did the heavy work of window and floor washing—while women did the dusting, sweeping, and wiping. The message was clear to a child: God's physical house needed to be clean before communion.

On the Friday evening before a Sunday morning communion, a special church service was held. It was called a preparatory service. There was a sermon followed by public confession. Men went into one room with a minister or ministers and women went into a second room with a minister or ministers. There were three questions that needed to be answered affirmatively if one were to take communion on the following Sunday: *Are you living in harmony with Scripture? Are you living in harmony with the teachings of the church? Are you living in harmony with your fellow church members?*[2] The message could not have been clearer: to be a part of this religious community of faith, one needed to be in agreement with its understanding of Scripture and of its practical teachings about the applied meanings of Scripture in daily life. In addition, one's lifestyle needed to be lived in harmony with the

---

2 These questions are worded now from my memory, and it has been decades since I needed to individually and publicly confess my faith before communion.

community and its common understandings of Scripture, faith, and spirituality.

My mother was my role model because, even as a very small child, I went with her for the biannual pre-communion confession. Her answers were always a firm *yes*—modified always with an additional comment: *as my conscience allows*. I do not remember hearing any other woman qualifying her answer in this manner. Twice a year the ministers, the bishops, and her fellow church members (and most importantly her daughter) heard my mother declare the primacy of her own conscience in matters of church discipline and in the daily management of her personal life.

An old woman now, I reflect on my life. When I do this, I become aware of the immense influence my family, childhood friends, and childhood's religious congregation have had on my life trajectory. As an adult, I have modified some of the ideals I was taught. I no longer live inside rigidly enforced dress and behavior codes.

These personal reminiscences set the context for the reflections that follow. These reflections are grounded inside an adult professional life devoted to the study of violence—in particular, affinity violence. As an adult, I have sought to live out my personal faith inside the context of a much larger community—that greater social order in which we all now live. In ways unknown to my childhood community and parents, I have encountered other world religions and their teachings about living peacefully and nonviolently. The desire to live with equanimity in the commons and to be a faithful advocate for a just peace in a dangerous world is the polar star of my spirituality and religious behaviors. I personally believe the Jesus-path is a path of peace and a path of justice. I believe that active peacemaking and justice-seeking are one pathway to healing for the world's victimized and traumatized individuals.

In addition, I believe that a mature adult life is one in which compassionate care for others is manifested. Compassionate and forthright care of the human commons is needed. When present, evil must be faced, recognized, and confronted. As an Anabaptist-

Mennonite, I believe in the accountability of individuals to the whole. In addition, I believe that personal integrity is the essential foundation for life. Personal and communal integrity are the rudders by which we can individually and collectively steer our lives.

What is the question?

How do you now address a community of pain, a community of agony, a community of trauma?[3]

Affinity violence is the violence that happens between people who know each other. It is not the chaotic violence of the street. It is not the random violence of strangers in chance encounters. It is not the organized violence of militarism and warfare. It is not the xenophobic violence between strangers from different ethnic groups. It is not the violence of hate speech and hate group actions. It is not unwanted sexual touch by a stranger on a crowded subway car. It is not the random obscene phone call in the middle of the night.

Rather, affinity violence is the violence that erupts between husbands and wives, parents and children, professionals, and those they are supposed to help, siblings, relatives, friends, and acquaintances. It occurs inside the trusted communities of our daily lives. Its ordinary names include spouse battering, child abuse, date rape, marital rape, professional misconduct, elder abuse, incest, workplace harassment, sexual harassment, playground bullying, and so on.

One aspect of affinity violence is that it betrays and shatters trust between people inside their intimate personal relationships and inside their communities.[4] Another is that it breaks down an individual's inner assumptive world about the safety and trustworthiness of his or her relational world with others.[5] A world in which principles of justice, fairness, kindness, and mutual respect

---

3 Quoted in Harris, *Irish Catholic.*

4 See Freyd, *Betrayal Trauma;* Carne, *Betrayal Bond.*

5 See Janoff-Bultmann, *Shattered Assumptions;* Kauffman, *Loss.*

guide individual and collective human behavior is replaced by traumatized inner and outer worlds in which others cannot be trusted.[6] Another aspect includes the changes that traumatic affinity violence creates in the victimized individual's physical, mental, and spiritual body.[7] The body/mind/spirit/self is both colonized by and changed by an individual's encounters with events of affinity violence. Each violation profoundly (and traumatically) damages an individual's life trajectory.

Over many years of professional work with survivors of affinity violence in a wide variety of settings, I have become convinced that the victimized individual's community also suffers. Families are destroyed. Friendship groups break apart. Suicides occur. Religious and spiritual communities shatter. That internal pain that begins inside an individual's suffering and desperation spreads like a toxic virus into the commons.

When the abusive person (the perpetrator of violence and violation) is in a trusted position of community authority (such as a minister), the damages are magnified. Not only have ordinary standards for an individual's behavior been violated; violations of power and authority compound the damages.[8] These damages have the power to destroy individual lives, families, and entire communities. For survivors and their surrounding community, there is also a spiritual dimension to these kinds of abuse. In many situations, the goodness of a compassionate and loving God can no longer be trusted.

Once incidents of affinity violence become public knowledge, they frequently create a traumatized and divided community.[9] When stories of affinity violation events and happenings surface into public view, not only victimized individuals but entire communities are faced with paralyzing questions: Who is telling the

---

6 Caruth, *Listening*.

7 See Van der Kolk, *Body Keeps the Score*.

8 See Krall, *Soul Betrayal*; Krall, *Clergy*.

9 Van der Kolk, *Traumatic Stress*.

truth here? Who can I trust? Who do I believe? Who is safe? Who else might be in danger?

Inasmuch as episodes of affinity violence occur outside the public gaze of the community, how is factual truth to be ascertained? In its essence, the community's question becomes this: What constitutes factual truthfulness? In contested narratives, the questions become these: Who do we believe? What is the evidence or criteria we can use to determine or to guide what we believe?

Inside the social commons of religious institutions (such as churches or church colleges), individuals are faced with the dilemma of believing or not believing complaints of affinity violations—most of which have occurred in private or isolated settings rather than in public ones. When faced with affinity violation complaints about community-trusted individuals (political leaders, religious leaders, civic leaders, teachers and professors, presidents of corporations, members of the press, entertainers, parents and grandparents, siblings and cousins, financial magnates, military officers, etc.), individuals and entire communities become bystanders to the actions of affinity abusers (i.e., perpetrators of violation and violence). One common community response is disbelief—that this individual could be a perpetrator of such violence; that the events of violation ever took place.

Without choosing or wanting to know about this situation of affinity abuse, once knowing, individuals must now respond. In short, when affinity abuse accusations become public information, there is no place of communal innocence to which to retreat. One's choices in situations of lost innocence are limited: one can choose to believe, disbelieve, or retreat into a false innocence of not seeing, not hearing, and not speaking—the false innocence of non-involvement (*This is not my problem; it has nothing to do with me; I have my own life to live; I didn't see or hear anything*).

The truth, however, is that whether one likes being in this situation, when complaints about affinity violations surface inside one's community, one is already involved. The questions then become: Now that I know about this accusation, this complaint, how do I personally respond to it? What, in this situation, mandates my response? What, if anything, do I need to do?

The questions are similar for members of the faith community: How do we individually and collectively respond? What in this situation mandates a communal response? Faced with rumors and allegations of affinity violence, what should our collective responses be? Seeing a badly bruised face, what do we need to do? Sensing terror in a friend's encounters with a rumored perpetrator, what do we need to do? Hearing a neighbor's child's terrified screams, what do we need to do?

Further questions arise: When a community splits wide open in disagreement about these matters, what is the pathway to individual and communal healing? When denial of factual truth pervades the community, what are survivors to do? Whom can they trust? Where can they find safety? How can they find a reliable pathway of healing? These questions are exacerbated in intensity when the community becomes hostile towards the survivor of an affinity violation. This overtly hostile behavior forms a second assault, a second betrayal of victimized individuals. Many survivors of clergy sexual assaults, for example, have reported that the disbelieving betrayal of their religious or spiritual community is a violation equal to the physical assault. The residual damages of a family's or a religious community's disbelief can be equal to or greater than the damages caused by the physical assault. It is often in this second assault that a survivor's connections with God and God's people are permanently severed.

Over the years I have come to the opinion that, if a given community is no longer safe for the survivors of affinity violation (for example, clergy sexual abuse of church members), it is no longer safe for anyone. I follow poet Mark Nepo's advice that in these complex situations of institutionalized betrayal (and here I paraphrase), *first get yourself to a place of safety; then do your needed spiritual healing work.*[10] I would add a third caution: *only then can you become a realistic helper of others.* Nepo's advice

---

10 Nepo, *One Life.*

follows the airlines' advice: *put on your own oxygen mask before attempting to help others with theirs.*

Inside complex situations where there are accusations, denial, and counter accusations, individuals and entire communities will inevitably need to make decisions about whom to believe and what to do. Their beliefs and opinions about truth will shape how they respond to the perpetrators and survivors of affinity violence. Social factors such as gender, race, sexual orientation, and an individual's status inside the community will all be factored in as individuals and entire communities make decisions about how to respond to accusations of affinity violence inside the faith community.

Anabaptist-Mennonite quagmires

One tricky area is lodged inside communal belief systems about social relationships and violence. I want to talk personally here. Anabaptist-Mennonites have a very and workable theology about nonviolence, peacemaking, and peacekeeping in times of militarism and organized war. However, we have almost no workable theology about acts of violence that occur inside our communities. Once the controlling authoritarianism of the bishops gave way in the last century to more egalitarian systems of congregational governance, individual congregations and church agencies were left on their own to name and then to monitor communal faithfulness.

In addition, I believe that some of our inherited theologies of forgiveness prevent us from developing adequate theologies and a praxis of peaceful and nonviolent conflict resolution inside our congregations and church agencies. Their absence prevents us from healing abuse-shattered individual lives and violence-shattered communities. In my opinion, we live in denial, individually and collectively, about the amount of affinity violence inside our communities. That which is denied inside of us and among us cannot be openly addressed; it cannot, therefore, be managed and healed. That which must remain a secret becomes the lie that destroys individual lives; it also destroys the community's life as a place of safety, healing, and spiritual maturation. It is that simple and that complex.

If I (or the collective we) believe, for example, that a parent has the right to beat his or her children into submission, it will be hard for me (or the collective) to believe the adolescent's or grown-up child's revelations about his or her experiences of affinity violence in childhood.[11] If I (or the collective we) believe that husbands are mandated by God to dominate their families and that it is acceptable spouse behavior to beat wives into submission, I (or the collective) will have a hard time making informed discernments about accusations of spouse abuse in divorce proceedings.[12]

Once more people than the perpetrator and his or her victim know about the events of affinity violence, the community is affected, and its choices will determine how these troublesome allegations of abuse are managed.[13] Whether or not an individual member of a congregation or denomination wishes to be involved, it is quite likely that she or he will become involved. Specific issues of abusive power, irrational control, and inept management of the accusations about affinity violation begin to be evident as the community and its individual members make decisions about how to proceed.

A short case study

Many years ago, I lived in a community in which a much-revered minister (a charismatic preacher, a superb liturgist, and gifted church administrator) was accused of sexually abusing several women who had sought pastoral counseling during and following difficult divorce proceedings. I was not a member of the congre-

---

11 "Spare the rod; spoil the child" comes to mind.

12 "Wives submit yourselves to your husband as if to the Lord" also comes to mind.

13 For a thorough multi-disciplinary discussion about ways in which individuals and communities deny that violence has occurred or is continuing to occur, see Cohen, *States of Denial*.

gation, but a good friend of mine sat on its governing board of elders.

As the congregation's board of elders and the denomination's presiding bishop investigated these multiple abuse accusations, the congregation became internally divided. Much enmity and disbelief were expressed toward the women. Some people in the congregation denounced the women as liars, troublemakers, and wanton seductresses. For these individuals, the minister was seen as innocent and seduced rather than as a perpetrator and seducer. In short, for these individuals, the minister became the victim. These members of the congregation rushed to his defense. Other members of the congregation denounced the minster as violating his ministerial responsibilities. He was openly reviled. Rumors sprouted like weeds after a rainstorm.

Some people blamed the board of elders for their management (mismanagement) of the situation. Others turned against the bishop—accusing him of making matters worse. Anger was directed at denominational executives. Individuals first shouted during and then stormed out of meetings. Longstanding friendships died in angry encounters and hotly conflicted arguments about who was right.

As I listened to my friend's anger and spiritual anguish, I remember thinking that in this congregation truth had already died a violent death. This excessively volatile verbal conflict created enemies. It nearly destroyed a congregation.[14] Eventually, my friend removed her membership from the congregation and stopped attending religious services anywhere. A former missionary and devoted church worker, she left all formal religious life behind. It took her many years to rebuild her inner sense of a meaningful spirituality. If we were in touch with each other, she remained alienated from her cradle denomination.

---

14 This case study is not about an Anabaptist or Mennonite congregation. I was not and have never been a member of this congregation. I was a total outsider. In addition, I have shaped some elements of this case study to protect the anonymity of the congregation and the identity of my now-deceased friend.

Eventually, the minister was removed from ministry; his ordination credentials were rescinded; and an interim minister was hired. However, almost two-thirds of the congregation's members had already removed their membership and walked away without looking back. Many of these individuals simultaneously left their cradle denomination.

More than thirty years later, I visited this church and discovered that this once vibrantly alive religious community was a mere shadow of its former self. Its once vital program of social ministry to its surrounding community was nearly nonexistent. Talking with some of the older members of the congregation, I discovered that the wounds of this ancient conflict were still very much alive in their minds and hearts. While they were the continuing members of this congregation—the folks who had stayed behind after everyone else had left—to me it seemed that they still refused to trust it and belong to each other. Worship became an individualized ritual; it was no longer a vital community of shared beliefs and practice.

Bearing witness

One of the items in the tool kit of individuals who seek to be healers in situations of violent conflict or peacemakers in situations of intractable hostility has come to be known as *bearing witness*. I have come to see the concept of bearing witness as essential to our understanding of individuals and entire communities whose lives have been ripped apart by affinity violence and betrayal.

Bearing witness includes several dimensions, and each one is important for effective work inside the toxic forests of affinity violence and betrayal violations. First, there is the task of *bearing witness to one's own personal experiences and to one's own response patterns to these forms of abusive violence*. The goal is to develop compassion for the self. Trauma experts know that trauma work affects their inner self. Trauma healing work will change the trauma worker's perceptions of the world and their perceptions of themselves. Thus, not only psychological work needs to be done to integrate the work one does into one's daily life. Inner spiritual work also needs to be done. When one is a member of the community in which affinity abuse has occurred and then become visible, one becomes a participant-observer. My personal experiences— as an advocate for Mennonite victims of affinity violence—have taught me that I do not stand above or outside the conflicted fray. My emotional health, physical wellbeing, and spiritual health have been deeply affected and sometimes compromised by the sexual violence advocacy work I have done. I have needed to take breaks in the work, and at times I have needed to go on extended retreats. I have needed other professionals to help me regain my inner equanimity and to find my own way once again. At times I have needed to find professional healers for my wounds. One consequence of my work is that I am no longer naïve; I am no longer trusting; I am no longer a true believer. I am much more cynical about the Mennonite Church and its formalized teachings about peace than I wish I were.

Second, there is the task of *bearing witness to the life events of violation inside the lives of survivors*. One needs to bear witness to the survival of victims—their own inner spirit's insistence that what happened to them is evil. One needs to listen carefully to find that aspect of the personality that will guide the healing process. I believe this aspect is a dimension of soul work. The living, human soul directs the healing process. It is essential to be able to listen compassionately, knowledgably, and non-judgmentally to survivors and to those who love them and accompany them. For professionals, I agree with Harvard psychiatrist Judith Herman: those who work with survivors need a supervisory support system.[15] Effective sexual violence advocacy work (bearing witness)—over the long haul of a professional lifetime—is not the work for lone rangers or lone wolves. A peer community is needed because the corrective of a knowledgeable community and the support of a compassionate and informed community are both needed.

Third, there is an aspect of *bearing witness that participates in the prophetic ministry of the church*. The Roman Catholic clerical sexual abuse and clericalism expert Richard Sipe describes this

---

15 Mendelsohn, et al., *Trauma Recovery Group*.

prophetic ministry as telling individuals things they don't want to hear.[16] When the institutional church, for example, protects an affinity violence perpetrator, the sexual violence worker and survivor advocate must be prepared to forthrightly address this form of denominational malfeasance. While in isolated situations, an individual may be called to be an isolated prophet, I believe that a small community of prophetic advocates is often more effective in bringing about needed institutional change.[17] Corrective institutional work often involves informed insiders and concerned outsiders. Alliances of concerned prophetic voices are needed.

Concluding remarks

This essay has represented an attempt to think about the issues of affinity violence inside Mennonite communities. I would prefer that it be read as a clarion call to Anabaptist communities for study and as a call for a denominational re-thinking of our approaches to affinity violations. It is also a call to the churches' theologians and ethicists to begin the work of updating Mennonite theologies of nonviolence to include affinity violations in their work. A vibrant peace witness to the violent worlds of militarism, economic exploitation, and ethnically or culturally motivated hate crimes has been and continues to be deeply compromised by the unacknowledged and unaddressed presence of affinity violations inside the Anabaptist-Mennonite community. As we bear witness

---

16   Richard Sipe, personal correspondence to author, 2018.

17   For an extended discussion of clericalism (the tendency of religious institutions and institutional insurance providers or legal consultants to protect themselves in situations of professional clergy sexual abuse), see Krall, *Elephants*. In many of his professional speeches and in personal conversations, Roman Catholic expert Thomas Doyle talks about the clericalism of his church and its mismanagement of clergy sexual abuse perpetrators as the "church outsourcing the gospel to its lawyers." I would add that the temptation of the institutional church in situations of professional sexual misconduct and sexual abuse is to protect the perpetrator and to abandon his victims as it "outsources the gospel to its lawyers and to its insurance providers."

to the affinity violence among us, my hope is that this will begin to change.

17

Anabaptists, Othering, and the Coming apart of a Community

Sylvia Klauser

> We do have choices. We're living through a certain part
> of history that needs us to live it and make it and write
> it. We can make that history with many others, people we
> will never know. Or, we can live in default, under protest
> perhaps, but neutered in our sense and in our sympathies.
> —Adrienne Rich, *Arts of the Possible*

I had often wanted to write my story. And then I thought,
Who cares? However, as a pastor and spiritual care educator,
I listened to the many stories of women and men who, like me,
grew up in conservative denominations and the cottage industries of Bible schools, summer camps, youth retreats, and quilting bees. Their stories were so much like my own. We lived
through a certain part of history, experienced similar things,
and yet, knew nothing about each other—except the experience
of abuse in the church was all the same, no matter the language
or creed or family relation. My upbringing in post–World War
II Germany was a jumble of abuse. That included being forced
to do certain things, believe in specific ways, and behave according to someone else's rules. The whole mess eventually put me
on a trajectory into pastoral theology and ethics. My experience has a name now: *adverse childhood experiences* (ACE) is a

set of measurable and classifiable traumas that effect the health and wellbeing of an individual. The Center for Disease Control (CDC) now acknowledges it as a public health issue. In the progressive tense, I am making my history my own. And I am writing my story for the many women, children, and men who have no voice—yet.

A certain part of history

The 1960s and 1970s in Germany were the tail-end of the post-war era, and churches were mostly introspective, familial places where people kept to themselves and their kind. The revolutionary renewal process of the Catholic Church called Vatican II went on at the same time without entering our consciousness. Our folks' energy flowed into birthing us, raising us, and making a living. Outwardly, that meant to build and keep a small, post-war house with a garden, chicken coop, fruit trees, berry bushes, and as little useless grass as possible. Every square meter contained an edible plant or tree. Flowers or decorative shrubs were frowned on and bickered about. But we always had roses, tons of rose bushes of all sizes and colors. We never ate them, though the hunger of the war years forced my parents to raise useful things—and children. We never had pets either, only consumable animals.

Our house, like thousands in post-war Germany, had the same simple, functional architecture. To this day you can spot the familiar layout of those streets in any German city and know that the *Siedler* (settlers) lived there. The new citizen-refugees came "home" from the places where previous centuries' geo-political development had taken them: Silesia, Prussia, the Southeast of Europe, even the Ukraine and Russia. The traumas of two world wars were deeply imprinted in the emotional and spiritual DNA of our parents and grandparents. We, the grandchildren of the war, learned instinctively how to keep the peace because our elders' emotional war turmoil dominated generational patterns of engagement. The German journalist and researcher Sabine Bode wrote extensively about the unspoken effects of wars.[1] My family and countless other refugee families survived and thrived by suppressing the trauma with physical labor, strong family bonds, and church loyalty. In Germany alone, the volume of inheritance between 2012 and 2027 is an estimate 400 billion Euros, according to the German Institute of Economy.[2] This legacy of my ancestors is indeed a *Wirtschaftswunder*, an economic miracle. But what is the toll of those years? Who carries the emotional and spiritual wounds of such outward success? What is the fallout of over seventy years of peace?

The success of us *Wirtschaftswunderkinder* (the miracle children of the economic success years, aided by the Marshall plan of 1950–1970) depended on the survival of our parents. Their behavior and proven strategy to stay alive through the war and the refugee years was family, church, and "your own kind." This became our credo for a long time. Like many families in the larger Anabaptist movement, we had a copy of *Martyrs Mirror*, and though it was read sparingly, the moral of the stories was clear: a follower of Christ is required to give up their life. Following Christ sets you apart from the rest of society. As Anabaptists and refugees, we were the others.

Church and the dualism of otherizing

We belonged to the ethnic and cultural group of the *Donauschwaben*.[3] They were Reformed with influences of Pietism. *Klauser Oma* (Grandma Klauser) told us about going to the *Schdund*—those Sunday afternoon hours of Bible study–like services conducted by itinerant preachers, which kept their faith and families together. My family must have somehow gotten in contact with

---

1 Bode, *Die vergessene Generation*.

2 "Erben Bekommen."

3 Melcher, *Borne on the Danube*. *Donau-schwaben* is a collective term for all Germans who floated down the Danube River in search of a better lives in the eighteenth century. Former Yugoslavia, Hungary, and Romania were the target countries for those settlers who moved there at the invitation of the Habsburg Empress Maria Theresia of Austria.

the followers of the preacher Samuel Heinrich Fröhlich.[4] They became *Nazarener,* apostolic Nazareans.[5] One could not just be an ordinary member of the Reformed church. One needed a conversion experience, followed by a *Prüfung,* a testing, a congregational questioning of sincerity before the baptism. My maternal grandmother was otherized early by her new family until she converted and was baptized into the fold.[6] Grandpa's family of 14 siblings exerted much shunning pressure on the young couple when he married her outside of the faith.

The dualistic boundaries between in-and-out, belonging and being other, right and wrong were set early and firmly and enforced swiftly. We drove into another country for church services, choir practice, and youth group. Our fifteen-minute car ride to Switzerland for church lasted for decades. The faithful met there in a beautiful nineteenth-century timber-framed villa in the shade of a huge Linden tree, overlooking the meandering Rhine River. We were located above, and removed from, most of the neighborhood. The church's location was yet another expression of being spiritually disconnected from our neighbors. Driving out of town, and into another country, also separated us from our own German neighbors and friends.

In church, before God, we are all the same, the preachers said. But we were never equal. And we were never the same as our neighbors who did not go to church with us. We did not participate in the cultural activities of the town, because they were *worldly,* the parents said. We were not encouraged to participate in municipal governance, the school board, or the local Lutheran church. We talked about the goings-on of the town at the dinner

---

4 Adler, *Die Tauf- und Kirchenfrage.*

5 Not to be confused with the Church of the Nazarene, they are the Apostolic Christian Church Nazarean. See http://www.acc-nazarean.org.

6 The Oxford English Dictionary defines *otherizing* as follows: "to view or treat (a person or group of people) as intrinsically different from, and alien to, oneself. Referring to them in these terms strips them of their identity and otherizes them as foreigners."

table, but we didn't get involved. We were clearly not the same as the neighbors.

Many Anabaptist-Mennonite churches are still a conglomerate of various family clans. The entire family system is always with you, breathing down your spirituality and controlling the output of your piety. Leaving the faith is leaving the fold, and vice versa. Even today, some family names are held in higher regard than others. I have a non-Mennonite last name, so the "Menno name game" during my undergraduate years at the Swiss-Mennonite Bible-school Bienenberg, in Switzerland, and later at the Mennonite Brethren seminary in California, held little attraction. My surname sounds a lot like Klassen, and establishing the proper progeny is important to Mennonites. I was often asked how many S's and A's are in my name. One S, one A, but it's still no Klassen of any sort. I was not connected and was therefore of little interest to the insiders. Again, I was other.

The Nazareans in the larger Anabaptist world self-identified as the called-out ones, those who *really* followed Jesus.[7] The plain dress code is still found in some conservative churches today. Such sociological reality of otherness is theologically named the *called-out community* within the larger church (*ekklesiola* in *ekklesia*). *Called-out* implied that we were better, set aside from the world. We followed Jesus, not the sword or the magistrate. We made it into the fold. We were saved (and safe). We were other, and other was better. Maybe it was a means of control or just a way to keep the tribe together. It is difficult internal and external work to adjust to a new land, new language, new customs. Our theological interpretations influenced ecclesiastical realities, which are recorded in many Mennonite history books. The story tells us that the plains of Saskatchewan, the hills of Chihuahua in Mexico, and the Bolivian bush were highly preferable to urban centers.

---

7 5 Adler, *Die Tauf- und Kirchenfrage*; Baker, *Traumatized*; Beck, *Stranger God*; Bode, *Die vergessene Generation*; Bode, *Kriegsenkel*; Bowler, *Blessed*; Crenshaw, *Intersectionality*; Dueck and Parsons, "Ethics," 271–82; B. Goossen, *Chosen Nation*; Halifax, *Standing*; Kahl, *Galatians*; Kerr, *Bowen Theory's Secrets*; Melcher, *Borne on the Danube*; Van der Kolk, *Body Keeps the Score*.

The city so easily diluted the faith and ensnared the faithful. Keep to the tribe, away from the sinful world. We otherized ourselves geographically and theologically. We were in the world but could not be part of that world, as Paul was fondly quoted. A theological dualism of in-and-out silently and forcefully permeated our Anabaptist reality.

The dualism and otherizing were not just theological and social; it was also visible inside the church and reinforced with laser precision. Men preached. Women listened. Women made the food—and talked. Women did the dishes—and talked. Men chose and married women, who then gave up their names and previous identity to become the wives. Blessed were those who had no burdens to bear, said the preachers, those who were not widowed (though there were many in those years), who were not physically handicapped (though we knew many wounded veterans), or mentally unstable, developmentally disabled, or single. These are still the categories of otherness in the church. If you were a man, had a job, a house, a wife, and healthy children; if there was enough food on the table and some extra produce to give to the more impoverished; if the kids were healthy and thriving, then life was blessed and good—except, it was so only externally.

Writing and living my story

I was an inquisitive child. I wanted to know how things worked, and that got me quite often in trouble. I wanted to figure things out for myself, but I was a girl. And I didn't trust anyone except myself.[8] From the ages of eleven to sixteen, I was in a constant state of high alert during summer vacations that we spent on the maternal family farm. I became hypervigilant and over-functioning, developed a sharp tongue, and quickly developed analytic and reflective reasoning skills. I became a keen observer of others, myself, and any given environment in which I found myself. I always had to be a step ahead of my sexual predators in order not

---

8 Kerr, *Bowen Theory's Secrets.* Multi-generational transmission processes as found in Murray Bowen's Family System Theory have had a strong influence on my differentiation and integration.

to get cornered, be unwantedly touched, or become the object of their sexual self-gratification. It was all about them. I was their object and plaything. I felt exposed for five years. I was othered. No one had my back. I had to fend for myself. And I couldn't tell anyone. Sexual sins and unwanted sexual attention were always the responsibility of the women and the girls. That was our sex education. Victim-blaming, like hard work and survival, were generationally transmitted. Don't look. Don't dress in a tempting way. Don't argue. Don't laugh too loud. Don't flirt. Don't, just don't. I felt cornered, caged, frozen. My grades nose-dived; I began to lie to my parents. Eventually I had to leave my school for a lower level of education because I could not concentrate. And church life went on as normal as ever.

Books saved me. Not God, or the church, but stories of other people and their adventures, how they overcame obstacles, how they made a life amid adversity. My safe space during those summers was the reading chair. Reading was acceptable during vacation—after the day's work was done. Sometime in those early teens years I knew with a bang that my parents could not teach me the things I wanted to know. They taught us their survival skills: work hard, be frugal, help your kin in need, trust in God and church, don't make waves, don't speak up, don't become a target. They transmitted these family survival patterns, including the severe corporal punishment they had received themselves. I was beaten to "save that curious child." Today I have words for such holistic abuse.[9] We continued our dichotomous lives in the church and at home. My journey of integration began when I left home at age seventeen.

---

9 Van der Kolk, *Body Keeps the Score*. A quick search of the terms *developmental trauma disorder* or *adverse childhood experience* (ACE) points to several websites that are potentially helpful to the interested reader. See, e.g., http://www.traumacenter.org/products/pdf_files/preprint_dev_trauma_disorder.pdf. Also useful is van der Kolk, *Body Keeps the Score*, even though he was recently accused of abuse of power in his workplace; Baker, *Traumatized*.

I often wonder how similar these dualisms are handled in other Anabaptist families. I wonder whether the cultural or regional contexts make any difference. We carry an air of humble simplicity and are secretly proud of our perfect lives. We focus on outward piety, yet unspoken abuse, repressed pain, off-record topics, and a disjointed church-and-private life have many congregations in turbulent waters today. Churches break apart, caused by a festering and molding pile of unspoken pain. Anabaptist-Mennonite churches and their scholars can do much better regarding the effects of adverse childhood experience. I am convinced that many good church people live with deep-seated, suppressed, even repressed trauma. Suppressing those experiences as not belonging in the church only cements power and privilege and a literal, biblicist theology.

As a woman who still hangs on to the church, I get increasingly frustrated with the incongruence of faith and life. I am deeply frustrated with the deliberate silence—and silencing—of many female and queer voices, and I am horrified about a categorical dualism that turns a blind eye to blatant privilege of white males and their abuse of power. The unacknowledged superiority by male leadership in the home and the church depends on the type-cast hermeneutic of literal interpretation and inerrancy of Scripture. Menno Simons's century-old question thunders back at us: Should the Bible be interpreted literally, or should its meaning be taken seriously? The prophets' mandate for justice, combined with Jesus's imperative to love the neighbor, is the light of truth that will shine a spotlight into the shadows in the peaceable kingdom.

Women who share their stories of pain and abuse crack open a fragile peace when they speak about their pain and abuse in the comfortable silence of privilege. We shun transparency with the people who mean most to us, our sisters and brothers in Christ. We do not talk about our daily experience of pain. I learned early that the church cared more about perfection, purity, and the afterlife than about a healthy and creatively transformative existence while we are alive.

Making my story with others

> Your silence will not protect you
> —Audrey Lourde

Reflecting on my story, analyzing my experiences, and sometimes rubbing the scars on my soul, I often wonder how many women like me are out there in Anabaptist-Mennonite land. As a pastor and chaplain, I listen to the horrific reality that a peace-loving and reconciliation-preaching church turns a deaf ear to the silent suffering of half its membership. I am unwilling to keep alive that soul-destroying cone of the quiet in the land. Speaking out gives power to and amplifies the voices of those whose silencing and otherizing is ongoing. A younger generation of activists leads the way, and I add my voice in support of all the women who have not yet been heard. These silent women of the church may live in much more difficult and soul-destroying circumstances than mine were. The silence about our experiences will no longer protect us or anyone else. Quite the opposite: it will stifle us and eventually kill our spirits. Such forced silence will be our early grave. We need to turn on the spotlight and shine out the shadows of abuse that thrives under the cover of privilege and silence. The voices of emotional pain and spiritual anguish must be amplified and heard. We need to write and re-write our stories to find our peace.

Spiritual, sexual, physical, and emotional abuse and boundary violations made me a fighter and defender of my inner core. I lived with a dualistic reality that undermined my integrative and reflective self-development for decades. During the week, I fought and fended for myself with a sharp, analytical wit. But on Sundays I needed to be a docile, agreeable girl who could not use her brain to question religious authorities and their theological interpretations. Requiring women to be the quiet, submissive, and subordinate members is denying their inherent equality in Christ. It is theological and spiritual violence that protects the ecclesiastical status quo. Denying the inclusive and saving grace of Christ for LGBTQI members of the church is a pastoral and congregational sin of continued exclusion and otherizing. Elevating ethnic and cultural minorities into denominational leadership is a thin veneer of tokenism to pacify the guilty conscience of white settlers who otherized the natives off their land in the past and now white knuckles "leadership" in trepidation of the possible loss of privilege.

After forty years of processing, reflecting, and learning more about my early start in life, I am a constructivist intersectional theologian and ethicist, which means that I believe our theology is always under construction in relation to our lived faith experience.[10] I propose four themes for continued close attention and research. Space permits only a brief sketch here, yet these themes will help to counteract the ongoing abuses that lives in the privileged mainstream of the church. We need to investigate (1) our continued theological dualism, (2) the persistent othering of those who are not us, and (3) the silencing of different voices in the church, and, the most difficult topic, we need to uncover, expose, and eradicate (4) the unchecked white (male) privilege that hides in our Anabaptist-Mennonite plain sight.

1. No to ongoing theological dualism

The largest and most basic obstacle for an integrated and contextual twenty-first–century Anabaptist-Mennonite theology is the ongoing binary preaching and theologizing. When I am invited to preach, I now avoid binary and exclusionary remarks about in-or-out, sinful-or-holy, we-the-church-they-the-world, and so on. Being inclusive requires more preparation time, deeper reflection, greater awareness of my audience, and stringent sensitivity to intersectional and intercultural realities. I must also scrutinize my own assumptions and prejudices through the hermeneutic of suspicion when preparing a sermon. Not only must I be suspicious of current cultural, social, and historical realities and experiences, but I also must be suspicious of my own pre-judging of self and others. The best sermons are those where we end up with a conversation about a text and its application in our daily life. *Con vertere* is one of the root words of conversation and means that

---

10 Crenshaw, *Intersectionality.*

we turn the words around and turn ourselves around the words of Scripture.

Counteracting abuse in the church and unlearning white privilege begins at the point of greatest influence: in Sunday worship where every voice (hopefully) has equal weight about their lived reality. Continued grappling with the dearly beloved tenets of non-involvement such as "in the world but not of the world" is a first step to becoming integrated and whole congregations where all voices count. In his blog called *Experimental Theology*, Richard Beck challenges the readers to deep engagement with self, other, and the world. The other is the divine in disguise, Beck learned in prison. The Reformation, with its off shoots of a perfectionist Protestant work ethic and a Calvinist pre-selection theology might come to an end when we acknowledge that we are not either/or but both/and. Distinguishing between worshiping Jesus and following Christ might be a good starting point. Being a follower of Christ is a fringe movement that depends on the glory of its broken people. We are no better than other folks.

2. No to ongoing otherizing

To paraphrasing of my favorite quote by Emmanuel Levinas: *Our mutual ethical reflection begins in the face of the other person.* This late French philosopher developed his life's work in the face of the Nazi occupiers in his native Lithuania. Levinas spoke German-Yiddish as part of his Jewish heritage and was faced with an almost unbearable choice: work with Nazis and perhaps live or refuse cooperation and be sent to extermination camp. Levinas's writing is a mind-bender, yet his challenge is clear. Ethical reasoning and moral obligation begin at the point of any relational encounter. Such engagement reaches far beyond established binary categories that make it easy to decide who belongs and who does not. Historical shadows loom in this definition: throughout Anabaptist history we have been otherized. In turn, we have otherized others, as Ben Goossen establishes in his research about Nazi Mennonites.[11] Our theological development enforced clear distinctions between *us* and *them*. We are in the world but not of the world. Our lived experience and generational transmission processes of *dos* and *don'ts* kept dualism alive and made otherizing easier. But such a thin reading of the other negates the thick lived spiritual experience of an integrated person.[12]

Privilege thrives on enforcing established categories, rigid boundaries, and the otherizing of entire groups. These processes and patterns were put in place in the sixteenth century and continue in force today. In her book *Galatians Re-Imagined*, Brigitte Kahl sheds light on our situation today: otherizing and abuse of power are the dirty underbelly of unchecked privilege.[13] Such was the case with the Roman Empire that killed Jesus, and it is the case today with the empire of Anabaptist theology that wants to vanquish the voices of the other.

In our quest to analyze rampant privilege in Anabaptist-Mennonite churches and to prevent abuse of power, Levinas's challenge is clear: in the face of the other person—in face-to-face meetings and in relationships—rests the creative beginning of our moral and ethical engagement with each other. We must accept the existentially endured pain of those silenced voices who finally speak of their raw experience. We need to accept that we failed masses of the silent in the land. When pain is spoken *and* heard, salvation happens in this life. A solid theology of grace might be the catalyst for such transformative experience.

3. No to the silencing of different voices

Some dearly held Anabaptist-Mennonite "characteristics" have long been my great irritants, especially enforced dress codes,

---

11 B. Goossen, *Chosen Nation*. Mennonite history slowly catches onto the fact that the settling in a new land goes hand-in-glove with otherizing native populations; B. Goossen, "Mennonite War Crimes."

12 Dueck and Parsons, "Ethics," 271–82.

13 Kahl's book traces the development of concepts such as inclusion and exclusion, dominion and subjection, and belonging and alienation back beyond the beginning of Christianity.

male-only preaching, and keeping women subordinate with less-
er ministries. My emotional and spiritual survival depended on
speaking up and refusing to become the object of another person's
satisfaction, but I lacked the resources and safe space to speak
early on about my traumatic experience. Selectively silencing the
stories of abuse is a means of control by the church hierarchy.
Sharing the pain forces the church to acknowledge and hold that
pain. Hearing about the whole-person destruction that abuse can
cause grows the knowledge that abuse is a raw and destructive
power that is wielded by the privileged to get their way.

Finding one's voice takes a long time, especially in a church
environment where the submission and docility of women and
girls are virtues. Speaking one's truth is even harder because it
makes one a target. The suffering humanity of the speaker is
objectified into a prayer request or an issue. Any pious expression
is easier than silently witnessing the destruction that a beloved
church leader has caused.[14] Speaking one's truth is tough business, and our denominations must put their tenets of justice and
reconciliation into practice and create more safe spaces for victims
of privilege and abuse. To this day, it is still not safe to speak, to
share, and to be heard.[15]

The ongoing work and advocacy of Our Stories Untold, Pink
Menno, the Brethren Mennonite Council for LGBT Interests
(BCM), the Mennonite chapter of the Survivors Network of those

---

14 Halifax, *Standing*. The three principles "Not-Knowing," "Bearing Witness," and "Compassionate Action" by the Zen Peacemaking Order, established by Roshi Bernie Glassman, can teach us Anabaptists how to support
victims of abuse in our own churches.

15 Speaking our truth may not protect us either—indeed, it is extremely
risky. I am married to my wife Susan, and my emotions flip-flop between
fierce fighting and withdrawn depression when I follow the ongoing ostra-
cizing of non-conforming persons in the denomination. Before I met the
love of my life a few years ago, I was deeply committed to a life of silence
about my abuse, a life of service, and a life of solitary singleness. And that
commitment nearly killed me. Women and men in the church may *never*
speak about their abuse, but especially for them we need to hold open a
space as we dismantle unchecked privilege in our denominations.

Abused by Priests (SNAP), and Into Account are important starting points for those who have never spoken of their abuse. Many of their experiences are included in this publication. Their stories teach us that speaking up is risky. Writing this is also risky. But not speaking about one's experience of sexual, verbal, emotional, and religious abuse inflicted by those with privilege and power only gives a free pass to perpetrators who are content with church business as usual. Look only at the number of church members among us who suffer from eating disorders, depression, anxiety, self-mutilation, addictions, and other self-harming, avoidant practices while attending church. Many members eventually drop out because they are literally sickened by being silenced and having to live with so much unacknowledged pain.

4. No to white (male) privilege

White (male) privilege thrives on easy theological dualisms and binary worldviews, and it is fueled by otherizing and tokenism.[16] However, when the token woman on the board or the token minority leader or the token victim dares to raise their voice and challenge the status quo of beloved history and process, privilege

---

16 I put *male* in parentheses because those of us Anabaptist-Mennonites with Euro-American background live in a cocoon of unacknowledged privilege wherever we go in the world. I am a German woman in my mid-fifties. I can use public transportation in Munich, Germany, or in New York City without being so much as glanced at. I am not pulled over by authorities while driving because no one feels threatened by a middle-age white lady, in contrast to how my friends of color are treated when driving. No one calls the police on me while ordering coffee. I am not mistaken as the Latinx wait staff at big church events. Even though my life has not been easy, I was able to study and obtain a PhD without the hassle of too many part-time jobs or dependents. I have been put in a box of *white female CPE supervisor* by students before or, worse, revered as a roshi. Such interactions continually raise my own awareness about how micro-aggressions hurt me. And they highlight my unexamined bias toward people who are not of my ethnic group, religious heritage, social class, and so on. I learn to engage with each person without otherizing and by holding my privilege loosely.

tightens its grip and holds on to power.[17] White (male) privilege lives with many unacknowledged shadows, including the unfounded notion that God will bless us when we do everything perfectly right. This definition of blessing is still much like the one I grew up with: healthy, prosperous, not disabled, not addicted, not gay, not an unwed mother, no disruption of the status quo. Nothing of that sort could be in our family or church. Kate Bowler, the author of *Blessed: A History of the American Prosperity Gospel*, puts her finger directly into this wound when she writes, "Though Mennonites are best known by their bonnets and horse-drawn buggies, they are, for the most part, plainclothes capitalists like the rest of us."[18] Now that we own what we never had before—relative safety and freedom, wealth, and acknowledgement—we must hold onto it all cost.

Privilege is a result of political processes and structural social injustice, but it is neither biblical nor humane. It keeps some in power and others under power.[19] Together, we must re-envision a gospel community where privilege is no more and no one is discriminated against, otherized, silenced, or abused. The time of privileged Christendom is ending. This crucial time in our history requires us to make our history our own and to create inclusive gospel communities that share all of who we are with all people.

---

17 Mennonite Central Committee's continuing debate about non-heteronormative ways of being constitutes privilege that clings to binary reasoning that harms and otherizes non-conforming individuals. Krehbiel, "Who Defines Celibacy?"

18 Bowler, "Death, the Prosperity Gospel and Me."

19 Indeed, the Oxford Dictionary defines *privilege* as "a special right, advantage, or immunity granted or available only to a particular person or group."

18

The Self Unveiled
The Dis-integration of Mennonite Women's Head Coverings

Sarah Ann Bixler

I remember the first time I saw my grandmother's hair. I was almost five, staying overnight at her house. That evening, it hung straight in long, grey strands all the way to her waist. As she brushed, it shimmered in the yellow-pink twilight that streamed through her bedroom window. It beckoned me, and I ran my eager fingers through its silky softness. I thought it was the most beautiful sight in the world. The next morning, my grandmother wound her glory around and around, twisting, tightening, and pinning until it was concealed beneath a white mesh head covering. Fifteen years later, she whispered to me, "Sometimes I wonder why I still wear this thing."[1]

---

1 My Mennonite grandmothers, however, were buried in the early 2000s in the white netted head coverings they had worn all their adult life. As a pastor's wife, my mother wore a small black prayer veil atop her contemporary hairstyle for Sunday worship until about 2004, when she sensed she could still show respect for the older generation without wearing it. When I was baptized as an early adolescent in 1993, the poured water fell onto a prayer veil. I never wore it again. Today I would not think of asking my own daughters to cover their heads for religious purposes.

A century of change—custom, ordinance, disappearance

Only a century ago, the woman's head covering was one of seven ordinances of the (Old) Mennonite Church.[2] Referred to as the head covering, cap, bonnet, or prayer veil, it came to occupy a significant position in church doctrine. In the past two or three generations, however, the head covering has largely fallen out of practice in Mennonite Church USA and Mennonite Church Canada.[3] Where are all these relics of women's piety and submission? Many lie forgotten in a drawer, their thin material yellowing and disintegrating with time.

Such a powerful symbol is not so easily discarded. The head covering is one of those "potent symbols whose power lingers even after the specific practices disappear."[4] Drawing on Carroll Saussy's insights on the self and the principles of common shock articulated by Kaethe Weingarten, I argue in this chapter that the head covering as a symbol of power wielded by men over women in the Mennonite tradition in the United States and Canada has an impact at the level of the self that may continue to be transmitted across generations. I am a Mennonite woman of Swiss-German descent who has inherited the intergenerational impact of a religious practice that, though I do not practice it now, still bears on me in some way. It is imperative to consciously examine this fading symbol as it relates to Mennonite women's current iden-

---

2 This paper focuses on the history of regulations on the head covering primarily in what is formerly the (Old) Mennonite Church. These communities have ethnic roots in the Swiss and South German regions of Western Europe and typically migrated directly from these regions to North America. This chapter tracks the symbol of the head covering among these particular forebears of what are now Mennonite Church USA and Mennonite Church Canada.

3 This chapter does not cover Mennonites and related Anabaptist groups in North America that retain a traditional position on women's head coverings, such as the Amish and conservative Mennonite groups, though a few clearly identified anecdotes will be used from these groups to illustrate a point.

4 Weaver, "Plain Clothes," 5.

tity.[5] A symbol of submission that was once imposed on women's selfhood and spirituality, the head covering is disintegrating from religious practice, but its legacy is in need of intentional analysis.

The religious mandate for women to cover their heads is a relatively recent phenomenon in Mennonite history. Prior to the 1890s, Mennonites rarely preached a biblical basis for this practice.[6] One Pennsylvania Mennonite testified that until 1898 he had not heard any preaching on the woman's head covering and was told it was merely worn as plain dress.[7] Examples abound of Mennonite women in the early nineteenth century wearing hats and a variety of bonnets but not for the reason of conforming to Scripture.[8] In the 1890s, evangelist John S. Coffman took married women's common custom of wearing a cap for worship and reframed it as a "prayer head covering" for all baptized women

---

5 One challenge of writing about the current impact of a historical practice is that we now recognize the limitations of the gender binary that was assumed during the time when "men" enforced the "women's" head covering. Though I will use these gender-based terms in this chapter, I want to acknowledge that categorizing persons as either male or female is a function of the politics of power. In arguing for the need for "women" to do integrative work, I want this term to be understood as encompassing all persons who feel the impact of the mandated head covering as an infringement on their body—no matter how that body is self-identified or characterized by others—and persons who experience common shock as a result.

6 Beyler, *Meaning and Relevance*, 73. There is evidence in Mennonite publications as early as 1864 referring to the head covering as a religious norm, but most Mennonites in the United States and Canada at that time did not preach a *biblical* basis for this practice. In 1879, the Southwestern Pennsylvania Conference passed a resolution for brethren to uncover and sisters to cover their heads during religious services, according to the teaching of Scripture. Yet this is the exception rather than the norm for this time period.

7 Ruth, *Earth*, 742.

8 Hershey, "Study," 26–27. Mennonite leaders in Ontario's Niagara district initially objected to the bonnet as an alternative to the wide-brimmed hats. In some communities such as in Pennsylvania and Iowa, bonnet boxes were standard in Mennonite meetinghouses for storing head coverings worn only in worship; Coffman, "Mennonite Dress," 126.

at all times, citing Paul's instructions in 1 Corinthians 11:2–16.[9] Coffman's son explains, "These times were among the first when many of our people ever heard I Cor. 11 expounded as signifying the purpose of the cap. It was a wonderful revelation throughout the whole church. From 1885 on through the early part of the 1890's this fresh appreciation of the subject was presented and accepted. *Young men* heard the exposition and accepted and taught it" (emphasis added).[10] Throughout this implementation period, male leaders promoted the head covering and wielded their power in such as a way as to dictate how women should present their bodies as a pleasing and acceptable sacrifice to the Lord.[11] And, as a convenient corollary, the head covering also served as the visible symbol of submission to the divine order of headship, always reminding women of their inferior place.

The 1890s saw the head covering rise to the status of an ordinance in the Mennonite Church. What had been merely a cultural custom and a symbol of plain dress,[12] practiced only by some women and in various forms, "took on a new, hallowed meaning: a biblical symbolism almost in a class with the Lord's Supper."[13] Daniel Kauffman's publication of *Manual of Bible Doctrines* in

---

9 Hurst, *Articulation*, 91–92. During the head covering's instatement in the 1890s and beyond, the rise of biblical fundamentalism and a reaction against women's rights advocacy likely motivated Coffman and his fellow advocates. These motivations were evident as late as 1972, when Richard Detweiler defended the practice in his study of 1 Corinthians 11 for the Christian Education Board of Lancaster Mennonite Conference. He writes that women's political involvement is one example of "misled desire," which results in the weakening of the woman's influence because it means she will "lose her most powerful position, the home." Women have influence if they have "guided men from infancy to greatness of character," which has greater impact on the nation than voting. According to Detweiler, this misled desire is also seen when women seek to look like men and do what they do; Detweiler, *Head-Veiling*, 5; Detweiler, "Historical Background," 12.

10 Gingerich, *Mennonite Attire*, 130.

11 My reference to Romans 12:1 is intentional.

12 Ruth, *Earth*, 742.

13 Gingerich, *Mennonite Attire*, 130–31.

1898 appears to be the first articulation of the head covering as an ordinance.[14] He regards Paul's instruction in 1 Corinthians 11:2 as forever establishing this status and lists the "woman's prayer-head-covering" as one of seven ordinances alongside baptism, communion, feet-washing, salutation of the holy kiss, anointing with oil, and marriage.[15] The head covering was to become the subject of numerous Mennonite conference resolutions and the most contentious article of clothing in the Mennonite Church.[16]

As the twentieth century dawned, the woman's head covering as an ordinance and biblical mandate gained traction across the Mennonite Church in the United States and Canada.[17] Thanks to "Daniel Kauffman's vigorous indoctrination program," most women in the (Old) Mennonite Church could be seen wearing a covering by the 1920s.[18] During this period, conferences ruled in favor of plain, undecorated coverings, sometimes giving specific regulations about its form.[19] The *Christian Fundamentals* of the 1921 Mennonite General Conference states in its article on ordinances, "Christian women praying or prophesying should have

---

14 Kauffman, *Manual of Bible Doctrines*, 150. Kauffman defines an ordinance as "an act or ceremony instituted by someone who has authority to do so. *An ordinance is not a sacrament* in the sense that the original meaning of the word *sacrament* implies."

15 Kauffman, *Manual*, 160.

16 Gingerich, *Mennonite Attire*, 119.

17 The impact of Kauffman's *Manual of Bible Doctrines* is illustrated by the timing of resolutions passed by Indiana-Michigan Conference. In 1891, the conference adopted the position of wearing the prayer covering as a required custom. By 1912, following Kauffman's publication, it listed it as an ordinance. Beyler, *Meaning and Relevance*, 77.

18 Wenger, *Prayer Veil*, 17–18.

19 Gingerich, *Mennonite Attire*, 118–19, 136. Franconia Conference in 1917 insisted on tying the cap's strings, and Lancaster Conference in 1937 mandated square-edged coverings with ties. "Round coverings are not allowed," Lancaster Conference stated in no uncertain terms, though this eventually changed.

their heads covered."[20] At the request of the 1925 Mennonite General Conference, Kauffman and a committee of twenty-one men compiled *Doctrines of the Bible,* reiterating much of what Kauffman wrote in *Manual of Bible Doctrines.*[21] This served as an authoritative text for the (Old) Mennonite Church (MC). In 1951, J. C. Wenger upheld the head covering mandate in *Separated unto God.* The General Conference Mennonite Church (GC), however, did not place such restrictions on the head covering.[22] A GC comprehensive theological statement of 1908, for instance, does not mention the issue.[23] Indeed, MC Mennonites in Lancaster, Pennsylvania, were startled when meeting Mennonite women from further west who did not wear the covering.[24]

During the 1950s, the head covering began to disappear in many Mennonite communities, though with notable delays in Pennsylvania and Virginia.[25] These shifts in practice occurred despite the 1963 *Mennonite Confession of Faith* identifying the Christian woman's veiling as an ordinance.[26] While in Lancaster the head covering was required into the 1970s at the Mennonite high school and even during recreation such as swimming, in most Mennonite communities it was only worn in public worship, if at all.[27] Documentation is scarce about exactly how it fell out of practice.[28] Denominational publications shed little light on its dis-

---

20 "Christian Fundamentals (Mennonite Church, 1921)." The Mennonite General Conference was the body of the (Old) Mennonite Church (MC), not to be confused with the General Conference Mennonite Church (GC).

21 Kauffman, ed., *Doctrines,* 7–8.

22 Nafziger Hartzler, *No Strings Attached,* 35; Yoder Nyce, "Head Covering."

23 Weaver, *History,* 188–90.

24 Ruth, *Earth,* 971.

25 Gingerich, *Mennonite Attire,* 119.

26 "Mennonite Confession of Faith, 1963."

27 Gingerich, *Mennonite Attire,* 131. Kraybill, "Veiling," 318.

28 Second-wave feminism and the departure from biblical fundamentalism likely influenced the head covering's disappearance. Changing occupa-

appearance. "In most congregations and conferences, the change in practice took place by default, rather than by some deliberate course of action."[29] I have concluded, along with my colleague Melody Pannell, that the practice disappeared as one Mennonite woman after another quietly left her head covering on her dresser before leaving for church on Sunday morning, or chose to leave it folded inside the cover of her Bible when arriving at church.[30] As the head covering disappeared, interestingly, the question of women's ordination came to the fore. Yet, even as the symbol disintegrates, we must ask if any ongoing impact of the head covering exists. What sense of self is unveiled with the disintegration of the head covering?

Symbol and self

Throughout the historical documentation advocating for women's head coverings, a recurring theme is the headship principle. According to 1 Corinthians 11:3, this divinely instituted order places God as the head of Christ, Christ as the head of the man and the man as the head of the woman.[31] The covering, then, functions as a sign of the woman's place in this order. As Kauffman writes, "The woman, to *show* her position with regard to the authority of the man over her, is here taught to put a covering on her head, when she prays or prophesies" (emphasis original).[32] Later advocates, such as J.C. Wenger, sought to nuance the headship principle by describing subordination not as a hierarchy, but as a matter of "function and administration . . . not of quality or importance."[33] Yet even after offering this nuance, Wenger subsequently feels a need to add the clarification that "woman was made for man, not

---

tions and levels of education also played a role.

29 John C. Wenger and Elmer S. Yoder, "Prayer Veil."

30 Sarah Bixler and Melody Pannell, "Uncovering Meanings of the Head Covering."

31 Detweiler, *Head-Veiling*, 4.

32 Kauffman, *Manual of Bible Doctrines*, 164.

33 Wenger, *Separated*, 199, 208.

228 • Sarah Ann Bixler

vice versa."[34] Without a doubt, the head covering at its height of practice was intended as "a symbol of submission."[35] This symbol subjected married and single women alike to male headship. It represents an expression of a patriarchal ideology.

In addition to the headship principle, the head covering also served the development of Mennonite group consciousness.[36] At first, women were not the only ones to dress in a distinctive way that marked them as belonging to the Mennonite community. From 1911-1919, two successive Dress Committees called for nonconformity and modesty in the Mennonite General Conference through simple, distinctive attire for both men and women.[37] The men's "plain coat," a coat without lapels that buttons to the neck, endured for ordained ministers almost as long as the head covering.[38] Yet as the twentieth century progressed, a double standard emerged as the church continued to regulate women's dress in the absence of men's distinctive attire.[39] As Marlene Epp notes, "Women's bodies were the mechanism for inventing and conveying group identity."[40] The head covering was the longest enduring symbol, marking women as belonging to the Mennonite commu-

---

34 Wenger, *Separated*, 209.

35 Martin, *Scriptural Headveiling*, 10.

36 Beyler, *Meaning and Relevance*, 89–90.

37 Hurst, *Articulation*, 181–85.

38 During the 1920s, numerous conferences required their male ministers to wear the plain coat when performing pastoral duties on behalf of the church, but not male laity. This caused some concern because it elevated the status of ministers above the laity. This regulation appears weak in contrast to the head covering that was required for all baptized women, at all times. Gingerich, *Mennonite Attire*, 54.

39 Elizabeth Landis Nissley recalls how she responded as a seventh grader to a revival meeting call in 1955. "I stood for the invitation, and the next day I went to the local public school with a covering. That was one of the hardest days of my life." Any young men who stood alongside her, however, were not required to adjust their appearance based on the spiritual commitment they had made. Stoltzfus, *Quiet Shouts*, 172.

40 Epp, *Mennonite Women in Canada*, 190.

nity and therefore signifying the nonconformity of the community as a whole.[41] "Long after men had moved in other directions, women were expected to be the social conservators of Mennonite culture . . . [through] clothing and hairstyles."[42] Indeed, some Mennonite women today who have given up the head covering yearn for such ready identification as part of the Mennonite group that used to be conferred by this symbol.[43] Submission and group belonging went hand-in-hand. This worked in such a way that the urge to be liberated from male headship was usually subdued by the pull toward a community of belonging, keeping women in their designated place. And in many cases, women internalized and strongly imposed the regulation upon other women. Some Mennonite women have conflicted feelings about the head covering, recognizing its positive elements in spite of the way it was manipulated to keep them in line. For these women, it is a symbol of solidarity with other religious women. It is worn out of respect for other women who wear it, and is a welcome coming-of-age ritual for entry into a feminine subset of a religious community.[44] Some Mennonite women continue to joyfully embrace the head covering, navigating the benefits of group identification even without the unwelcome demands of submission. Esther Stenson, a state university professor, is one example. She selectively wears her head covering because it reminds her of her Mennonite values and the people to whom she belongs.[45] In wearing the head covering in the spirit of freedom, Stenson apparently has not internalized the subjection that her Amish Mennonite community of

---

41 Hurst, *Articulation*, 94–95. Epp, *Mennonite Women in Canada*, 195.

42 Wiebe, "Me Tarzan," 16.

43 Showalter, "Mennonite Bonnet and Covering Stories."

44 Bixler and Pannell, "Uncovering Meanings of the Head Covering." The Mennonite women in attendance at this conference session shared some of these positive meanings of the head covering from their own experiences.

45 Esther Stenson, "Veiled and Free."

origin intended.[46] Other Mennonite women still choose to wear the head covering because it reminds them of their spiritual commitments and empowers them to pray and prophesy. Ordained Mennonite pastor Seferina de León, now retired, still finds meaning in wearing her prayer veil in the privacy of her own home when engaging in intercessory prayer.[47] Piety is a strong factor in women's choosing to wear the head covering, as a testimony to herself and others that she is set apart as a follower of Jesus.[48]

For other Mennonite women, though, the head covering as a symbol of submission confers a negative impact on their sense of self. Women's objections to the head covering were present as soon as Kauffman embarked on his campaign to institutionalize the practice in the 1890s. This is evident in his replies to a lengthy list of objections in *Manual of Bible Doctrines*, wherein he uses the pronoun "you," which signals that he is replying to women's objections.[49] Moreover, some female scholars interpret the head covering unequivocally as a "visible sign of subjection."[50] Brenda Martin Hurst explains, "Male church leaders required women to *show* the world their acceptance of submission to men on their female bodies. Church leaders did so to reinforce their identity as strong Mennonite men. The prayer head covering served as a visible reminder to men of their authority over women."[51] This located women's sense of self within in a patriarchal system. The head covering stands as a reminder of the power men have wielded over

---

46   As an Amish Mennonite publication states, "The very reason [a woman] wears the veiling is because she recognizes that she is not equal to [the man], and that she wants to be subject to him. . . . In fact, she wears the veiling to show that she is. The man and the woman are equal in spiritual privilege, but they are not equal in social relationships." Martin, *Scriptural Headveiling*, 3.

47   Phone call with Seferina de León, October 29, 2018.

48   This is the spiritual meaning one of my own grandmothers attributed to wearing the head covering.

49   Kauffman, *Manual of Bible Doctrines*, 166–68.

50   Hurst, *Articulation of Mennonite Beliefs*, 94.

51   Hurst, *Articulation of Mennonite Beliefs*, 97.

women in the Mennonite church, a symbol of what women have worked to overcome in their beloved communities—the desire for belonging without subjection, piety without dominance.

What, specifically, might the imposed and constant wearing of a symbol of submission do to a woman's sense of self? Considering the self as representing "what is most personal and unique about an individual," Carroll Saussy believes the self incorporates "the body, mind, and spirit; abilities and limitations; and repressed and remembered experiences both positive and negative: bodily experience, relational experience, cultural experience, religious experience."[52] She writes about a "theology of submission and obedience" that prevents women from having faith in their intrinsic worth.[53] This theology is embedded in a patriarchal ideology.[54] Women under patriarchy may develop what Saussy identifies as "a false self, an adapted self that lives according to other people's expectations."[55] This blocks the expression of the true self, which depends on the ability to communicate one's feelings, sensations, needs, ideas and emotions. When expressions of the true self meet rejection, "the true self is violated."[56]

The theology of submission and obedience, exemplified in the Mennonite ordinance of the head covering, tells a woman that in her natural state she cannot pray, she cannot communicate her feelings, sensations, needs, ideas and emotions and find acceptance. Her true self cannot communicate directly with God or others in the community; it needs to be repressed and veiled under the pretense of a false self. This false, submissive self represents the expectations that the male-dominated religious institution gives Mennonite women in the symbol of the head covering, "an idealized image others have held up to them as to who they ought

---

52 Saussy, *God Images and Self Esteem*, 39.

53 Saussy, *God Images and Self Esteem*, 13.

54 Saussy, *God Images and Self Esteem*, 16.

55 Saussy, *God Images and Self Esteem*, 34.

56 Saussy, *God Images and Self Esteem*, 34.

to be."[57] This is given to women most clearly in baptism. When the baptismal waters flow over a man's head, he is liberated for leadership and authority in the religious community; when the baptismal waters flow over a woman's head, she receives the head covering as a sign of her piety and subjection. It is only under the veil that women can become that whom God and men intend them to be.

Women's internalization of the head covering as a symbol is a theological problem. It obscures the relationship between outward expression of faith and inner reality. On the one hand, Anabaptists have affirmed the distinction between symbol and reality, keeping with Augustine's view of sacraments as "an outward and visible sign of an inward and invisible grace." Performing religious rituals does not automatically mean someone is a sincere follower of Christ; yet, such signs are expected as a natural outgrowth of a dynamic spiritual life. But when the outward sign is imposed upon a believer and regulated by someone with power over them, this cause-and-effect relationship changes direction. In the case of the head covering, "appearance standards are used as a means of interpreting a woman's inner religious qualities."[58] Wenger, for instance, clarifies that external ordinances are symbols of spiritual attitudes, and calls Christian women to align their inner attitudes with the outward sign worn on their heads.[59] Wenger's call points to the assumption that an outward sign, i.e. what a woman wears on her head, is distinct from her true inner self, which must conform to the outward sign under the pretense of a false self. Regulating the head covering is an exercise of power that intends to reshape a woman's self as submissive and compliant. The true self is manipulated through an act of violence and violation, the abuse of power.

---

57 Saussy, *God Images and Self Esteem*, 39.

58 Graybill and Arthur, "Social Control," 21.

59 Wenger, *Separated unto God*, 212.

From shock to unveiling the power of the true self

When men acting within the system of patriarchy wield their power in a way that places women in an inferior and submissive position, they commit acts of violence and violation that confer a form of trauma called common shock.[60] In establishing this theory, Kaethe Weingarten identifies sexism specifically as a process that produces victims by threatening their sense of security and safety.[61] She identifies three positions involved in the experience of common shock: perpetrator, victim and witness. When someone witnesses a perpetrator subjecting a victim to violence or violation, the witness likely experiences a common shock response.[62] In the case of instituting the head covering as an ordinance, male leaders inflicted violence on women's psyches and spiritual lives and perpetrated physical violation by requiring them to affix a foreign object to their bodies. In many cases, the head covering was secured on a woman's hair with straight pins.[63] The insidious nature of common shock is that, because it does not reach the same level of intensity or duration as full-fledged trauma, it often goes unaddressed. Yet, it has a cumulative effect both on the individual and on those whom she influences.

The theology of submission represented by the head covering does not only affect women who wear it; it is transmitted through common shock to the next generations.[64] I believe some Mennonite women today experience common shock from the recent history of male domination over women's bodies through the mandated head covering. Some women were of the era that

---

60 Bixler, "Can I Get a Witness?," 9–25.

61 Weingarten, *Common Shock*, 23.

62 Weingarten, *Common Shock*, 3–4.

63 We might imagine further connections between the perilous task of affixing something to one's head with sharp objects and the potential for pain and harm from wearing the head covering as a symbol.

64 Weingarten, *Common Shock*, 119. This intergenerational transmission is not solely negative; positive behavioral adaptations may be conferred as well.

they themselves wore the head covering, and are engaged in the challenging task of discovering their true self that was repressed by the false self under the veil. For some of them, parting with the covering—an act of their own desire—was a traumatic experience.[65] Others, such as myself, may be more in the position of witnessing to those women of a previous generation. And still others may be, as Saussy writes, "frozen in a false self . . . blind to the patriarchal rules and values that dictate their lives."[66] What can be done to reckon with the reality of the head covering as it relates to Mennonite women's selves today, in order to stop the impact of common shock?

The first step toward healing requires awareness. Mennonites don't often talk about this recent history of the head covering. Many don't know why the practice started, or only vaguely remember how or when it ended. We need safe spaces for truth-telling to break the silence around the traumatic impact of the head covering.[67] In my research and in listening to Mennonite women reflect on this surprisingly recent practice, I have learned many stories of Mennonite women with a conflicted sense of self because the head covering was imposed upon them as a requirement for belonging to the community and a symbol of their religious devotion. This impact is particularly poignant for women of color in Mennonite history, who were subject to the most severe regulations. As one African American Mennonite woman shared with me, she and her female peers of color in Philadelphia were subject to stricter guidelines than young Mennonite women in rural Lancaster County, in terms of their head covering size and amount of hair concealed under it. She recalls that wearing the head covering "wasn't something that we liked."[68] Yet, she

65 Weaver, "Writing about the Covering," 4.

66 Saussy, *God Images and Self Esteem*, 87.

67 Literature in trauma studies identifies truth-telling, mourning and responsibility taking as essential tasks for healing from trauma. See Bixler, "Can I Get a Witness?," 23.

68 Barbara Baynard in phone conversation with author, June 19, 2018.

and her peers complied, even to the extent of being discredited by their own African American community. The truth is largely unknown and untold about these intersectional harms in the head covering's legacy.

As we seek healing, I envision a truth-telling space that brings together Mennonite women who are in the various positions of witnesses, along with those who consider themselves victims of the abuse of power in relation to the head covering. These resilient women could tell the truth about the trauma and common shock they have experienced and the veiled self that resulted, using their agency to combat the "silence [that] plays a crucial role in passing trauma and common shock from one generation to the next."[69] Consciously bearing witness to oneself and to one another, by being present with and communicating one's feelings, sensations, needs, ideas and emotions, helps to cultivate the true self and break the transmission of common shock.[70] Because the head covering was an ordinance of the Mennonite church, it would be most significant if this truth-telling space could be protected by the religious institution: for instance, at the invitation of a subgroup within Mennonite Church Canada and Mennonite Church USA. At a later point, provision could be made for pre-screened men, who either directly or indirectly supported the head covering practice at some point in their lives, to hear a select group of women who volunteer to share their stories.

In these intentionally crafted spaces, truth-telling could open the way for communal mourning as those present wrestle with the realities of the past and its ongoing impact in the present.[71] Healing from trauma and integrating its reality into the self is, after all, impossible without mourning. I also imagine a church-wide ritual of mourning—whether an event at a national gathering or a designated week for observance across the country—to mourn the damaged selves and lost contributions of women whom the

---

69 Weingarten, *Common Shock*, 142.

70 Weingarten, *Common Shock*, 151.

71 Sheppard, *Self, Culture, and Others*, 139–40.

Mennonite church banned from leadership and denied equality over the years. The head covering is a tangible and visible symbol of this abuse of power. I offer these ideas as possible steps toward awareness and healing from the ongoing impact of the trauma that has occurred in Mennonite women's bodies and selves.

In order for the cycle of common shock to be broken, responsibility taking must occur. As we saw in the historical overview, those male church leaders who first implemented the head covering are no longer with us. Others now occupy formal positions of power in the Mennonite church, and I look to them to take responsibility on behalf of the institution for the harm that has occurred, whether through a public apology from the religious institution, a public ritual or another creative response crafted in conjunction with Mennonite women who are passionate about this work. Yet, this is largely a symbolic act of responsibility taking. There is also a component of responsibility taking that empowers women who themselves are impacted by trauma and common shock. Women have agency to integrate the veiled false self of the past with the emerging true self in the present. This is work for which we can take responsibility, together in a community of witnesses that seeks to reclaim and restore that which was taken away.

It is time not only to unveil the Mennonite woman's head, but to unveil her true self. This is an act of repossession, reclaiming oneself for oneself in the presence of God rather than putting on a self that is imposed by someone in a more powerful position.[72] Emerging from under the veil, Mennonite women have the power to bear witness to the violence and violation endured when church leaders effectively integrated the head covering into the woman's self. Even as this symbol of submission disintegrates from the practices of Mennonite communities, remnants of the abuse of power and domination remain. This chapter has represented one attempt to acknowledge the history and ideology behind the mandate of the woman's head covering, in hopes of fostering the conscious reintegration of this disintegrating practice into the narrative of women's experience in Mennonite

---

72 Herman, *Trauma and Recovery*, 202.

communities. Each woman who has been impacted by the head covering, either directly or indirectly, will have to do this work not by herself, but for herself. In this way, the Mennonite church can move forward into a new era where women can better express their true selves unveiled before God and persons in their religious community.

19

Run, Dirk, Run!
Wrestling with the Willems Story
Kimberly D. Schmidt

Introduction

Dirk Willems (d. 1569) is a local folk hero in the Netherlands and universally lauded among Mennonites who
claim spiritual descent from Anabaptism, a socio-religious
movement in sixteenth-century Europe. Anabaptists challenged both the ecclesiastical and magisterial authorities of
their day. They baptized adults at a time when the Catholic
Church taught infant baptism. They adhered to nonviolence
at a time when European monarchs counted on mercenaries
and foot soldiers to fill their armies. They worshiped freely as
a "priesthood of all believers" at a time when Catholic priests
controlled access to God. For these and other radical beliefs and
practices, Anabaptists were labeled heretics, hunted, jailed, tortured, and killed.

One such Anabaptist was Willems, whose story is examined
more fully below. While escaping over a frozen river from certain
death, he turned back to rescue his pursuing jailer who had fallen
through the ice. He is held up as the embodiment of nonviolence.
But how should abuse victims engage with his story? Must we
always rescue those who commit violence against us and on us?

I am the ex-wife of an abuser. Turning back to rescue my
now ex-husband only led to more victimization. This short essay,

originally a sermon, focuses on how I, as an abuse survivor, have wrestled with Dirk Willems's story, which has seemingly become the defining narrative for North American Mennonites.

Dirk Willems as the Mennonite story

He's everywhere.[1] Pick up just about any Mennonite publication, online or print, and I'll bet my grandmother's sacred recipe for *zwiebach* that Dirk Willems makes his ubiquitous appearance.[2] It seems every Mennonite church foyer, periodical, publication, brochure and pamphlet contains his image.[3] As historian James C. Juhnke writes, his image can be found "on church banners, Sunday School curriculum publications, church bulletins, conference brochures, periodical mastheads, newspapers, books, and even on the label for a [failed] Mennonite beer."[4] Apparently, he also inspires Tom and Jerry cartoon knock-offs and dog sweaters, which one can easily find images of on the internet.[5]

---

1 This article was first presented as a sermon at Hyattsville Mennonite Church, Maryland, on January 21, 2018, and published as such on Sixoh6, a blog of sociologist Rebecca Barrett-Fox. Since that publication I've expanded the research and commentary to engage with scholars from a range of disciplines, all of whom claim an Anabaptist background (Mennonite and Church of the Brethren). Their writings have taken me deeper into the analysis and helped me clarify my own evolving thoughts and interactions with current interpretations of Dirk Willem's actions and what they mean for women of Anabaptist traditions.

2 Mennonite *zwiebach* does not refer to the crackers that folks in Germany use for teething babies. *Zwiebach* is a soft bread made up of two small rolls that sit atop one another like a headless snowperson. For many North American Mennonites, this simple double roll is sacred food. See Epp, "Semiotics of Zwieback," 416–31.

3 Luthy, *Dirk Willems*. James C. Junhke, in a review of Luthy's book, noted that Luthy has collected over 400 Willems artifacts. See Juhnke, "Martyr We Remember Most."

4 Juhnke, "Rightly Remembering."

5 The Tom and Jerry cartoons were part of a series produced by Ian Huebert, an illustrator, for inclusion in Beachy, *Tongue Screws and Testimonies*.

There's Dirk, in 1569, skinny from being jailed. The charge? Baptizing adults. Willems did not adhere to the Catholic practice of infant baptism and had not only undergone baptism as an adult but had also performed several adult baptisms, a heretical act in sixteenth-century Holland. According to Thieleman J. van Braght, the seventeenth-century author of *Martyrs Mirror*, after eating nothing but watery gruel, descending with knotted rags from his jail cell window, and skimming across a frozen pond, he was close to escaping a certain death when his pursuer, a well-fed and hapless member of the local brute squad, fell through the ice.

What did Dirk do? As many school-aged Mennonites can tell you, Dirk turned, reached back, and hauled his would-be captor from the icy currents. For his selfless heroism and compassion, he was promptly re-jailed, tortured, tried, and sentenced to be burned at the stake at dawn.

That's as far as most Mennonites telling the story get. However, the story continues. The pyre refused to burn. The wind was too strong and kept blowing out the "lingering fire," leaving Dirk burned from the waist down but alive. Thieleman J. van Braght wrote that Dirk cried out in agony at least seventy times before the constable in charge implored the nearby executioner to find a way to quickly and mercifully dispatch Dirk.[6]

Mennonites are people of the book. Our sixteenth-century Anabaptist reformation was fueled not only by missionary zeal and disgust with indulgences and the corruption of the Catholic Church at that time but also by the printed page. Many early Anabaptist leaders were writers, printers, booksellers, and theologians. We are named after Menno Simons, who chronicled our belief in nonresistance, but I think it's fair to say that, more than Menno, Dirk captures our imaginations. Dirk is our most popu-

---

6 David L. Weaver-Zercher gives a compelling account of Dirk Willems's recapture and persecution and how it continues to shape North American Mennonite identity today. See Weaver-Zercher, *Martyrs Mirror: A Social History*, especially the chapter on Dirk Willems, "The Most Usable Martyr: Putting Dirk Willems to Work," 264–91.

lar martyr,[7] and his story has endured on the printed page in the *Martyrs Mirror*.

Martyrs Mirror documents the martyrdom of eight hundred and three early Anabaptists in well over one thousand pages accompanied by one hundred and four etchings by Dutch Mennonite artist Jan Luyken.[8] First published in 1660, "*Martyrs Mirror* has functioned, and continues to function, as a measure of Christian faithfulness," writes religious historian, David L. Weaver-Zercher.[9] Historian Benjamin W. Goossen adds, "Put differently, martyr tales are always about power, especially the power to induce social and theological conformity."[10] Writer and poet Julia Kasdorf makes a similar observation in her review of the *Martyrs Mirror*'s migration from Europe to North America, noting that the book was the largest book published during colonial times and served to "reinforce an ideology of nonviolence in the New World."[11] The book reminded Mennonites and related groups of their beliefs in nonresistance. As Kasdorf writes, "We can trace a relationship between the printing of the big book in the United States to the nation's military history."[12] It was the largest book published in colonial America. However, as scholars have noted, for most Mennonites the martyrs' stories and images have been reduced to one: Dirk Willems.[13]

Dirk's *Martyrs Mirror* story defines Anabaptist-identifying people. In his article on Dirk, Juhnke cites "a mission worker" who

---

7 Juhnke, "Martyr We Remember Most."

8 The full title of the book is *The Bloody Theater or Martyrs Mirror of the Defenseless Christians who baptized only upon confession of faith, and who suffered and died for the testimony of Jesus, their Saviour, from the time of Christ to the year A.D. 1660.*

9 Weaver-Zercher, *Martyrs Mirror: A Social History*, x.

10 B. Goossen, "Book Review: Martyrs Mirror."

11 Kasdorf, "Mightier than the Sword," 44–62.

12 Kasdorf, "Mightier than the Sword," 52.

13 Leichty, "Staying Mennonite." See also the chapter on Dirk Willems in Weaver-Zercher, *Martyrs Mirror: A Social History*, 264–91.

claimed, "This story is quite possibly *the* most potent illustration in the Mennonite subconscious."[14] I agree. Except for the Jesus story, it is the most defining narrative of contemporary Mennonite collective identity. The Dirk Willems story does many things: "Dirk Willems warns Mennonites not to expect to be rewarded for good works—a sharp contradiction to the American gospel of success."[15] He teaches us to have compassion for the enemy. He teaches us about self-sacrificial love. He teaches us about dying for our beliefs. He teaches us how to follow Jesus's words and "turn the other cheek"—that is, to not respond to violence with violence. He teaches us that following Christ's example of nonresistance will not necessarily be rewarded. There is much to applaud about the Dirk Willems narrative, and I'm not here to dismiss it. But there's a problem.

The problem with the Willems story

In 1997, I gave a paper at the symposium "Mennonite and Jewish Ethnic Identity in America," held at the University of Maryland at College Park. In attendance at the conference were a number of adult children and grandchildren of Holocaust survivors and also Mennonite scholars and community people. When Juhnke told the Dirk Willems story, the Jews in the audience erupted with surprised laughter. They asked, "Why on earth would you go back to rescue your captor? Jews would never rescue Nazis. How stupid can you get?" The Mennonites in the audience were dumbfounded. I've never forgotten the Jewish reaction to our most highly revered story.

Why has the Jewish reaction to Dirk Willems remained so powerful for me? Probably because of its relevance to my life. I am a Mennonite woman, activist, scholar, and feminist who suffered years of marital abuse. Mennonite women suffering from abuse and harassment and who are encouraged to embody the Dirk Willems story face a double bind. First, they must rescue

---

14 Juhnke, "Rightly Remembering."
15 Juhnke, "Rightly Remembering."

their abusers. Second, they must submit to their abusers. I would argue that rescuing an abuser is an act of self-harmful submission and not an act of virtue or moral courage. What happens when victims adhere to the martyr story because it induces social and theological conformity? To decide not to go back, to not reach back and rescue your captor, goes against our primary theological identity. It is something most of us are not willing to challenge.

How many times did I go back and try to "rescue" an abusive husband? I still wonder at how naive I was. During our courtship, I should have paid more attention to his court records, his run-ins with police, his lack of boundaries with female friends, and his belligerent behavior at parties and with waiters, shop owners, and those who are hired to serve in businesses where "the customer is always right." These confrontations during courtship escalated in marriage to fits of anger, violent rages directed not only at others but also at me and our children, including physical, psychological, and emotional abuse. By the end of our marriage, when I had finally given up any hope of redemption, I remember thinking, *Don't go back. Don't pull him out of the water again. Just let him drown.*

The Dirk Willems story as understood by many Mennonites today—when taken with no criticism, no thoughtful analysis, and no alternate narratives—can hold people in abusive, trapped places, especially when relational power dynamics are skewed. Mary Sprunger, historian of Early Modern Dutch Mennonites, has said that in the Netherlands Dirk Willems is remembered as actively resisting Spanish imperialism. His story is primarily political, not religious, and he is remembered differently. I find this recasting of Dirk helpful. He was politically active and courageous.[16]

The struggle I had with rescuing my now ex-husband resulted in revictimization. I knew that pulling him out of the water would result in once again having to protect myself and my children from his violence. I knew that pulling him out of the water would result in codependency. I had stayed with him in spite of

---

16 Kasdorf notes Sprunger's comment in "Mightier than the Sword," 47. And Kasdorf is right: "Some of us just call him 'Dirk'" (59).

his unhealthy behaviors and supported him at the cost of my own mental, emotional, and physical health. Pulling him out of the water was not a healthy choice. Pulling him out of the water resulted in years of shame and silence. Yes, the Willems story holds powerful lessons, but we've taken it too far.

I'm not the first to question Mennonite fidelity to Dirk. In 1992, Melvin Goering argued that the *Martyrs Mirror* was hardly relevant in today's world: "The theological assumptions and social context of Mennonites at the end of the 20th century are so different from the world of Dirk Willems, a comparison raises doubts whether the martyr stories can provide guidance for the 21st century."[17] Goering was also concerned with the dual kingdom worlds of the martyrs—good versus evil, sanctified Anabaptists versus corrupt papists, and so on. In 2002, Ross L. Bender questioned how wealthy BMW-driving Mennonites could possibly identify with a sixteenth-century outcast.[18]

I am focusing on gender as an analytical tool and dynamic. How does the Willems story change when gender is introduced? Weaver-Zercher, in his thorough and insightful chapter on the responses of assimilated Mennonites to *Martyrs Mirror*, notes that "the most vigorous critics of *Martyrs Mirror* in the contemporary Mennonite world have been women, some of whom . . . have underscored the book's potential to sanctify victimization."[19] Stephanie Krehbiel has written that the *Martyrs Mirror* taught her that to be a Mennonite was to self-identify as a victim.[20] I was an abused wife, and the Willems story was not helpful. I needed an alternate narrative, one that pushed me across that frozen river and shouted at me to keep running.

This is not just one woman's story. Let me remind you of the #MeToo Movement, now bringing down men in high places. Let me remind you of United States Senate candidate Roy Moore's

---

17 Goering, "Dying to be Pure," 9–15.

18 Bender, "Writing for Mennos," 260–61.

19 Weaver-Zercher, *Martyrs Mirror: A Social History*, 251.

20 Krehbiel, "Staying Alive," 133–44.

alleged sexual abuse of teen-aged girls, which thankfully cost him a senate bid in 2017, if nothing else.[21] Let me remind you of the women's marches held across the country and around the world in response to President Trump's inauguration.[22] And let me remind you of the legions of women who came forward to finally level charges at the celebrated Mennonite theologian, John Howard Yoder.[23] In these cases, the personal has become unabashedly and powerfully political.

When one considers domestic violence statistics in the United States alone, one must confront that women are still being martyred. The answer to questions posed by Goering and Bender about the relevance of martyr stories to today's North American Mennonite communities becomes clear when one considers that in 2017, according to the National Coalition Against Domestic Violence, "72% of all murder-suicides involved an intimate partner; 94% of the victims of these murder-suicides were female."[24] One might argue that women might not be harmed or killed for their beliefs, but they are being harmed and killed for something even more fundamental: their biology or gender identity. In these cases, Dirk is a woman, and Dirk needs to run. *Run, Dirk, Run.*[25]

---

21   Roy Moore was a prominent judge in Alabama who decided to run for a senate seat vacated by Jeff Sessions, then tapped by President Trump to be the US Attorney General. The *Washington Post* broke the story: McCrummen, Reinhard, and Crites, "Roy Moore."

22   Donald Trump was elected President of the United States in 2016 and inaugurated in January 2017. During his campaign a number of sexual misconduct allegations were levied against him. He also bragged while being taped about sexually assaulting women, saying, "You can do anything. . . . Grab them by the pussy. You can do anything." The *Washington Post* published the video on October 6, 2016.

23   See R. Goossen, "Defanging the Beast."

24   See the National Coalition Against Domestic Violence stats page at https://ncadv.org/STATISTICS.

25   Thank you to Sarah Pearson of Hyattsville Mennonite Church for giving me the title to this sermon.

One might also argue that women are not being harmed by state authorities, that violence against women is not state sanctioned as persecuting and killing Anabaptists was in Early Modern Europe. This is tricky because, although violence against women is not stated policy, the prevalence of gynocide, of men killing women, is so common that it is sanctioned by our culture, if not our laws and policies. Perhaps because Donald Trump, a self-acknowledged sexual predator, rose to the White House, so-called women's issues, sexual harassment, and abuse of power have been more prevalent in the headlines in recent years. I say *so-called* women's issues because the great majority of perpetrators are men. Women are predominantly the victims of these crimes, and men are the abusers, so why are these called "women's issues"? It seems to me that abusive men are the ones with the issues. So how can we as a community respond to the overuse of Willems while taking gender into account? I suggest we come up with alternate, equally powerful narratives. One is that of Helena Von Freyburg.

Helena Von Freyburg's story

Helena Von Freyburg, another early Anabaptist leader, ran.[26] She was a noble woman in Kitzbühel, in present-day Austria, under fire from ruling Hapsburg authorities during the Anabaptist reformation. When her position, title, connections, marriage to a powerful man, and personal wealth couldn't protect her, she did not submit. She did not rescue. She ran, first to Constanze, in present-day Switzerland, then to Augsburg, in present-day Germany. In all three locations, Kitzbühel, Constanze, and Augsburg, she formed congregations, testified, and used her considerable resources to protect her fellow fleeing Anabaptist refugees. She did not submit to authorities. Indeed, she outwitted them on several occasions. The Swiss authorities were so frustrated with her that they called her *die bose Freybergerin* (the evil Freybergerin)— a "nasty woman" of her day.

---

26 For biographical information on Helena Von Freyberg, see Snyder and Hecht, *Profiles of Anabaptist Women*, 124–35.

At one point the ecclesiastical leaders of Kitzbühel said they would allow her back into the city without imprisonment if she would renounce her faith, publicly, on Sunday morning during church services. It was thought that her public renunciation would severely damage the local Anabaptist cause. She agreed to this plan. But, then, she must have thought better of it. She contacted a low level vicar and gave her testimony in private. There was no public recantation. Soon she was back to her usual habits of harboring Anabaptist refugees in her castle, hosting church services, planning debates between theological luminaries, and teaching and praying with locals. Much to the frustration of the Hapsburgs, the congregation began to grow again. *Auch meine gute. Diese Bose Frau*—Oh my goodness, that evil woman! Eventually the pressure became too great, and she once again fled from Kitzbühel. She eventually died in Augsburg, one of just a handful of early leaders to die a peaceful death. In Helena's case, Dirk was a woman, and she kept on running.

Helena's story presents an alternative narrative, one in which the would-be martyr outwits authorities and escapes. Her escape should be just as celebrated as Dirk's martyrdom. After all, are not Mennonites also a people of the road? Until settling in North America, we were migratory. Stories that didn't make it into the *Martyrs Mirror* but that have been passed down include sliding through hidden trap doors in barns to escape the *Täuferjäger*, the Anabaptist Hunters.[27] Helena's story presents an equally powerful, moral narrative where a woman takes smart, life-affirming

---

27 In "Mightier than the Sword," 55–57, Kasdorf mentions two women martyrs, Ursula of Essen and Christina Haring, both of whom "actively resisted" their tormentors. However, both of these women were martyred. I'm interested in accessing stories of women who escaped, who survived. Thank you to Daniel Shenk-Evans's response to my original sermon in which he reminded me that stories about foiling authorities and fleeing also have a place in the Mennonite collective consciousness.

action. She escapes oppression and actively builds and leads a strong supportive community.[28]

Re-narrating the story

Another response to Dirk's overuse is to come up with alternate visions of Dirk. If Dirk becomes a woman, he can also become a group of people. What if Dirk is not alone? What if that ubiquitous lithograph from the *Martyrs Mirror* pictures a group of people, standing on the ice, pulling the jailer out of the water but also blocking him from reaching Dirk. The jailer is confronted. Dirk gets away. Dirk doesn't get burned.

This second response involves more community involvement, something contemporary Mennonites like to emphasize. I know from personal experience that in some cases you can't keep turning the other cheek in Christian love and expect the situation to change. Here I turn to the work of Marty Langelan, a community safety expert who teaches anti-harassment workshops throughout the Washington, DC, region. Someone other than the victim needs to call the perpetrator out. Someone other than the victim needs to box him in.[29] Someone other than the victim needs to come up with accountability measures. The victim shouldn't have to be the only one doing all the rescuing. Langelan writes, "We all have a moral imperative to take action—individually as [active] bystanders and collectively as a community. It's our responsibility to provide escape routes, resources, and a community moral framework that frees the oppressed (and does not burden the victims with the duty to rescue their oppressors)."[30]

Good men must recognize that this is a men's issue. Good men must step up. Women confronting abusive men on their own are rarely successful without male allies. It is not anti-feminist to recognize the gender imbalance still present in our society and to

---

28 Marty Langelan, email correspondence with the author, January 22, 2018.

29 Marty Langelan, email correspondence.

30 Marty Langelan, email correspondence.

call on men to help do the rescuing. Until our culture shifts—and I think it's shifting now—women need men to help do the heavy lifting. Not just women but men, too, must confront the chasing, abusive men and call them out to change their behavior. They must be willing to take risks and run out onto the river and over that frozen ice. They must risk drowning to support the victims. If they stay on shore, they remain silent bystanders; they perpetuate the power imbalance and embolden and validate the abusers. And Dirk gets burned once again. Abusers and bullies look to other men for validation. When this stops, they will stop. I'm tired of watching women burn. I'm tired of being burned.

I ask that, if Mennonites change the images and pictures of Dirk, they should include a host of people on the ice. Not just two men but women and men, shielding Dirk, hauling the jailor from the ice, calling him into account. Protecting and rescuing. The community, women and men, need to stand with Dirk. But until that happens, until our culture truly shifts, and victims of any gender aren't alone on that ice, I say this:

Run, Helena, Run!
Run, Kim, Run!
Run, Dirk, Run!
Amen.

20

Sexual Harms in Mennonite Contexts

Lisa Schirch

Sexual harms in the Mennonite Church have had a significant impact on my life both as an individual and as an advocate for survivors of sexual harm. Mennonite survivors have told me they were harmed first by an offender, second by institutional leaders who insisted they stay quiet, and third by Mennonite community members who shunned them for speaking out. This chapter provides examples, analysis, and recommendations for this "triple threat" of abuse, institutional backlash, and community shunning.

Sexual abuse in a Mennonite context shares similar patterns with other religious and secular communities where members value patriarchal authority, loyalty, and community over individual safety. Starting with my own story and those of Mennonite survivors in my community, I then describe six patterns of Mennonite institutional responses to reports of sexual abuse. This includes an emphasis on institutional reputations over individual harms, a focus on secrecy rather than transparency, a reliance on private accountability rather than public knowledge, a reliance on the interpretation of sexual harm framed as "consensual affair" rather than understanding it as an abuse of power, and a systematic, multi-tiered effort to blame victims for the harm they experienced. Mennonite theology, culture, and community contribute to these patterns.

I conclude this chapter with an outline of what is needed to prevent sexual harm, help survivors heal, and address the root causes of harm in the church. The fields of restorative justice and peacebuilding, shaped in large part by Mennonites, could inform and shape a better way of preventing and responding to sexual harms.

Understanding sexual harm in a pacifist church

Sexual violence is not a crime of sex. It is a crime of power, domination, and humiliation. The US Center for Disease Control defines sexual violence as an umbrella term including the following types of behavior: (1) "verbal sexual harassment (e.g., making sexual comments)"; (2) "unwanted sexual contact . . . including touching"; (3) abuses of power "through intimidation or misuse of authority" and "feeling pressured by being lied to, or being told promises that were untrue; having someone threaten to end a relationship or spread rumors; and sexual pressure by use of influence or authority"; (4) "alcohol or drug-facilitated sexual contact"; and (5) forcible sexual contact including "pinning the victim's arms . . . using one's body weight . . . using a weapon, or . . . threatening a victim with physical harm."[1]

For over thirty years, I have listened to dozens of Mennonites recall experiences of sexual abuse, and I have seen the women and men who speak out against sexual abuse be vilified and scapegoated by their Mennonite communities. The following examples document five experiences told to me at one Mennonite institution. In each case, there is an initial sexual harm followed by an institutional harm and in some cases a community harm.

Case 1. On a Mennonite school's sports team, team captains and other upperclassmen sexually assault younger players in a hazing ritual known to happen on sports teams. The hazing happens with their coach's consent, as he tells the team it is time to play "lights on/lights off" on the way home from a sports event.

---

1 Center for Disease Control, "Sexual Violence."

At other universities, similar assaults result in formal charges and prison time.[2] But at the Mennonite school, the survivor of the attack is referred to a counselor. The school never publicly names, reports to law enforcement, or sanctions the team captains who commit sexual assault or the team coach who is the responsible authority. And the university never asks other team players if they too were assaulted.

Case 2. A male coach for a Mennonite school's sports team grabs and twists a female player's hand behind her back, pins her against a wall, and grinds his groin into her backside as he chastises her for her sport performance. A second female athlete reports to the university that the coach took her to a secluded spot and sexually assaulted her. Female team members write a letter of complaint to university administrators. The coach quietly leaves his position. The university protects the privacy of the offender, who is rehired at a Mennonite high school.[3]

Case 3. Several young women at a Mennonite university report to their friends that the two sons of a Mennonite school administrator sexually assaulted them when they were drunk after the sons had pushed them to drink. These brothers sometimes publicly boasted of this strategy on "how to get laid" to their friends. In their minds, the boys used alcohol to get "consent" for casual sex from girls. But according to legal definitions from the US Center for Disease Control, no one can give consent when under the influence of alcohol. Consent must be granted before consumption of alcohol. Sex while drunk without prior consent is rape. Yet at the university hearing on the case of reported rape, the panel and the wider community chastise the women for being drunk and conclude that little can be done. The other women choose not to come forward for fear of further victim shaming and retribution.

Case 4. Another young woman writes of her rape at this university in a blog, "How my report of rape at a Christian school

---

2 See, for example, this news article of a similar type of hazing: Blackburn, "Five Maryland prep football players charged."

3 For more details on this account, see Cassel, "I, Anje."

made things worse," and speaks of her experience in a spoken word video of all the unhelpful responses she received when she reported rape.[4] As in other cases, the university hires the man who raped her when he graduates. She leaves the university while he retains his community status.

Case 5. When a Mennonite university wants to hire a leader for the seminary, female advocates contact the university with details of a prior report of abuse of power by this pastor with a female member of his congregation. A Mennonite conference committee undertakes a private, internal accountability process. A group of Mennonite men decide this "private affair" does not need to be part of the public deliberation since the man has a record of doing "so much good."

My story

Throughout my life, older Mennonite men have asked me for prolonged hugs, left their hands on my knees, lower back, and head for too long, and made unwanted sexual advances. At a recent Mennonite conference, an older married Mennonite man came up to me, interrupting a conversation I was having with a female colleague. He told me, in front of her, that I looked "tense" and that he wanted to give me a backrub while he talked to me about his work. I said no to the backrub three times before he backed off. When I reported this to the conference organizers, there was sympathy but no action. "This happens all the time," they responded. They proceeded to tell me their own stories of sexual harassment by "nice old Mennonite men." And, therefore, according to this prevalence of the problem, in the Mennonite world where women aim to please and men call the shots, there was nothing to be done. This man's pesky demands to give me a backrub left me upset at myself. Why was I so afraid of hurting his feelings instead of expressing anger at his disrespect, sense of entitlement, and rude and inappropriate touches and questions? As a "nice Mennonite woman," I have never been able to find

---

4 M.G. "We Can Do Better"; M.G. "Save the Apology."

my voice to express anger directly at men who sexually harass me. For me, sexual harm has been a psychologically exhausting inconvenience. For other women and men in the Mennonite context, sexual harms have been much worse and have led to lifelong physical and emotional impacts.

In each of these examples above, students or staff at Mennonite institutions sought me out to ask for help addressing a case of sexual harm on a campus with few public advocates for survivors. I have a bookshelf full of research on sexual violence, and I have taught courses on this topic beginning in 2004, after returning from spending a year as a Fulbright Fellow in East and West Africa learning how local women responded to sexual harms and how it impacted broader peacebuilding processes. I have published multiple articles on sexual abuse and sexual integrity for the Mennonite press.[5] I have provided training on responding to sexual violence at the United Nations, at the Pentagon, and to the Swedish government. Being an advocate for survivors of sexual abuse seems like a natural part of my job as a professor of peacebuilding. Peacebuilding processes emphasize right relationships, listening to victims, and doing justice. Yet applying these same ethics or peacebuilding processes to address sexual abuse in Mennonite contexts resulted in institutional scapegoating and community shunning for survivors, other advocates, and myself. I have spent most of my life living in Mennonite communities and attending and working for Mennonite institutions throughout the United States and Canada. Ironically, my decision to be an advocate for survivors of sexual abuse is a result of ethical commitments to victims of violence—commitments that are themselves a result of my Mennonite education.

Fifteen years after one of the first students confided in me about a sexual assault that he experienced on a Mennonite university sports team, he asked me why I did not do more to speak out for him. When he first reported to me, I had asked him if he had reported the abuse to the university and assumed the univer-

5 Schirch, "Sexual abuse in Mennonite contexts"; Schirch, "Afterword"; Schirch, "Toward Mennonite sexual integrity."

sity had addressed the abuse. I was wrong. The university Title IX system that is set up to address sexual harms on US college campuses was not working for him or other students. I felt personally responsible for not doing more for students who had confided in me over two decades of teaching. I could see the impact of sexual abuse over decades of their lives. Many have had lasting trauma from abuse, have left the church, relive memories of humiliation, and refuse to donate to church institutions.

In 2014, I realized I needed to use my power as a full professor at the university to speak out as an advocate for survivors and prevent further sexual abuse. I became a member of SNAP-Anabaptist, a group of Mennonites who volunteer our time and take legal and personal risks to investigate, name, and suffer the consequences of naming those who perpetrate and enable sexual violence in Mennonite institutions. SNAP stands for the Survivors Network for those Abused by Priests and began within the Catholic context. The National SNAP organization has several chapters affiliated with denominations outside of the Catholic Church. SNAP-Anabaptist formed to learn from the Catholic experience of addressing clergy sexual violence. The most common lesson shared by Catholic advocates aiming to address sexual abuse is that whistleblowers will always face a backlash.[6]

Survivors wanted to meet directly with the president of the Mennonite university to share the triple threat of sexual harm, institutional harm, and community shunning they had experienced. They had specific complaints about how the university handled their cases and suggestions for how to improve campus support for survivors. Initial requests for meetings were denied.

I began meeting with my colleagues and institutional leaders up the chain of command to ask for their support and advice. I met repeatedly with the campus ombudsperson, Title IX coordinator, Human Resources director, and the campus pastors to attempt to build support for survivors. I offered that the university could provide a safer, healthier campus community resistant to sexu-

---

6   See also the history of Barbra Graber in Graber, "Timeline of What Happened."

al abuse in a way that would both address survivors' needs and improve the university's reputation. I turned down invitations from national news media outlets who wanted to do a story on sexual abuse at the university, hoping that it would be possible for survivors to get acknowledgment and healing without being put in the media spotlight themselves. But all this effort was for naught.

In a final mediated meeting with the university president, he initially agreed to but then later canceled a meeting with one of the victims. Despite years of efforts to convince the university of the ethical necessity of listening to victims and creating better policies for preventing and handling sexual abuse, the Mennonite administrators began to scapegoat victims as "attacking the university" and threatening its survival. They deflected blame for the legal risks they had brought to the university by repeatedly hiring known sexual offenders. When they spent hundreds of thousands of dollars on lawyers and public relations consultants to help them manage rumors of administrative wrongdoing, they accused advocates for creating rumors.

Instead of viewing advocates like myself as a resource to help Mennonite administrators manage the significant number of sexual abuse cases at the university, Mennonite administrators chose to target me as a scapegoat. In most institutional settings, survivors and advocates take legal risks by naming offenders and those who enable abuse. Survivors who speak out risk additional violations of their privacy as well as widespread judgment that something that they said, wore, or did somehow "invited" sexual abuse and further hostility from Mennonite institutions and communities that want them to stay silent. Survivors and advocates lose professional status, with several of us losing our teaching jobs for challenging the institutions we work for to address their responsibility in hiring known sexual offenders. We lose paying work in order to volunteer our time to prevent sexual violence. We lose friends and colleagues who think we are trying to destroy Mennonite institutions.

The campus ombudsperson mediated a conversation between the provost and myself, in which the provost argued that if I were more "sex positive," I would not be upset about what he viewed as sexual "affairs" rather than "abuse of power." The provost then fired the ombudsperson who witnessed this conversation and hired his sister-in-law to run the Title IX office. With other key administrators, they created false accusations against both victims and advocates and spread false rumors to others in the community that we posed an existential threat to the university's survival. One administrator falsely accused me of breaking into the campus system to identify and contact victims and spread paranoid rumors of lawsuits or boycotts, even though there have not been any attempts at this. They spread false rumors to family members of some of those credibly accused of sexual abuse suggesting that I was threatening their jobs. The provost gathered my academic colleagues in a meeting with the goal of discrediting and denouncing my advocacy for survivors. The provost's strategies for deflecting away from the legal risks he brought to the university created a widespread culture of disdain for survivors and their advocates.

In 2017, the provost cancelled a major program I had been planning for two years that involved multiyear planning for twenty university students. By all accounts from faculty and others in the university leadership, this was a transparent effort to punish me for victim advocacy. He was pressured to retract the cancellation. But at this point, the provost's falsehoods and the community antagonism toward me made it impossible for me to continue working at this Mennonite institution, and I formally resigned.

Mennonite theology and sexual harm

Sexual harm in a Mennonite context is unique in several ways. Mennonites emphasize the need to take all of the scriptures seriously. In the Mennonite church, leaders rush to love the enemy (Luke 6:27) or the offender in cases of sexual harm. The Mennonite theology of love of enemies contributes to Mennonites' emphasis on forgiveness of sexual offenders. Victims are pressed to forgive offenders who, in most cases, have never confessed wrongdoing or taken responsibility for their harms. This cheap forgiveness is no gift to an offender or their family, as it does not stop the offender's behavior. Forgiveness without public accountability is dangerous; it makes institutions responsible for the harm these offenders may do to other vulnerable people. Love for offender means recognizing their humanity *and* holding them accountable so they cannot hurt other people.

The passage from Luke 6 certainly must not be an excuse to ignore Jesus's warning that "just as you did it to one of the least of these who are members of my family, you did it to me" (Matthew 25:40) or Jesus's uncharacteristically strong denouncement of those who hurt children (Matthew 18:6). The integrity of Mennonite theology—and its practice of caring for victims in restorative justice and peacebuilding—depends upon our ability to listen to and respect those who have experienced sexual harm.

For pacifists concerned with following the nonviolent way of Jesus, stopping sexual harm should be a top priority. Yet often the Mennonite church focuses its attention on state violence rather than sexual and gender-based violence. Progressive Mennonites speak out against war and racism, and many support LGBTQ inclusion. When it comes to sexual violence in the church, few are willing to speak out on behalf of victims. Some Mennonites diminish the seriousness of sexual violence. Yet the most brutal armies and terrorist groups in the world routinely use sexual violence because it is deemed the most humiliating and traumatic form of violence. The United Nations, governments around the world, and public universities have taken more significant measures to stop sexual violence than church institutions have.[7]

---

7 United Nations General Assembly, Declaration on the Elimination of Violence against Women.

Mennonite survivors

Mennonite culture impacts how survivors respond to sexual harm. In Anabaptist theology, suffering is often seen as redemptive.[8] In this theological context, victims of sexual abuse are told suffering is a religious experience, bringing one close to understanding Jesus's suffering on the cross as an act of redemption. The *Martyrs Mirror* is a book of stories of how Mennonites and other Christians have suffered for their faith. Through the telling of heroic martyr stories, the book coaxes Mennonites to understand suffering as a religious call.[9] Mennonites chastised women who spoke out on sexual abuse from prominent Mennonite theologian John Howard Yoder's widespread abuse for not "bearing the cross silently, as Jesus did."[10]

Mennonite culture encourages obedience to male authority. Boys and girls are taught to defer to authority and to suppress anger. Girls in particular are taught to smile, be nice, and be cooperative. This cultural training makes many women afraid of hurting men's feelings when they harass us. This cultural training is a significant problem for Mennonites trying to stop sexual violence. When a Mennonite uses their position of authority to gain emotional intimacy and groom younger people by flirting with them and suggesting that they would like to have sex, it is not the young person's fault. Power imbalances negate consent.

As with non-Mennonite sexual abuse, many Mennonite victims are young, have already been the victim of child sexual abuse, and have been carefully "groomed" by older, more powerful offenders who manipulate and deceive them. Offenders use their power and authority as a lever to gain trust and sexual access to young people. Sexual offenders offer love and gifts as "bait." Then these potential victims who seek out the approval and attention of the offender—often a respected and charismatic man—can be cast as consenting. Too many people, including survivors,

---

8 Oyer, "Suffering."

9 Van Braght and Sohm, *The bloody theater, or Martyrs mirror.*

10 Cited originally in Schirch, "Afterword."

end up believing that the victim has "ruined a good man's life."[11] Most cases of sexual violence are never reported. Many victims underestimate, minimize, or dismiss what has happened to them. Many victims never speak out because they fear further humiliation from those who may disbelieve them. There are hundreds of reasons why people who suffer sexual violence do not speak out. We do not know how many remain silent. But we do know that those who do speak out are too often not believed.

Mennonite offenders

Anna Salter observes that most people expect that sexual offenders will be "monsters" that can be clearly recognized. Because most Mennonites seem to assume they can spot someone who would sexually abuse others, they disbelieve that Mennonite youth pastors, sports coaches, and beloved professors can commit sexual violence. Salter documents countless stories of offenders describing how they deceived others. For many offenders, the thrill of sexual violence is not the sex. It is the deception and secrecy. The thrill is grooming, deceiving, and coercing a victim, their family, and the wider community. Offenders use power over others, often relying on a mix of persuasion, manipulation, and coercion. Highly personable in public, they recognize how they can gain the trust of potential victims and their families. Offenders "groom" people they sense as vulnerable—those who may be compliant with their intent to cause sexual harm. They also groom their colleagues, the family and friends of potential victims, and the wider community. Offenders want to make sure that if they are ever accused of sexual harm, they will have others who will testify to their character. It takes planning and strategy to carry out sexual harm.[12]

Sexual offenders often cannot stop themselves from abusing others. Sexual offending is an addiction. It is a set of behaviors that controls both victims and the offender. The Association for the Treatment of Sexual Abusers (ATSA) states that there is

---

11   Fortune, *Sexual Violence*.

12   Salter, *Predators*.

no definitive "cure" for many of those who commit sexual abuse. Rather, it takes lifelong management strategies to prevent those who feel tempted to commit sexual abuse.[13] An offender can "promise" to stop offending in a secret meeting, away from the eyes of the public. But public safety requires that everyone know that someone has a sex addiction because this is the only way for an offender to be accountable to the whole community to prevent further abuse.

There is some evidence that a small number of victims go on to become offenders. The trauma of being victimized can create, in some people, a desire to offend and control others. There can be a cycle of abuse. But this is also a dangerous path of analysis. While it can help to humanize offenders and recognize their own woundedness, it can also create more obstacles to victims in reporting. Victims already face tremendous pressure. If communities also ostracize victims because they may become offenders, this does not break the cycle of violence.[14]

I have met personally with a variety of Mennonite men who are credibly accused of sexual harm. They are professors, sports coaches, pastors, executives, students, and youth in Mennonite institutions. They are often well-liked and trusted by their communities. For me, love of offenders requires both seeing their humanity and holding them to account for the harm they have caused others.

Patterns of sexual harms in Mennonite contexts

Mennonite administrators and institutional leaders rely on six strategies for managing sexual abuse. First, a fog of *silence and secrets* surrounds the stories of sexual abuse in the Mennonite Church by pastors, professors, Sunday school teachers, youth group leaders, the sons of church officials, sports team coaches and captains, and in the homes of too many Mennonite families. Secrecy works to protect the privacy of offenders and prevent

---

13 Association for the Treatment of Sexual Abusers.

14 Baril, "Sexual Abuse."

public scrutiny. In her research listening to and documenting the strategies used by sexual offenders, Anna Salter concludes, "secrecy is the lifeblood of sexual aggression."[15] Those who commit sexual violence groom their victims and their communities, convincing them of their goodness while keeping the secret of the inner sickness to control, humiliate, and hurt others. Some Mennonite executives assert that the reputations of accused leaders are more important than public knowledge of reports of sexual abuse. They insist all reports of sexual abuse be kept private. Some Mennonite leaders reported to me that they had "no files" on cases where multiple survivors insisted they had sent letters and information to the Mennonite university detailing a history of sexual abuse. It appears that some Mennonite leaders, like their Catholic peers, purposefully do not keep files of reports of sexual abuse or destroy files when asked.[16]

Second, Mennonite leaders are often most concerned with *the institution's reputation* rather than the safety of community members. Ironically, this strategy often creates a lose/lose outcome where survivors and their communities live in unsafe environments and institutions lose credibility because of their inability to communicate authentically about the challenge of sexual abuse. Administrators invest hundreds of thousands of dollars with lawyers and expensive consultants whose stated primary aim is to prevent and protect the university from legal risk by ensuring "compliance" with the law. These profit-motivated, reputation management consultants are part of what is known as the "rape industrial complex." They aim to protect institutions while doing little to improve community safety. Research indicates that institutional leaders who acknowledge the problem of sexual abuse and address it openly have a greater chance of improving community safety and protecting institutional reputations.[17]

---

15 Salter, *Predators*, 4.

16 RFI, "Catholic Church."

17 Crossley and Correll, "Leader Messaging."

Third, some Mennonite institutions *refuse to acknowledge or apologize to victims*. This tactic has a significant cost to Mennonite ethics, the main asset and recruiting message of most Mennonite institutions. The Mennonite university where I taught is world-renowned for advocating restorative justice—a "victim-centered approach" that listens to and responds to victim needs. Yet on multiple occasions, Mennonite administrators have delayed, cancelled, or refused to meet with victims of sexual abuse. Lawyers advise that universities should not meet with victims or apologize for harms on campus because, in their view, an apology opens up the university to legal risk. But research on apologies in medical institutions finds that the risk of lawsuits decreases when doctors apologize.[18] The same is also true with sexual abuse in the church. When churches can let go of their fears of lawsuits and act from their theology and ethics, reconciliation is possible. In Vienna, Virginia, a Presbyterian church took responsibility for its youth pastor's sexual abuse of over a dozen young women. This apology led to greater healing. "We failed as leaders to extend the compassion and mercy that you needed. . . . Some of you felt uncared for, neglected and even blamed for this abuse. I am sorry. The church is sorry."[19]

Fourth, Mennonite leaders have a pattern of holding an *internal accountability process* to quietly and secretly put mild pressure on an offender to stop abuse. Private accountability processes are usually run by male church authorities who have an interest in suppressing cases of sexual harm and have little understanding of sexual abuse and the patriarchal, sexist culture that enables it. As Father Thomas Doyle has said, "Church culture creates, nurtures, protects and defends sex offenders."[20] Institutional leaders lack basic competencies to address sexual abuse; most have little training about the complex psychological, social, physical, and legal implications of sexual violence. Some institutional leaders

---

18 Robbennolt, "Apologies," 376–82.

19 White, "Vienna Presbyterian Church."

20 Clohessy, "Clergy sex abuse."

actively work to protect sexual offenders and discredit outspoken survivors, witnesses, and whistleblowers. They create detractors and smear campaigns and sow seeds of doubt or rumors against survivor-activist networks. Church officials frequently fail to understand that sexual abuse is an addiction that is difficult to stop. If not publicly exposed or motivated to go into rehabilitation, repeat offenders can and will often continue to perpetrate sexual abuse throughout their lives.

Fifth, institutional leaders often *ignore significant power imbalance* between a pastor, professor, Sunday school teacher, choir director, camp counselor, or sports team coach or captain and their student, congregant, employee, or younger team member. Mennonite institutions refer to "sexual misconduct," "relationships," or "consensual affairs" between older married men in positions of authority and younger, single people. The offender's abuse is reframed as an "affair" or sexual misconduct without an understanding of the abuse of power, the offender's addiction to harming others, or the harm done to victims. *Mennonite institutions continue to show by their actions and public statements that they do not know how to distinguish between consensual affairs and sexual harm.* Sexual affairs occur between two people of roughly equal power and capacity. Sexual harm includes acts of grooming, coercion, manipulation, and control by one person who holds a position of power over another.

Finally, in many cases Mennonite institutions quietly and covertly *blame and shun victims* who report sexual violence. People tend to view victims of other crimes as innocent. If someone paints their house a bright color, leaves alcohol on their porch, and leaves the door unlocked, it is still an obvious crime to walk into their house and take something. But with sexual violence, those who report abuse often find themselves under investigation. In meetings with Mennonite administrators, I have heard leaders say, "She needs to take responsibility for her clothing choices," and even, "She should have let him down easy; she was hard on his self-esteem!" During a Title IX campus hearing, I witnessed a review panel asking a survivor if she was drinking when she was raped, if she had had sex previously, and why she didn't fight off the rape more forcefully. These questions are irrelevant to the crime of rape and illustrate a pattern of victim blaming. In Mennonite communities, victim blaming often includes wide community pressure to keep victims from reporting in the first place. Speaking out about abuse seems to be viewed as worse than the abuse itself, especially if survivors identify abuses by a popular, powerful, or influential church worker. In a patriarchy where men hold most of the power, the community rallies around the historical propaganda that "ladies lie." [21] Research indicates that 95 to 99.9 percent of those who report sexual violence tell the truth. And most people never report sexual abuse, making the percent of those who lie even smaller.[22] The myth that sexual violence is a matter of "he said/she said" is a strategy to silence dissent.

Improving Mennonite institutional responses

The pressure to address sexual harm has never been stronger. The #MeToo movement, the scale of revelations and reports within the Catholic Church, and media reports are all contributing to an avalanche of evidence that sexual harm is widespread, causes life-long impacts, and requires a civil rights movement to address it. The film *Spotlight* won an Oscar for Best Picture for its portrayal of the sexual abuse crisis in the Catholic Church. *Spotlight* rightly emphasizes that it not only takes a village to raise a child—it also takes a village to abuse a child. Solving the problem of sexual violence in the Mennonite church does not just require removing sexual offenders and enablers from their institutional posts. Preventing sexual violence requires bold religious, cultural, and institutional change to address the triple threat from offenders, Mennonite administrators who enable them, and Mennonite communities that shun and blame victims and advocates for speaking out.

---

21 Leotta, "I Was a Sex-Crimes Prosecutor."
22 Heaney, "Almost No One."

In the last few years, Mennonite institutions have taken some positive steps to address the problem of sexual violence. Yet there continue to be persistent problems and concerns with Mennonite institutional policies and procedures related to sexual violence. Mennonites' expertise in the fields of peacebuilding and restorative justice could provide healing for victims, transformation for offenders, and safety for communities.[23] New types of programs such as Callisto make it easier and safer for victims to report sexual abuse and find others who name the same offender to build a stronger case.[24] Non-Mennonite universities are paving the way to illustrate how to improve public communication by naming reported offenders and inviting others to come forward with information. Institutions build trust with survivors and become credible in their efforts to prevent sexual violence when they become willing to name predators and enablers. Mennonite institutions can do more to prioritize community safety and recognize that their institutional reputation is damaged by short term tactics like secrecy and cover ups. Mennonite survivors of sexual abuse deserve institutions who will hold offenders to account, offer authentic apologies and support to victims, and identify wider community paths for restitution, accountability, and healing.

---

23 Oudshoorn, Amstutz, and Jackett, *Restorative Justice.*
24 Khazan, "Game Theory."

21

Bearing Witness for Molly and Me
Two Stories of Clergy Sexual Abuse
Cameron Altaras

The following chapter relays two incidents of abuse of power by two separate Mennonite pastors, both perpetrators of sexual abuse. In the first case, I was in the role of bearing witness for a friend, whom I shall call "Molly" to protect her identity. The second story is my own; in it I speak of the moral injury of clergy sexual abuse and of the many who were in the roles of supporting and bearing witness for me.

Speaking up for Molly

Molly sent me a letter. She revealed to me that she had been sexually abused as a young teenager—by, of all people, a Mennonite pastor.

I remember an older Mennonite woman telling me to be careful around that pastor just a day before I was to drive with him to a meeting—a warning from one generation of Mennonite women to the next. I remember her exact words: "He likes to take young women under his wing to mentor them." She told me this because I had just shared with her that he had invited me to drive with him to a meeting. I dismissed her comments as irrelevant to me, thanked her, and told her, "I have enough mentors already."

After reading Molly's letter, though, I knew why the older woman had warned me—indirect though the warning was. She didn't elaborate or say anything about him crossing sexual boundaries. But the sense of urgency in her voice told me she knew more than she let on. I have often wondered why her warning wasn't more direct, why she didn't just come right out and tell me to stay away from him. Why not say something like, *Given half the chance, he's the kind of man who molests women; don't be fooled just because he's a pastor?* Whatever clue I did pick up from her confirmed the veracity of my internal, illogical, alarm-bell voice shouting *Ick!* in contrast to my reasonable voice, which assured me there were no grounds for me to feel that way: *He's a pastor, after all.* But I did feel that way. From the first moment I met him, I just knew this man wanted more than a seemingly harmless pastoral conversation.

Before we got to the meeting, he reached over and put his hand on my hand in that ever-so-gentle, overly pastoral, tentative, sickeningly caring sort of way, and said what a "special person" I was. It made me gag. It sounded so fake, so phony, so much like rehearsed pastoral garbage.

I've often fantasized that I'd had the guts to turn to him and yell, *That's just b---s---! You are so full of s---! Now get your slimy pastoral paw off me!* Instead, I smiled a meek smile and—remembering the words of warning from the older woman and my own alarm system—carefully, so as not to upset him, removed my hand from under his. I wanted to puke right through my nice-Mennonite-girl face—the humble one, the one that will never make waves, the always-so-calm, pacifist face. It makes me ill just to think what might have happened if I had ignored my gut or not had that warning.

I never made an effort to meet with him—ever. I only returned calls out of obligation; he was a pastor, and I didn't want to offend a pastor. He always called me and asked me to meet, said they needed me to go to that meeting.

Molly told me that what he did to her messed her up for life. Everyone knows he had a mental breakdown. I wonder if he had his mental breakdown because he knew he did wrong and couldn't handle his own hypocrisy, or if his mental breakdown severely warped his mind and that is why he abused her. I found myself fanning the flames of a secret hope that the breakdown happened after he touched her—divine retribution!

Thanks to him, Molly wrote, her second marriage was in shambles, and she had been in therapy for years to deal with not having been able to say *no*, not having been able to protect her body, to claim it as her own, as if she has no right to—feeling like she started it, and so she must let it finish. She was feeling guilty about all of it—kissing and petting and going all the way at an early age—but she couldn't stop it. She was feeling like her self-worth had been corrupted and wrapped up in the false attention of flattery and sex—behaviors, she had come to understand, that were directly linked to early abuse. And it went back further, she wrote, back to when she was younger and seeing that other kids her age were so happy and she wasn't—like, somehow, she was different and couldn't be thoroughly joyful and like she was always apart from and observing, never in the game.

I understand that. I know what Molly is talking about. I wonder if it's because I was abused when I was a child. Three different therapists over twenty-five years asked me if I had been abused as a child. Three different therapists living in two different countries all suspected the same thing: as in Molly's case, they, too, saw my behaviors as symptomatic of early abuse. I didn't put it together until I was in my late forties.[1] That's when the flashbacks started.

---

1 As E. Sue Blume writes:

Amnesia, or "blocking," is the most common feature of Post-Incest Syndrome. It can take many forms, affecting memory, feelings, or perceptions. It can result from efforts the victim makes to separate from what is happening to her at the time of the abuse, or from techniques that she resorts to after the abuse. It is achieved through dissociation. . . . The impact of this aftereffect cannot be underestimated. I have found that most incest survivors have limited recall about the abuse. Indeed, so few incest survivors in my experience have identified themselves as abused in the beginning of therapy that I have concluded that perhaps half of all incest survivors do not remember

That's when deep, intense, petrifyingly painful therapy unraveled the onion layers of my very self. I sobbed in the face of two undeniable memories of an uncle—the one around whom I always felt gross, the same feeling I had around that disgusting pastor.[2] Do those kinds of men have a sixth sense for me, like they did for Molly, men who sniff out the dissociation from unhealed wounds of abuse and calculate how to set the hook?

Molly wrote me that she was filing a Pastoral Abuse complaint with Mennonite Church leaders. She asked if I were willing to be a witness, to tell them about his hand on my hand in the car, how he called me a lot and the attention he paid me, about my gross, icky feelings. Of course, I would! I promised I would do whatever she needed me to do. He had ruined her life, and he did it under a pastoral guise.

And so, I found myself in a room with church officials, bearing witness for Molly and bearing the details of those feelings I had had, the warning I had received, his phone calls, his use of that "special person" phrase about me, and that pastoral paw on my hand.

Then it became public; the pastor that molested Molly was stripped of his ordination credentials because the allegations against him were substantiated. Molly had told her story, got it off her chest, peeled the secret shame from between her legs, exposed the whole sordid tale. That pastor got what was coming

---

that the abuse occurred. These women cannot understand their lives and do not know why things seem so out of control. They therefore cannot seek the help they need. . . . For many incest survivors, the process of remembering after the initial acknowledgment never feels complete. (Blume, *Secret Survivors*, 81–82.)

2 Blume writes: "Flashbacks can be frightening, astonishing, painful, and overwhelming for the therapist with whom they are shared as well as for the incest survivor herself. . . . However, flashbacks do not represent mental illness; they are not psychotic. They are controlled experiences –events relived to release, cleanse, and heal. That they occur at all indicates that the incest survivor is strong enough to face her memories." Blume, *Secret Survivors*, 101.

to him. Molly's name did not become public—nor did mine or any of the other "Mollys" who came forward.

Another Mennonite Pastor, who told me he would be my mentor, talked to me about that pastor who lost his credentials: "You can't trust him," he said—which I now recognize as just another hook cloaked in a purportedly caring phrase, used to build a net of illusory trust. I told him I had been a witness in the case.

"Good for you," he said and then handed me a glass of red wine.

Moral injury of clergy sexual abuse

I can't believe I saw what had happened to Molly and didn't see that I was living the same thing—except that often, when you are in the middle of it, you don't know what you are in the middle of. That second Mennonite pastor groomed me for two years.[3] What I mistook for sincere words and gestures of concern for my well-being were simply calculated hooks labeled *pastoral caring*. And I swallowed them whole, washing every one of them down with coffee or—so unpastoral-like and therefore secretly special—with wine he bought me with lunch or from a bottle he brought to my parents' home, when he knew I'd be there alone. It took me more than twenty years to see how much power I had allowed him to have over me, how I had consented to flattery's disconnection of the alarm bells that clanged the first time I met him, how I had dismissed the sudden attention out of nowhere. I had convinced myself to believe that he did think I was a "special person" and that anything he did for me was for my benefit and not just for

---

3 As I write elsewhere, "When pastors overstep professional boundaries with someone under their care, they become sexual predators and interact with their victims in the same destructive ways as non-clergy offenders. They slyly spin their web around a potential victim in what is referred to as 'the grooming process.' The first step is to gain her trust. Then it's easy to slide innocuously into her life, seep under her skin and into her places of least resistance and greatest need. This grooming can take a few days or last a few years, depending upon both the skill and patience of the perpetrator." Altaras, "Can Sex with a Pastor Be an Affair?" For an oral retelling of this article, see Altaras, "Sex with a Pastor Is Never an Affair."

his. Somehow, I allowed twisted thinking to take over and gave in to actions I knew were inherently wrong at the hands of someone whom I inherently trusted, actions that flew directly in the face of my internal sense of right and wrong.

This, I have come to understand, is precisely why such betrayal is so damaging. It is betrayal not only by one in whom one has placed a great deal of trust; it is also betrayal by and to oneself. This is moral injury, and this is betrayal at a soul level.

Moral injury is "perpetrating, failing to prevent, bearing witness to, or learning about acts that transgress deeply held moral beliefs and expectations."[4] Failing to prevent, bearing witness to, allowing things to happen to oneself that transgress deeply what one holds to be the morally right thing to do—all of this, in aggregate and individually, brings about a great deal of shame and self-blame. Those who have experienced moral injury sit with this and in this. With one hand, many drive their shame down deep enough so they can keep it just out of view as, with their other hand, they drive themselves to achieve whatever goals they have set. And the shame stays put, for a while. Eventually, though, it rears its ugly head in a physical or mental health crisis or a marriage crisis or a career crisis.

Sometimes, though, it's the tiniest straw that breaks the thin veneer covering the anxiety swirling in the pit of those who have experienced moral injury—anxiety because they know they took a wrong turn at a moment of vulnerability, and somehow their internal clock got stuck at that undeniably life-altering moment. And that moment is for them as present now as it was when it happened; no matter how many decades have passed, they could tell you precisely who said what, when and where it happened, and even what they were wearing because they have relived that moment repeatedly in their head to the point where it has dug neurological routes that are now ruts. *Now* has no timeframe for such moments.

The spirits of many are flattened under the weight of the moral injury that occurs in moments such as this and many never

---

4 Litz, Stein, Delany, Lebowitz, Nash, Silva, et al., "Moral Injury," 222.

come out from under the shame of that injury to achieve any sort of life they had at one time imagined possible. Many become numb because they couldn't stop it or they didn't stop it, and shedding the weight of the shame of not having put a stop to it, to express any emotion, is just too heavy. Moral injury is for others a catalyst that unhinges their rage so that they strike out at anyone who crosses their path. And still many others die in their isolation under their moral injury; either the betrayal brought about by moral injury sucks the life out of them, or they can't stand to bear it anymore, so they bring their own end on themselves.

I had no awareness of the moral injury occurring as I was living through it. Somehow, I had convinced myself that Molly's situation seemed different. Now I realize that the fact that I was older than Molly was when it happened to me makes no difference whatsoever. A part of me had responded to betrayal by retreating into numbness. I looked on as slowly and methodically the strands of my moral fiber were being torn apart at the hands of someone who had come to me as a beacon of moral uprightness. Worse, I had allowed myself to be convinced to participate in my own moral shredding. Worse still, I had somehow figured out how to set goals and achieve those goals and build up that thin veneer over the lie I had consented to live so I could appear to be living a normal life. There was no older Mennonite woman in this case who warned me, either directly or indirectly, to be careful around that second pastor, to see past the flattery, to sniff out the saccharine coating on the caring, to see through to how his advice for my future was to benefit him, and especially, to question why he would share with me intimate details of his own marital unhappiness. And I didn't know of any of the several Mollys he had already victimized. He was a senior pastor, a conference and national leader. In my world, he was almost God. And then he died. Who would have been a witness for me?

Who shall bear witness for me?

More than twenty years later, I came to understand what had happened. It took me more than twenty years and the unravelling of my own marriage and the safety of the pastor's death to begin writing the wretched, hard-to-face details of my story: me and my weaknesses being taken advantage of and played like a pawn on the chess board of a well-regarded Mennonite pastor. It was as if he worked from the same playbook as the other pastor: he frequently called, frequently used the word *special*—about me, about our relationship—and wouldn't keep his sickeningly caring-pastoral paws off me.

As with Molly, so too for me: the day had come to tell my story.

I wrote it all down and read it all aloud to my family—the entire story, all the gory, injurious details, nailing them all down on Good Friday ("the darkest Good Friday," in my dad's words). My brothers were furious and ready to kill. My Mom, sister, and sisters-in-law cried with me. My dad expressed as much anger as his pacifist theology would allow—and then recommended I tell my pastor.

The Tuesday following Easter Monday, I dutifully made an appointment to tell my pastor and the Congregational Chairman, both Mennonite men much older than me. My dad agreed to be present. I read the whole story again—the entire grooming and abusing story—from start to finish. They listened. They let me cry all the way through to the end. They expressed no shock. "We never knew him personally," they replied, "but we knew about him and are not surprised." They recommended I tell the Mennonite Church pastoral misconduct committee.

And so, once again, I found myself in a room with church officials: bearing witness this time for myself and bearing the details of those meetings in coffee shops and wine in my parents' home and wine with lunch and on and on. This time, though, I had to admit that any icky feelings I had had in response to his pastoral paws had been assuaged by his flattery, and that there had been no words of warning, and that it was my marriage that had ended in shambles, and that it was my life that didn't go along the path I had originally imagined it might, and that my shame tainted the atmosphere in that room—my shame for not putting a stop to the whole ordeal weighing heavily on the self that was me, sitting in that room.

There were other differences. This time, a female Mennonite pastor was leading that committee—how things had changed in twenty years! And this time, I asked both of my parents to go with me, to be in the room, to support me. They agreed.

I read my story for a third time. The tattered pages were stained by tears and travel, and I knew where I had cried last time I read it; and, sure enough, even though it was the third time through, I cried again. The church officials listened, and I knew I was being heard. They witnessed my grief. They said, "We knew him, and we are not surprised. The problem is, he is dead."

My parents said little. They left it up to me. I am their oldest child. I am articulate. I am educated. I am an adult. I can tell my own story. My parents barely let on how my revelation had thoroughly shaken the foundation of their world. They did not disclose their confusion at the ruins of their daughter's life or their shame for not seeing what had been going on under their watch. They stumbled over their Amish roots in their attempt to understand my anger. But the female pastor got it. She knew the fury forming my words. She felt the depth of my despair. She knew, and I knew she knew.

Over the next two months she kept in touch with me. She called. She accepted my calls. She wrote me emails. She responded promptly. She shepherded me through the process. She explained when she would be sharing my story with the whole committee responsible for issues of pastoral misconduct, and she was careful to ask my permission before doing anything. She would bear witness for me. And when I finally told her that I would not, because I really could not, remain a member of the Mennonite Church, she did not condemn. She understood. She told me she was honored to share in my story and to be entrusted with my truth. But no, it is I who felt honored—for the first time throughout this whole ordeal.

There were many emails and phone calls and meetings that followed. I learned what it means to nurture the virtues of

276 • Cameron Altaras

patience and perseverance, waiting and wading through administrative process, legal consultation, and committee deliberation.

My soon-to-be new husband, J, accompanied my parents and me to another of the many meetings. He was surprised at how seemingly void of emotion my parents were when faced with an opportunity to seek justice for wrongs done their daughter by a man of the church. Not yet understanding the cellular level of Amish pacifism directing their beings, shaping their inaction, and molding their silence, J, fueled by his Jewish need to seek justice, encouraged my parents to speak up. My timid mother who learned from her mother the importance of knowing when a woman may speak, especially in church and especially when seated next to her husband, finally blurted out, "If you can't trust a pastor, who can you trust? I don't know what to believe anymore!" Her comment named the unnamable sinkhole that had suddenly swallowed her entire world: betrayal by a pastor, someone she had assumed she could trust without question, made her question everything.

The church officials in the room shared with us the response of the larger committee, on hearing my story: "They were not surprised. They knew him. The problem is," they all repeated, "he is dead." They believed my story, they told me they did, and they could see the evidence of damage in my promising-life-not-lived and in my marriage-that-did-not-last, but they couldn't do anything to the pastor. They couldn't strip him of his ordination credentials like the pastor who had molested Molly. All they could do was tell me they believed me.

Weeks became months, and finally of my own accord I arranged to meet with my pastor once again. I told him I was removing my name from the book of names of those who are members of the Mennonite Church. I was surprised at his response: "You have more integrity than most people who show up Sunday morning because they have just always shown up Sunday morning, or because their parents insist they continue to show up Sunday morning, or because it's good for their status in the community to show up Sunday morning. Yes, I understand." He was bearing witness to my need to live in integrity.

After I spent several years of Skype meetings and phone calls and emails too numerous to count and several trips across the continent and gathering a support group of friends and leaders in the church who went to meetings in person for me, finally church officials had what they needed to publicly release the name of the dead-pastoral-perpetrator-of-sexual-abuse. Among the backlash, there were also more revelations. More women—more Mollys—came forward with their own allegations against him. Somewhere, somehow, I always knew that no matter how "special" he told me I was, I could not have been his only target. Men who do this and get away with it rarely do it only once. It becomes like an addiction. It feeds something in them, fills some wounded place they have left unhealed.

At one time, I had worried about hurting a pastor's feelings when his hands went where they had no business going. And at that time, I didn't want to mess up my nice-Mennonite-girl face. Then when I clearly saw what I had lived and came to understand the nature of the injuries I had endured and allowed, I unearthed anger churning like lava deep below the layers of my calm exterior. Inside, I was fanning the flames of another secret hope—this time, hope for divine retribution in an afterlife, that somewhere in some place and space beyond time this second pastor was paying for his actions in the lives of me and the other "Mollys."

I mustered up the daring to untie the Amish meekness that had stopped up my throat like head-covering strings and allowed myself to mouth furious fantasies of ramming a dead pastoral body on a meat hook on the walls of the frozen center of Inferno— that ninth circle, Dante's circle of treachery, reserved for those who commit fraudulent acts on someone with whom they share a special bond of love and trust. I was sure Dante was thinking of a pastor who ensnares a young female church member, gains her trust, designates himself as her mentor, and grooms her to use for his own sick game. Surely Dante knew this kind of story.

I went through long un-pacifist-like periods hurling rocks at myself. Like a good martyr, I succumbed to self-chastisement directed at my much younger self for not protecting myself, not grabbing words from somewhere to express my disgust, not throwing off the distorted scriptural condemnation of anger as a sin, and not screaming my rage instead of turning it inward and living it in reverse, in the shame-filled darkness of isolated depression-that-is-anger-on-the-inside.

Now I find myself sitting in the middle of a big question: How can the theology of peacemaking within which we—me, Molly, the other Mollys, and both pastors—grew up and to which we all subscribed be untwisted to help me navigate a way to some settled place in my middle-aged self? What about the theological prohibition against anger—the theology that says that anger is a sin—that I and the other Mollys grew up with? How did that shape my nice-Mennonite-girl composure, the not-screaming-to-make-the-whole-ordeal-stop composure? Why didn't I grab on to the arms of Jesus overturning the table of the moneychangers in front of the temple and plead with him to turn over the game board on which I was being played? Jesus had been angry, and he did something about it. I did not. My anger came only late in the game, more than twenty years after the fact. And I had to learn to give myself permission to even feel that anger, write that anger, scream it at my therapist.

I have come to understand the value of anger. In the words of philosopher Martha Nussbaum: "The experience of anger can make a previously unaware person aware of her values and the way in which another's wrongful act can violate them."[5] Experiencing this anger, sitting in this anger, and finally forming this anger into words proved more helpful than I could have believed possible. Anger propelled me to give form to the fury I had denied for so long, fury about the nature of the moral injuries I had permitted to be enacted on my very self and, in the end, allowed to change the course of the life that I had wanted, deep within myself, to live.

But remaining stuck in anger is not of value. Nussbaum asserts that "the angry person is always well advised to begin moving beyond anger as soon as possible, in the direction of the

5 Nussbaum, *Anger and Forgiveness*, 38.

Transition"—a transition, she explains, from "anger to compassionate hope" for justice and the welfare of all.[6] That is where I now find myself: I am moving on from and releasing the anger. I see little value in dragging behind me the fomenting, now-rotting anger at myself and at the uncle and at the pastor to whom I fell prey. I want to stop revisiting the moss-covered, decades-old, grudge-filled memories of moments I have re-lived too many times to count. And, with every ounce of strength I still have, I would like to dump the whole trainload of debris in shambles. Transitioning to seeking justice was why I had to take my story to the church authorities. Somehow, I knew that telling my story would provide some light to the other Mollys I was certain were hiding somewhere under the shame of their own stories of violation at the hands of a pastor they, too, had trusted. And indeed, they did come forward. One of them told me how it saved her life to finally be able to come forward and be heard. From my Jewish husband, I learned the following quote from the Talmud: "To save a soul, it is as if one saves an entire universe."[7] In my estimation, this makes it a worthwhile choice to let go of anger and take actions that transition the second half of my life in the direction of compassionate hope.

A circle of witnesses

I see the circle, and it is not just a fantasy. There has been and there is the circling of bearing witness: me for Molly, my parents, my brothers and sister and sisters-in-law, and my husband J, the female pastor and her committee, and my own male pastor and the other friends and other church leaders who heard my story and wrestled with how to bring the name of a dead perpetrator of clergy sexual abuse to the public—all of them bore witness for me

---

6 Nussbaum, *Anger and Forgiveness*, 31, 38.

7 The quote from the Jerusalem Talmud, Sanhedrin 4:1 (22a), is as follows: "Whoever destroys a soul, it is considered as if he destroyed an entire world. And whoever saves a life, it is considered as if he saved an entire world."

and, in the end, for all the other Mollys who found the courage within to come forward.[8]

And I, in turn, once again bear witness to the evolution of my being of Amish Mennonite roots, to baptized Mennonite member in good standing, to graduate of a Mennonite college, to bride getting married in a Mennonite church, to now, a middle-aged, remarried woman peering back in over the edge of the Mennonite world from which I came, writing about and transitioning beyond what has been seen and what has been lived. In this process of bearing witness and of gathering those parts of my being to form a whole, there are undeniably wounded parts. There is wisdom to be gleaned from those wounds, many of which I licked clean so often it has taken years for scars to begin to form. With that wisdom, I can begin to see the possibility of tapping into a source of forgiveness for my younger self, the one who didn't protect me or my dreams for my life, who permitted perpetration of actions that transgressed my soul, who bore witness to my own moral injury.

I have gleaned another piece of wisdom as well. For this, I have once again to thank the anger that I finally allowed myself to feel. Getting angry was the catalyst I needed to begin to shed my shame, that sense that I am bad—not that I did a bad thing but that I *am* bad. That's shame. It's hard to heal under a cloud of a sense of being so flawed. Shedding shame, even bit by bit, has moved me toward developing a sense of compassion for a self I could not love because I could not love something I considered so inherently bad. This is the most difficult part of the whole journey. However, to transition to a path pointed forward requires forgiving myself and finding compassion for a part of myself that for so long I had been ashamed of and refused to love.

It's a long road—two steps forward, one step back, looking forward, praying as I go: *Make of my heart an inner sanctuary of love and forgiveness, and may it begin here and now.*

---

8 For a more complete understanding of just how important it is to have the support of a trusted group during a time when one breaks the silence of pastoral abuse, see Altaras, "Naming," 25–27.

22

Speech + Action + Community
Power at Work in Sexual Abuse

Catherine Thiel Lee

Power is at once obvious and complex, shadowed and simple. Power is a force at work in all our interactions with others, yet we struggle to articulate what power is and how it shapes our lives, even as we feel its daily presence. Philosophers of power seek to shed light on how power works so that we can understand and embrace its benefits and change harmful power dynamics to protect ourselves and others. Hannah Arendt developed theories of power that concentrate on speech, action, and the work of community. Her theories offer helpful insights into the dynamics of power at work in sexual abuse and provide cues for how Anabaptists can intervene to dismantle abuse and nurture healing and wholeness.[1]

Power and sexual abuse

It's about power.

---

1 As an ally to several survivors of sexual abuse, it is important that I acknowledge that I am not myself an abuse survivor. I acknowledge this social location as a position of privilege and distance from personal experience regarding sexual abuse. Some of my support work with survivors has been in the formal context of my profession and training as a chaplain, but much has been as a friend and in informal support roles. Other aspects of my social location include my identity as a cisgender woman, a US citizen, and a licensed minister in the Mennonite Church USA.

A graduate student endures sexual pressure and advances from a professor, knowing that if she protests either quietly or publicly, her abuser can permanently derail her professional future.

It's about power.

A physically and emotionally abused woman finally separates from her husband. She stayed for twenty years out of fear for the safety of her four children, economic dependence, and pressure from her religious community who told her to "make it work, no matter what."

It's about power.

A popular pastor resigns unexpectedly and moves to a new community. Years later reports surface about sexual misconduct and assault against youth in multiple churches and knowledge of denominational leadership who expedited quick new appointments each time allegations were raised.

It's about power.

These are stories of sexual abuse, instances of unwanted sexual behavior by one person on another, perpetrated by force, threat, or taking advantage of victims. They are stories about violence—physical, verbal, and psychological—in profoundly broken relationships. And they are always stories about power.[2]

Stories of sexual abuse assail us. We hear reports of individual and institutional complicacy, from #MeToo bios to secret keeping in Catholic hierarchies to revelations within our own Anabaptist organizations.[3] Christians are finally beginning to grapple with abuse within our walls of worship. As we wake up to the devastat-

---

2 In this chapter *sexual abuse* generally refers to instances and patterns of unwanted sexual behavior perpetrated by force, threat, or coercion. At times, I also refer to *sexual assault* as a more specific crime of sexual violence. While I attempt to use the terms consistently, their meanings are overlapping and, in some contexts, interchangeable.

3 Here the term *Anabaptist* includes institutions and individuals who embrace beliefs and practices consistent with historical Christian Anabaptist movements, including Mennonite and Mennonite Brethren denominations.

ing and persistent reality of abuse in the church, Anabaptists have the chance to join in the work of responding to abuse and working for its end.

If we are going to talk about sexual abuse, we are going to have to talk about power. But what is power? How does it work? How does it work in sexual abuse? And what can we do to prevent and shift the power dynamics that allow and enable sexual abuse?

Arendt, Anabaptism, and what power is not

Hannah Arendt, a political theorist and scholar, wrote and taught on the nature of totalitarianism, revolution, and action. A German-born Jew, she escaped Europe during the Holocaust in 1933 and eventually made her way to the United States. Arendt was fascinated with power, its nature and inner workings. As we attempt to understand the ways power functions in sexual abuse, Arendt's theories can provide us with insights into power's essential ingredients, how they intersect, and how Anabaptist communities can dismantle abusers' power and generate power, instead, alongside survivors.[4]

Power is a dynamic force. Arendt identifies power's three essential ingredients as speech, action, and community, defining power as the human capacity to act and speak together.[5] Power is something that *happens* among people, rather than a thing to be held or welded. Power "springs up between [people] when they act together."[6] It "is always a power potential . . . and not an unchangeable, measurable, and reliable entity like force or strength." It is not a commodity; it cannot "be possessed . . . or

---

4 Though I argue below for the utility and helpful nature of Arendt's theories, her analysis lacks a consideration of intersectionality and forms of oppression, including gender identity, race, and indigeneity. The failure to address systems of patriarchy and provide gender analysis is especially problematic for discussion of an overwhelmingly gendered crime.

5 Arendt, *Human Condition*, 203, 209.

6 Arendt, *Human Condition*, 200. I have edited Arendt's consistent usage of *men* to a more inclusive *people* or *we*, indicated by brackets where I have changed her original text.

applied." Power's immateriality renders it boundless, limited only by the willingness of people to act together.[7]

Her definition of power shares several affinities with Anabaptist thought. Anabaptism grounds its theology in the importance of *Word*. God speaks the world into being, Jesus lives as the incarnation of the Divine Logos (Word), and the Holy Spirit breathes life into believers and speaks for them in times of persecution. The prophets testify and the gift of revelation comes through the holy words of Scripture. For Anabaptists, speech is sacred and full of power.

Anabaptists also believe in the centrality of action. Following Christ is important not only in word but also in deed. "Work and worship are one."[8] Active practice, and particularly the active pursuit of justice, is a hallmark of life in Anabaptist communities.

What's more, Anabaptists embrace community as a foundational value. We define the church as a community committed to one another in shared life, collective discernment, consensus, and mutual aid.[9] Definitions of power that center the work of community, asserting that power *only* exists in contexts of relationship and never in individual hands, are congruent with Anabaptist values. As Arendt observes, "*Power* corresponds to the human ability not just to act but to act in concert. Power is never the property of an individual; it belongs to a group and remains in existence only so long as the group keeps together."[10]

Before we examine in greater depth what power *is* (i.e., the additive ingredients of speech + action + community), we can say what power *is not*, especially in the context of sexual abuse. Common misunderstandings of power—particularly the conflation of power and violence and our tendency to associate a lack of strength with powerlessness—make the dismantling of sexual

---

7 Arendt, *Human Condition*, 180, 200.

8 *Hymnal: A Worship Book*, #749.

9 Cf. Articles 9 and 16, *Confession of Faith in a Mennonite Perspective*, 40–41, 62–63.

10 Arendt, *On Violence*, 44.

abuse difficult. Arendt's rejection of violence and of language of disempowerment both show further congruence with Anabaptist thought.[11]

Power and violence are not the same. Frequently we intertwine power and violence in our thinking, due to their problematic relationship and the ways men have for centuries defined violence as power and vice versa. While Arendt acknowledges that "nothing is more common than the combination of violence and power,"[12] she refuses to collapse power and violence into one another. We conflate power and violence because individuals, governments, and hierarchies tend to use violence "as a last resort to keep power structure[s] intact against individual challengers," creating the illusion that violence is "a prerequisite for power."[13] The illusion is so strong that it can be difficult for us to imagine power apart from violence.

Power and violence are opposites.[14] Violence destroys power. Power is vulnerable, a potentiality dependent on the collective will of a group of people speaking and acting together. Violence includes physical attacks using tools of strength, such as muscular brawn and weapons. It also includes the threat of force, as well as attempts to squelch speech, block action, and disrupt communal bonds of support, aid, and encouragement.

Yet, according to Arendt, violence appears "where power is in jeopardy." Violence is a sign of power's waning, rather than its accumulation. Though "violence can destroy power . . . it is utterly incapable of creating [power]."[15]

---

11 Arendt was not a pacifist. Many of her theories, however, include critiques and dissections of violence, including violence's futility, which are helpful for Anabaptist constructions of pacifism and the importance of peacemaking. Cf., *On Violence*, especially 80.

12 Arendt, *On Violence*, 47.

13 Arendt, *On Violence*, 56.

14 Arendt, *On Violence*, 56.

15 Arendt, *On Violence*, 47, 51, 56.

Where violence is a sign of the disintegration of power, it can signal an opportunity for people to gather, act, and speak to shift power in new directions. The distinction of power from violence frees Anabaptist pacifist traditions to understand and embrace power apart from violence and dominion.

Misunderstandings of power pervade our everyday language. We tend to talk about who "holds power" or how oppressors "wield power" over others. When we say, "It's about power," we usually mean one person has power, while another person does not. When we think about power, we imagine a struggle, a zero-sum competition for goods.[16] Power is an object over which we tussle.

Not so for Arendt. Her notions of power are far less concrete. She refuses to believe that power is a thing, a resource to be stockpiled or traded. "Power cannot be stored up or kept in reserve for emergencies, like the instruments of violence, but exists only in its actualization."[17] Rather than a noun, a possession that can be hoarded and doled out, power functions more like a verb. Power happens; it "springs up."[18] Power cannot be saved or wielded as a weapon like strength or force, which is why power can shift quickly and unexpectedly. We find power even in places where people and societies are weak, under-resourced, and vulnerable.

Those who are weak can still be powerful. This is because, for Arendt, power is not the same thing as strength. Survivors are often the victims of crimes of physical domination, the exertion or threat of physical strength; frequently the bodies of victims are overcome by larger, stronger bodies. In contrast to the strength of their abusers, victims may be labeled as "powerless." Their weakness and lack of resources, and the instances of assault and harm, are conceived of as a persistent power void. Even advocates who

---

16 Or, in more benevolent scenarios, we speak of a search for a way to "share power." Even then, we imagine power as a limited, "concrete" resource.

17 Arendt, *Human Condition*, 200.

18 Arendt is among a number of thinkers who conceptualize power in a more "verbal" capacity, rather than as a concrete commodity.

helpfully seek to reclaim power and reject victimization commonly focus on a quasi-quantifiable differential of power between survivors and their abusers. But such an articulation of abuse can perpetuate the notion that survivors are "outside of power" or "powerless."

Abusers tell survivors they have no power to change their situation, reinforcing abusers' control. Focusing on power as a concrete resource that survivors lack can mirror and reinforce their experience of abuse. In contrast, Arendt's conceptualizations of power challenge the nature of survivors' disempowered state. She imagines that power is not something to be brought in, handed down, marshalled, or resourced from elsewhere. It does not need to be given by those with privilege. We do not muster it from our own mental and emotional wells. Power is not secret inner strength, a charitable gift, or an earned commodity. Power is not a resource to grasp or amass. It is more like "an attribute or even a verb," rather than a possession.[19]

Thus, rather than attempting to "hold onto" or "take back" power from abusers, survivors and their allies can focus on generating new power. Allies and supporters of victims can talk about power in terms that remain open to survivors since speech and action are available to everyone. Power is therefore available to all, even people actively experiencing oppression—including those who are in abusive relationships.

Arendt's conception of power also makes room to recognize the power survivors actively employ during and after abuse, power that keeps them alive, protects others around them, and allows many to live and thrive despite scathing wounds. Arendt provides a dignifying argument that survivors are not necessarily without power, even when they are weak. Sexual abuse negates neither survivors' power potential nor the possibility of new power that springs up when others join them in their struggles, testimonies, and healing.

---

19 As suggested by the classicist Mary Beard in Beard, "Women in Power."

Power = *speech*

Stories of sexual abuse are filled with words about speech. Elizabeth Bruenig tells the story of Amber Wyatt who, in 2006, reported being raped by two high-school classmates. Despite immediate reporting and significant physical evidence, no charges were filed, and the boys were never questioned by police. Community peers and parents castigated the survivor. Bruenig writes that "she wasn't just doubted but hated, not simply mocked but exiled."[20]

As Bruenig revisits the story of Wyatt's sexual assault, she uses more than one hundred distinct words related to speech: reported, gossiped, questioned, repeated, published, mocked, called the police; rumors, slurs, documents, allegations, threats; watched mutely, filed a complaint, sworn statement, denied hearing, declined to comment, competing version of events; "It was a 'he said, she said' thing." It is surprising to consider how many of the descriptions of Wyatt's experience of trauma focus on speech—what and how things were said—leading up to, during, and in the aftermath of a crime of profound physical violence.

Other stories echo with similar dynamics. Cameron Altaras journeyed through the clergy misconduct process with Mennonite Church of Eastern Canada following experiences of sexual abuse. Her account also zeroes in on speech: "I foraged about for words." Altaras describes a process in which she and her supportive community repeatedly faced the challenge to "speak unapologetic truth to power."[21] Her speech to power was a means of dismantling the abusive power at work against her and of generating power for herself.

The nonprofit Into Account and its online project Our Stories Untold are networks supporting survivors of sexual abuse, birthed from an Anabaptist context. Both center on the power that operates through and is generated by speech. Our Stories Untold helps survivors speak publicly about past experiences of abuse to promote healing and awareness. They believe that speech

20 Bruenig, "What Do We Owe Her Now?"
21 Altaras, "Naming," 25–27.

is "a powerful part of survivors' processes of rebuilding ourselves and our lives" and is also "an act that cracks away at systemic perpetuation of sexualized violence in our communities."[22] Into Account provides advocacy and resources for survivors seeking accountability, including "strategies for holding institutions, perpetrators, and enablers accountable for violence, harm, and cover-ups."[23] Their names reflect the centrality of speech's power—*stories, account*—in the pursuit of healing and justice.

We also see the power of speech at work in the impact of silencing and disbelief. Often when survivors speak about their experiences of abuse, others refuse to listen to or believe their accounts. Disbelief douses power. When we fail to listen and receive the truthful speech of those who tell their stories, we cut off the potential for power to spring up among us. Disbelief destroys speech and squelches power along with it.

Moreover, when we silence the stories of others, we cannot act. *Accountability* involves speech; an *account* must be given and received. Without speech and belief, accountability cannot exist. Where there is no account, there is no justice.

But in cases of sexual abuse, survivors are not the only ones speaking. Abusers engage and manipulate the power of speech as well in order to justify or explain away their actions. Communities determined to defend individual perpetrators, or the reputations of particular organizations, shield abusers and attack survivors with their speech.

Altaras's story highlights how institutions and individuals work to control the outcome of survivors' speech through rebuttal. Like many survivors, Altaras was subject to "callous rumors and vicious lies" and scathing letters to the editor of *Canadian Mennonite* when she brought her claims forward.[24] Survivors, who have already endured physical trauma, frequently are also the

---

22 See the *Our Stories Untold* website at http://www.ourstoriesuntold.com/.

23 See the *Into Account* website at https://intoaccount.org/.

24 Altaras, "Naming."

victims of verbal backlash if they dare to speak. Rebuttals come in the form of vicious speech: slurs, name calling, threats, smears of reputation, death threats, or encouragements to suicide.[25] Vicious speech becomes a tool of linguistic violence, deployed by perpetrators or communities who are threatened by the power of a survivor's speech in reporting. Sexual abuse is not only a power struggle of physical altercations. Sometimes the primary tool of coercive power is in the web of social relationships and communication. And the aftermath of abuse often involves a power struggle of words.[26]

If Arendt's view that "violence appears where power is in jeopardy" is accurate,[27] then verbal backlash from abusers can, paradoxically, signal an opportunity for survivors and their allies. As Arendt's analysis of power suggests, backlash can be a sign that the power dynamic of the abusive relationship may be shifting. Allies and institutions can look for eruptions of violent speech as attempts to destroy the power of survivors who speak out. When allies hear violent speech, they can take action to protect survivors. Survivors can, with support, recognize attacks not as a sign of a lack of power relative to their abusers but as its opposite—a sign that power dynamics are shifting, leaving abusers on shakier ground and survivors in a new, if vulnerable, space of strength and possibility.

Other kinds of speech can bolster survivors' power. Allies can provide supportive speech that compounds the power of the survivors' speech. Altaras talks about the importance of "calls of reassurance that [she had] done the right thing, emails of concern for [her] well-being, prayers for continuing strength." In the face of attack, the encouraging speech of Altaras's community—

---

25 Cf. Bruenig, "What Do We Owe?" Amber Wyatt's story is also filled with details of the speech of backlash used against her when she made her allegations.

26 Many times it does not since as many as two out of three cases of sexual assault go unreported.

27 Arendt, *On Violence*, 56.

"written, spoken, and prayed"—shored up her resilience and generated power.[28]

Power = speech + *action*

Power is also about action. Definitions of power focus on the ability to act and to influence and control the action of others. And action is tied closely to speech. According to Arendt, speech and action are "interrelated faculties" fundamental to our humanity.[29] The tight intersections of speech and action, and of silence and inaction, are apparent in sexual abuse.

When survivors are silenced, their ability to change their situation, exit abusive relationships, and protect themselves and others decreases. Hindering survivors' ability to speak about their abuse hinders their ability to act, to stop the abuse. Abusers can silence survivors through physical harm or intimidation, cultural or economic restraint,[30] threats, and isolation. Robbing survivors of speech impinges directly on their ability to act because speech and action are so intertwined. Limiting speech limits action. And power potential fizzles.

"If she would have kept her mouth shut then nothing would have ever happened."[31] Amber Wyatt heard this phrase repeatedly, often by defenders of her abusers, after she reported her rape. The comment represents an erasure of Wyatt's assault, a devastation that *did* happen to her. But the comment also illustrates the importance of the relationship of speech and action in power.

---

28 Altaras, "Naming."

29 In *The Human Condition*, Arendt painstakingly argues for the climactic importance of action in human life. She centers the importance of speech in the chapter "Action," titling the opening section "The Disclosure of the Agent in Speech and Action." Arendt links human agency not only to doing (action) but also to voice (speech). Arendt, *Human Condition*, 175, 178, 236.

30 Examples include culturally deferential or economically dependent spouses and employees who fear job or wage loss when abused by professional superiors.

31 Bruenig, "What Do We Owe?"

Wyatt spoke. Things happened. When Wyatt reported her rape, the power of her speech set in motion a web of action, like a cue ball rolling across a pool table. An investigation commenced. Waves of shock, shame, and anxiety rippled through her small Texas community.

When Wyatt voiced her allegations, her community answered and acted in response. Unfortunately for Wyatt, many people chose speech and action in defense of her attackers rather than with and for her as a survivor. Parents, school officials, and law enforcement minimized Wyatt's accusations, diminishing her speech and its power, and rushed to exonerate her attackers. Rumors, insults, and death threats created a tide of backlash speech that silenced Wyatt from speaking more, muffling her speech in disbelief and intimidating Wyatt into paralysis from further action. Power shifted again as the speech and action of the community shifted.

We see Wyatt's power realized as she reports her attack and engages an investigation. We also see Wyatt's power reflected in the intense response it elicits from her community. The community's response was swift and harsh because it recognized the power Wyatt exercised. The violence of their words of backlash and cover-up needed to be thorough because Wyatt, and her speech, exercised so much power potential. Wyatt had shown she was able to generate power by reaching out to her parents and the police. Others, who had much to lose, reacted quickly to destroy her power. "If she had kept her mouth shut then nothing would have ever happened." But Wyatt chose instead to speak and act, unleashing the power of her testimony in her community.

Survivors engage power in other ways as well. Survivors speak, name, and define abuse. Survivors' naming of abuse becomes more powerful when spoken with others who strengthen their speech through acceptance and belief. Acceptance is the opposite of backlash. Where disbelief douses the power of survivors' speech, belief magnifies it.

Survivors also act to leave, displace, or change patterns of behavior and exposure. They create structures of protection through safety plans, boundaries, and separation from abuse and abusers. The follow-through of action protects the speaker, creates physical and psychological safety, and completes a cycle of change and resistance that disrupts abusive patterns.

This combination of speech and action is powerful. It is, according to Arendt, the very definition of power. It generates power for the survivor, among her supporters, and crucially between herself and her abuser. The power that arises from a survivor speaking and acting in the face of abuse is generative and can be cataclysmic to the abusive relationship when it is able to subvert the structures of abuse.

Often abusive relationships function according to power generated by the abuser's speech and action. Abusers use speech to dictate control, boundaries, and the terms of relationship through threats, shame, gaslighting, or direct commands. Abusers curtail survivors' abilities to speak and act independently. Abusers also use action, whether physical violence, threats of violence, or the demonstration of violence (e.g., smashing walls, pounding tables, breaking household objects). Abusers activate more subtle forms of control like policing victims' social contacts. Abusers maintain control of the power dynamic over their victims through an effective use of speech and action.

Patterns of abuse limit and douse the power of survivors through physical and linguistic violence, yet even in severe cases, power is still available to them. Power is not merely a commodity that must be obtained from another source or in greater quantities than the abuser holds, as we often conceive of it. Power is also latent, though not in the sense that survivors are at fault for failing to access untapped power in relation to their abusers.[32] The latency of power is more like a seed "lying dormant or hidden until circumstances are suitable for . . . manifestation."[33] Speech and action by victims and their supportive communities can alter the circumstances of victims' experiences of violence and oppression, allowing hope for the manifestation of power.

---

32 Victim-blaming is one of abusers' oldest tools in the belt of linguistic violence and manipulation.

33 Lexico.com, "latent."

If power "springs up" between people, then when survivors find supporters, when their speech is heard and believed, when their actions are supported by others joining them in their attempts at change and newness, power is restored and generated anew for the survivor. This is power for herself and in the relationship with her abuser. Power dynamics shift. The ability of the abuser to speak and act, to direct the relationship, the energy, the power flowing between the two people can fundamentally change. Abusive power can be disrupted and has the chance to wane and dissipate. The same can be true structurally when institutions change their speech and action and generate power with and for survivors rather than in defense of abusers.

The shifts in power may be weak. They may, as in the case of Amber Wyatt, sway to and fro. Survivors and institutions may continue to ask themselves how and why the abuse happened. But the potential for shifts in power is possible, especially when survivors' voices are magnified by listening, belief, and reassurance from allies.

Shifts in power elicit retaliation. Abusers may double down and recruit defensive speech for themselves. They may attempt to destroy the power generated on behalf of survivors through verbal or physical violence. It is therefore important for survivors to speak and act only when they are ready and ideally in the context of supportive community.[34] They will likely be the victims of backlash when they speak up. But Arendt helps us to see that it is not because they are powerless. It is precisely the opposite. It is because survivors, when they speak and act, are generating power.

The word *hero*, as originally used in Homer, was "no more than a name given to each free man who participated" in the Trojan enterprise.[35] Free people are capable of *heroic* behavior. The connotations of a hero's courage are "already present in a will-

---

34 Cf. Stephanie Krehbiel's article on the fallacy of mandatory reporting policies and the need for survivor-directed accountability. Krehbiel, "Our Rock Is the Truth."

35 Arendt, *Human Condition*, 186.

ingness to act and speak at all."[36] All survivors retain the basic human capacity of heroism. The exercise of their freedom, their willingness to speak and act, can render heroic, powerful results. And while victims of abuse are often not free in significant ways, Arendt offers us a way in, a crack in the oppressive weight of abusive relationships, insights into how power works and flows among people and institutions, even those who are oppressed and lack strength.

We can nurture liberation by creating conditions in which survivors are more sufficiently free to speak and act, and in so doing we can shift the power dynamics of their abuse. When we speak and act, power will arise—not because we hope it will or because we, as individuals or institutions, have any particular strength or courage or resources but simply because that is how power works.

Power = speech + action + *community*

"Power always stands in need of numbers," Arendt declares.[37] If we increase the numbers of people willing to speak and believe stories of abuse and engage the problems that exist in our communities, we may begin to shift and change the power dynamics that led to violations of abuse in the first place. As Arendt writes, "The only indispensable material factor in the generation of power is the living together of people."[38] Arendt is clear that sharing life is "the most important prerequisite for power." Her requirements for power are refreshingly simple and clear. Moreover, they are at the fingertips of Anabaptist communities of worship committed to living together in a "spiritual, social, and economic reality, demonstrating now the justice, righteousness, love, and peace of the age to come."[39] The nature of our life together offers us the hope of power realized, springing up in the world.

---

36 Arendt, *Human Condition*, 186.

37 Arendt, *On Violence*, 42.

38 Arendt, *Human Condition*, 201.

39 *Confession of Faith in a Mennonite Perspective*, Article 24, 89–90.

Anabaptist communities, churches, and institutions can be places for the nurture and protection of power for survivors of sexual abuse. Our first step must be to stop protecting abusers. Anabaptist institutions have in numerous instances engaged in cover-ups for leaders accused of sexual abuse, from Mennonite educators like Luke Hartman to theological luminaries like John Howard Yoder.[40] We must no longer protect the power of those accused of abuse, squelching the power of their alleged victims and adding to their trauma.

But we can do more than reform injustices of the past. Anabaptist communities can also take constructive action. We can believe survivors when they engage in costly acts of speech, preserving the power that springs up among us and nurturing their power for the present and future. We can generate power for and among survivors through the speech of reassurance, support, protection, and justice. We can resist the power-destroying physical and linguistic violence survivors face from their abusers and communities who resist the change and shifts of power that accompany accountability. We can hold abusers accountable, refusing to enable behaviors and structures that perpetuate violence and secrecy. We can refuse language of "powerlessness" for survivors, recognizing the power survivors generate from their speech and action among others.

Power, Arendt is clear, is "dependent on the unreliable and only temporary agreement of many wills and intentions."[41] Power is delicate, unpredictable.[42] Our job is to protect its possibility, to keep gathering together and speaking truth with a willingness to act. In facing sexual abuse, the work of the church is to listen when survivors speak, allow their power potential to be realized, and reverse the domination of silencing which has limited and destroyed their power in the past. Rather than being a

---

40 Houser and Heinzekehr, "Church acknowledges reports"; Preheim, "Mennonites apologize."

41 Arendt, *Human Condition*, 201.

42 Arendt, *Human Condition*, 191.

place of dominion and silence, the church can be a place of vibrant speech and sharing, bubbling with power. And from this boundless spring, we can move forward together with survivors into healing and new life so that action can follow, things can change, and prisoners of abuse and violence can be free.

Conclusion: The beginning of power

Arendt writes, "To act, in its most general sense, means to take initiative, to begin . . . to set something in motion. . . . The new always happens against the overwhelming odds. . . . The new therefore always appears in the guise of a miracle. The fact that [we] are capable of action means the unexpected can be expected."[43] She believed in the power of beginning. Power is present in the spark, the flare that springs up in the moment of people speaking and acting. It rolls forward into unpredictable freedom from a moment of wellspring. Arendt's vision of power is filled with hope and possibility, for she affirms our power even as we begin new tasks and new conversations. The task of addressing sexual abuse in our churches is fraught with discouragement and resistance, but perhaps Arendt would tell us to take heart. Even when we do not know where we are going, we are powerful, precisely in the moment we begin. Beginning is the task. We can begin today to speak and act, to listen to survivors as they speak and fight for safe spaces for their voices to be heard. We can begin to change the tides, for power is here among us.

---

43 Arendt, *Human Condition*, 177–78.

23

A Pass
A Poem

Julia Spicher Kasdorf

Forgive us our trespasses
as we forgive, I softly recite

among strangers, remembering
the hand of an older man

gliding up my thin dress.
I twist free of him,

keep speaking as if he is just
a rich family friend chatting,

and I am still safe
in the shape of my skin.

Of course it sets me back,
as each death resurrects

the memory of all other deaths,
and you must return to mourn

your full store of passings afresh.
A child cannot be accused

Of seducing a neighbor man,
but as the girl grows, the bones

of her cheeks and pelvis jut
like blades beneath her skin,

gorgeous weapons of revenge.
At last, the lusts of those

who trespass against us bear
some resemblance to our own:

shame and rage, heavy as coins
sewn in the lining of an exile's coat.

When an immigrant ship went down
In Lake Erie, passengers who refused

To shed their heavy garments
drowned, yards from shore.[1]

---

1 "A Pass" from *Eve's Striptease* by Julia Kasdorf, © 1998. Reprinted by
permission of the University of Pittsburgh Press.

24

Lessons Learned
Sexual Abuse, Power, and Church Administrators
David Martin

S eminary did not prepare me to confront sexual abuse in the church, and neither did it teach me how to respond when the perpetrators were ordained leaders. Likewise, my twenty-five years of pastoral ministry did little to teach me about accompanying victims of sexual abuse. As a white male pastor moving into denominational administration, I was ill-equipped to deal with the complexities and emotional dynamics of relating to victims or navigating the institutional power structures that come with the office of church executive.

Nonetheless, in my role as a denominational leader, I have not been immune to instances of sexual misconduct by credentialed leaders or the need to confront the prevailing culture of denial around sexual abuse in the church, whether from within the pew or from other church leaders. I have learned the hard way what it means for the church to address the challenging issues surrounding sexual abuse. My education has come through the crucible of being thrust into situations that I would rather have avoided. I have learned primarily from the courage and vulnerability of victims, the thoughtfulness and compassion of others, and the willingness of those who had power to choose to do the right thing.

Sexual abuse in the church has not been an area of academic study for me. Rather, my learnings have been derived from the practical experience I have gained from being required to deal with a number of difficult incidents of clergy misconduct in my role as a volunteer on clergy credentialing committees and my time as a church executive. In addition, I have learned from workshops,[1] boundary training seminars, and other continuing education opportunities. What follows are reflections of my experience and the lessons learned along the way. I share what I have learned through a series of vignettes that are based in real-life experience. These stories reflect actual experience but have been altered to protect the confidentiality of all parties involved.[2] The most important lesson I have learned through all of this is that *when we act with integrity, courage, and compassion, we make room for healing and hope to emerge for those whose lives have been shattered by sexual misconduct.*

Lessons learned from victims

I have learned that one of the most important things we can do to change the culture around sexual abuse in the church is to take steps to become communities of faith that survivors experience as safe, just, and compassionate, whether that is at the congregational, institutional, or denominational level. As the following vignettes illustrate, this requires several fundamental attitudinal shifts. Most important, we need to learn from victims themselves.

> *Vignette 1.* Jennifer sat in the chair in front of me, angry, nervous, and agitated as she recounted her allegation of

---

1 FaithTrust Institute is an invaluable resource for training about clergy sexual abuse. The organization was founded by Marie Fortune, a pioneer in the field of clergy sexual abuse and someone to whom the church owes a great debt for her ground-breaking work.

2 Over a period of about twenty years, I have engaged with over a dozen cases of alleged clergy sexual misconduct, so the details of the stories herein should not be connected to any particular case that one may be aware of. I tell these stories to relate what I have learned and not to convey any private or confidential information, which is why I have altered details throughout.

long-ago abuse by a church leader. Her demands seemed unreasonable—so unreasonable that it was tempting to write her off as an angry young woman who didn't have a clue what she was demanding. Despite my inclinations to the contrary, I forced myself to listen, to hear her pain, and to empathize as best I knew how. Later, a call to our legal counsel confirmed what I already knew: "You owe her absolutely nothing. Your misconduct policy doesn't apply to this. If you don't engage with her, your legal risks are extremely low."

How am I to respond as an older male executive leader with institutional power and legal precedence on my side to what seems to me an unreasonable demand? Do I walk away or engage? Do I conveniently dismiss what appears to be a legitimate allegation of clergy sexual misconduct because I am not obliged to address it? Do I run for shelter behind the walls of institutional and legal power that are at my disposal? Or do I dare to begin a vulnerable conversation with Jennifer about what I can and cannot do in relation to her pain and suffering? Thankfully, I chose to begin a conversation. Jennifer became my teacher and mentor, and much of what I have learned about sexual abuse in the church is a result of my willingness to enter a long-term conversation that has supported her healing journey and deepened my understanding of how the church can relate to survivors of sexual abuse. By doing so, I learned my first lesson: *Having the courage and vulnerability to engage in authentic relationship with victims of abuse can foster their healing and deepen our personal and corporate understanding of how the church can be a compassionate community for survivors of abuse.*

> *Vignette 2.* Don made it clear to his friends at church that he knew who this confidential complainant was: "We were in youth group together. You all know what she was like. Misconduct? Fat chance! She is the one that seduced the music director! Now look who is getting the blame!"

Vignette 3. As Ruth listened to the angry words of the young adult who blurted out her painful allegation of abuse by her youth pastor, she thought to herself, *This is an angry, volatile young woman. I wonder if her version of this story is true. And, I must admit, I've always thought she dresses a little too provocatively.*

Don's accusation that the complainant had a history of promiscuity is a common tactic used to blame the victim. Does a person's past sexual behavior automatically discount the truth of a particular incident? Individuals who have been promiscuous may struggle with low self-esteem and poor personal boundaries, which makes them an ideal target for a predator. Ruth's assumptions about a provocatively dressed young woman inviting her own abuse reflect a misunderstanding of professional power and responsibility. Even if the woman was provocatively dressed, even if her behavior was inviting or flirtatious, does it matter? When it comes to professional misconduct, it is always the responsibility of the professional or the person with the greater power to set the boundaries and maintain them. No further qualifications need to be added.

Drawing attention to a victim's emotional intensity, irrationality, or anger is another strategy used to minimize the experience of the complainant and to ignore the truth. Do strong, angry emotions discount a painful story? Or are we just afraid of anger? What kind of emotions do we expect an abused person to have? While it is uncomfortable to be on the receiving end of an emotional tirade, assessing the validity of a victim's allegation based on their degree of emotional intensity or level of composure is essentially an abuse of professional power by the person receiving the disclosure. In my experience, an individual's history of emotional vulnerability or promiscuity may be indicators that validate the complainant's story of abuse more than discredit it.

Stories like these taught me a second lesson: *Angry emotions, provocative dress, and previous sexual history are not grounds for dismissing allegations of abuse. If the culture around sexual abuse*

*in the church is going to change, everyone must resist the knee-jerk
reaction to blame the victim.*

> *Vignette 4.* The conversation in the church hallways and
> over coffee was furtive and low. Wendy was overheard
> saying, "I hate to put him down, but I just don't believe
> it. Pastor Wilson would never do something like that.
> Many of us know that Jonathan has a history of emo-
> tional struggles. Don't you think emotional instability
> has something to do with these crazy allegations?"

An individual's history of emotional or mental health issues
should never automatically discount their allegation of abuse.
Jonathan's emotional problems may or may not be related to his
so-called crazy allegations but may be the result of his abuse.
Predators often seek out, either intentionally or intuitively, individuals who are vulnerable because of an emotional weakness or
poor boundaries. Jonathan's situation illustrates a third lesson:
*Rarely are sexual misconduct allegations the product of emotional
instability, and mental health issues should never be grounds to
automatically dismiss an allegation.*

> *Vignette 5.* Jessie is an elderly woman, nearing the final
> years of her life. As she sat with her counselor, sharing
> the painful story of abuse from many years ago, she felt
> the sharpness of the shame and pain as if it were yes-
> terday. "Why did I wait thirty years to talk to a trusted
> professional like you? I guess it was that announcement
> in church that Pastor Richards was found guilty of sex-
> ual misconduct at his new church. That's when I realized
> that I wasn't the only one. It gave me the courage to
> come talk to you. You know, it will be a relief to make
> peace with myself and God while I still can."

One of the things I have learned about sexual abuse and professional misconduct from stories like Jessie's is that victim pain does
not have an expiration date. Whether it has been one, ten, or thirty
years, unless the pain is disclosed and addressed and healing steps

have been pursued, the pain can fester for years due to feelings of guilt, shame, or fear of the abuser. This is a hard lesson for many to understand. Many people dismiss disclosures about incidents like Jessie's that occurred decades in the past. They wonder how anything that happened that long ego can still be relevant. I have learned from victims, however, that the amount of time that has elapsed between the abuse and the disclosure does not correlate to the level of pain and distress that they may experience. Some victims do not come forward until after their abuser has died, and it finally feels like the environment is safe to disclose their experience of pain.

Other factors can also dissuade victims from immediately reporting. A victim's perception and experience of the abuse might change over time. It is not uncommon for an eighteen-year-old to think that she had an affair with her professor. Years later, through life experience or counseling, this same person may come to the realization that what happened was not consensual but was an instance of grooming and predatory abuse.

For the same reasons, financial support for survivors to pursue counseling, or in some circumstances to be compensated for grievous harms, may be required decades after the original experience of abuse. While the denomination and congregation have a role to play in financially supporting the healing journey of survivors, the perpetrator should also bear the brunt of these costs. If the perpetrator refuses to financially support the healing process, perhaps the civil courts are an appropriate avenue of redress.

If our goal is to support victims, those in power need to accept that disclosures can be expected decades after the initial abuse. And so, a fourth lesson I have learned is this: *When we recognize that emotional pain does not have an expiration date, we can relate to victims with much greater care and compassion.*

> *Vignette 6.* Sandra called to inquire about an investigation of clergy sexual misconduct. It was clear from her questions that she had doubts about the investigation. She informed me that she had workplace experience with investigating matters like this. At one point she

asked, "Do you have any DNA evidence? I am presuming you don't. That really makes it hard in cases like this to determine guilt, doesn't it?"

If the church is going to abide by Sandra's expectations that we have definitive DNA evidence as the standard of proof in its investigation procedures, then we may as well just hand all the power to the perpetrator and make disempowerment the norm for victims. A temptation for church administrators is to adopt investigative procedures that assess allegations of abuse using the legal standards that apply to criminal courts. It is important, though, that church investigations do not replace due legal process. If the sexual misconduct allegation is potentially a criminal offense, then the first step is to encourage the victim to report the offense to the police and have it investigated by civil authorities. This is mandatory procedure when a minor is involved. The church is not equipped to investigate criminal offenses. After the legal process has concluded, it is still obligatory for the church to conduct its own disciplinary process and to use the legal findings as a component in its investigation.

In my experience, most allegations of sexual abuse do not fall into the definition of a criminal offense. Non-criminal offenses can still constitute misconduct and are incredibly damaging to victims and require investigation. The church can conduct these investigations in a manner that is much different than a criminal investigation and in ways that are more supportive and compassionate both for the victim and the perpetrator. The legal standard for conviction in the criminal court is based on the evidence being "beyond a reasonable doubt." This exceptionally high bar is one that most victims and their advocates would find difficult to achieve unless they have definitive DNA evidence.

Alternatively, the standard of evidence required in many denominational investigative procedures is proof based on the "balance of probabilities." In other words, the standard is that it is *more likely than not* that the alleged perpetrator engaged in sexual misconduct. This reflects the standard of proof that is used in civil courts. When the church evaluates a complainant's allegation of abuse, it can be treated with more dignity than what often occurs in criminal or civil courts. If victims are to have the courage to disclose their burden of pain, it is imperative that they experience the church as being safer than the legal system. Victims need to be convinced that church is a place that is more likely than not to believe their accounts of abuse.

The accused person also needs to be assured that that they, too, will have the opportunity to be heard and to defend themselves. It is incumbent on the church to demonstrate to the victim and the accused that it is a faith community dedicated to truth and justice.

My point here is that church investigations should not be based on the criteria of a criminal court proceeding but rather on the "balance of probability" criterion that is used in the civil courts. The church is only removing a credential, not imprisoning someone, and so the civil court criterion is more appropriate. Furthermore, church investigations should never be used to avoid reporting a criminal offense. Some victims, though, are reluctant to engage the court process and would prefer a church investigation. This is only appropriate when the allegations do not constitute a criminal offense. Church administrators can help a survivor to review their options for addressing an allegation, encourage them to seek independent legal counsel when appropriate. In addition, good investigative policies appoint an advocate to walk with the survivor through the entire process. Survivors need to be assured that church investigations are designed to provide a humane, safe, and dignified process for addressing their complaint.

A significant learning for me has been the value of moving from appointing lay investigators to hiring an external, third-party investigator to handle an investigation. Even if they are professionals in their respective vocations, lay investigators simply do not have the investigative experience or training to handle most complaints. External investigators also represent a commitment to impartiality as they are one step removed from the institution. This can help the survivor, the accused, and the church constituency to have confidence in the process. External investigators can be expensive for the church, but my experience is that they are worth every cent.

As a church administrator who has dealt with multiple allegations, I have learned that when complainants have the courage to come forward and share their story of pain, we can normally assume that what they are sharing is true. Experience has shown that it is more often the perpetrator who is lying or distorting the truth. At the same time, we must always ensure that our listening and evaluation protocols include robust safeguards to ensure that truthfulness, due process, and natural justice are respected for both the complainant and the accused.

On the side of caution, however, we must always remain open to the possibility that an allegation may not be substantiated. The life, vocation, and reputation of the accused are all at stake. Misunderstandings can happen, and misperceptions of what constitutes abuse or sexual harassment are possible. This is why it is critical that the congregation, denomination, or church institution have robust investigative policies.

The fifth lesson I have learned, then, is this: *An assumption that allegations of abuse are usually true and a commitment by the church to hear the stories of victims without applying the evidential standards of a criminal court will create a disclosure culture in which victims can trust that they will be treated with respect, dignity, and due process.*

At the same time, I have learned this sixth lesson: *The best way to test the validity of an allegation and safeguard all concerned is a strong policy and procedure for investigation.*

> *Vignette 7.* A member of the local press called the denominational office and wanted to know everything about this new allegation of misconduct. "Who is this woman?" he demanded. "If someone is going to make an allegation like this, the least they can do is to have the decency to stand up and be counted. The church hasn't given us a name, and the public has a right to know who the accuser is. Besides, how serious was it? Did he rape

her? Was it just an affair? Was it intercourse or just sexual harassment?"

Whether it is the person next to you in the pew, the curious folk in the congregation down the road, or the inquiring minds of the press and the wider public, none of them are owed or deserve the confidential details of another's life or pain. In my experience, one of the biggest fears for victims is the fear of their identity becoming public without their consent. Victims deserve the right to define the extent to which information is shared about their experience. The church is not a viewing gallery for the inquisitive or for those who think they have the right to make their own evaluation of the evidence. No one other than those dealing directly with the disclosure, or those required to make decisions about it, should be privy to the confidential details of the abuse itself or the identity of the complainant.

Victims are more likely to come forward if they can trust that their identity and the explicit details of their experience will not become the subject of public voyeurism. I have encountered cases where victims have not come forward for this very reason. If a victim does not come forward, and the church never learns about the abuse, the perpetrator may never be held to account. A perpetrator not held to account may be a perpetrator who continues to offend. This is not in the best interests and health of the church and its members. Confidentiality related to the identity of victim and the allegation is critical to making the church a safe space for victims and survivors. The identity of the perpetrator is a different matter that we will address later.

One of the best ways to ensure that victims are safe and in charge of their experience is to have them be as fully in control of their story as possible. A victim may choose to publicly share their identity and story, but that is their decision to make. Survivors need to discern what level of confidentiality best promotes their journey towards healing. This does not mean, however, that they get to control the investigation process, the decisions made, or the disciplinary actions that may be taken. The seventh lesson I have learned from victims, then, is this: *If victims are going to be empowered to speak their truth about abuse, the church must learn to respond to disclosures in ways that (unlike criminal courts) maintain strict confidentiality, which protects the identity and dignity of the victim.*

These lessons I have learned from victims have not always been ones that the church and its leaders have embraced. The church often has used its power to promote a culture of silencing, disbelieving, minimizing, and victim blaming. Rather than address allegations head on, church leaders have often found it easier for the church to simply sweep the allegations under the rug or blame the misconduct on the victim. If we open ourselves to learning from victims of abuse, we will discover that the church can model new ways of responding that will honor victims, hold perpetrators accountable, and foster a culture of healing and justice.

Lessons learned in navigating corporate power

Church structures are vehicles for the channeling of power. That power can be directed toward the church's vocation to embody Jesus's purposes and healing presence in the world. If misused or misdirected, that same institutional power can undermine the purposes for which the church was commissioned by Christ. Dealing with victims, survivors, and perpetrators is one of the starkest experiences I have had of navigating power in ministry. The awareness of wielding power has never been more palpable for me than when facing the complexities of addressing clergy misconduct and abuse. Here I share some vignettes based on my experiences and some of the lessons that have emerged for me regarding navigating the appropriate use of power in relation to clergy abuse.

> *Vignette 8.* Before she left the meeting, the lawyer reminded the board members that it was her responsibility to advise on a course of action that would expose the organization to the least risk. "My advice to you is to stay out of this. What you choose to do, however, is up to

you. I am giving you legal advice, not moral advice. As a church, you might decide to respond differently."

The board members looked at each other, knowing that they faced a stark decision. The church had no insurance coverage for liability. They and the denomination were on their own. Ingrid put it bluntly, "We know that doing nothing has the least risk. If we engage with the victim, we may be opening an unpredictable can of worms. There is no way of knowing what else we might unleash." Peter responded immediately, "If there is a can of worms, there's a can of worms. We will deal with it. We need to do the right thing!" The nods around the board table spoke volumes.

In my experience, legal counsel is always a helpful resource when navigating allegations of clergy abuse. On matters like this, church leaders are always in over their heads. Legal guidance is critically important and relevant to making wise and informed decisions. In the final analysis, though, the church needs to make the decision of how to proceed with an allegation. As the lawyer said, legal advice is not always moral advice. As a church, we also stand for compassion, justice, courage, and doing the right thing. We are not in the business of sacrificing victims on the altar of expediency or risk avoidance.

This can be a tough decision when a church does not know the legal or financial implications of their decision. Church leaders may have the corporate power to shield themselves from risk. They may also have the corporate power to reach out to a hurting victim, to hear their story, and to see where that conversation leads. The question is which application of power is more in keeping with the values and vocation of the church. Organizations are never called to be reckless with the financial or legal outcomes of their decision-making, but churches are invited to place those decisions within the context of their vocation to be the body of Christ in the world. A key thing that I have learned in relation to corporate power is this: *While legal counsel is important, it is imperative to place that counsel within the context of the values and vocation of the church.*

> *Vignette 9.* Sitting across the desk, the niece of Pastor Williams exclaimed, "How can you do this to our family? Some slutty woman seduces my uncle, and you turn around and strip him of his ministerial credential and parade him before the public like some criminal. I thought the church was about compassion and forgiveness! Maybe he made a mistake, but it wasn't his fault. You've ruined his life. You've ruined all our lives! I am done with this hellhole you call church!" With that, she got up, slammed the door behind her, and left the church—possibly for good.

Situations like Pastor Williams's are some of the most difficult and painful that I have had to navigate. The reality is that whenever we deal with professional misconduct and take an action that supports the victim and holds the perpetrator to account, the circle of pain will widen.

This is challenging. It does not take long before persons connected to the perpetrator begin to feel victimized: spouse, children, siblings, parents, aunts and uncles, nieces and nephews, grandchildren, friends, colleagues, church members, and the list goes on. All these people, through no fault of their own, will have shame and pain inflicted on them. They may become angry, confused, and emotionally distressed. They may even leave the church.

And then there is the congregation, or the college, or the camp community that suffers because of the abuse. It can take decades for a congregation to recover from an incident of sexual abuse. Everyone suffers. There is no lack of shame, pain, and suffering to go around. It is easy to see why it is so tempting to sweep misconduct under the rug and go on pretending as if nothing happened. Dealing with the pain of sexual abuse will always result in more pain.

The question is whose pain is given preference: the victim or those related to the perpetrator. The victim, like the perpetrator, may also have a spouse, children, parents, and other family and friends. What about their pain? What about their shame and suffering? Is their pain not also worthy of our concern? If we are not willing to appropriately disclose misconduct, we abandon the victim and sacrifice them on the altar of least resistance.

I believe that if we fail to act or support the victim for fear of widening the circle of pain, then we risk abandoning what is right and just. It is difficult to be the one whose decisions create pain for others. When I have faced decisions like this, I have found it helpful to remind myself that the perpetrator, not the church, is responsible for creating victims of their families and social networks. As a church, we cannot own the perpetrator's decisions and their impact; we just have to live with them. We can, however, still support those, who through no fault of their own, find themselves carrying an unexpected burden of pain because of someone else's actions. I would encourage denominations to consider offering professional support to the "secondary victims" who have been significantly impacted by misconduct. So, the second lesson I have learned from such situations is this: *Church leaders are not responsible for the ripple effects of the perpetrator's actions; perpetrators are the ones whose choices and actions inflict pain on their relational network.*

Vignette 10. Sunday morning it was announced that Pastor Stewart, the congregation's former pastor, was being investigated for an allegation of sexual abuse at the church he was currently serving. Afterward, the conversation at coffee time was animated. "I can't believe it," said Joe. "The allegation is over a decade old!" June added, "Best pastor we ever had! He made everyone feel like they belonged." Barbara, however, sat silently throughout the conversation and then slipped out the side door and went home. After a long night, Barbara picked up the phone in the morning and called a friend. "Robert, can you go with me to the denominational office tomorrow? I want to lodge a complaint with them about Pastor Stewart."

In my experience, public communication is critical when it comes to professional misconduct. Communication is itself an exercise of power. What we choose to say (or not say) can have a significant impact on the accused, the survivor, and other potential victims.

Effective communication can be a significant part of a victim's healing journey. Once an investigation has confirmed that professional misconduct has occurred, publicly naming the perpetrator's abuse can be an important validation for the victim. It is essential for victims to know that what they experienced was categorically wrong. It was not their fault. To have that spoken officially and publicly can be an important part of the healing journey for the victim.

Communication is also critical because experience has shown that there is often more than one victim. Public communication is a way to inform other victims that they are not alone and that they can seek help for their experience of abuse. In the above vignette, Barbara found the courage to make a complaint because she realized she was not the only one.

When we communicate publicly about a finding of misconduct, only the accused is named, not the victim. Confidentiality regarding the identity of the victim is paramount. Providing minimal details also protects the accused from being put on unnecessary public display. In my view, what is communicated is strictly the misconduct charge, a few details about the process, and the disciplinary actions taken.

At the same time, transparency about the process is appropriate and important. Trust will be built in the wider constituency when those dealing with a disclosure can be fully transparent about the process used to address the allegation. For instance, we can communicate the existence of an official complaint, the process that was used to receive and evaluate it, and the names of those who are involved with managing the complaint process. On the process side, we can offer full transparency and as much detail as appropriate in terms of steps taken, decisions made, and even missteps or errors of judgment that may have occurred along the way, or long-ago complaints that were mishandled at the time.

Both the survivor and the church constituency need to be confident that the church is committed to transparency and will in no way dismiss allegations or cover up evidence of misconduct. On the personal side, we need to ensure protection for the identity of the complainant and confidentiality in terms of the details of the allegation. Those viewing it from the outside need to be assured that good process is being utilized and that the church is acting in good faith and is being fully transparent. They can be encouraged to trust those who are mandated to manage the investigation process and can be reassured that policies and procedures are being followed.

Those managing the misconduct process have the power to contain information to a small circle of awareness or to circulate information much more broadly. My experience suggests that the circle of communication needs to extend at least as far as the sphere of influence in which the perpetrator was active. If the professional's work was regional, the communication might remain regional. If the individual worked nationally or internationally, then communication should correspond to that sphere of influence. Ultimately, communication of misconduct is a public matter. Those credentialed to serve the church are acting within the public sphere, which is why communication about findings of misconduct requires public transparency. Communication should also include an invitation for anyone impacted by professional misconduct to share their experience with the appropriate denominational staff person.

Communication is a form of power, and the purpose of exercising that power is twofold. Public communication signals to both professionals and parishioners that the church will not tolerate sexual misconduct. Furthermore, it is an explicit invitation for other victims to disclose abuse, whether that abuse is directly related to the announcement being made or to another circumstance. To summarize, a third lesson I have learned about navigating corporate power is this: *Church executives can use their power to communicate publicly about sexual misconduct in ways that sup-*

port the healing of victims, respect the dignity of the accused, and invite others who have been harmed by clergy abuse to seek healing.

> *Vignette 11.* James was adamant that he did not want any public announcements about the investigation into his sexual abuse by Pastor Georgina. "I know what she did was wrong, but at this point I am getting the help that I need. I don't want to see her entire life ruined because of this. I still care about her as a human being."

Sometimes the survivor's goals conflict with the goals and purposes of the church. James, for instance, did not want *any* public communication, but this is at odds with what the church believes is in everyone's best interest. The legitimate task of the survivor is to focus on their personal healing path, while the church's responsibility is to use its power to seek the welfare of the entire constituency that it oversees. While supporting victims and their healing path should be at the forefront, the church has other obligations as well. It is also called to support the welfare of the perpetrator, the perpetrator's family, the congregation, its wider constituency, and the organization itself. It is the mandate of the church executives to exercise power in a way that places the victim's needs and demands within the context of the wellbeing of the whole. Finding balance, justice, and equity for all stakeholders when it comes to sexual abuse cases can be a challenge, but it is one that must be navigated by taking the best interests of all parties into consideration. The fourth lesson I have learned about institutional power is this: *The church is not beholden only to the interests of one party who has been impacted by misconduct; the vocation of the church is to seek the healing and welfare of the whole community.*

> *Vignette 12.* "Oh man, not another boundary crossing workshop!" grumbled Pastor Simmons. "We used to have to do these courses every five years, and now they are making them mandatory every three years! When is enough, enough?"

I am sure that Pastor Simmons has more than enough on her plate, but when it comes to protecting pastors and lay people from clergy sexual abuse, rarely has the church done too much. In my tenure as a church administrator, we used our executive judicatory powers to develop a variety of initiatives to enhance prevention efforts in the constituency. We increased the frequency of mandatory boundary training for pastors from every five years to every three years; we refined our screening protocols for credentialing pastors; we published story-based print and online educational materials for youth and adults; we encouraged congregations to use the *Circle of Grace* prevention curriculum for children and youth, originally developed by the Archdiocese of Omaha; and we commissioned a theatrical production on sexual abuse that toured throughout our churches. In addition, we invited Marie Fortune and staff from FaithTrust Institute to lead day-long training sessions for church executives, denominational staff, not-for-profit directors, and congregational leaders. We also sent judicatory staff and leaders from cultures new to our denomination to FaithTrust Institute to be certified in teaching boundary training to pastors. This enabled them to instruct pastors from those cultures in their own language and with greater cultural sensitivity. There is still always more do be done, and church executives have the power to make change. The fifth thing that I have learned is this: *Executive power does and can make a difference! When our power as church administrators is used well, the church can increasingly become a safe and just community for all.*

Conclusion

Vignette 13. "I have been living with this hell for fifteen years," said Corina. "This abuse stuff just never goes away! Some days are good; some days are bad; it's impacted my relationship to my spouse and kids; it's affected my career. But I think I am finally seeing a bit of light at the end of the tunnel."

Vignette 14. "Our decision as a board to go public on this misconduct file has cost my daughter one of her best friends," said Rachel. "She *can't* forgive us for hurting Pastor Dan's family."

Vignette 15. "This misconduct impacts so many people!" said Nathan. "And it's not just the victims. Last week I saw Pastor Luke in line at the unemployment office. How sad!"

Vignette 16. At the denominational office, Linda, the financial manager, sat staring at the pile of bills. "I wonder where we are going to get the money for that $15,000 legal bill! Oh, and I almost forgot about that $11,000 bill for the investigation. I expect we are looking at a deficit this year."

Vignette 17. "Our denominational leaders are way off base on this sexual abuse stuff," declared Amber to her friends during coffee hour. "They certainly aren't getting a year-end gift from me this year!"

Vignette 18. Holding the divorce papers in her hand, Mandy wiped a tear from her eye as the last box was moved into the small apartment. It was a big change from the four-bedroom parsonage in Jamesville, but the kids would just have to get used to it. "Damn it, Jim, why did you do it!"

In my experience as a denominational administrator, I have seen that professional misconduct comes with horrendous costs. God wants better for our faith communities. As church executives, we have the power to follow the prophet Nathan's lead in calling out King David's sexual misconduct, no matter how daunting that action might be or how imposing the powers being confronted. What is at stake are the lives of individual church members and the health of the church itself. In a world plagued by sexual misconduct at all levels of society, the church is called to lead the way in embracing a profound culture shift both within and beyond the church. Through the careful exercise of the power at our disposal, we can foster a culture that builds resilience and prevention into the fabric of our communities. In doing so, we can ensure that the costs of professional misconduct are minimized. We can envision a church culture in which victims and survivors feel safe to disclose their pain and abuse and know that they will be supported on their path towards healing.

As I have navigated these painful stories, I take heart in the powerful symbol of resurrection. Christians embrace the conviction that no matter how horrendous the evil or how grievous the sin, pain and death do not have the last word. As church leaders, we cannot allow sexual abuse to have the last word.

In my journey with victims of clergy abuse, I have seen God at work bringing life out of death, healing out of incredible pain, and restoration out of brokenness. I am left with the simple yet profound hope that when we journey with God and are faithful stewards of the power entrusted to us, brokenness and pain can begin to heal through the promise of resurrection and the seeds of new life. As daunting as the realities of clergy sexual abuse can be, I invite us to be confident in the power of resurrection that courses through our lives and our world. We can choose to open ourselves to the power of this renewing, life-giving Spirit and allow it to bind up wounds, restore what is broken, and direct us along healing paths.

25

Opportunity or Curse?
An Institution Responds to Its Past

Bryan Born

On March 4, 2017, I received an email from a victim of Murray Phillips, a Columbia Bible College professor from 1975 to 1991, who had engaged in professional sexual misconduct with a number of women connected with our college. The victim-survivor's message arrived months before the #MeToo movement gained worldwide attention, and I was caught unprepared as the college president. She recounted her horrific experiences with Phillips and told me how it had impacted her life and family and the lives of other victims she knew. Near the end of her note, she challenged me with these words: "None of it happened under your watch, but it is part of the school's history. I hope you will accept my invitation to participate in this as an ally of the women Murray abused. Be their voice. I'm trusting you will do the right thing, Bryan. Be strong, and do not fear. Stand with the victims—past and present, living and deceased. Truth is light, and the Light overpowers darkness."[1]

Most leaders do not like surprises, especially those that threaten their institution's reputation and ability to fulfill their stated mission and vision. A story of professional sexual misconduct implicating a faculty or staff member—no matter when it

---

1 I have not provided the victim-survivor's name in order to protect her privacy.

took place—is never good news for a college president. Neverthe-less, how leadership deals with these situations—even those cir-cumstances for which the current administration bears no respon-sibility—can well become a defining moment for those tasked with providing direction for a community. This was our challenge at Columbia Bible College, and what follows is our story.[2]

Background

In 1991, following the attempted suicide of one of the women Phillips had victimized, allegations of professional sexual miscon-duct were first made public concerning this long-time professor. Phillips had just resigned from his role at Columbia after teaching at the college for seventeen years and running his own counseling office on campus.

As the matter was investigated, it came to light that Phillips had abused at least nine women, the majority of whom had been Columbia students at one point in their lives. Further revelations indicated that a few college and denominational leaders had been aware of some of his sexual misconduct but had forgiven him after he assured them that his "indiscretions" were isolated incidents. His confessions appeared sincere, and he promised never to repeat his behavior. It turned out that Phillips was a master manipula-tor, and he tricked these leaders, just as he had deceived his vic-tims. A brilliant intellectual—devious and charismatic—Phillips was allowed to continue his abusive behavior long after he should have been confronted and stopped.

In the years prior to the revelation of his misconduct, Phillips had been a sought-after speaker and counselor, even described by one church leader as a Mennonite "guru." This image was further bolstered by his leadership of the Second Mile Christian Commu-nity in Kenora, Ontario (a type of Christian commune devoted to exploring Christian theology during the summer months). One

2 Columbia Bible College, located in Abbotsford, British Columbia, is one of Canada's largest Bible colleges. It is affiliated with the British Columbia Conference of Mennonite Brethren Churches and Mennonite Church Brit-ish Columbia.

322 • Bryan Born

prominent Vancouver evangelical leader at the time described Phillips as perhaps "the most gifted young preacher in B.C."[3] His personality and giftedness drew many to him and allowed him to victimize the vulnerable women with whom he came into contact.

When Phillips's reprehensible behavior was first revealed, it was treated as sexual sin—as adultery or a sexual affair. However, as his victims and their advocates challenged college and denominational leadership to dig deeper and understand the root issues, the larger Mennonite community was forced to confront the reality of clergy or professional sexual misconduct. It became more clear that the significant power differential between a professor or counselor and his students or clients made this kind of behavior a matter of abuse of power and exploitation rather than illicit sexual conduct. Professor Carol Penner of Conrad Grebel College explains it well: "It is a violation of the role (to protect and care), it is a misuse of God-given power and authority, it is taking advantage of vulnerability, and there is an absence of meaningful consent to sexual contact."[4]

Phillips operated from a position of power, and he used it to fulfill his own twisted desires. Phillips's capacity to manipulate and deceive began with his victims and then drew in people from the college and church community. Deception is the trademark of professional sexual misconduct, and it allowed him to repeat this activity over a long period of time. Penner provides additional insight:

> The church leader often couches the abuse in the language of love, leading the woman to think that she is entering a mutual relationship. Men who abuse often choose or groom women who are hurting, or whose

---

3 For more on this story, see Jantz, "Women and Community," 20. Pages 18–22 of the same *Christian Week* are full of the best reporting on professional sexual misconduct to be found in Christian literature of that time period.

4 C. Penner, "Violence against Women," 193.

personal boundaries have already been violated. An abusive pastor will often justify himself by saying that God approved the relationship, or that the woman is central to his functioning as a minister. Sometimes he will manipulate his victims by threatening to take his own life, or to physically harm them if they tell anyone.[5]

According to Phillips's victims and others who knew him, this description of the abuser's mode of operation accurately reflects his words and activities. One of those he abused put it this way: "He created an alternative reality in which he redefined his victims' values. It was mental and spiritual seduction first."[6] The effects on those who experience this type of abuse are disastrous and far-reaching. As mentioned at the outset, the original impetus for reporting Phillips was the attempted suicide of one of his victims. One of those abused by Phillips describes the impact his actions have had on her life as not only "physical rape" but also a "soul rape."

Another painful aspect of this story is the initial response of college and denominational leadership. More than twenty-five years provides some perspective, and those in leadership at that time had little experience and few resources for dealing with a crisis of this nature. Yet Phillips's victims repeatedly expressed frustration with the mediation process and spoke of being re-victimized by those who were supposed to be their advocates.

It took nearly three years before the process resulted in an apology and a clear acknowledgement from the College Mediation Recovery Team that Phillips had engaged in professional sexual misconduct. Eventually, the college and Mennonite Brethren and Mennonite Church Conferences provided some financial help for victim counseling and small cash settlements for two of the victims. In retrospect, some observers have suggested that the process moved too quickly from acknowledging the reality of the events to mediation and largely missed the important role

---

5   C. Penner, "Violence against Women."

6   Jantz, "Women and Community," 20.

of ensuring accountability for the abuser and vindication for the victims. FaithTrust Institute (formerly known as The Center for the Prevention of Sexual and Domestic Violence) reminds us that "there can be no healing without justice-making." According to founding director, Marie Fortune, such justice-making involves truth-telling, acknowledging the violation, compassion, protecting the vulnerable, accountability, restitution, and vindication.[7] Much of this process was left undone when I received the email in 2017 inviting me to stand with the victims.

Responding to the past

When confronted with our past, I had to decide what we were to do about it in the present. What was our responsibility now that this evil and painful chapter from our past had resurfaced? I confess that my initial gut reaction was not a courageous determination to stand up for justice. Instead, my first inclination was to retreat to the safe position of the college administrator who duly does everything possible to protect the reputation of the institution. I was selfishly frustrated by having to clean up a mess that I had done nothing to create. I wanted to find a way to make this complaint quietly go away. But fortunately God got my attention, and my first thoughts were soon replaced by a commitment to meet this courageous woman.

Before long I had the opportunity to sit down with this determined woman, her advocate, and one of our college board members. Listening to her story impacted us deeply, but as college leadership we were still unsure about what to do. I personally felt a need to protect our reputation and ensure that our ability to fulfill our mission would not be harmed, and I delayed doing anything public. Instead we focused on our internal structures. In the years following the Murray Phillips scandal, Columbia had put in place various boundaries, policies, and procedures to prevent a reoccurrence of this type of activity. Now, having been challenged by the re-emergence of this story, we re-checked and reinforced

---

7 These elements of justice-making are drawn from Fortune, *Is Nothing Sacred?*

our commitment to training and protecting our students against professional sexual misconduct, but we did not do or say anything publicly.

Two things happened to spur us to public action. First, in the fall of 2017, the #MeToo movement burst onto the scene with almost daily revelations of horrendous misbehavior perpetrated by powerful men, and it became clear that the public landscape on issues of sexual misconduct had shifted dramatically. Second, the woman who had told me her story took me to task. In another email message, she asked, "What's taking so long?" I had no good answer. I knew I needed to come up with a response, and I knew I needed to do what was right by these women.

I soon met with a crisis management expert, and along with much other good counsel, she provided me with an article that radically challenged my thinking: "Urgency. Accountability. Transparency: Lessons from Maple Leaf Foods SVP Randy Huffman."[8] It just turns out that much of the content of this article on a food processing company is remarkably applicable to responding to professional sexual misconduct. Here was an account of a public company, with no overtly Christian connections, acting the way the Bible teaches us to treat those who have been victimized. Here was an example of a righteous response when an institution fails badly.

In 2008, Maple Leaf food products were contaminated by the listeria bacteria, which resulted in twenty-three deaths and fifty-seven other cases of serious illness. Maple Leaf's Huffman tells of how they determined they would respond to the victims and their families: act with urgency, take accountability, dare to be transparent. That sounded like integrity in action. Indeed, that is the kind of response Christians are called to exhibit, especially leaders of faith-based institutions. Rather than hiding their history, Huffman owns it. Often when Huffman begins a presentation, he starts by telling his audience that he works for a company that took the lives of twenty-three Canadians. Moreover, Maple Leaf's

---

8 "Urgency. Accountability. Transparency," *NEWS@IVEY*.

corporate training videos show a hearse arriving at a cemetery to drive home the point that bad decisions have bad consequences.

Huffman also emphasizes that organizations must be accountable. According to the article, "There were two groups he didn't take advice from: the accountants and the lawyers, . . . emphasizing that he was more concerned about clear, honest, and humane communication than the prospect of legal battles or lost sales." I do not know if Huffman has any faith commitment, but that is one of the most Christian declarations I have read. Do what is right, not what is cheapest, what is most expedient, or what simply makes the problem go away.

Prompted by the perseverance of a survivor, and inspired by a crisis management expert, our Columbia lead team and college board came together with denominational leadership in December 2017. Together we determined to schedule a conference on professional sexual misconduct for mid-May 2018, which would be held at Columbia Bible College. Partner organizations would be invited to assist in planning and organizing the event.[9] We would provide a press release in early 2018 for the *MB Herald* and *Canadian Mennonite* announcing the conference. This press release would also provide some historical context explaining what happened with Murray Phillips while employed at Columbia. Columbia would advertise the event in our Mennonite churches but also reach out to other denominations and invite them to participate. In organizing the conference, we would invite the victim to share some of her story and appoint someone from Columbia to lead a workshop on the Columbia response to how professional and personal sexual misconduct is addressed both in the curriculum and on campus. And we would invite someone from the *Mennonite Brethren Herald* or *Canadian Mennonite* to write about the conference, including information about what happened with Murray Phillips at Columbia, an explanation of professional sexual misconduct, and a discussion of the dynamics surrounding power imbalance and factors such as gender and age.

---

9 Mennonite Central Committee British Columbia's End Abuse program coordinator proved especially helpful.

Once the commitment was made to go public, we immediately went to work. The first person to contact was the survivor who had first brought her story to my attention. I communicated to her that Columbia was willing to own the Murray Phillips chapter of our history in an open and transparent manner. In addition, our leadership believed that the moment provided us with a way to seize the opportunity for hope and healing instead of hiding from the curse of shame. We wanted to develop and promote practices, policies, and procedures that would protect the vulnerable and lead to healthy interactions between women and men. Her response to our planning committee was full of grace, and although she eventually declined our invitation to tell her story publicly, she repeatedly expressed her support for the conference and her gratitude that we had responded to her challenge.[10]

Organizing the conference went smoothly. Representatives from the B.C. Mennonite Brethren, Mennonite Church B.C., and Mennonite Central Committee B.C.'s End Abuse program were determined to ensure we had a strong program.[11] Almost everyone who was invited as plenary speakers, workshop presenters, or panel participants quickly agreed. A number of our Columbia staff were especially engaged in looking after organizational details and communications pieces.[12] Aften Thiessen, a member of our planning group, teamed together with Columbia faculty member David Warkentin to serve as co-hosts for the conference. Everyone involved carried out their responsibilities with diligence, sensitivity for the topic, and considerable creativity.

---

10 I support and respect the survivor's decision to decline our invitation. She has experienced an enormous amount of pain on account of Phillips's actions. She displayed an incredible amount of courage in contacting me and challenging me to address those events from years ago. I will always be thankful to her for not giving up, even when I was moving much too slowly.

11 Denis Federau (B.C. Mennonite Brethren), Aften Thiessen (Mennonite Church B.C.), and Elsie Goerzen (Mennonite Central Committee B.C.'s End Abuse program) all played an important role on the planning committee.

12 Erica Bain and Laura Abraham were especially helpful with organization and Stephanie Jantzen with communications.

Early in the planning process I was contacted by Glenn Fro-
ese, the spouse of one of Phillips's victims, and invited to meet
with him for coffee. This turned out to be another deeply forma-
tive experience for me. Glenn is a big man, and if he so chose,
he could be rather intimidating. Considering that I represented
the institution that had caused him and his wife so much pain, I
went into our meeting with some trepidation. Glenn turned out
to be a kind and gracious man who has walked a painful journey
with his wife. He wanted me to hear their experience and share
what Columbia and other Mennonite organizations were doing to
prevent this type of activity from ever happening. He recounted
their story and shared some of the deep emotional and relational
waters they had traversed. Listening to the ways that they had
been abused was gut-wrenching, and I emerged from that meeting with a new level of understanding of the devastating consequences of professional sexual misconduct. His willingness to be
vulnerable with us all at the conference was a precious gift, and
his words touched us all.

A number of people, some quite close to me, asked me why
we held a conference on professional sexual misconduct. But as
we met with some of those who were abused and reflected on
their stories in light of what it means to follow Jesus, we knew
that sweeping it under the rug was not an option. We are called to
be those "who hunger and thirst for righteousness" (Matt. 5:6).
We had a responsibility.

Moving forward

As we at Columbia communicated at the outset of our conference,
if someone was victimized by Murray Phillips while he taught
at Columbia Bible College and would benefit from counseling
services, Columbia is committed to assisting with the health and
healing God wants each of God's children to experience. We are
committed to doing the right thing. A long-running, horrible set
of events with far-reaching consequences happened at Columbia Bible College some three decades ago, and that same type of
behavior still takes place in many organizations today. For us at

Columbia, we were provided with an opportunity to own our past. Doing so means that we are committed to doing whatever we can to ensure that professional sexual misconduct never happens on our campus again. And if, God forbid, it ever does re-occur, we will deal with it with urgency, accountability, and transparency. We are committed to acting with integrity, justice, and courage.

When I first met with the person who brought our curse into the light, she challenged me to see the situation as an opportunity. It took time for me to come around to that point of view, but she was right. As the church, we have too often avoided the conversation. However, we should be out ahead on the issue of professional sexual misconduct, not lagging behind. As disciples of Jesus, we are called to invite people into transformed, redemptive communities. This means doing everything in our power to make sure people are safe from sexual misconduct within our church and ministry settings and learning how to respond faithfully and well when we encounter people who disclose that they have been harmed.[13]

I conclude with a prayer of repentance and appeal for forgiveness that I offered at the conclusion of my opening address for our #ChurchToo conference:

Tonight we lift our prayer to you, O God of love, healing, and forgiveness. God the Father, you breathe life into your whole Creation. Jesus, help us rest deeply in your presence. Help us give our fear, pain, and grief to you.

Holy Spirit, you move through our lives in unexpected, and sometimes unwanted, ways. Lord, I confess that I did not want to re-open this wretched story of deceit, abuse, and manipulation. But we believe that it is only as your Light pierces the darkness that true forgiveness and healing are possible.

---

13 The date of the #ChurchToo conference was May 25–26, 2018. The opening statement made at the conference can be found here: https://vimeo.com/274113638.

Lord, the leaders of Columbia Bible College tried to deal with this sin decades ago. We cannot speak of their motives, and we struggle to judge what could or should have happened at that time. In many ways, we are without knowledge. But what we know is that sin exercised its power through a man and through a system; we know that women were deceived, abused, and re-victimized; and we know that for many, justice-making failed to take place. For all these sins, we express our sorrow.

Today, as a Columbia community, we admit that we have been too slow to acknowledge the depths of the victims' pain, too unwilling to own our past, and too quiet about confronting the sins of abuse of power and sexual misconduct. For these sins, we repent.

Lord God, we are not unaware of the battle raging around us. "For our struggle is not against enemies of blood and flesh, but against the rulers, against the authorities, against the cosmic powers of this present darkness, against the spiritual forces of evil in the heavenly places" (Ephesians 6:12). We take responsibility for our attitudes and actions, while acknowledging that we desperately need your presence, power, and love to help us defeat the dark forces that seek to tear apart our relationships, our families, our churches, and our communities. Save and strengthen us, Lord Jesus.

Lord of Life, hold in the palm of your hand all who are most affected by sexual misconduct in your church both in these days and throughout the generations. May our repentance move us towards a renewed life as a community of the Beloved. Grant all who turn to you the courage to participate with you in restoring this broken world to wholeness, so that everyone and everything may share in the hope of your kingdom.

Lord God, who calls us to new life: Touch us with your presence and power: Heal us, restore us, and transform us. All this we ask in the name of Jesus, the one betrayed and yet the bearer of perfect love. Amen.

26

Poems

Elizabeth Wenger

Elizabeth (Liz) Wenger (1946–2022) was an artist and poet from Goshen, Indiana. She created many pieces of art using the medium of needlepoint, had exhibitions of her work in both the United States and Canada, and published three volumes of poetry. In an introduction to her 2017 art exhibit through the Goshen Historical Society, Wenger was described as "an artist of vivid imagination and emotional depth" whose "needlepoint paintings are vibrant and sometimes painful meditations on life, faith and what it means to be alive."

Wenger's poetry addresses a wide range of themes, including the theme of disability because Wenger lived with a physical disability her entire life. Another important theme in her work is the pain of sexual abuse. Wenger was born in 1946 in Goshen, Indiana, to parents Ruth Derstine Detweiler and John Christian (J. C.) Wenger, who was a prolific author, popular speaker, and professor of theology at Goshen College and Goshen Biblical Seminary. The following poems were previously published in Elizabeth Wenger, *Foretaste: Poems* (Goshen, IN: Pinchpenny, 1972), or Elizabeth Wenger, *Heal on Monday: 31 Poems with Line Drawings* (Goshen, IN: Pinchpenny, 1974), and are reprinted here with permission from the publisher.

Psalm 139:8

"It's up to you,   If
It's up to you,
It's up to you," he said,   I
"I'll turn away,   ascend
I'll close my eyes.
Just see me turn my head!" he said.   to
"Just see me turn my head."   heaven

    "I know for sure,
    I know for sure,
    I know for sure," I said,
"You'll turn again,   thou
You'll look at me   art
And disapprove my bed!" I said.   there!
"And disapprove my bed."

    "Because I care,   If
    Because I care,   I
    Because I care," he said,   make
"I'll watch you close,   my
Your man will go   bed
And you'll have me instead!" he said.   in
"And you'll have me instead."   Sheol,

    "Because I care,
    Because I care,   thou
    Because I care," I said.
I'll turn my love   art
To willful ways

And wish that you were dead!" I said.
"And wish that you were dead."   there![1]

---

1 Wenger, *Foretaste*, 14.

conFRONTation

if tears won't pay
  I rare
  to rush
the Finished blush
that mouths "O—K"

if words won't sway
  I flair
  my bait
at large-head weight
that drops "You—may"

if hands won't pray
  I dare
  Four Fears
in beard laced ears
that shake "Don't stay"

if eyes won't play
  I stare
  unKissed—
the high-rise fist
that thrusts "No—way"[2]

---

2 Wenger, *Foretaste*, 13.

I Am Who I Am

I don't know why I removed my rings.
My shoe slips, my skirts laugh
And I can forgive the frizzies
When my hair hangs—Most becoming,
That rubberband won't force
A fallen style that betrays the cynic
(I believe.)
I don't know why I removed my rings.

I don't know why my Hero sings.
His hold slips, his sons laugh
And he can forgive the Lizzies
When his Word hangs—Most becoming,
That poppycock which won't force
A fallen style that betrays the cynic
(I believe.)
I don't know why my Hero sings.

If I am too weak to cry out,
Let me laugh at the frizzies
And Lizzies. May I sing and forgive
To Lay aside my rings—Most becoming,
That ceremony which won't force
A fallen style that betrays the cynic
(I believe.)
If I am too weak to cry out.[3]

---

3 Wenger, *Foretaste*, 36.

The Rent

Teased, I match my caller by cunning
And, angled through a throat lined with blood,
My clear questions splice his carved eyelids.—
This skeptic's humor whirls to fling
One shrapnel view against a heartish iron.

I've heard the logic he outlines now:
Prepare with steel! An easy recluse,
The antithesis rusts in corners,
Its lame overture too aslant
To beacon its comely, witty stance.

The steel is his, a respected head
Which ego-posts its boundaries
And seldom steadies an orphan to tack
Extra sheeting that buckles on the joints
Or dreams to craft my thoughtful stronghold.

The floor lies level. The mat between
Our shoes hesitates on reflections
Of a guarded doorframe and we, startled
That my rich blood could beg for a furnace,
Can simply forget past resurrections.[4]

---

4 Wenger, *Heal on Monday*, 8–9.

Uncrossing the Bar

Fevered upon
   dry sand, iced & dark,
      legs seem peninsulas

Kisses are blown
   to forge empty air—
      boomerang, flat

Dock shrugs away—
   a mannered, wet dot—
      bare feet float, drowned

Fingers work up—
   smear vapored wreakage;
      sanded weeds—crumbled

Water will sound,—
   a gag to my breath:
      holy, as His!

Craft turns to sand—
   castles to smoke-stacks—
      me, to—me, only

Crying, exploring
   pools, bony rock—
      eyes, a firm 'no'[5]

---

5 Wenger, *Heal on Monday*, 46–47.

27

Confronting Power inside a Peace Church
A Congolese and North American Dialogue

Sylvia Shirk and SWANA FALAGA Sidonie

In this chapter, the two of us—a Congolese Mennonite woman, Rev. SWANA FALAGA Sidonie from the Democratic Republic of Congo, and a North American Mennonite woman, Rev. Dr. Sylvia Shirk from the United States—engage in dialogue about abuse in our respective Anabaptist churches.[1] We are both theologians and pastors. We talk about abuses of power in our own respective cultural context and about sexual abuse and sexual violence as manifestations of abuse of power. Our theological collaboration has been an unfolding journey of partnership. We met for the first time at the 2003 Mennonite World Conference in Bulawayo, Zimbabwe. SWANA was a representative of the African Mennonite Women Theologians of Congo. Sylvia was an interpreter for a research project collecting the stories of international Mennonite women leaders. SWANA was one of the women interviewed by Sylvia and her colleagues during the conference. Since that time, we have en-

---

1 This chapter uses the authors' names as each is used in her own context—formal surname in capital letters for Rev. SWANA and first name for Sylvia.

joyed other opportunities to build friendship through letters, phone calls, and visits in Canada, Paraguay, and Congo. Our contacts have allowed us to deepen a dialogue concerning the passions we hold in common—theological work, pastoral vocation, and women's experience.

Our dialogue reveals contextual differences and similarities and helps each of us to reflect on our own respective context in order to minister more effectively. We are inspired by the example of Jesus Christ who came to this world to offer not suffering but abundant Life (John 10:10). Below we take turns reflecting on abuse of power and the church's response from our respective contexts before offering some joint theological and practical reflections.[2]

A Congolese perspective (SWANA)

The African Bantu tradition does not like to dishonor a leader.[3] This example concerns both power abuse and sexual abuse. My maternal aunt lost her two daughters, who died on the same day in 1980 because she reported that the village chief had solicited her for intimate relations. According to custom, after having resisted his demand, my aunt should have kept the solicitation a secret. By speaking out, she had dishonored the guilty chief, and for this reason she became the victim of a double human loss. With his magic power, the chief caused the death of my two maternal cousins in order to punish and harm my aunt who had revealed "that which should not be reported." The chief is viewed in our culture as extraterrestrial, untouchable, superior, extraordinary, immune to condemnation and disparagement, infallible—in spite of his bad character.

---

2 Sylvia has translated SWANA's reflections from French to English, and both of their reflections have been lightly edited for clarity.

3 Bantu refers to a group of more than 200 languages belonging to the Niger-Congo language subfamily, including Swahili, Xhosa, and Zulu, or to a member of any of the Bantu-speaking peoples living throughout the southern half of the African continent.

In an effort to gain broader perspective on the topic of power and sex abuse in the Congolese church, I conducted interviews in 2018 with several colleagues where I live in Kinshasa, the capital city of the Democratic Republic of Congo.

In one of my interviews, I spoke with ABONAFANGA HATA Evelyne who is a Baptist pastor and professor-colleague of mine at the Christian University of Kinshasa. In addition, I interviewed two male Mennonite pastors, FALANGA GITULO Leonard and SHA FIMBO a Gimeya Delfin.

Pastor FALANGA GITULO explains familiar cultural practices: "The Bantu leader is replaced by someone else only after the death of a predecessor." According to Pastor SHA FIMBO a Gimeya, continual power by a ruler is justified in order to protect their own people from fear, so that the latter will not be avenged or judged by an incoming government administration. ABOFANGA Evelyne says,

> We see the same thing concerning training for the leaders' replacement. The spirit of tribalism and nepotism and corruption is present even in the Anabaptist church. We see unlimited arrogance. Leaders lack the humility and resignation exemplified by Jesus Christ (Mark 10:42–45) and by President Mandela of South Africa. Many African leaders, and Congolese in particular, always expect to be promoted, despite their record of chaotic mismanagement. Bad advisors like Job's [in the Hebrew Bible] are those who say to leaders: "Now it's your turn to be in charge, a chance you get only once, so take advantage of it." Protection of the leader by their supporters in the name of partisan interests regardless of the failings of the leader, dictatorship, lack of a transformational spirit—for example, like Moses in Exodus 15:22–25—and lack of initiative, magic power . . . These are also abuses of power.

Lack of clear vision or a plan of action, inattention to the past life and the behavior of the candidate to whom the church intends to give authority, is equally one of the causes of their abuse of power when in office. Additional causes are greed (thirst for money), egotism, poorly defined criteria for election, undeserved honors, and lack of training before their term in office. There is also a misinterpretation of Anabaptist doctrine in Congo concerning nonviolence: people erroneously think that to denounce evil is a form of violence.

These conversations with peers reveal a number of factors that contribute to abuse. The lack of term limits allows leaders to remain in office for life. Power passes down within the family or ethnic group. Future leaders are not properly screened, and their past failings are minimized. Those in authority are not given adequate training for leadership. Abusers contort Anabaptist theology to justify abuse.

A North American perspective (Sylvia)

Reflecting on a lifetime of experience in the North American Mennonite church, I have observed that pastors and church leaders abuse because they can. They can abuse because they are often more educated and more articulate than members of their congregation. In many cases they are older than the people to whom they minister. The majority of pastors in Anabaptist congregations enjoy the privileges of patriarchy. As religious leaders, representatives of the Divine, pastors are granted an authority which is out of proportion to their humanity.

In contrast to the leaders, the congregants are children, women, and men who are taught to trust in the care of their pastoral leaders. Anabaptist congregants in many churches have learned submission to the authority of the leadership. Many Mennonite communities stress obedience as a virtue, especially for women and children. Communities transmit to their children a culture of shame related to sex and the body, with little education for healthy sexuality.

A scenario in which leaders are overly empowered and congregants are disempowered is ripe for abuse. Church leaders abuse because the opportunities for abuse present themselves on a regular basis. They abuse because the likelihood of being caught or challenged seems minimal. In a church culture where the lesson of the Gospel hymn "Trust and Obey" is applied not to only God but also to the pastor, leaders can abuse their followers.[4] And they do.

Further reflections on Congo (SWANA)

One example of an appropriate use of power is the story of a pastor named GHYMALU Enos who told his congregation, "Despite any gift you may give me, I must reproach you in the case of any fault you commit." This pastor's behavior is to be applauded and encouraged. Churches are not firm when confronting sexual abuse because the abusers are among the major donors. To speak of their faults or to punish them or to seek their expulsion from membership would result in the church's financial loss.

In the Congo I heard a story about US churches that confirms that power abuse is rampant on both continents: A Christian who was a great American donor asked his pastor not to preach about sin—or else he would leave the church. As the man of God chose not to bow before the evil requirement of his solicitor, the donor eventually left the congregation. This pastor in the United States acted as had the previously mentioned Congolese pastor GHYMALU because he recognized that the quality of the people in a congregation counts more than a great quantity of unscrupulous members. One cannot allow oneself to be corrupted by an offender at the expense of the other believers who need eternal life. It is not just the threat of lost financial gifts to the church that keeps pastors from denouncing abusers. A good number of pastors are themselves sexual abusers, and for this reason, they cannot condemn persons like themselves or preach on this subject.

For my master's thesis, I researched the sexuality tradition of my Pende ethnic community in Congo, which offered insights into the sexual behavior of church leaders.[5] Pastors often lack

---

4 Sammis, "Trust and Obey."

5 The thesis is titled, "La vie sexuelle chez les Pende hier et aujourd'hui: cas des Pende du territoire de Gungu, Province de Bandundu, RDC" [Sexual

sexual maturity and self-awareness. Aside from their abuses of power, there are also those related to human sexuality. These abuses are committed by Christians and pastors. Certain causes mentioned below are at the source of the evil which gnaws at the Anabaptist church.

Created in the image of God, pastors often lack the fear of God in sexual matters and have little self-control and discernment when they experience an unexpected sexual desire.

Despite their honorific titles, pastors receive neither premarital training in matters of conjugal or dysfunctional sexuality nor training in leading seminars or preaching about sexual abuse. There is also the problem of sexual obsession, of Bantu culture that authorizes polygamy and polyandry and promotes the superiority of man over woman despite both man and woman being created in the image of God (Genesis 1:27).

Pornography in films, on television, in print, and via radio programs are also a means of facilitating sexual abuse. Preoccupation with pornographic images is a reality in the United States just as it is in Bantu cultures.

Another root of sexual misconduct has to do with monotony. Some believe that by going elsewhere, they can have a change of flavor with different partners. These sexual abusers say, in other words, that it is impossible for them to consume the same food every day, ignoring what God says in Genesis 2:18, "It is not good that the man should be alone; I will make him a helper as his partner," and in Genesis 2:24, "Therefore a man leaves his father and his mother and clings to his wife, and they become one flesh."

To justify sexual abuse, some argue that Kings David and Solomon had many wives, forgetting that these stories are told to us to inform us and not to promote this point of view, which is

---

life of the Pende yesterday and today: The case of the Pende of the Territory of Gungu, Bandundu Province]. An article of the same title based on the thesis was published by the Circle of Concerned African Women Theologians in Theologiennes a l'epoque des realites africaines, 2007. For an English article based on this thesis research, see Swana, "Marriage is words," 82–86.

not authorized by God (Gen. 2:18, 24). Humans are called to cling to one spouse.

In my master's thesis, I highlight several additional causes of sexual abuse. Poor sexual practice in the marriage leads to other problems. Many husbands do not know how to prepare for genital relations throughout the day, nor do they observe the position of spouses in bed suggested by Song of Songs 2:6 and 8:3. They do not know what they should do before, during, and after the genital act, important moments in which to convey their attachment as God wills. According to Genesis 4:1, "the man *knew* his wife Eve!"

Furthermore, many marital relations are not affectionate because they are not carried out in a way that is desired by both partners. For this reason, there is need for organizing seminars, conferences, and retreat days on the theme of marital life in order to instruct partners to properly carry out their genital relationship.

Other causes of abuse I discuss in my thesis include forced marriages due to an unplanned pregnancy and the loss of traditional Pende schools that prepared young people for marital life. In some marriages there is conflict over the sex of the children, and a husband goes elsewhere to seek a child of the sex he prefers, especially male. He does this even though, biologically, the determination of sex depends on him.

Marital privacy is a problem in some Congolese homes, due to the position of the parents' bedrooms in relation to those of children. This is especially true in houses without ceilings. In those living conditions, the marital partners cannot fully enjoy their lovemaking. Other difficulties include the inability of the spouses to live together consistently, due to work and other constraints. The arrival of children in the marriage may lead the wife to orient her love toward them and to neglect the emotional needs of her husband. Lack of understanding, insults, curses, slander, and authoritarian attitudes between marriage partners also open the door to sexual abuse.

Married life is a part of our social life about which pastors speak very little. It is the same for the taboo related to the term *sex*. The Anabaptist church in my context does not apply firm sanctions for sexual abusers. All the causes already listed, among others, lead married partners and pastors into sexual abuse.

Why the church doesn't respond

Churches don't want to react to sexual abuse by a pastor because they are used to hypocrisy and covering up evil. They have fallen into the habit of always whispering what should be shouted, for fear of being excommunicated by the powers-that-be and thus becoming alienated within the community. There is also a lack of courage and the protection of family and friend relationships. Churches are corrupted by materially and financially powerful persons who take charge and take hostage.

When a victim accuses a pastor, the church is hampered in its response by its image of their leader as a person who they expect will be benevolent, trustworthy, even sinless. The abused person in contrast is seen as a morally weak individual. If it's a matter of believing the accusing victim or the accused church leader, the church wants to believe that their pastor would not have committed an immoral act. Blaming the victim, especially if that person can be dismissed and silenced, is an effort to do away with unpleasantness while the church continues its façade of saintly religious practice.

Biblical and theological resources

Christ came to destroy the works of the devil and to reestablish right relations for human beings one with another and with their Creator. New Testament passages such as Titus 2:1–13 and 2 Peter 3:11–14 show that, even though fallen, those who turn toward Christ in repentance receive pardon. Pastors and those who sexually abuse should remember these texts.

The letter of Titus was written to the early Christian church to guide the emerging movement and to promote ethical behavior within the community, especially on the part of leaders. Biblical scholar Joanna Dewey writes about Titus, "The letter opening is followed by an exhortation to appoint elders in the towns of Crete, a list of qualifications for elders and bishops, and a warning against those the author considers false teachers who upset households."[6] The biblical writer speaks of training (2:12) and of hope for a glorious future (2:13). The tone of the 2 Peter text is one of envisioning new personhood, expecting the dawn of a new heaven and a new earth.

Both of these texts are useful for the church. These biblical passages call church leaders to account for abusive behavior and hold up standards of integrity. The texts suggest the need to actively train the whole community, to strive holistically for justice and peace. Living into a vision of new heaven and new earth, the church is urged in these texts to pursue restoration for both the abused and the abusers.

Liberation and Anabaptism are two useful theological resources for those who confront abuse in the context of a peace church. Liberation theology lifts up the epistemological privilege of those oppressed by the abuse of sex and power. In the confrontation between abuser and victim, it is the voice of the one abused that receives preference. Anabaptism rejects hierarchies and sees the church as an egalitarian assembly of believers, where no sister or brother is more holy than another.

Moving toward grace and all things new

Based on SWANA's research, training emerges as a preferred way of preventing abuse of power and sexual abuse in the church. Those who are preparing to hold office need to be trained to steward the power of their positions. Pastors need to be trained to understand and take responsibility for their own mature sexuality and marital relationships. Both in the USA and Congo, church communities, inspired by the Pende ethnic tradition, need to provide consistent training in healthy sexuality for children and young people.

Perversions of Anabaptist theology allow abuse to fester. The church needs to be clear that denouncing abuse and holding abus-

---

6 Newsom and Ringe, *Women's Bible*, 452.

ers accountable is in the spirit of Anabaptist nonviolence. Christian peacemakers confront abuse as they pursue the biblical vision of a new heaven and a new earth where justice is at home. This work includes creating seminars for Congolese Mennonite pastors and their spouses to address the causes of sexual abuse and expanding use of resources such as the Healthy Boundaries training being provided within Mennonite Church USA. Attendance at these trainings, designed by the FaithTrust Institute, is now being required by regional church conferences for all credentialed leaders.[7]

While abhorring the destruction and violence of sexual and power abuse, we also desire to extend God's grace to abusers. Those who turn to Christ in repentance receive absolute pardon. Leaders must renounce abuse of power in order to avoid the fate of Moses who, at the end of his life, did not have permission to enter the Promised Land (Numbers 27:12–14). Echoing Jesus's call to a person caught in adultery to "Go your way, and from now on do not sin again" (John 8:10–11), sexual abusers are called to renounce their abuse to avoid God's judgment (Hebrews 13:4) and find the joy in heaven for the sinner who repents (Luke 15:7).

Turning toward those who know the devastation of sexual abuse and trauma, including the abused, the abusers, and their families in church communities around the world, we move in a positive direction by gathering resources. Church leaders can be trained. Congregations can create safe(er) space. Policies and procedures can be put in place so that the church is prepared to handle reports of abuse. We move in a positive direction by dismantling structures that give unchecked power to church leaders. We move in a positive direction by breaking the silence about abuse, telling both about the pain and about the healing. We move in a positive direction by exercising the courage to stand with victims and survivors. We walk with sisters and brothers on the road to justice and healing. Hope rings out in the words of a hymn that echoes

---

7 FaithTrust Institute, based in Seattle, Washington, is a national, multi-faith, multicultural training and education organization with global reach working to end sexual and domestic violence.

the biblical text: "New earth, heavens new, Spirit of God moving. Sing a new song of the One who has said, I make all things new."[8] May it be so.

---

8   Loewen, "New Earth, Heavens New."

28

Untangling Life on Wednesday
A Journal of Healing from Abuse

Brenda Gerber

This chapter comprises a compilation of journal entries. It is a monologue, unravelling the long and twisted strands of surviving childhood sexual abuse—here, one Wednesday at a time. Writing has become a means of both venting and healing, of talking to God and digging deep into the peace theology of my Mennonite faith. I was born into a large Conservative Mennonite family, grew up on a farm in rural Ontario, Canada, and continue to attend a Conservative Mennonite congregation. However, if a family or faith group or sports group can maintain a good name only by suppressing stories of misbehavior and evil—

It is a façade.[1]

Our hearts long for perfection and I'm intrigued by how many people become very resistant to factual stories that reveal dark under threads of violence in plain communities. This begins to make sense if having perceived safe places where all is well and the sun shines and children's laughter fills farm fields lets these people have the golden reality that somewhere right now all is

---

1 My sister broke the silence hidden by the façade when she wrote about our experience growing up on the farm and, in particular, about the sexual abuse she experienced. C. Burkholder, *No More Silence*.

as it should be. To have that come undone is to hit at the heart of humanity. Our longing to be home in paradise.

But.

I won't be silent. Children are being offered to maintain that façade. Where the peace and wholeness is real, it will outlive any and all exposure of cult-like leader control, mothers turning a blind eye to their children being abused, fathers using daughters to gratify lust, house fathers crossing boundaries of trust and respect, and sons sexually attacking animals.

Gold is not destroyed by fire.

—untangling life on Wednesday

* * *

Deeper or forward, there have been times I was told straight up and other times round about to not feel discouraged because I had regressed. Or to not forget to keep moving forward. But. Going deeper can look like moving backward. Old ways of coping pop up. Old neural tracks are reactivated. Sleeplessness and hyper awareness are there like a weed that refuses to die. And no amount of cheerful talk can really provide the muscle needed to live in wholeness. Many times, I think we shut off that part crying out to be heard and find socially acceptable ways to numb the pain and dull our thoughts. Work. Church. Doing good. Quiet time check list (oddly enough). Looking for praise. When instead the way of life often leads through dark and quiet places. Those caverns of mystery in the heart waiting to be descended into. There are plenty of shortcuts available, but the treasure of wholeness requires willingness to be still. To feel. To ask. To search. To descend. God has written eternity on our hearts and part of that is a discomfort which accompanies cosmetic fixes to our wounds. Here's the thing. In the same territory as the wound, lies the purest desire. If we can find the courage to walk and crawl our way into those places, we will discover a savior like no book can describe and His words about himself will begin to glow and warm on the pages. And as those desires that lay buried beside the wounds gasp back to life, eternity will begin here on earth

—life on Wednesday

⁎

Until about six years ago, I lived with condemnation nipping at my heels. A constant low-key hum of fear. On sunny days, it receded. Sometimes. But there were nights when I'd wake up in cold sweats of fear with a deep darkness so physical as to be tasted and felt. Fear is too weak a word. I don't yet fully see all the links connecting this powerful prison, but I know one of the key holders was the belief that any day, any time, with one small choice, I could be on the wrong side of eternity. The goat. On the left. The worm never dying in the unquenchable fire. And there was nothing offered in those dark times as an option. Nothing that was warmth and invitation. The path out of this torment didn't look like a miracle. It looked like a coming undone. It looked like losing all I had believed. It looked like foundations crumbling. It looked like loneliness. It looked like climbing into my car in the evening and driving to one more appointment with my therapist, Helga. It looked like just getting out of bed and facing one more day, even though getting out of bed required more energy than I use now in one day.

And the change happened. I was meeting Jesus. In ways that defy human speech, he was freeing me from intolerable powers and generational forces. He was showing up as I screamed my throat so raw it hurt a long time after. He was putting his nail scarred hands over the claws squeezing my throat (and taking them into His own dear hands ohsweetJesus) He was dancing me into truth. Light. And laughter. And then one night I woke up. Last summer I think it was. And the dread was there. The metal in my mouth. The panic. And even in the grog of midnight, I recognized this enemy who had cohabitated with me for years and with the confidence I once could only dream of as one hears of interstellar travel, I rebuked that spirit. And. It left. Today I am held. I am loved. I am pursued. And I'm safe because my friend tells me when I'm straying. I saw the wolves tear at his flesh when he came to rescue me. So, in His truth and His love for me, I rest. I am saved. I am sealed. I am marked as His

—untangling Wednesday

***

A significant player in my untangling has been the Presence of the Spirit of God. And my learning to lean on him rather than my own understanding. Trust does not come easily for me, especially when my body and brain are on scream alert. But. He doesn't seem put off by that. Unlike the spirit I grew up hearing about. The one who would leave at a moment's notice. The one who had feelings so easily offended that I barely dared breathe, let alone blab out my thought of distrust and unbelief. The one who, like a dark malevolence, crept up and down the aisles during "revival" meetings. Looking with those red eyes. Just like the nighttime monsters. And only by sitting motionless and breathing really, really shallow did I have a hope in hell of escaping attack. And one day I looked square at that monster and renounced him, the multi-headed beast, and in a drench of icy metallic sweat, invited the sweet Presence of God to come. I was not yet ready to invite beyond a friend beside me. And yes, I was in my thirties. And yes, I've been a Christian since my teens. And yes, my life changed. But. I see how he was with me when I couldn't yet see hear smell or feel him. And now. Dot to dot. Our children like the 1000-plus numbered dot to dots, and one day I looked at a partly completed picture and thought: This. This is how it is to walk in the spirit. The whole picture is there. In the dots. But I can't see it. I follow him from 1 to 2 to 3 to 4. Some moves are very tiny. Some cross the page. Some don't make any sense. But always, there's that moment when, *Aha! There's the picture!* And no, don't spoil the quest by looking at the back of the book. Let the beauty of discovery and exploration unfold one dot at a time

—(and there I end a quite, to me, unexpected)
untangling Wednesday

***

Does knowing chapter and verse add authority to your Bible quote? Are the verses there to aid your ability to out-quote the person arguing with you? What do you do when the leather-bound book gives icy shivers when it's opened in front of you? How do you reconcile the fact that slavery is condoned, incest excused, oppression validated, all with a verse to back up the policy? How do you come to terms with the gray fog that descends on your brain when 1 John 1:9 is recited?[2] What do you think is really going on when someone holds a certain version in such high regard that they are adamantly unwilling to examine and test in comparison to the text from which it came? My relationship with the Bible has been complex. Today I am struggling to be honest. But sometimes honesty carries a price tag. Especially honesty about what is inside my own heart and mind. Today as I ponder my belief about the Bible, I see parts of a large stained glass window. I see the 3:00 a.m. spiritual battles where verses whispered through my mind and I spoke them out in defiance against the dark hordes. I see the dream where I spoke out the prayer Jesus prayed, and as the words giving the glory, power, and honor to the Father were said, violence erupted all around me and I woke into battle. I think of the day as in tears I pled with God to just please cut through all the voices, and I did a straight read right through 1 Corinthians 11–14. And how I broke down sobbing as God turned me around and showed such abundant life that I could only equally rejoice and grieve. I think of the year I felt something akin to physical hunger to read the whole book in three hundred and sixty-five days and again whisper the idea to have chapters come as email and find an accountability friend. And I read quickly, lightly, and free from the heavy voices laying *shoulds* and *musts* on my head. And chain by iron chain, link by rusty link, neuron and cell one after the other, God is freeing and renewing my mind. Far from finished but delighting in how God again and again shows me pathways hidden. Sometimes through low doorways. Through tangled brush. Through packs of wild dogs. But truly I am finding the vitally living truth of "thou wilt show me the path of life, in thy presence is fullness of joy, at thy right hand are pleasures forevermore."

—untangling Wednesday
(thank you Spirit of God; you gave me words)

---

2 "In the beginning was the Word, and the Word was with God, and the Word was God" (1 John 1:9).

***

Don't be afraid of your pain story. Many times, your most meaningful life work will rise out of it. Find a safe person. Start talking. Draw. Paint. Sing. If you are a follower, ask Jesus to teach you redemption. Listen to those around you, but don't put their voices above Jesus's.

Words. Drop. Lost in the fog. Resonance dulled. Muffled. So much to be said. But no one within hearing distance. Vocabulary distorted. Events for which no English word exists. Eyeless and earless listeners. Echoing turning corners into obstacles. Speech fragmented. This is how it is to speak of spiritual abuse.

Ten years ago, I knew deep in my bones that I was on the side of right and God when I confronted abuse in my family. Even when church leaders called my husband and I on the carpet to tell us how wrong we were. Even when my parents told me to be quiet and that my husband and I were tools in Satan's hands. I knew one thing. I would *not* be silent. Never again. And as my foundations began crumbling and fury like I never had experienced was unleashed on me and the ones near, I never stopped choosing to *not* be silent. The last year has brought a shaking of generations-old silence that is stunning and awe inspiring. Today I do not regret the bloody last ten years. I'm not the woman I was. And I'm so proud of the woman I was. I call back and say, *Go, girl! You feel utterly alone most days. But you're not!* And I don't feel alone anymore.

Forgiveness. If I am to forgive like God does, and I believe God waits to forgive until the offender repents, then—. But what if? What if all have been forgiven? What if when Jesus took on all sins and curses and said *It is finished* it really was finished and a thunderously heavy door that had been barred and locked since Eden swung wide open and the Father stood there with tears pouring down his face as his children came home? But. We get to choose. The door is open, but the reunion happens when we choose to stand up and walk through. So I chose and keep choosing to forgive the one who preyed on my innocence and those who still refuse to call evil evil. But the reunion has not yet happened. The door is wide open. And I wait. Because of Jesus I get to partner in this tremendous gift of forgiveness. Too often the Christian world tries to hang forgiveness as a cruel and heavy burden on those who already have been stripped and beaten instead of presenting it as a beautiful gift of freedom and empowerment. When I forgave the man who had chained me to him, the chains shattered, and I walked out of the cell into the light. There's nothing better than light—for me there isn't. But the reunion has not yet happened. And I wonder. I wonder about what surprises await those who have forgiven unspeakably wicked actions. So, yes, I will forgive as my Father forgives. And at this point in my life, I have a lot of questions about the mystery in that statement.

—untangling Wednesday

* * *

Dissociate: to sever oneself. I can still at times feel it. The slow crawl of my skin. The moving darkness in my periphery. The helmet weighing heavier and heavier. The inner stillness and outer trembling. Sometimes I left and hovered. Other times I crept inward too deep to be found. Nowadays this topic brings lessened reactions but still my body shakes uncontrollably, and I fight to remain present.

—untangling Wednesday

* * *

I remember the day I discovered that the moon's cycle and the female cycle run approximately twenty-nine days. Later I found out that when women live in or near nature, they are at the ovulation stretch at the same time the moon reaches its fullest point. Full moon. When I sit and think deeply about this and let its reality seep into my mind, I realize—I already knew. I knew that comments about *the curse* and *look out, she's at that time of the month* and *oh, I'm just hormonal* did not reflect the whole truth. I knew that locked into my DNA as a woman was something deeper and broader than anyone had taught or spoken. And only recently have I been discovering the untapped spiritual authority I have as a waxing and waning, ebbing and flowing, sad and delighted, singing and crying, silent and hollering woman. There is a reason so much shame has shrouded women's emotions and reproductive cycles. There is a reason that at certain times as women our actual body just swells up and we have had *enough*. There is a reason we and the moon run in sync when not blocked. And as a woman, I want to continue learning why my creator put this power of new life, this deep hunger to be a conduit of new life, this cell-level knowing that life is in constant flow, this cell-level inability to let life flatten into an unbroken monotone—all of this plus much more. Into me. A woman. Teach me God.

—untangling Wednesday

* * *

I remember the fear and the steady reminders via sermons, encouragement, books, and tracts. Don't stray from the straight and narrow path. The repeated theme was *once off, forever off*. And although a small hidden flame guarded by the Source of Life never believed, my will and mind tried valiantly to walk in The Way. So, when the day came that my world went through a series of seismic events and I was left under the rubble, what I didn't see as clearly as now is that The Way had also vanished. There is little in my inherited vocabulary and theology I can draw from to explain what happened next. The one story that made sense was the children of Israel's flight out of Egypt and long walk through the wilderness. But here's the thing. First, I had to go, with the Lamb of God, back into Egypt. We went from house to house and fought a bloody war to release all the pieces of me that were locked, trapped, and guarded for years. The other picture that made sense in those years was nesting dolls. I was the big doll, but all my stackables that should have been carried inside were strewn through Egypt's houses. During that time, I didn't talk much about what was happening. Mostly I felt like I was in a parallel universe where small talk didn't even make sense, much less hold relevance with my reality seven days a week. But during that time, I saw power structures and ancient lies in ways that equipped and prepared me for a task that only my heavenly Father knows the scope of. And although he has shown parts and revealed glimpses, I do not see what all he has in mind. One thing he has made crystal clear though, is that all he asks is my honesty. Just be honest, he says, when I'm in tears after yet another vision on a Sunday morning in a venue where no space is provided for visions. Just be honest, he says, when I'm feeling utterly crushed and bruised from the horror of the past. Just be honest, he whispers, after I've raged and screamed and asked why he gave me these gifts and then sent me as a girl into a Mennonite home. And every time this comes as a relief. I can't change much around me. I can't make anyone see. I can't find the magic sequence of words or the correct theological phrases that open eyes to the wickedness hiding inside the Temple. But—and it's a big *but*, I can be honest—somehow his advice or imperative always holds a warmly scented welcome. His words carry his breath. And in him I rest.

—life on Wednesday

* * *

Peace. Safety. Wholeness. Harmony. How ironic that I took on the role of *peacemaker* in my family. I looked the other way when I stumbled on nasty stuff. I tried (unsuccessfully) to defuse escalating arguments. I hid feelings of fear and anger. Because that was avoiding conflict. That was keeping peace. I grew up hearing that we are peaceful people. Don't fight. Don't sue. Turn the other cheek. Don't take anyone to court. Don't resist evil. Don't ever say no. This was the definition of peace. But it's not. Peace is not an interval of nothing. It's not avoidance. It's not an agreement to silence. Peace is a living, muscular force. It is choosing to look at wickedness inside our communities. It is open-eyed examination of my own heart. It is sitting down and taking time to explore my thoughts and feelings around difficult topics. It is, first and foremost, following the Shepherd who not only defines peace but is peace. He is the one who breaks down the walls of hostility. He is the one who witnesses fingering and groping and rubbing and patting and poking. He is the one who leads down dark halls into shadowy corners. He is Light. Healing. Freedom. And this is peace.

—life on Wednesday

* * *

Out of the hardest and most painful experiences emerges the diamond hard core of being that cannot be shaken. This center, this core, this eternal flame of truth is guarded by the father of light in whom there is no shadow of turning. A few years ago, in the middle of the night, I had a vision in which I stood at the front of the church of my childhood and told my story, which at that time was one of danger and an enemy breathing down my neck. The audience sat quietly unsure by all appearances, and then the back door flew open and a handful of men in black swaggered down the aisle breathing scorn and mockery with every step. *Ha,* they mocked. *Don't listen to her. She's making it all up.* I saw the red hatred flames in their eyes and knew. As soon as we left that building, I'd be dragged into the nearby grain field and got rid of. Desperately I cried out, *They're evil! They're hiding as men. Someone. Anyone. Please help.* But I saw each person on the benches had shuttered their eyes. A wild fear shook my body. I had no hope, if no one believed me. As we exited the building, I saw dark shapes moving through the hedge around the churchyard and knew that the helpers were biding their time until everyone had gone home. The sky turned black, and I went from one person to another, but no one would look at me. It was like I didn't exist. Bile rose in my throat.

I realized no one was going to help, but then, one young woman met my eyes. That's all it took.

And I woke up.

All day I lived in two worlds. One as real as the other. And I wondered how this was going to unfold. The fear was still present. And the knowledge of dozens of beings prowling and pacing the churchyard perimeter. But something unexpected happened. I saw the church again. The yard. The fence. The hedge. And I asked God's spirit, *What now? What happens next?* And here's what happened. He entered that building and rose into a great column of shimmering light and wind and swept up one aisle, across the front, and back the "women's" side, and there was an immediate blaze of glory light so radiant it sparkled as his presence cleansed all shadows and dirt. The sky was pure. The clouds fluffed. Grass fresh scented. No hearses at the front gate. And the sun shone on the hedges where only birds and chipmunks busily lived their cry of praise. Then he, Spirit of God, invited me, and I climbed the steps beside him, a child filled with joy so indescribable it could be expressed only by twirling and laughing. And so, I twirled. And the walls of the church were clear like glass, and there were no shadows, and he had done the work, and it was so beautiful that it healed.

—untangling life on Wednesday

29

Is There No Balm in Gilead?
When There Is No Healing for the Wounded in the Community of Faith

Elsie Goerzen

This chapter explores the reality of the pain experienced by those who are in a relationship with an abusive partner and find no place to go with their pain, even though they are part of the community of faith.[1] Two women share their stories of hurt not only by their partner but also by their church family.[2] I examine how a church can be helpful to someone experiencing abuse and take a look at how the practice of confrontation described in Matthew 18 can be applied in a way that can bring healing and hope.

For over three decades, I have had the opportunity to be a support to many women who have experienced intimate partner abuse—the last fifteen years with the Mennonite Central Committee British Columbia (MCC BC) End Abuse program. The

---

1 "Is there no balm in Gilead? Is there no physician there? Why then has the health of my poor people not been restored?" (Jeremiah 8:22). In the NIV translation, the last half of the verse uses these words: "Why then is there no healing for the wound of my people?" Gilead is a region in Palestine with groves of balsam poplar trees, which have a resin that can be harvested and made into a soothing healing balm. The old spiritual, "There is a Balm in Gilead, to make the wounded whole," is a familiar use of the term.

2 Names and other details have been changed to protect identities.

courage of the women I have met continues to astound me as they raise children, manage households, hold jobs, and often continue to deal with the abusive behavior of their partner or ex-partner. MCC BC End Abuse offers hope to the women who come to us through individual and group support. Every week, forty women come into one of four ten-week phases of the healing journey work through the When Love Hurts groups. These groups are facilitated by trained women, and over the years of my involvement, over four hundred women have experienced the healing and change that this opportunity brings them.

The End Abuse program also offers accountability and support groups to men who want to learn to be healthier in their relationships. Home Improvement has seen several hundred men over the last nine years of that program, and change at times is evident, as the men learn healthy ways of relating to their partners. Many of the men have wives and partners in our women's groups. We are also aware that at times men experience abuse by their partner. However, the percent of men in this situation is much smaller than it is for the women.

Research conducted over many years by a number of scholars indicates that the rate of abuse in Christian families is similar to that of the general population: at least one in four families are impacted by intimate partner abuse.[3] The difference is that Christian women stay in their relationship longer because of the commitment they have made and the vows they have spoken before God.

Everyone in the family is affected, not only the one being actively abused. Children suffer, and the one behaving abusively is not living a healthy life. The most important person to support is the one experiencing the abuse. When friends and family say they want to be neutral and not take sides, they are actually siding with the person with the power: the abusive person.[4]

---

3 Nason-Clark, Fisher-Townsend, Holtman, and McMullin, *Religion and Intimate Partner Violence*, 106.

4 Bancroft, *Why Does He Do That?*, 287.

Over and over, we who work in the End Abuse program have heard how pastors and churches simply do not understand the pain and impact of abuse and offer unhelpful and often dangerous advice to the woman who risks coming to them looking for help. The End Abuse program offers an annual three-day training for pastors, advocates, students, and counselors, and yet it is rare that a pastor attends. Pastors hold a position of power in the church, and their lack of education in this area of life puts them at risk of doing great harm to families who come looking for help. Below we hear from two women directly about their experiences of abuse and how their church responded, beginning with Leona.

Leona's story: My church let me down

The emotional and verbal abuse by my husband had escalated to the point that it was unbearable. I had become a shell of the person I had been when we married. His angry outbursts accompanied by bizarre, unexplainable behavior were becoming regular occurrences. He spoke to me in commands and with sarcasm, and I felt more and more like his servant, employee, student, or child, not a wife loved in the way the Bible tells husbands to love their wives as Christ loved the church. He regularly told me how "stupid" and of "below average intelligence" I was with those exact words and in variations like "I miss having intelligent conversation" or "I married for love not brains" or "I rescued you when I married you."

Any time I tried to discuss a marital conflict, he would simply tell me to leave if I was not happy. I had shared with him my regret over not having attended university, and he also knew how much value I placed on marriage and all my relationships, whether with friends or family. He used that knowledge to attack me where he could hurt me the most. He often told me how boring I was.

A turning point

Shortly before our thirteenth anniversary, I asked him if he was committed to our marriage and he replied, "No." I can pinpoint that as the moment I lost hope of things ever improving. Hope deferred makes the heart sick. The confident, independent, capable, resourceful, fun-loving woman I had been when we married was slipping away. I spoke very little because I felt my voice counted for nothing. I hardly ever laughed. I had gained weight by masking my pain with food and alcohol. I felt confused most of the time.

A wolf in sheep's clothing

I thought I was marrying a man who loved the Lord and loved me. I had been excited about serving the Lord side by side wherever God would lead us. I was horrified the first time my husband exploded after we were married and told me I was seeing a side of him he had hoped I would never see. He was a wolf in sheep's clothing who was unable to keep up his religious façade in an intimate setting. Throughout our marriage we were actively involved in whatever church we were attending: in home groups, Alpha, kids' vacation Bible camps, and food programs. I was on staff in one church. My husband sang in the choir and was treasurer for a widely known mission group. Despite his good works it was clear that I had fallen in love with the man my husband had only pretended to be.

Education on abuse comes to our church

In the fall of 2017, I attended a seminar facilitated by Karen McAndless-Davis, co-author of the book *When Love Hurts: Understanding Abuse in Relationship*. Karen was invited to put on her seminar by the Community Care Coordinator of the church where I attended, and extensive fund-raising had been done to make her seminar affordable for the women in my community.

For me, the seminar was a godsend because, although I had read Karen's book years ago, during the first time I left my husband, it was while listening to Karen that my denial finally fell away and I clearly saw that what I had been enduring in my marriage was abuse. It now had a name. I decided soon after the seminar to make a plan to leave my marriage and begin a journey of healing.

364 • Elsie Goerzen

Part of my plan was to speak to my pastor and let him know what had been going on behind closed doors and why I was leaving. Naively, I felt confident that he would understand because he had attended Karen's seminar along with an elder of the church. The pastor told me that he understood the situation but that I should expect that not everyone in the church would and that there would be a taking of sides. While I was in his office, someone opened the door without knocking and saw me sitting there. It was awkward and uncomfortable, especially because it was the elder and his wife, who were the leaders of the home group that my husband and I attended.

Abandoned by the church

Since I left my husband and had the meeting with my pastor, I have not been contacted again by the pastor or anyone in leadership at the church. *Out of sight, out of mind,* I guess. I know that my husband sang in the Christmas choir, has had regular coffee visits with the elder who attended the seminar, is treasurer of a Christian ministry in the community, and continues to attend the home group. The home group leaders have come alongside him and I am told by a third party that because they were working with him, they could not talk to me. He has had counseling sessions with a Christian counselor from our church who attempted to teach him empathy.

I left the church and moved away from my community. One woman in the home group has called me twice in the ten months since I moved away, and one couple in our group from a different church have remained in touch. I also had one kind and encouraging email from the church secretary. But that is it.

I see my husband as a wolf in sheep's clothing. He has fooled a lot of people and gathered many allies within the church. That is hurtful to me, to say the least. My only solace is that God knows my heart, how much I value relationship, and how hard I worked on my part in our marriage.

The pain when the church response is unhelpful

Leona's story demonstrates the pain caused when a church does not understand the dynamics of abuse in relationship. The abusive person has a different persona when in the company of church family and friends than when they are in their own home, behind closed doors.

Even pastors who have some knowledge of the dynamics of abuse in relationship can be misguided if they do not listen carefully to the one who is experiencing abuse. The abusive person is good at presenting their version of events in a way that blames their partner for the difficulties, often projecting their own behavior on the victim. This creates a heart-breaking situation for the one who is already beaten down by the abuse, whether physical, emotional, psychological, spiritual, sexual, or verbal. The cycle of abuse is driven by the motivation to have power and control over one's partner.

The one who is abused cannot believe that the person they fell in love with has disappeared once the relationship is solidified, whether through marriage, pregnancy, or simply time invested in the relationship. Then to lose the support of their church adds a double layer of pain and anguish. The pastor must recognize the power they have, as well as the power of the words they use have, to heal and help or to harm. We see this power on display in Olivia's story.

Olivia's story: Love wins

I must have sat at my computer one hundred times, trying to put into words what I have seen, felt, and experienced in the last chunk of my life. I am a domestic violence survivor. That in and of itself is a fairly miraculous statement—that I survived. The culmination of my experiences left me dangling by the throat from my husband's hands, his fingers increasingly tightly circled as my four-year-old and twenty-three-month-old children looked into my reddening face. You might wonder how that moment came to be. My answer is this: the church.

The courtship leading up to my marriage was a fairy tale; unbeknownst to me, it was a thinly veiled fairy tale hiding a nearly deadly, horror-like story that no one around me seemed to believe. My husband was the church treasurer, as thick as thieves with elders and pastors alike. Everyone knew and loved him. It was absolutely unthinkable to our church that he could possibly have done the things I was whispering about as I begged for help and reached out to my church family for support and love. As the first days of our marriage passed, the doting, idolizing, adoring, and wonderful man I had known and come to love melted away into a monster who pushed, shoved, controlled, screamed, and seemed to take sadistic pleasure from every small physical and mental torment he could squeeze into our days.

Fast forward to two years later. I was heavily pregnant, a boisterous toddler in tow, and I had finally fled to safety while my husband was at work, hiding at my parents' home a short drive away. The abuse had culminated in multiple nighttime attacks, leaving me exhausted and struggling to cope with my child and my pregnancy. I could not trust my husband or sleep in his vicinity. My church family, the women I had come to be close to, were well aware of the series of events leading to my exit. It was such a relief to be living in safety in my parents' home.

The pastor's advice

Before I left my husband, the pastor had sent us to a counselor tied closely to our congregation, who had much experience with what he called "difficult" relationships. There was the insinuation that I had failed to submit properly and that I had not respected my partner. "Contracts" were made where we would erase the past and start afresh, as long as I was willing to forget what he had done and have an open forgiving heart like Christ suggested Christians should. I heard a lot of verses and Bible-based idioms like how "God hates divorce" and that I needed to try harder.

I am a life-long Christian. I grew up in a strong, stable, warm, and loving Christian family. I accepted Christ at about three or four years of age, having seen my mother frequently sharing the message of Christ's love with women's groups—and truly modeling Christ's love as a wife, mother, and active community and church member. However, I was raised to believe that the pastor had the final word. He *knew* things the rest of us did not know about God and the Bible. He was *the* authority on God's Word. I *knew* that God hated divorce and that divorcing was a sin as unforgiveable as murder.

I had also witnessed my parents' deep and unending support of other church members experiencing divorce. Looking back, I knew that these people had become pariahs in the church and my parents showed Christ's love in ways most Christians do not. These people were loved unconditionally, welcomed into our home, and treated as Jesus would have treated them: with love, in spite of their "sin," or maybe it was because of it. I knew that divorce was sin, but I also knew that our home saw it not as sin but rather as a circumstance.

Safety at last, but again the pastor's dangerous advice

I was now living in safety in my parents' home. My husband had been arrested and charged, and there was a protection order in place. During this time of separation, the pastor of our church had pursued me actively, having a strong desire for me to "work it out" with my spouse. He had urged me more than once to drop the assault charges because it was not "Christ-like" to press charges.[5] He was aware, or so he said, of the violence that had previously transpired and kept insisting that my husband could and would change. Finally, after we had been separated almost six months, my pastor urged me to meet with him. We met, and I listened, again, to his homily of information about love and marriage, forgiveness, submission, Christ-like behavior, and my need as a godly woman to move past this and begin our marital healing. After hearing this numerous times, I gave in. Every fiber of my being wanted my husband to return to the person I knew before I signed the marriage license. I wanted to believe this was a bad

---

5 In British Columbia, the Crown Counsel lays charges following the police investigation. The victim does not have the right to "drop charges."

dream and I could wake up and find this horror movie over. Our pastor unintentionally played into my deepest longings.

My pastor urged me to allow my husband back into my life. I did so, and the end result was his hands around my throat and my children watching, wide eyed. I breathed and prayed what I believed was my last prayer on this earth: *Father, may I be calm and brave in this moment, that my children will know I fought for them to my last breath.*

I am grateful to this day that I did not meet a tragic end that day, though it was extremely close. I do not know how long I was in his grasp, for as I struggled for breath, I saw the light fading away and just tried with every fiber of my being to stay coherent for my babies.

No balm in Gilead

It is heartbreaking to say that I have never found healing inside church walls. The institution I grew up placing my faith in, the one I was raised and formed in, failed me in the most spectacular of ways in the time of my most dire need. I was pushed out of our core group—pulled aside and quietly told that "you can't both come" because it was too stressful for the others in the group and that my husband had decided that he would go one week and I would go the other. Communication from the group started out well, and then gradually over weeks and months I would only get last-minute notice that he had canceled on his week and that he had shown up before me on my week, and thus I could not come. Group members stopped answering or returning my calls, and the close-knit group of moms I had come to know and love shunned me and left me without any support or person to turn to when I needed love and support. The same was true at church on Sundays, on the days I was brave enough to attend. I was treated like a pariah. Women would not speak to me or acknowledge me, and if they did, conversation was brief and peppered with excuses to walk away or promises to catch up later in the week, which was a cycle of unreturned calls and texts that led me to give up altogether.

My experience initially pushed me into an extremely deep depression, which, if properly labeled, was not really a depression at all. I was treated for depression for several years and then, on realizing that depression was not my issue, began to actively strive to pinpoint, mitigate, and heal my despair. By God's power and the blessings of friends and family around me, I was able to rejuvenate my soul with the only thing capable of repairing its undoing: Love.

While I have stopped attending church, and I do not know if I ever will again, I have a strong handle on the cloud of despair that once entangled me. It is overhead and hovers nearby, but it no longer consumes me or defines my life. I have a deeper understanding of who God—Love—is. God is visible all around me: in my survival, my daily growth, my desire to be present and loving for my children, my ability to see the church for who and what it is and to forgive it. Forgiving the church and the people in it will in no way bring a desire for me to be a part of it, but it does give me freedom from the almost unrecoverable wounds the church inflicted.

These days, I am regularly confronted with my abuser. He is the father of my children and will be present in their lives and in mine until the courts say otherwise. He is a pillar of the church we attended and a leader there as well. His behavior has not changed, and he shows no movement toward stopping or slowing the pathologies that led him to harm me in such intimate ways. It is still fascinating to encounter old church "friends" who inquisitively and inappropriately question why I would so unilaterally remove my husband from my life. Why am I unwilling to work on my marriage? Do my children not deserve a loving two-parent home? It is almost funny to me now, having felt these spiritual jabs so many times. I am nearly to the point of immunity.

Love wins

In the words of the lovely and wise Glennon Doyle Melton, *Love wins*.[6] It truly does. Wounds do not define me, abuse did not end me, the church did not destroy me, and the people sitting in it and "acting in Christian love" did not do anything less than revolutionize my understanding and practice of Love—to myself, to my children, and to those around me.

Love gives me the strength to tell my story, the resolve to continue doing so, and the desire to build whatever awareness I can, in order that the church can learn the true meaning of Love: the kind of Love that shows up when women call to it in despair, that provides the safe haven and support. It can even love the men who abuse women: instead of harboring and perpetuating their abuse and isolating the victims of it, the church can recognize it, come alongside, and be the Love needed to stop the perpetuating harm and devastation domestic violence brings.

The power of the church leader

The church has this incredible power. It can envelop us, give us safety, provide the fertile grounds for spiritual growth, and offer refuge like no other place on earth. It is supposed to feed us and enrich us, and give knowledge and insight as we search to be closer to Christ. The flip side of this, unfortunately, is a poorly understood devastating minefield of spiritually based abuse that is both insidious and radically obvious for those of us whose lives encounter a "taboo" like domestic violence or issues with gender or sexuality. The loving church family we know then becomes a decisive instrument of pain. Armed with verses and misconstrued attributes of God's love, the abuse victim is ushered back to their perpetrator to try harder, to overlook, and to suffer alone. Domestic violence is perpetuated by silence, lack of education, and well-meaning people who think they can pray it away.

---

6 Glennon Doyle Melton is an author, activist, advocate, philanthropist, founder, and president of Together Rising, a non-profit for women and children in crisis.

The church can be a place of healing

Olivia's story dramatically shows how dangerous a pastor's lack of understanding of abuse can be. The role brings a lot of power with it, and lives can be endangered, as Olivia's was. Fortunately, there are also churches that have educated, compassionate pastors, who listen and believe when a woman experiencing abuse in relationship comes to get help. I spoke in a church several years ago, and invited people into a conference room after the service for discussion. Fifteen women came with the pastor and shared their stories of abuse and their stories of how the pastor had been helpful to them. That pastor had previously attended the MCC BC End Abuse program weekend training, "Understanding Abuse in Relationship." He responded to the women from an informed, understanding place, and the significance of that was huge for the women. To be believed, understood, and supported without the pastor giving advice was so helpful. The women asked how they could find a support group, and with the support of the church, a When Love Hurts group was established in their own facility. This pastor also provided opportunity for accountability and support to the abusive spouse. The pastor is now on the advisory committee of the MCC BC End Abuse program, adding wise counsel and perspective to our program. This is an example of the impact a well-educated pastor can have to support healing for women experiencing abuse.[7]

The pastor provides pastoral care but encourages the victim to pursue professional counseling. Funds needed for the counseling should be provided by the church. Couples counseling is not recommended. Because of the power imbalance, and the possible danger to the woman, it is not appropriate in situations of intimate partner abuse. The pastor should also be aware that, in our experience, when an abusive person senses that his partner is telling the truth of the relationship and getting some support, they will make sure they develop a close relationship with the leadership of the church, volunteering for positions, telling their "side

---

7   See Mennonite Central Committee's guide, "Abuse: Response and prevention."

of the story," often accusing their partner of the behaviors they are themselves using to control her. The pastor may try to be supportive to both individuals, thus believing themself to be neutral in the situation. This is not possible, as Lundy Bancroft explains, drawing on the insights of Judith Herman: "It is not possible to be truly balanced in one's views of an abuser and an abused woman." As Dr. Judith Herman explains eloquently in her masterwork *Trauma and Recovery*, neutrality actually serves the interests of the perpetrator much more than those of the victim and so is not neutral. Although an abuser prefers to have you wholeheartedly on his side, he will settle contentedly for your decision to take a middle stance. To him, that means you see the couple's problems as partly her fault and partly his fault, which means it isn't abuse. Bancroft thus summarizes: "In reality, to remain neutral is to collude with the abusive man, whether or not that is your goal."[8]

Restorative justice: Matthew 18 and situations of abuse

For a church experiencing a disclosure of abuse, guidance from Matthew 18:15–18 may cause harm, if there is not an awareness of the power imbalance in a relationship where one partner is controlling the other. Verse 15 states: "If another member of the church sins against you, go and point out the fault when the two of you are alone." This text assumes an equality of power. However, if we think of the woman who has been abused, trapped in a cycle of abuse by her husband, we know that she has likely resisted the abuse for years to no effect, in any way that is safe for her. The abuse has only gotten worse with time. Because of the power imbalance in a relationship where one partner controls the other, it would be dangerous for her to take the step verse 15 describes and confront her abuser on her own. She is one of the "little ones" referred to in verses 6–10. She must make the decisions affecting her life, and the church confronting her husband may make her situation even more difficult. Confidentiality and safety are essential in order to protect her.

---

8 Bancroft, *Why Does He Do That?*, 287.

Too often in church circles, women who have experienced abuse have been exhorted to "just forgive" their husbands, which only serves to perpetuate the cycle of violence, as in Olivia's story.[9] However, if the woman agrees, the church could take the next step described in verse 16. It is very important that the woman is always consulted before any action is taken by the church.

The woman is believed, and the pastor arranges a meeting with the husband in the company of two to three others, perhaps including a friend of his. The group may strongly urge him to go to an accountability group for those who abuse, such as the Home Improvement: Men in Relationship group, which MCC BC's End Abuse program offers for men who want to learn healthier ways of being in relationship. This accountability group might help him feel less alone and assist him in learning tools for healthy relationship building. It is hard work to change the basic beliefs that feed his abusive behavior of needing to have power and control. If the husband responds, and is willing to participate in the group, healing and restoration may be available for him once he is willing to do the hard work.

The woman who has experienced the abuse could be referred to a support group, such as the When Love Hurts: Understanding Abuse in Relationship group that MCC BC offers to women experiencing abuse. If she chooses to go to the When Love Hurts group, she will find clarity in the crazymaking that abuse brings to a woman's life, and she will find the support of other women affirming and life-giving. The church must support her in leaving her abusive partner, if that is what she chooses to do. Often, separation is essential for her safety and for her healing to begin. Financial support by the church may be necessary for her and her children. Maya Angelou has said, "There is no greater agony than bearing an untold story inside you."[10] The effect of being heard and believed by the pastor and the church is profound for the victim.

---

9 Myers and Enns, *Ambassadors of Reconciliation*, 66.

10 Angelou, *I Know Why*.

374 • Elsie Goerzen

If her partner continues to resist the help and discipline the church is offering him, he has chosen not to be accountable, to be an outsider. A change takes place in the community's response to the offender. He is the lost one, the straying sheep.[11] This is not about shunning but about nonviolent resistance to the abusive behavior that is unacceptable to the community. But Jesus is the friend of sinners, and so the community's strategy is to reestablish the relationship with the abusive one, to reach out to him, proclaiming the good news of the gospel, offering "sight to his blindness" as we read in Luke 4.

The restorative justice process described above is challenging and time consuming but could be much more redemptive than a long drawn-out court process, which is the way domestic violence issues are often resolved, at great cost and pain to everyone. The husband and wife may never be reconciled. There may be too much pain in the past for her to ever trust him again. However, he may one day be in relationship again and will be much better equipped to thrive in that relationship. When we engage in the redemptive process of supporting victims and holding offenders accountable, Jesus promises to be in our midst. The health of the whole community is at stake. It will not be easy for anyone as we practice the principles of kingdom living. It will be a long journey, but with God's presence and our willingness to participate in the work of restorative justice, healing is possible for victim and offender and for the whole community.

---

11   Myers and Enns, *Ambassadors of Reconciliation*, 67.

30

Sexual Assault and Pacifist Theology

Joanne Gallardo

L oving your enemy does not seem hard until you have an enemy. In this chapter I share about how sexual violence challenged everything I believed as a pacifist and the journey I took to pick up the pieces after intimate violence changed my life.

I will never forget when I became a pacifist. I was twelve and was not a part of any church at that point in my life. My dad bought an old VHS tape for us to watch the movie "Friendly Persuasion" starring Gary Cooper. Cooper plays a Quaker man whose family refuses to engage in violence, including enlisting in the military, during the time of the Civil War. His reason was that the Bible teaches us to love our neighbors and enemies. He labeled his belief "pacifism," and I knew for sure I must be a Quaker—or at least a pacifist. Even though Cooper goes on to fight in the war, I knew I had encountered a theology with which I agreed.

When I became a Mennonite, I was pleased to find pacifism as a core belief. This was quite a transformative theology to have— regarding an enemy, for instance, with the same love as we have for ourselves. At first I found this easy. As a teenage Mennonite, I tried to see people I did not like the way God would see them. It transformed me. Growing into young adulthood with a strong personality, there were many people who fit into "enemy" territory. After particularly fractious encounters, I would take a step back, breathe, and remember that this person was a beloved child of God. Most of the time, I was able to take the high road and remember Christ's teachings. In fact, I reasoned, maybe I wasn't so different from these so-called "enemies." Weren't we all just trying to do our best at any given moment?

I found quite the rub with this theology when I entered seminary. This pacifist theology taught women to take abuse and transform it into a spiritual experience of "letting go." This theology gave permission for oppressors to impose epistemological, emotional, and physical violence on minority groups because, as Christians, we are taught not to resist but to give permission. This theology perpetuated a culture of abuse within the church, especially at the hands of those with power. My mind waged a battle between offering Christian grace (something I was taught as a teenager) and fighting back (something I was taught growing up). My twenties involved a messy battle between my theological instruction and my lived experience as a brown body moving in mostly white settings where not fighting meant getting stepped on or over. This meant there were many people I was in opposition with, but I had no one that I would label as "enemy."

A new concept of "enemy" entered my life when I turned thirty-one. I had moved to work in Washington, DC, as a case manager to the chronically homeless and severely mentally ill. I loved my clients, and I loved my job. I saw what I was doing as a different type of pastoral ministry, one for which my master of divinity really trained me.

Then something terrible happened.

A few months into my job, a client of mine sexually assaulted me while I was in his home delivering groceries. I did everything I had learned to do as a woman living in a world where this happens to one in four of us at some point in our lives. I told my sex crimes detective that I wanted to press charges. This, I thought, would bring me justice. I looked to the criminal justice system for my salvation, and as with many of survivors of sexual assault, it let me down immensely.

This man was my enemy. He had personally wronged me in such an intimate way, and I hated him. I wanted him locked up and for him to spend the rest of his days rotting in a jail cell. But this was not to be. After a week on a psychiatric hospital unit, he was released and continued to be a client of my non-profit agency. I did not have to work with him again, but knowing that he was still around and that he was a short drive from my home caused me anxiety. Knowing that he was still a client of my open-door, people-first, empowering-the-powerless agency caused me to shake every time I saw someone of his stature enter the property.

All of my highly held theology, the entirety of my seminary degree, and my indoctrination of forgiving and forgetting was tossed out the window and replaced with anger, hatred, and a want for vigilante justice. I dreamed of breaking into his house and hurting him. My blood boiled every time I drove by his apartment. I wished horrible things would happen to him, and there were days I wanted him dead. I sat in these feelings for quite a bit of time.

I learned an important lesson, and it is one I carry with me even now in my work as a pastor. There are people who say they care for you. And they very likely do. But people are flawed, broken, and selfish when there is a fire burning and no extinguisher in sight. That old safety mantra of helping yourself before helping others is an accurate metaphor for life. No one is going to look out for you the way you can. You need to look out for your needs because there is no guarantee that your needs will be thought of by others. Being completely selfless is something many Mennonites have been taught, but following that to its logical end at all costs and at all times leads to no sense of self, or tragically, no self at all. Being your own advocate, your own lover, and your own protector is essential to surviving life as a woman in this time and this space.

I soon learned to become all of those things for myself. I entered counseling where I found healthy ways to deal with my anger. Many times this meant letting it all out, which is scary when you are taught to be scared of strong feelings. I took medication that lifted my mood and helped me see the good in life again. I met with friends as well as my pastor to talk about what happened, and bit by bit, I began to heal. But I did not address what the sexual assault did to me in regards to my faith. I avoided thinking theologically about this, as I did not want my faith in God to be tainted by this life event.

This did not last long, as I am wont to think theologically. "Love your enemies" was the mantra in the back of my mind every time I tried to reconcile what happened with what I believed to be the moral character of God. I knew that what had happened to me was not God's will but the choice of an ill man. I could not "love" this enemy. And I did not know why.

I realized after some time that part of this block in my ability to love my enemy was my inability to love myself. At the root of it all, I blamed myself for what happened. I hated myself for having fallen for what was clearly a trap. As much hate as I had for this man, I hated myself even more. This was blocking my ability to love my enemy, or even my neighbor. I needed to first love myself the way God loved me.

Loving myself did not come easy, and it is still in process. But after I started loving and forgiving myself, old hurts and grudges from years past started to melt away and become less and less painful. I was able to see others the way I saw my young adult self: flawed but ultimately a child of the Creator. I would be careful in dealing with people who had wronged me because I had not forgotten what happened, but I could forgive them and allow myself the freedom to move on with my life. Simultaneously, I still acted as my own protector and resisted that which was not mine to own.

This left me thinking of my assailant. I drew on strength from my community, the empowerment and joy I found in music, and my faith in an all-powerful God to release this man from the tangled roots of my mind and the snares of my anger and wrath. I imagined the roots unraveling from the image of this man and replacing themselves in rich soil, thereby anchoring me more firmly in the ground. The snares of my anger and wrath were pulled out of his skin and transformed into leaves and greenery to show strength and life. I released this man. I released him to God.

To think about loving and forgiving my enemy, my assailant, is a bit of a stretch for me at this point if I am wanting to be intellectually and theologically honest with myself. I respect the love God has for this man, but I also believe God will be the harbinger of justice for me. I do forgive him in the sense that I no longer want to harbor ill will toward him; I would rather put my fire-fueled thoughts toward social justice and kingdom work. In that sense, I have forgiven him. To love him is more difficult. At this point in my spiritual life, I can say that I love that God can love him. And I pray that God might move my heart one day to look at him with the same love and compassion that God's self is capable of. I am also content with this never happening.

This has been my own singular journey with sexual assault. The journey of forgiveness is different for each person, and I in no way offer a prescribed way of loving or forgiving one's enemy after such a violation. That is between a survivor and God. As I have talked with others who have had an experience like mine, many feel they will never get to the point of forgiveness, let alone love. It is my opinion that this is completely fine. No one from the outside can understand the journey of someone who has experienced this form of violence, and as children of God, we are here to listen and not judge or dictate. It may be best to let God work in God's own ways in the hearts and minds of others. I admire survivors for simply surviving. I think everything survivors do along the lines of being a functioning human is a massive hat trick after such a disorienting trauma.

I have had a major lesson in loving my enemy, and I wish no one would ever have to learn it in the same way. I am thankful to God, my community, and my faith tradition for helping me navigate waters I never intended to encounter. Maybe most central of all, I am thankful to the teachings of Jesus, the voice of God incarnate, for helping me find the soil in which I want to grow.

31

Forgiveness
Neither Indiscriminate nor Arbitrary
Johannes van der Meer

Can abuse be forgiven? Can there be reconciliation? Who makes the final decisions in this extremely complicated process? What is the role and the position of the victims in all of this? This chapter explores the topic of forgiveness regarding the abuse of power. I set the stage by sharing from my experience pastoring in the Mennonite church in the Netherlands, then reflect on what I have seen in the Mennonite world regarding and in reaction to abuses of power. I distinguish between power and authority, discuss the abuse of power, and then turn to the relationship among repentance, forgiveness, and reconciliation. I suggest that a Jewish rabbinical approach might be helpful in the search for answers to these questions.

Pastoral context

The Mennonite congregation in the village in the Netherlands where I grew up had a close-knit, active youth group, in which no subject was taboo and where we felt free to express anything and everything about faith, beliefs, and ideology. One of our pastors exhibited great understanding and truly listened. When I would drive home late on Saturday evenings and see there was still a light on in her room, I knew she was wrestling with her sermon. On one of those evenings, I knocked on her door and found her seated in a sea of books, with a notepad and a pen. She said she had not been able to write one word of her sermon. We started talking. After a couple of hours, the sermon was finished. Naturally I was in church the next morning to hear how she had assimilated our discussion.

That became a regularly recurring ritual: talking together about the sermon, then hearing the result the next morning. One time she asked me what I thought of the sermon. I told her the truth: "Rubbish." She smiled and said aloud, "Brothers and sisters, Johannes thought the sermon was rubbish this morning. So, he is going to preach on the same biblical text next week, and he can show us that he can do it better!" That was a challenge I had to accept. The next Sunday I preached for the first time. I was nineteen years old. More sermons followed. She taught me what I should watch out for, what was possible and what not. I learned a lot from her, including when I saw her struggle: writing sermons, pastoral care, the way she dealt with people. She found it difficult, and perhaps that was the reason she was so good at her job. When I had almost completed my teaching degree, I realized there were plenty of people in education but too few in the pulpit and in pastoral care. Thus, I embarked on a new course of study—theology—with all the associated disciplines: languages, psychology, history, homiletics, exegesis, pastoral care, and so on.

Much of what I learned, whether at seminary or while pastoring, I put into practice. Many other things, I have since dismissed and replaced with acting according to my best judgment. In one of the first congregations where I served, a young girl died in her sleep. She was twelve; I was twenty-four; the parents were in their thirties. They were completely desolate, bereft, and I had no words for them—none whatsoever. I did have two arms and broad shoulders. We stood for a long time, with my arms around them, completely contrary to everything I had been taught about distance—especially about no physical contact. But it was the only thing they needed at that moment, and it was right and comforting.

I have encountered innumerable personal situations in my more than forty years of pastoring, all kinds of highlights and low points in people's lives. Where I could, I offered comfort, tried to help them back on the right track, listened, heard things, kept secrets, laughed, cried, cursed, prayed, been confounded, and perplexed. I have also blundered many times and learned a great deal from my mistakes. But *never* has my integrity been at issue. Perhaps this is more a matter of grace than merit, I am not sure, but it does make me thankful.

I know the stories about ministers and other church workers in the Netherlands, where things went terribly wrong. We have developed protocols about how to deal with situations in which there are instances of inappropriate and unacceptable behavior, sexual abuse, and abuse of power. These protocols work, but the often-deep wounds that have been struck endure. It remains necessary to face fully the enormous destruction that has been inflicted and to see the impact of the trust that has been so devastatingly violated. The oft-heard simple call to forgive and forget frequently backfires, proves impossible, or is undesirable.

All these experiences have led to this: nothing really surprises me anymore; nothing amazes or astonishes me. However, this does not mean that certain things no longer affect me or raise my hackles of resistance. Somewhere in the Talmud it states that the greatest sin of humankind is indifference. Thank God, I have not become indifferent. It is out of these experiences, and my study of Jewish interpretive tradition, that I offer the following reflections on the challenges of forgiveness.[1]

Power

According to Maximilian Carl Emil (Max) Weber (1864–1930), the German economist, historian, and academic lawyer—who is

---

1 In the Netherlands, I am on a committee within the Dutch Mennonite Society, which has been working to publish study material titled "Weg van de Tora" (Way of the Torah). These study guides contain lesson material of Jewish exegesis, which teachers of *leerhuizen* (learning houses) can use. Much of my thinking—including, with her consent, in this present chapter—has been influenced by the work of Dodo J. van Uden (MTh). See van Uden, "Weg van de Tora VII," 104–107.

generally considered to be the founder of modern-day sociology—power is the ability of persons or groups to force their will on other people, groups, or matters, possibly against the wishes or interests of the other.[2] Power can be distinguished from authority because authority is legitimized, and power is not.

Power often degenerates into abuse of power. Unfortunately, those who are guilty of such corruption and abuse too often also get away with it. Sadly, we must acknowledge that within the church context, power has not always been appropriately wielded and such abuses have not always been appropriately addressed.

One particularly disturbing story of power abuse that has stayed with me from within a church setting is that of a woman who suspected that she was lesbian. She went to her pastor to discuss it. Wanting to test it out, he raped her and then concluded, "Nope, you're not lesbian." He got away with it. People have no idea how much power other people can have over someone else's life. One of the problems is the unquestioning acceptance of power, where it is claimed to have been given by God.

An additional problem in this is that both a family and a church are reasonably closed communities. Naturally, much has changed. Formerly the complaints of victims of abuse in the church were trivialized, much was concealed and covered up, and perpetrators loudly denied the abuse with large displays of power. Fortunately, a sharp corner has been turned, thanks to the influence of such movements as #MeToo, which has revealed how widespread and extensive the abuse of power is. It seems we have reached some kind of boundary. Those who have been victimized are no longer keeping silent but are insisting their voices be heard. Women and children, the largest category of victims of abuse within religious circles, are being heard more often than in the past, at least within some corners of our Mennonite churches and communities. Their voices are listened to, perpetrators deny allegations, protocols are set up, and mediation processes are started. Simultaneously, it is becoming increasingly clear how complicated it is to make a clean sweep and to clear the mess and put one's house in order.

---

2 Weber, *From Max Weber.*

While these processes move full steam ahead, all sorts of things go wrong again. Shrewd lawyers have their hands full absolving the perpetrators, smoke screens are put up, word games are created, and, through all this, attention is being drawn away from the main issue. Things have happened that never should have happened, and often no one recognizes how much the victims have been wounded and damaged.

In short, when a point is reached in which it becomes clear that someone is guilty of misconduct and someone has been harmed, then within the processes that have been started, we shall have to tread carefully around concepts such as expressions of regret and repentance, forgiveness, and reconciliation. To this end we explore the relationship between repentance, forgiveness, and reconciliation.

Making amends

In the Jewish tradition, making amends is the central element of repentance. In the Mishnah (compiled ca. AD 200 in Israel), we find an elaboration on what making amends means concretely in a certain case. Whoever harms or wounds another person owes them compensation for five things: (1) material (physical) damages, (2) pain, (3) the cost of recovery, (4) time lost (when the victim could not work due to injury), and (5) immaterial damage of insult or defamation.[3]

A few paragraphs further, the Mishnah adds that in addition to compensation for damages, asking for forgiveness is also necessary.[4] Maimonides (1135–1204) formulates this idea more extensively. He underscores that God will forgive us the transgressions we have committed against God but not the transgressions we have committed against a fellow human, unless we first make amends with the one we have injured.[5]

---

3 *Mishnah Bava Kama* 8.1.

4 *Mishnah Bava Kama* 8.7.

5 *Maimonides, Mishneh Torah, Hilchoth Teshuvah* 2.9.

A parable is recounted regarding this in the Talmud (compiled ca. AD 500 in Babylonia), which basically explains it as follows: You can ask God for forgiveness for what you have done to God, and God will forgive you too. But there is no point in asking God for forgiveness for what you have done to another fellow human. You must take that up with that person. You must first restore the disrupted relations with your fellow human before you can restore your disrupted relationship with God (cf. Matthew 5:23–24). Likewise, it is pointless to ask forgiveness from anyone other than the person whom you have wronged because forgiveness is something between the injured party and the transgressor. You cannot forgive someone for what he or she did to another person. Only the person wronged can do that him or herself.[6]

Refusal

The rabbis also reflected on the possibility that an injured person may refuse to forgive the perpetrator. According to Maimonides, not only should the perpetrator repent and ask the victim for forgiveness, but the victim is asked to forgive the perpetrator—at least ultimately. However, it is crucial that the perpetrator actively shows repentance. Forgiveness on the one side cannot be asked for without repentance on the other side. Repentance and forgiveness are two elements of the restoration process that takes place between the perpetrator and the victim.

This does not mean that you cannot forgive another person even if he does not show repentance. However, no one can *require* you to forgive the other person. In a case of no repentance, the forgiveness is unilateral, not a component of a reciprocal process, and, therefore, there is no reconciliation.[7]

Atonement

One of the consequences of a transgression is that it damages relationships, the relationship with your fellow humans, the rela-

---

6 *Babylonian Talmud, Rosh HaShanah* 17b.
7 *Maimonides, Mishneh Torah, Hilchot Teshuvah* 2.9.

tionship with yourself, and the relationship with God. Repentance is necessary on one side and forgiveness on the other side, in order to restore the damaged relationship. The traditional word for restoration of a relationship is *atonement*. Atonement is a possible result of repentance coupled with forgiveness.

The first ten verses of Deuteronomy 30 make it clear that repentance is a process. If the transgression was minor and can be easily restored, then it is a short process. It takes more time with serious transgressions. The same applies to forgiveness and thus also to reconciliation. According to the Mishnah, in some cases, repentance is enough for reconciliation; in other cases, repentance may be indispensable but is not enough. It takes time for the reconciliation process to ripen and mature.[8] A more detailed version of this idea can be found in various places in the rabbinical literature. The Midrash collection Mekhiltah (compiled third century AD in Israel) asks a question of Rabbi Elaszar haKapar in Lod, Israel, about four kinds of reconciliation in the Scripture, which all state conflicting things about repentance and forgiveness. He asks how these four statements can simultaneously be true.[9] According to the version found in the Talmud, forgiveness and atonement are dependent on the severity of the violation. This is a tricky text because not every detail is clear, but it does make apparent that the process of atonement or reconciliation is dependent on the nature and the severity of the transgression.[10] In brief, the process as spoken of in this text can be understood in the following manner. Sometimes, you do or say something wrong, whereby you only need to apologize, and the matter is finished. Other times, the damage to the relationship caused by what you have done is greater, and more time, and perhaps a particular opportunity, is needed to restore the relationship. In the case of a serious crime, even more is necessary than just repentance and time and the perpetrator should suffer visibly having

---

8 *Mishnah Yoma* 8.8.
9 *Mekhiltah Yitro*, Bachodesh tract, *parasha* 7 (about Exodus 20:7).
10 *Babylonian Talmud, Yoma* 86a.

understood the consequences of his deed. Finally, there are deeds which obscure the goodness and justice of the Eternal to such an extent that they can only be closed when the perpetrator dies—at least, if the other three elements are also present.

The challenges of forgiveness: neither indiscriminate nor arbitrary

We must view religion in all its breadth, while determining how and when organized religion may be capable of helping people and improving life and not simply be reduced to proclaiming that the church is no good. However, being open to the ways in which religion can spiritually free, enrich the spirit, and ethically deepen human beings in no way means that you should close your eyes to the perils. It is shocking that people have been severely damaged, that church leaders are not held accountable, and that this abuse is partially brought about because church leaders have the advantage of special status, privilege, and protection. This is a procedural mistake in many churches. However, we cannot generalize about all churches. We shall have to look at the wrongdoers and at the undermining structures within church associations. And we must put into practice unconditional solidarity with the victims.

The call to find an answer as to why it is so difficult to get a grip on the abuse scandals that have afflicted the Mennonite world for years is growing increasingly loud. God's love is measureless and unconditional, and no one is excluded from it, but that does not mean that you must take a forgiving stance in advance. Nor can we say that it is not ours to judge or that he who is without sin should cast the first stone or that one must forgive seventy times seven, after all. This last argument wreaks a great deal of havoc when it is indiscriminately ripped from its context and used arbitrarily. The rabbis teach us in Amos 1:3 that one must forgive three times, no more. This seems to agree with what is written in Matthew 18:15—17. But then, the seventy times seven makes an appearance in Matthew 18:18 and the following verses. These words may not be seen separately from Genesis 4, where, in the context of Cain, the Bible speaks of sevenfold revenge, while seventy times seven is the case with Lamech. The use of these numbers in Daniel 9 raises even more questions that require much more explanation, more than can be discussed within the scope of this chapter.

The essential point is that whenever the emphasis is placed only on forgiveness, this will lead irrevocably to a failed approach. If everything is forgiven, then everything is permissible. Perpetrators and those who protect them understand this all too well. What is bad is bad, and what is wrong is wrong, and saying this, naming it, and hearing it will only help to clarify the situation. No matter who the perpetrator is, whether we are talking about the professor or the pastor, the youth worker or the lay person working in God's church, "who has done so much good" and who, based on this work, has built up good will with the congregation and thus has earned the benefit of the doubt, or even worse, is elevated above all suspicion and doubt, and thus—worst of all—*deserves* to be forgiven. This is a disastrous stance, one that is an enormous blow to the victims, and which does them a huge injustice. The wrong interpretation of forgiveness feeds a permissive culture and appears to uphold it. Forgiveness is not an unfounded acquittal of one's share in damage inflicted. It is not an obligation but a gift, which only the victim is entitled to give. This gift, this deed of love, which is stronger than the desire for retaliation or revenge, cannot be forced on them nor taken from them.

No matter how eagerly some would wish it otherwise, forgiveness and absolution must come from the victim. The victim is in charge of this story. In addition to proclaiming the good news, congregational leaders are also charged with protecting their flock from the wolves. *This* is the role that church leaders must play in this situation, and they must take great care to do so.

Concluding remarks

In this chapter, I have drawn from the wisdom of Jewish interpretive tradition. However, my nieces and nephews in Canada would oft refer to the question, *What would Jesus do?* Yes, what would Jesus, the teacher, the rabbi, have done regarding the question of forgiveness in the context of abuse of power? It is guesswork. We do not know which school Jesus attended to prepare for his teaching. Some scholars believe he was a student of the school of Sjammai, others assert the Hillel school. There is something to be said for both opinions. However, considering that no reports of Jesus's education were recorded by his disciples or eyewitnesses, but that it was all written after the stories of his death and resurrection, makes it difficult to distinguish between reality and proclamation.

I am inclined to believe that Jesus, as Rabbi, explained the Scriptures (that is, the Hebrew Bible) according to the rabbinical rules and practice. When explaining the Scriptures, there is one applicable condition: that each word in the Torah contains seventy possibilities to explain its meaning—just like the biblical number of the seventy nations known at that time. This includes the understanding that there is no one authority that can elevate *one* exegesis to doctrine, thereby denouncing the others. All seventy have equal validity to God, according to an ancient rabbinical principle that had already existed when Jesus walked this earth. However, his explanation does concern what we call the Holy Scriptures.

In following Jesus, we have learned to read these Holy Scriptures from the Torah tradition as the vision of the righteous world, of the Kingdom of God. These scriptures are called holy because they stand up for the *holy* rights of each person. Simultaneously, they formulate the holy *duty* of each person toward his or her fellow creature.

Jesus's connection to and solidarity with the Jewish background he came from is indisputable. The Gospels are records of the Jewish faith, set out by faithful Jews, and, in the first instance, for faithful Jews. No editorial processing or ripping out of context by well-meaning Christians can rob the gospel of its Jewish foundation. This concerns a holy tradition, a continuity, a language, and a style, all of which are at our disposal to help us to better understand and place the Gospels, and thus Jesus, in context. If you were to take scissors and cut out of the New Testament all four hundred and fifty-two passages and quotations that originate in the Hebrew Bible, nothing but a fragmentary body of text would be left, which no sensible person could decipher as a coherent story.[11] Moreover, words such as *amen, hosanna, hallelujah, Sabbath, Messiah,* and another two dozen Hebrew and Aramaic words are untranslatable loan words that still echo Jesus's voice. The Gospel writers themselves admit that they were constantly translating both of Jesus's mother tongues.

Immanuel, which means "God with us," is found in Matthew 1:23. *Korban,* which is an offering, is written in Mark 7:11. But even in that process, linguistic mistakes have crept in. This has also happened with the translation of the title "Son of man," which is the most authentic statement Jesus says about himself, appearing over fifty times in the Gospels, and forming the basis for a whole structure of hypotheses built by various Christologies. The Hebrew *ben adam* and the Aramaic *bar-enasj*—namely, "son of Adam"—mean something like "normal person." Therefore, "son of man" should not be used but "person" or "someone like us," in accordance with the original meaning.

Someone like us. That was Jesus, too. Someone like us, who came to teach, completely in the old tradition, not changing the smallest letter or stroke of a pen (Matt. 5:17), but returning to the Torah and to the explanation, in mutual dialogue, in conversation, to ensure that no one is damaged, and everyone has justice done to them and for them. It is my conviction that that is what Jesus would have done.

11 Lapide, *Er predigte.*

32

Abuse, Worship, and Power in Community

Carol Penner

When I preach or lead worship, I am keenly aware that there are people in the pew who have experienced abuse or sexual assault and people who are abusers. The majority of victims are women, children, and LGBTQ+ people. The majority of abusers are men. How do we lead worship faithfully knowing that our congregation includes both perpetrators and victims? How do we do that in churches historically shaped by a patriarchal worldview to not speak about this type of violence? More particularly, what does it mean to lead contextually appropriate worship in Anabaptist churches that are part of a peace church tradition? What difference can talking about violence make? In this chapter, I explore these questions, drawing on feminist theology, my own life stories, and practical examples of worship resources I have written.

Talking about violence close to home

I grew up in a Mennonite church that said it rejected violence. I remember our pastor outlining the history of our peace position in a catechism class when I was seventeen: "And that's why Mennonites don't believe in violence. We won't participate in wars. Mennonites become conscientious objectors to military service."

In church we prayed for peace, but it was always about wars far away.

I went on to study at a Mennonite Bible college where the peace position was emphasized, connecting it to Jesus's willingness to absorb violence rather than be violent himself. Our professors mostly talked about conflict in relation to war. The year after I graduated from college, I worked as a homemaker for a single mom. When her ex-husband broke into the house and assaulted her in front of me, it was traumatic in many ways. She survived. What did not survive intact was the theology I had received in the Mennonite church. I did not know what it meant to believe in peace when a man was assaulting a woman in front of me. My theology did not fit my life. I simply had no idea how to faithfully respond to violence happening in a family setting.

Over the next months and years, female friends and relatives told me stories about their experiences with violence. One shared how she had been sexually abused as a child. Another talked about how her husband beat her. Another told me how she was sexually assaulted in a campground by a stranger. Two sisters revealed that their uncle sexually abused them as teenagers. Another was sexually harassed and stalked by a theology professor. I recalled the sexual harassment I and every woman I knew had experienced.

The most difficult story for me was from my stepmother, who told me that my late father used to hit her. This was the strangest story of all, because I had not known he hit her, but as soon as the words came out of her mouth, I had a flashback: a strong bodily memory of me lying in my bed in the middle of the night and hearing an angry exchange, the sound of chairs overturning, and my stepmother's voice, "Don't you dare hit me again!" This had never been a conscious memory—I cannot remember ever thinking it before—but it was crystal clear, as if it was happening to me at that very moment.

When I talked to my older sisters about what my stepmother had told me, they said they had witnessed that violence. We had never spoken of it. They also told me that when I was very little and our birth mother still lived with us, she ran into our room in the middle of the night, shaking us awake and crying, "Girls, wake up; Daddy's trying to kill me." I had never heard that story before. Violence was, indeed, close to home.

With newly opened eyes, I wrote a doctoral dissertation on violence against women and Mennonite peace theology. As I studied and dialogued with others, I came to realize more about the violence in our society. I learned that color of skin, economic class, culture, gender identity, and immigration status all influence the rates at which people face violence and how they are treated if they talk about it. Patriarchal violence, where power is used to oppress and hurt those below you on the ladder, is a pervasive and horrible reality. It is a silent war, waged in the homes and neighborhoods in which we live. The casualties are real but mostly uncounted. I wondered why we had never talked about this in church.

The patriarchal power of silence

The early Anabaptists in the sixteenth century were reformers who took issue with a number of the practices and ideas of the churches they were attending. They believed that church membership should be voluntary; adults should make a decision whether to join a church. This theological idea was reflected in their worship, where they baptized adults, not infants. They believed in the priesthood of all believers. There were no special sacraments that designated certain people to be intermediaries between God and the common person. In this new way of thinking about church, everyone should read Scripture, witness to their faith, and follow in the footsteps of Jesus. They believed that God was most clearly understood when the community read Scripture together. The community was the vehicle for divine revelation, as they faithfully interpreted what the Bible said together.

With this theological underpinning, one might assume that women would lead alongside men, sharing their insights from Scripture. Early in the Anabaptist movement, women shared their faith and were persecuted for it, along with men, but the patriarchal worldview shaping the way people related to each other at that time soon diverted women away from leadership. While over

394 • Carol Penner

the centuries exceptional Mennonite women found ways to influence their communities, when it came to leading the congregation
in worship, women were continually sidelined.

When I was a child and teenager growing up in a Mennonite
church in the 1960s and 70s in Canada, all of my pastors were
men. The first time I saw a woman leading worship was in 1983,
which was right around the time I witnessed the woman being
assaulted in her home. I never heard anyone talk from the pulpit
or in Sunday School about sexual assault or abuse in the home
until I began preaching a decade later.

The patriarchal rules that only men could speak in church
meant that women's experiences and stories could not be shared
publicly. Theologian Marjorie Proctor-Smith talks about the "sto-
rylessness" of women and how this impoverishes worship and
limits women.[1] When women have no public venues to share
their stories and the religious meaning of those stories, individual
women facing abuse have to create the theological wheel again
and again, trying to make sense alone of violations they endure.

How is someone experiencing violence to interpret the silence
of the church on this issue? The silence is not simply a void; it carries a lot of freight. They can interpret it to mean that this violence
is not important enough to mention. Aren't the most important
issues talked about in church? If it is important, wouldn't pastors
and theologians be talking about it? Or the silence reinforces the
message that society often gives to survivors: your abuse makes
you soiled or dirty, and it is shameful for you to speak about this
out loud. Or the silence can suggest that perhaps violence is not
even happening at all because, if it is happening, it would be discussed; if it is real, it would be part of our peace theology. The
silence in the church about abuse is a type of gaslighting, a type
of crazy-making. Silence about violence close to home means that
there is no space in the church for people who are abused to name
their suffering publicly before God or to strategize together on
how to change their situation. Silence about this issue in church
suggests that God does not care about the pain of abuse. Silence

---

1 Proctor-Smith, *Praying*, 58–59.

can assure abusers that they can violate with impunity because no one will hold them to account.

A gradual change: Power to break the silence

This worldwide, age-old silence about sexual violence and abuse began to crack as various waves of feminism gained momentum in the twentieth century. The first wave of feminism in the late nineteenth and early twentieth centuries saw campaigns for women's rights. Feminists fought for a woman's right to divorce her husband, own property, and have custody of children—all essential if a woman wants to leave her abusive partner. A second wave of feminism beginning in the 1960s campaigned for wage parity and rape laws inclusive of more types of violence. This second wave of feminism brought the issue of sexual violence and abuse into the public forum of society in North America in the 1970s and 80s. However, this topic was slow to trickle into Mennonite church contexts. There was an occasional article about rape or child abuse in the Mennonite church press in the 1980s; however, it was talked about as if it was a problem "out there" in society and not in good Christian homes. These issues were not raised in any worship settings that I attended.

In the late 1970s and 80s, women started moving into ministry positions in my denomination, the Conference of Mennonites in Canada (CMC), empowered by feminist writers and theologians from the wider church. Mennonite women in CMC interested in leadership met together in Women in Leadership conferences that were held in various locations in Canada and with a sister conference in the United States. Mennonite Central Committee Peace Section started a Women's Concerns Committee in the 1970s, and it put out a bi-monthly report where women were able to discuss, among other things, a theology of abuse and strategies for survival and prevention.[2] Women Doing Theology conferences gave women the spaces to share their stories and find their voices.[3]

---

2 See C. Penner, "Jesus and the Stories of our Lives," 33–52.

3 For a description of the significance of these conferences, see C. Penner, "Mennonite Women Doing Theology," 53–76.

Feminist theology in North America and around the world was blossoming in the 1990s. A theology around sexual violence and abuse was developing.[4] There were hundreds of books and articles published on abuse of various kinds, by writers like Marie Fortune, Phyllis Trible, Delores Williams, Kelly Brown-Douglas, James Poling, and Nancy Nason-Clark.[5] Mennonite theologians like Carolyn Holderread Heggen, Melissa Miller, and many others wrote about how our theology must change to address the reality of sexual assault and abuse.[6] In the Mennonite church, this work was galvanized by a group of survivors who persisted in the face of enormous institutional opposition to expose the abusive behavior of the Mennonite church's most famous theologian, John Howard Yoder.[7] Mennonites organized various conferences about abuse, and numerous writers published articles in church magazines and newspapers on this topic. The repeated message was that abuse and sexual assault was happening and should be exposed. Justice for survivors and accountability for offenders was essential, and safeguards needed to be put in place to prevent abuse from happening.[8]

In the new millennium, there was less talk about abuse. Fewer books were published, there were almost no conferences, and it was rarely mentioned in church periodicals. It was as if the church had reached a saturation point in the 1990s and then veered away from the topic. Abuse issues did percolate at a local level since

---

4 For a thorough history of how this theology was developed in the Canadian church context, see Trothen, *Shattering the Illusion*.

5 Fortune, *Sexual Violence*; Trible, *Texts of Terror*; Williams, *Sisters in the Wilderness*; Douglas, *Subjugated*, 37–43. Poling, *Abuse of Power*. Nason-Clark, *Battered Wife*.

6 Heggen, *Sexual Abuse*; Miller, *Family Violence*; E. Yoder, *Peace Theology*. This theological project was paralleled by feminist historians who documented sexual violence and abuse in Mennonite communities. See, for example, Epp, "Memory"; Klassen, *Going by the Moon*.

7 For a thorough examination of the history of what happened, see R. Goossen, "Defanging the Beast."

8 For an excellent summary of this time period, see Peachey, "Naming."

many churches were mandated by their insurance companies to write and implement sexual abuse policies (sometimes called "safe place" policies) for their churches. But discussion about patriarchy and the gendered nature of violence were harder to find.

The issue of abuse has recently come to the fore again, especially since 2017 and the social media campaign called #MeToo, where women started talking more openly about their experiences of being sexually assaulted and harassed. Perhaps the new openness to naming assault and abuse will result in greater accountability for offenders and justice for survivors, but that remains to be seen. Hopefully for people in the church, it means a resurgence of interest in naming the violence that happens in the home and the bedroom and the other everyday places we live and work. I also hope that we will begin talking more openly about this type of violence in our worship services. Toward that end, in the next sections I briefly outline different ways that the context of violence close to home can be addressed in our worship times together and why that is important.

Scripture: Speaking the word of God

The Bible contains quite a few stories about abuse and sexual violence; however, these passages are rarely read in public. Rape and incest happened in biblical times, and these stories made their way into the biblical text, even if rarely told from the victim's point of view. Phyllis Trible's classic book, *Texts of Terror: Literary Feminist Readings of Biblical Narratives,* was my first real introduction to the stories of Hagar, Jephthah's daughter, and the unnamed woman in Judges 19. Stories like the false accusation of Joseph by Potiphar's wife speak directly to the topic of power and abuse. King David's daughter Tamar chooses to publicly name her violation, and she is ignored by her father; ironically, David's psalms are read in churches continually, while her story is mostly still ignored. Stories about sexual violence need to be read in worship because they resonate with the people in the pews. They should not be passed over, ignored, or considered "not suitable" reading for Sunday morning. Mennonite churches, like most denominations, are reluctant to talk about sex in any context, and when the sex involves violence, there is an added disincentive.

Many churches use a set schedule, called a lectionary, of which scriptures are read each Sunday of the year. Feminist theologians analyze which scriptures are used in lectionary collections and how they are paired with each other.[9] Lectionaries, which were often compiled by male scholars, often pass over stories of women and stories of violence against women, while including scriptures that advocate the subordination of women to men.[10] As Elizabeth J. Smith describes, "A lectionary manages the community's exposure to Scripture by restricting the amount heard in a given liturgy and by combining passages so as to encourage interpretation to go in certain directions. For feminists, manageable Scripture will mean that passages that are oppressive to women are combined with passages proclaiming women's full humanity and religious agency, encouraging interpretation for the liberation of women."[11] Feminists have written lectionaries that are more inclusive of women's experiences.[12] When men's stories from the Bible continually dominate times of public worship, people are taught the patriarchal message that men's stories in our communities should be prioritized.

Some churches in Anabaptist denominations use a lectionary, but it is voluntary; there is no central authority that mandates that churches have to use it. In the Mennonite tradition, and many other Protestant denominations, worship committees, worship leaders, and preachers are given the freedom to choose which scriptures they will read each Sunday. The community commissions them to listen to the Spirit of God as they do the work of worship planning. The planners hold the community in mind as they read the Bible and make selections. Does the worship committee, worship leader, or preacher take into account the

---

9 See, for example, Paris, "The Bible on Steroids," 21–31.

10 Proctor-Smith, "Lectionaries," 88.

11 Smith, *Bearing Fruit*, 84.

12 See, for example, *Inclusive Language Lectionary*; Winter, *WomanWord*.

many people hurt by abuse? Do they imagine how certain scriptures will land in that context? People in charge of worship have power to hurt, ignore, help, or heal through their judicious choice of scriptures.

Translations of the Bible that use sexist language for humanity are often still read in public worship contexts. As Letty Russell notes, "The writings of the Bible took shape in a variety of cultures, but they were all patriarchal, and it is not possible to expect or desire the original manuscripts to reflect sex-inclusive language. Yet it is important that translations be as accurate as possible in conveying the sense of the message in contemporary speech."[13] Choosing more modern Bible translations that use inclusive language for people sends a powerful message that the love of God extends to all, not just to men. Our choice of language in worship can either confirm or challenge the reality of male dominance in our communities.

Sermons: Interpreting the word of God for the people of God

Preachers are given time each week to make the connection between the word of God in Scripture and the word of God in our lives. They are empowered to do this by the community that selects them to preach. Allowing more than just men to preach is essential if we are to hear the word of God fully as a hermeneutical community.

In the late 1980s, I attended a Mennonite congregation that invited me to be part of the preaching team, which included lay members. It was the first time they had asked a woman to participate. It was not then, when I felt unsure on my preaching feet, but five or six years later that I preached a sermon in which I talked about rape. My sermon was about violence, and as an illustration, I told a story about someone who was sexually assaulted. As I preached, when I came to the part where I was going to use the word *rape*, my heart was racing, and I felt my knees starting to shake. To name that reality from the pulpit seemed incredibly risky. This only makes sense if you understand what it means to

---

13   Russell, "Inclusive Language," 586–587.

grow up with this type of violence being unnamed. Similarly, I remember the first sermon where I talked about incest and the first sermon where I talked about pornography. My communities heard sermons about those topics because they invited me to preach. They were open to hearing my words. I will never forget one woman who came and shook my hand after the service where I talked about sexual assault. She did not say anything to me, but I will never forget her meaningful gaze and that one side of her face was bruised with a black eye.

Our pulpits should provide a venue for many different people in the congregation to share their perspectives. Women preachers speak from the experience of being women. When the pulpit is closed to people of color, LGBTQ+ people, or those who live with disabilities, we do not hear their interpretations of Scripture. People preach from their experiences; if that includes abuse or sexual violence, they are more likely to consider that context when they choose their texts and illustrations and make their theological observations.

A person who has left an abusive marriage is going to preach differently about "taking up your cross," for example—perhaps pointing out that not every cross needs to be picked up, nor do they have to be carried forever. They may choose to preach instead on a different major biblical theme like God's call to flee oppression and claim liberation, like in the book of Exodus. A person who was sexually assaulted by their father when they were a child might choose not to preach on the commandment to respect your mother and father, or they might choose to preach on that text in the light of Jesus's words about punishment for those who hurt little ones (Matthew 18:6). A person who did not get justice in the courts after being date-raped might not choose to preach on loving your enemies because they find that impossible, but they might rather choose a passage from the prophets about iniquity catching up with the wicked.

Communities give preachers power by giving them an audience and listening. Preachers can use that power to name the reality of abuse or to mask it, and this can have a powerful effect on people's lives. A male preacher I know named sexual abuse in a sermon; that week a member of his congregation found courage to share her own history of abuse with him. It was the first time she told the story to anyone outside her family. Sermons can be a way to open the church's pastoral care door; they signal that the preacher acknowledges the reality of this type of pain. Sermons can be a conduit for healing. They can convey not just the preacher's concern and care but also God's care and concern for victims of abuse.

Whenever we preach, we should be keenly aware that not only are there people in the pews who are experiencing abuse or violence; there are people who are perpetrators. How is our message good news?[14] We should hear sermons in church where this type of violence is named as both a sin and a crime. Preachers should encourage church members to flee abuse and to seek help from the police. This is good news for the victims, who are encouraged to find safety. In the long run, it is also good news for people who abuse because they are being called to accountability and to repentance. It is important not to demonize people who commit sexual offences in sermons because people are less likely to seek help in the church if they assume they will be rejected completely.[15]

Mennonite theology, with its strong emphasis on turning the other cheek, obedience, and forgiving your oppressor, needs to be interpreted carefully in the context of abuse since this theology has encouraged submission to abuse.[16] Preachers and worship leaders need to resource themselves with books that are written

---

14 For examples of sermons that deal with the topic of sexual violence and abuse, see Sojourners, "100 Sermons."

15 For a discussion of how people who have committed sexual offences can be included in church life, see Yantzi, *Sexual Offending*; C. Penner, "How Inclusive Is the Inclusive Church?"

16 For a summary of the issues around Mennonite peace theology and violence against women, see C. Penner, "Mennonite Peace Theology," 280–92.

not just by white men; many excellent books have been written on the intersection of abuse and theology.[17]

Occasions in the church year

There are times in the church year when speaking about abuse and sexual violence is especially appropriate. On Good Friday we remember the crucifixion of Jesus. We say Jesus was "abused" because he was whipped and his body was nailed to a cross, but there was another element to that abuse. Matthew 27:26–31 and Mark 15:16–20 record that, surrounded by a group of soldiers, Jesus was stripped of his clothes, a cloak was put on him, and then he was stripped of that, and his own clothes were put on him again. His clothes were stripped from him again before he was crucified (Mark 15:24; Luke 23:34); he hung naked on a cross. We do not usually think of this because most artists depicting the crucifixion give Jesus a loincloth for modesty's sake. We do not want to picture Jesus humiliatingly exposed, being mocked by onlookers while naked. Taking someone's clothes off by force and exposing their nakedness against their will is sexual abuse; it is degrading and dehumanizing. It was one element of the torture he endured.[18] Mentioning the sexual humiliation that Jesus experienced may make us uncomfortable; however, it can open up a new dimension of his human suffering. It can encourage survivors to turn to the community of faith as a place where abuse can be named.

Another time of the year where abuse can be discussed in worship is Mother's Day or Father's Day. Churches often have special presentations by children on these occasions, or parents are honored or thanked in special prayers. Many people abused by their parents find these holidays extremely distressing. Churches can fall into the trap of idealizing parenthood, marginalizing

---

17 See, for example, Albrecht, *Family Violence*; Everhart, *#MeToo Reckoning*; O'Donnell and Cross, *Feminist Trauma Theologies*; Rambo, *Resurrecting Wounds*; Robinson, *Embodied Peacebuilding*.

18 For a thorough discussion of how and when this understanding of Jesus as a sexual abuse victim developed, see Reaves and Toombs, "#MeToo Jesus."

those who were hurt by their parents. In a Mother's Day prayer, after giving thanks for a mother's love, I included these words:

> Others have felt other things;
> putdowns, ridicule, judgement,
> cruelty and abuse, neglect and abandonment,
> made all the more bitter since it comes
> from one whose love we so crave.[19]

In another Mother's Day prayer, I address the people who may have been abusive:

> Thank you, God, that even though mothers may fail us, you
>   never fail us
> and that you mother us through your love.
> We are not perfect people, and in our intimate relationships,
>   we are imperfect.
> For all the ways we have as mothers, disappointed or failed
>   our children, forgive us.
> Give us the grace to say, "I'm sorry," and the wisdom to
>   make amends.

Prayers that name the reality of abuse are extremely important. Confessional prayers are extremely sensitive because too often the church has offered assurance, spiritualizing forgiveness so that it is something that is just between God and the individuals. In this prayer, I was careful to connect asking forgiveness from God with apologies and restitution.

In one church I pastored, we had a special prayer each Sunday of Advent for people living with violence. This prayer is for people living with violence in their homes:

---

19 This prayer, and all of the other prayers in this chapter, were written by me and can be found on my worship resource website, https://www.leadinginworship.com.

At this time of year as we sing "Silent night"
    with its echoes of calm and heavenly peace,
    we say a prayer for all who live in homes
    where peace is absent.
We pray for children who live with fear,
    whose homes are not a place of safety,
    who live with beatings, both physical and verbal.
We pray for seniors and other vulnerable people
    whose caregivers do not care
    as they are neglected or degraded.
We pray for all who are emotionally abused,
    and who are not loved, honored and cherished.
We pray for women who have had to flee their homes
    or are afraid to flee their homes.
We pray for people of all genders who have been sexually
    violated,
    and who are haunted by terrible memories and a
    continual fear of violation.

While it may seem jarring to talk about violence at Christmas, imagine how jarring it is to live in a home where you feel unsafe at Christmas. Imagine what it is like to go to a service hiding bruises and hear the whole congregation talking only about joy and light. Worship leaders can use the power given them by the community to make a home for hurting people, or they can choose words which ignore and exclude them.

Congregational prayers

Who we mention in our public prayers of intercession communicates a lot about how we see the world. How we pray for people conveys the solutions that we see as viable. I have heard many prayers for interpersonal relationships, asking God to help us forgive the people who hurt us. This is important and is found even in the Lord's Prayer. But only praying like that can leave the impression that the only faithful response to being hurt is to absorb violence and forgive the abuser. In this prayer I open the possibility that sometimes the faithful option is to leave a situation of violence:

> Give us love for our families, accepting them as they are,
> encouraging them to be all they can be,
> appreciating them as we want to be appreciated.
> Sometimes the people we love the most
> can be the people with whom we have the most conflict,
> help us persevere in our love. . . .
> Jesus, you walked a fine line of love with your own
> family;
> help us know when to stay, and when to walk away,
> when to hope, and when to draw a line.
> Help us to live in peace while still respecting ourselves;
> to refuse to abuse, and not to let others abuse us either.

As worship leaders, our prayers should encompass the concerns of our communities, our country, and our world. One week when a mother and her children were murdered by her partner, I prayed this way:

> God of hope, hear our lament.
> Since we heard the news of the ____ family being
> murdered,
> our minds are reeling.
> This is violence happening in our own neighborhood.
> Some of us knew the victims, some know people who
> knew them.
> Our community is grieving.
> We pray for family and friends of the victims.
> We pray for police officers who responded.
> We pray for counsellors called in,
> and everyone touched by this crime.
> We need your help because this crime is not singular.
> Every year women are murdered by their partners,
> in their homes, in their own bedrooms,
> or even when they try to flee the violence.
> Help us do better. Help us believe victims of abuse,

help us protect them when they try to leave.
Help us work on changing a culture that teaches men
that women are property, that women must obey,
and that women who disobey deserve death.
We pray for our local women's shelter
that right now is sheltering women who have stories
just like the story of the woman who was murdered.
Give them strength and courage to do their work,
and show us how we can best support them.

One might pray for this same situation as if it were a unique tragedy, but that would be a missed opportunity. By showing the connection between this crime and the larger system of gendered violence, we are addressing the powers and principalities of sinfulness
in our world. Lament about sin and its effects is a strong biblical
tradition on which we rarely draw; naming sin, and even questioning where God was when it happened, is a faithful response.

Sometimes the order of the service does not allow time for a
prayer devoted to a particular situation such as the example I just
gave. Prayers about abuse can be printed in the bulletin, projected
on a screen before the service, or posted on a bulletin board or
church blog. The following prayer that I wrote is not appropriate
for most public worship services, but providing it to your congregation through some medium could be the difference between life
and death for a survivor of abuse:

Lord, make me an instrument of your peace.
When I think I can change another person,
remind me that I can change only myself.
When I think that being hurt is your will,
remind me of your exodus call to flee from oppression.
When I think I should sacrifice myself unto death,
remind me that you died for our sins, so I don't have to.

O Lord grant that I may not so much seek to endure abuse,
as to escape it entirely;
that I may not so much seek to model victimization,
as to model being a faithful survivor.

For it is in new beginnings that we find your grace,
it is in standing on our own two feet that we find your
   strength,
it is in leading our children to safety, that we find peace.

A prayer like this can be a powerful message for someone who is being abused. It can be a lifeline after a lifetime of hearing prayers about forgiving those who hurt you and carrying your cross. It provides a theological framework for faithful departure from an abusive situation.

A prayer for survivors of abuse does not serve just as a request to God for help. These prayers have a pastoral function in transforming us, the people who are praying. It is a powerful message of identity: this community stands against abuse, and we will not tolerate it in our community. It teaches us that we are people of peace. This helps create an environment where people who are abused can come forward and get help. It can convict those who are abusing to seek help.

In the prayers of confession I have heard in church, I have rarely heard sexual abuse or assault mentioned. This prayer points out that abusive people are hurting themselves as well:

This prayer is for all who are making a big mistake today,
   especially those who are committing a sexual assault
   or abusing someone who trusts them.
God of truth, you know their actions, you hear their words.
Lies, manipulations, plotting.
Threatening, hunting, cornering.
Overpowering, hurting, dominating.
All of these actions devastate the victim.
They also lead the one who does them towards death:
each act obliterating tenderness,
squelching compassion, extinguishing the ability to love.

Prayers of confession can include acknowledging the temptation to hurt children or act out on sexual thoughts about them. These are quite common temptations, which we never name in church. We need to draw on God's strength to resist these temptations because so much is at stake. We must remember that children are praying with us on Sunday morning. It is important that children hear the church talking about sexual abuse so they might find courage to name what is happening to them if they are being hurt.

Intercessory prayer is important not only to call on God's help but also to remind the community about our shared commitments and concerns. There can be prayers for people who work in shelters, for law enforcement and parole officers, and for social workers who work with people who have offended. Scripture encourages us to pray for prisoners; naming people who have committed sexual assault who are in prison is both a prayer for them and a reminder to the congregation that sexual assault is a crime. We can also pray for survivors of abuse or assault who have never told anyone their story or who would like to seek justice but are afraid of the criminal justice system. We need to pray for people with bruises and people whose bruises cannot be seen because they are survivors of emotional abuse.

This is just a brief survey of how violence and abuse can and should be named in worship. Those involved in planning worship have the power to recognize and acknowledge what has long been unrecognized and unacknowledged. This can help people who are feeling marginalized and isolated to feel gathered into the care of the community. It can communicate that God cares.

Conclusion

I do not have the space here to discuss the importance of inclusive names for God or how communion services can be more sensitive to abuse survivors. Wedding services can spell out what love and honor means, and funeral services need to sensitively name how complicated grief can be when someone who was abusive dies. How we spend our money in church, and what causes we support with our offerings, is also communicated in worship. And I did not talk at all about how the lyrics of our music convey our theology about abuse.

If you are a worship leader, think about how and when you could speak about sexual assault and abuse the next time you lead worship. Not every worship leader feels equally empowered to name this type of violence. (I remember my shaking knees when I spoke the word *rape* in a sermon.) People who are confident in their positions, or who are willing to take risks, have the opportunity to make a real difference in their community. Worship committees can reflect together on how the themes and scriptures they are choosing might be received by both survivors and perpetrators of abuse.

I am keenly aware that the movement toward allowing women to lead worship that I spoke of at the beginning of this paper and that is modeled in my examples above completely bypassed huge parts of the Anabaptist family of churches. The branch of the Mennonite church I am in is relatively small on the Anabaptist tree. The larger groups are more patriarchal. In some Mennonite groups, like the Mennonite Brethren, women leaders are still a small minority. In the largest Anabaptist churches in North America—the Amish, Old Order, and Conservative Mennonites—women are still strictly prohibited from being pastors or leading worship services. I lament that there are so many churches that do not allow women or LGBTQ+ people to lead worship and preach. Keeping them from these roles is not just stopping some from using their gifts; it impoverishes the whole church.

Our worshipping communities are warped by power dynamics in the church that put men in charge and force others to be silent. We need the whole community on board as we listen for God's leading. Churches need to think critically about power—who has it and who is kept from having it, who is invited to lead worship and who is not invited. We need to lead worship thoughtfully, with our hearts tuned both to the pain of the community and the promise of Scripture. Our words in worship are the signposts on the map of our theology. Are we leading people to the Promised Land of freedom from oppression or away from it? Our faithfulness depends on this vital theological work.

33

My Tradition
A Poem

Jerry Holsopple

My tradition should have remembered
  What it felt like to be silenced
  They should have remembered the pain of the tongue
    screw
  They should have noticed how many women wore them
  Wore them to their death
  Into ashes
  The ultimate silencing,

But no
  Silencing the victims of sexual abuse
  Was also part of my tradition.

Institutional leaders often remain silent while seeking to silence the victims of sexual abuse. Silencing is accomplished
in multiple ways: victim shaming and blaming, complicit bystanders, and enablers. A twisted theology of forgiveness can
allow powerful leaders to remain in their positions while a forgiving victim is expected to be silent about what transpired.
If the victim resists offering forgiveness, they are accused of
not being Christian. When forgiveness becomes an expectation
rather than a choice, it has forfeited its grounding of truth-
telling and accountability. This type of forgiveness theology

rarely interrogates the reality that confession is active and involves removing oneself from positions of power, taking public accountability for actions, and recognizing that you have no expectation that forgiveness will be offered.

As Elie Wiesel writes, "We must take sides. Neutrality helps the oppressor, never the victim. Silence encourages the tormentor, never the tormented."[1] So leaders often make a clear choice—an unacknowledged choice. To be silent is to speak for those in power or to speak for the perpetrator. The silent leaders are complicit with this violence. This silence normalizes the behavior of the perpetrator and once again wields power in a destructive manner.

> You assured me
>> that you would handle it
>> That you would make sure it was taken care of
>> Things will happen
>
> But your action was
>
> SILENT.
>
> And then
>> You tried to mute God
>> To make God seem silent
>> To hold your spiritual power
>> Over me
>> To make me submit
>> To the abuse
>> Once more
>> Just so I could glimpse
>> What you called grace
>> What you traded for love
>> What you desired
>> So you could twist
>> Tighter
>> And tighter

---

1 Wiesel, *Night Trilogy*, 22.

Until
I was

Silent
Forever.

34

Power, Violence, and Peace Church Ethics

Kimberly L. Penner

Growing up Mennonite—in Mennonite churches (Mennonite Church Canada), a Mennonite family, and as a baptized member of the Mennonite church—I at times felt a disconnect between the peace theology of my church family and faith, on the one hand, and my own experiences of God, on the other. In high school, my parents expressed hesitancy about me learning self-defense in gym class because it seemed "violent." Their concern seemed odd to me considering I already felt some fear about my safety as a young woman living in a society in which one in three women experience some kind of sexual violence in their lifetime. Was I just supposed to submit to this violence? I joined my high school's rugby team in the eleventh grade. The response from my church friends and people who knew I was Mennonite was surprise and concern: "How can you justify playing this violent sport as someone committed to non-violence?" I was crushed. For me, rugby was liberating. As a rugby player, I was welcomed onto a team of thirty women who worked together and prided themselves on physical strength and toughness—not traits that I typically saw valued in women. Finding my physical strength made me feel confident and brave and appreciate my body and what it could do. It seemed to me that the supposedly contradictory nature of a Mennonite woman playing rugby was illustrative of a larger problem regarding how violence is defined and what difference gender makes for conversations about power.

I experienced a similar disconnect between what I experienced as empowering and what others considered wrong, or at odds, in university. University or college years are a common time for self-exploration and sexual experimentation or growth. The Mennonite university residence I lived in was full of young women who were no different. A group of women on my residence floor created the Vaginal Wonder Club—a club committed to our own empowerment as women. We wanted to gain greater understanding and love for our bodies and sexualities. While the club was a natural reflection of the time of life we were in, it was also a response to a need for something that was missing. Residence rules and our observation of how these rules were enforced led us to see that the university's prevailing concern was appearances of sexual morality that included keeping "male" and "female" bodies separate. We did not find messages of support regarding the importance of women developing self-esteem and talking about how to embody an ethic of peacemaking in intimate relationships. Instead, sexual abstinence, or the appearance of sexual abstinence, in heterosexual relationships was the primary focus. Open and closed residence hours sought to keep students who identified as female from visiting students who identified as male (to say nothing of transgender or non-binary students) and vice versa in their dorm rooms during much of the day and night. The assumption was that this would prevent premarital sex and give each gender important time to bond with those who identified similarly. The extent of the sexual ethics we received was this: premarital heterosexual sex is unethical, so refrain; men and women cannot be "just friends" and therefore need to be kept separate in residence; gender is binary; and LGBTQ students do not exist at our institution. These experiences, and others like them, motivated me to pursue an academic career in theological ethics.

My experiences led me to ask a number of questions about my inherited Mennonite faith: How has the lack of a lifegiving, character based, body-positive, sexual ethics—one that includes a commitment to nonviolence as a commitment to shared power (equality)—negatively impacted Mennonites? Could it be that abuse in our churches and homes is perpetuated or justified by the very discipleship ethics and peace theology of our community of faith? Alternatively, is it possible for a church to be well prepared to resist controlling relationships of power and to embody relationships in which power is shared because of its ethics? If so, how?

In this chapter, I offer some possible responses to these questions. I begin with a brief history of the complex relationships that Mennonite institutions and leaders have had with power—or what is often referred to as "worldly power." I find that many Mennonites have largely understood power with suspicion and associated it with political and social structures, choosing to invest, instead, in the "Godly power" of "powerlessness," synonymous with nonviolent discipleship ethics, which values obedience to Christ and therefore a willingness to submit to suffering, just as Christ suffered.

I then point out that this discipleship ethic committed to nonviolence has not adequately considered violence in all its forms—including gender-based, sexualized, racialized, classist, and ableist violence *within* the community of faith. Normative, male contributions to discipleship ethics have also not painted a moral vision of what peacemaking on each of these levels looks like and why it is necessary for peace in all relationships. As a result, violence within the community of faith has largely gone unacknowledged and unaddressed by those in leadership—who are often men—allowing it to spread. Furthermore, as feminist Mennonite theologians such as Carol Penner, Lydia Neufeld Harder, and Malinda Berry have noted, a Mennonite theology of obedience and submission has kept Mennonite women who have experienced abuse silent.

I conclude by arguing that the absence of a broad definition of violence, the lack of a lifegiving theology of God's power as shared power, and the presence of a theology of obedience and submission have been and continue to be dangerous for all—but especially for women and others with less social and ecclesial privilege. Constructively, I propose that a theology of shared power is part of what is required for Mennonite understandings of the church and commitments to nonviolence.

What is power?

In agreement with psychologists Dena Rosenbloom and Mary Beth Williams, I hold that, generally speaking, power is the ability to make something happen and that this includes the ability to act and to have an effect.[1] Any act that has an effect contains power. Power, though, can have varying effects. Power need not be controlling, but control is a form of power; control "is the ability to make happen what you want to happen."[2] In agreement with French philosopher Michel Foucault, I also find that power is relational—that is, arising out of particular relationships and shaped by discourse.[3] And, I claim, it is only when power is shared in relationships of mutual dependence that power empowers people to be "active and full participants in the decisions and environment that affect their lives" and nurtures community.[4]

There are many biblical examples of God's power as relational (shared with humans and all of creation in mutuality). God creates *for* relationship. We can trace God's desire to be in a mutual and loving relationship with God's good creation from Genesis through to Revelation. God acts with and through us. In the New Testament, the Greek word *dunamis* is used to refer to power. According to feminist theologian Carter Heyward, this kind of

---

1 Rosenbloom and Williams, *Life after Trauma*, 150.

2 Rosenbloom and Williams, *Life after Trauma*, 150.

3 My understanding of power as relational is informed by French philosopher Michel Foucault's articulation of power as the effect of particular configurations of relations through discourse, rather than a thing that can be owned. Foucault, *History of Sexuality*. Foucault uses the term *discourse* to denote how knowledge and meaning are produced by historically contingent social systems. Foucault, *Archaeology of Knowledge*, 135–40.

4 Lederach, *Preparing for Peace*, 21.

power is transpersonal and rooted in our own agency. In other words, it is not like authority, which is bestowed on or granted to us by others. It is raw and dynamic, springing from within us to work with God, ourselves, and others for inclusion, wholeness, and equality.[5]

Jesus embodies this same power. He does not possess power; instead he facilitates relationships of shared power. He facilitates the revelation of God as the creative power of intimate relationships of mutual respect and valuing. In the healing narratives of Jesus, for example, we find that Jesus works with others to heal. In the story of the hemorrhaging women (Mark 5:20–30), the woman is an agent in her own healing. She reaches out and touches Jesus and is healed. Jesus, the healer, is also affected by the healing. He feels it happen and addresses her. As Heyward notes, "The healing was enabled not by Jesus 'in himself', but by Jesus in relation. Healing, and the intimacy that grounds it in relation, is a reciprocal process in which the healer is affected by the healed."[6] Jesus reveals to humans the possibility of their own potential to participate in God's good, healing, power.[7]

Normative Anabaptist understandings of power

It is common for those who identify as Mennonite, historically and presently, to speak and write primarily about power in relation to the state, which is often viewed negatively. Many do so within an ecclesiological (church centered) framework that considers how the church is called to live into the kingdom of God as disciples of Jesus. Just as Jesus modeled an alternative to state power (coercive) in the form of God's power (understood either as powerlessness or as shared power that is empowering for life-giving actions as people build each other up), so too we as disciples of Jesus are called to embody relationships of powerlessness or shared power. The difference here is that for some, Jesus was pow-

5 Heyward, *Redemption of God*, 42.

6 Heyward, *Redemption of God*, 42.

7 I draw here on Julie Hopkins's work in Hopkins, "Epiphany," 285–309.

erless, and therefore power itself is immoral; for others, power is not a moral issue, and therefore the question for Christian ethics becomes what kind of relationships of power we are called to embody.

In *Power, Authority, and the Anabaptist Tradition*, Benjamin Redekop and Calvin Redekop describe the "Anabaptist/Mennonite relationship to power" as paradoxical.[8] In the Radical Reformation, they note, those who would come to be known as Anabaptists rejected a close relationship between church and state and the abuse of power by church leaders in positions of authority. On the one hand, since then the Anabaptist movement has continued to represent "a break with the inherited system of intermingled religious and political power."[9] "Power and authority were not vested in traditional and inherited political power or in the ritually sanctioned offices of the ecclesiastical hierarchy, but rather in the individual will and the community of the faithful."[10] On the other hand, "this radical and innovative stance has the potential to yield its opposite, and even worse, can provide a deceptive, benign cover behind which naked power may operate as though invisible . . . power is renounced yet not in truth forsaken."[11]

There were, and continue to be, differences in the various Anabaptist and Mennonite relationships to power—in theory and in practice. What concerns me most is the view that communities of faith can be powerless or power neutral and therefore incapable of abusing power in ways that seek to dominate, silence, or harm others.

Peace in all relationships?

While many normative Anabaptist-Mennonite understandings of violence have focused primarily on state violence and have emphasized—for example, conscientious objection to war—femi-

---

8 Redekop and Redekop, *Power*, vii.
9 Redekop and Redekop, *Power*, vii.
10 Redekop and Redekop, *Power*, xi
11 Redekop and Redekop, *Power*, vii.

nist Mennonite scholars from a variety of disciplines have been, and continue to be, instrumental in expanding definitions of violence for peace theology and discipleship practice. Cynthia Hess notes that in the history of the Mennonite church, its practice of nonviolence, primarily in the form of refusal of military service, "does not explicitly attend to the reality of internal violence,"[12] which Hess names as "violence that is incorporated into the identity of Christian communities and those who constitute them."[13] In my own work, I have added to Hess's claim that not only has Mennonite pacifism not attended to internalized forms of violence and its effects, but it has elided or ignored the violence done among people who identify as "Mennonite." "Outside of wartime circumstances," writes Marlene Epp, "the gendered meanings of pacifism have only begun to be explored. Feminist analyses of nonresistant/pacifist beliefs have drawn attention to the ways in which notions of peace and nonviolence, espoused as key markers of Mennonites past and present, have overlapped with gendered character traits such as humility, submission, and service,"[14] which have proven dangerous for women in many cases. Likewise, Gayle Gerber Koontz observes,

> Historically most Mennonite peace theology and ethics has been engaged with questions of and arguments for Christian pacifism in the face of violence that was being justified by others. Catholic, Lutheran, and Calvinist traditions developed complex systems of theological-ethical thought justifying violence in war. . . . There is no comparable major Christian tradition which has sought to explicitly justify the use of violence against women. On the surface, such violence has been assumed to be wrong (therefore ethical debate was not needed) while actual

---

12 Hess, *Sites of Violence*, 24.

13 Hess, *Sites of Violence*, 12.

14 Epp, *Mennonite Women in Canada*, 215.

practice has frequently been cloaked in silence and self-deception.[15]

Carol Penner reiterates this point: "Mennonites have endured great hardship for their unwillingness to hurt other people through military service. Yet Mennonites have tolerated violence directed against vulnerable people in their own communities. Mennonite theologians have been blind to this dichotomy."[16] As Lydia Neufeld Harder argues, "The theology of peace, justice, and non-violence that has characterized the Mennonite community has generally not examined the power relationships between women and men."[17] Hess, Epp, Koontz, Penner, and Harder are a few examples of scholars who highlight the need for an expanded definition of violence for Mennonite peace theology and practice that includes gender-based and sexualized violence.

Obedience and submission

An expanded definition of violence would complicate and raise questions about Mennonite commitments to obedience and submission as defining features of Christian discipleship—the result of confession of Jesus Christ as Lord and Savior.[18] Attention to context and power inequalities reveals that obedience as the guiding principal may encourage people in positions of greater vulnerability to endure suffering they never chose in the first place. Differences in experience and context highlight the problems with obedience and submission as appropriate rhetoric and commitments for *all* disciples of Christ. Who are we submitting to? Should suffering as disciples of Christ be freely chosen?

Carol Penner demonstrates the risks of a theology of submission and servanthood and an emphasis on suffering for women in relation to sexual violence and abuse. For example, she is critical of attempts to reclaim the New Testament Household Codes,

---

15 Koontz, "Introduction," 1.

16 C. Penner, "Mennonite Silences," 17.

17 Harder, *Obedience*, 10–11.

18 Harder, *Obedience*, 15–16.

or *Haustafeln* (Colossians 3:18–4:1; Ephesians 5:22–6:9; 1 Peter 2:13–3:7; 1 Timothy 2:9–15; and Titus 2:2–10), as liberative rather than essentially conservative. The passages outline the behavior that Christian members of the household are expected to embody within a patriarchal framework. Penner helpfully reveals that reclaiming obedience and subordination as radical acts of love make "no difference to the abused woman for both obedience and subordination require her to stay in an abusive situation." The only difference is that reclaiming obedience and subordination as liberating for women assures a woman "that by accepting her suffering she is being a moral agent and can thus have a meaningful witness and ministry."[19] How dangerous—a discipleship ethic that encourages and even praises women for enduring suffering "as Jesus did"! It is only when depictions of subordination adequately value the experiences of those who are already socially subordinated (i.e., relationships of unequal power) for ethics that they stand a chance of being radical or liberating.[20]

We need to examine how suffering happens *because of* the roles and rules governing relationships within patriarchal, white supremacist, and classed systems as they function to keep some dominant and others subordinate. If they are not examined, experiences of "involuntary suffering" or "unjust suffering" can be interpreted as "voluntary" and therefore "just" and function to provide theological justification for abuse. As Penner asserts, many Mennonite women have endured abuse because they submitted themselves to what they believed was the God-given authority of male members. This happens because patriarchy was left unexamined.[21]

In this way, relationships of unequal power operating within the community of faith impact the community's ethics. They also complicate understanding of voluntary suffering and signal the need for character formation and moral action guided by suspi-

---

19 C. Penner, "Mennonite Silences," 46–47.

20 K. Penner, "Erotic Peacemaking," 43.

21 C. Penner, "Content to Suffer," 103–104.

cion of unequal relationships of power and the biblical values of love, justice, and peace.

According to feminist Mennonite theologian Lydia Neufeld Harder, a necessary tension must remain between vulnerability and obedience when it comes to the biblical text as a source for Christian ethics.[22] She writes, "Neither a suspicion that rejects these texts completely nor an easy obedience that fails to see the freedom of living a new life in Christ does justice to these texts in which the human and divine are so thoroughly intertwined."[23]

Toward a theology of shared power

The ecclesial community is the place in which, ideally, we as Mennonites are formed to be disciples of peace through an awareness of the ways in which power operates among us—in our churches, our institutions, and our society. What kind of community do we seek to be considering the fact that relationships of unequal power exist within the church? What knowledge of God and Jesus act as our inspiration? And how do we grapple honestly with the fact that during this time, before the full inbreaking of the Kingdom of God, we will live with inequality? Furthermore, what do we do about the fact that we will fail at living up to the expectations of emulating Christ?

High moral standards, such as a commitment to nonviolence, are not in and of themselves problematic. However, they must be coupled with a certain realism that acknowledges the present brokenness of the church—including the potential for destructive and dominating relations of power that enable some to exploit, manipulate, and coerce to exist within the church.[24] In order to

---

22 C. Penner, "Content to Suffer," 148.

23 C. Penner, "Content to Suffer," 149.

24 I am thinking in particular of Reinhold Niebuhr's emphasis on the biblical paradox that humans are both good, a reflection of the *imago Dei*, and also finite and sinful, which he articulates in *The Nature and Destiny of Man*. Malinda Berry has done ground-breaking work on the value of Niebuhr's realism for Mennonite peace theology and ethics. See, for example, Berry, "Shalom Political Theology."

be life-giving—that is, to be justice-seeking and peace-oriented—ethical reflection must, as Eleanor Haney articulates, "move between the poles of analysis of what exists and construction [or vision] of what might be."[25] An ideal moral vision and a realistic view of relationships of power within the church presently are both necessary.

I appreciate the importance of looking to Scripture to answer these questions. However, as a feminist, I am committed first and foremost to seeking God's wisdom revealed to us through experiences of injustice "for what they reveal about victimization as well as courageous resistance."[26] Women's experiences of abuse and empowerment, for example, ought to be the starting point for discerning the leading of the Holy Spirit with regard to peacemaking and discipleship.

For me, a commitment to shared power means working toward relationships of nonviolence with a commitment to the well-being of all our ecological and social relationships. It names the fact that there is no outside to power and that power itself is neither good nor bad. A commitment to shared power is critical of relationships of unequal power and domination. It provokes us to ask questions of who can affect decision making and who cannot, what we are doing with our decision-making abilities, and how we can work together to effect change and reflect the gospel's commitment to love and justice.

In my own life, there are many examples of how power can be, or is currently being, shared. Power is shared when my tenured professor friend invites me to guest lecture in her class and connects me with potential publishers for my dissertation. Power is shared in the church process on LGBTQ inclusion that I am facilitating as members give special value to the experiences of LGBTQ persons as a source for ethics. Power is shared when Mennonites in Canada privilege the experiences of Canada's Indigenous people in conversations about pipeline projects on

---

25 Davies and Haney, *Redefining Sexual Ethics*, xi.

26 West, *Disruptive Christian Ethics*, xvi.

Indigenous land. Power is shared at the academic conferences that I am part of when they create space for a diversity of voices and encourage a relational approach to learning through panel discussions, group conversations, and an appreciation for teaching as facilitation as well as dispensation of knowledge. Relationships of shared power are those characterized by giving and receiving, teaching and learning, speaking and listening.[27] Shared power is also informed by the understanding that relationships of power intersect with one another. As a result, a commitment to justice and equality necessarily requires a commitment to these values in all relationships.[28]

A suspicion of unequal relationships of power and a commitment to sharing power can also nuance our understandings of violence and nonviolence. Or, put differently, a commitment to nonviolence necessarily requires a commitment to creating relationships of equality and shared power. Such a commitment changes the common definition of violence. Returning to the example from my introduction, a woman engaging in an act of self-defense against her attacker could be considered an example of "active nonviolence" rather than violence. Because she is at a disadvantage, or position of less privilege because she is a woman in a patriarchal society, her engagement in self-defense is an equalizer. In defending herself, she claims her agency and her ability to affect change, rather than perpetuating the status quo.

---

27 Harrison, *Making the Connections*, 175.

28 The theory of intersectionality recognizes that relationships and power dynamics between social locations and processes (e.g., racism, classism, heterosexism, ableism, ageism, sexism) are linked and can change over time and differ by geographic setting. Law professor Kimberlé Crenshaw developed intersectionality as "a way of framing the various interactions of race and gender in the context of violence against women of color" but recognized its potential more broadly "as a way of mediating the tension between assertions of multiple identities and the ongoing necessity of group politics." Crenshaw, "Mapping the Margins." For helpful introductions to intersectionality, see Dhamoon, "Considerations"; Collins, *Black Feminist Thought*; Kim and Shaw, *Intersectional Theology*.

In this case, violence is interpreted with attention to how relationships of power operate.

Conclusion

Can theology justify abuse? Yes, and any theology of nonviolence that advocates for redemptive suffering and is inattentive to relationships of power is at risk of doing so. Is it possible for ethics and theology to resist controlling and dominating relationships of power? Yes, through a commitment to nonviolence that includes a nuanced view of how power operates within systems and relationships of inequality and a commitment to relationships of shared power. We cannot remain unaware of the social inequalities that inform our experiences in the world—our experiences of privilege and disadvantage. We do not live and worship in communities that are power neutral or powerless. Because of this, we must explore in greater detail what it means to share power with others as Jesus did. If we are committed to this theological and ethical task, then we are working toward a moral vision of the kingdom of God without abuse.

Contributors

Cameron Altaras, PhD (University of Toronto), is retired, remarried, and living in Washington State. Cameron was born into a Canadian Amish Mennonite community and raised in the Mennonite church. Her doctoral work focused on the Frankfurt School's critical theory of the ideological manipulation of power, in particular as manifested in the manipulation of art by religious institutions. She spent her career in the corporate world in business ethics, leadership development, and coaching. With the unraveling of the marriage to the father of her children, she began to come to terms with how the course of her life had been shaped by her religious upbringing, gender oppression, abuse of power, clergy sexual misconduct, and moral injury. Part of her healing journey included choosing to legally change her name (previously, Cheryl Nafziger-Leis). In her retirement, she and her husband create audio recordings of her poetry, available on her website https://www.vocem-redisuum.com/.

Carol Penner, PhD (University of St. Michael's College, Toronto), teaches practical theology at Conrad Grebel University College in Waterloo, Ontario. She has been a pastor for thirteen years in three different congregations. She was raised in the Mennonite church and has been active in it her whole life. She authors a worship resource blog (leadinginworship.com). Her doctoral work was in the area of Mennonite peace theology and violence against women, and she has written extensively about abuse issues. She has two adult children, and she lives with her partner in Vineland, Ontario, in a house surrounded by apricot trees on the traditional territory of Anishinaabeg, Ojibway/Chippewa, and Haudenosaunee peoples.

Sarah Augustine, MA (Antioch University, Seattle, Washington), is cofounder of the Dismantling the Doctrine of Discovery Coalition and executive director of the Dispute Resolution Center of Yakima and Kittitas Counties. She is the cofounder of Suriname Indigenous Health Fund, where she has advocated for Indigenous Peoples whose health and communities are threatened by resource extraction since 2004. Sarah has represented the interests of Indigenous community partners to their own governments, the Inter-American development bank, the United Nations, the Organization for American States Inter-American Commission on Human Rights, the World Health Organization and a host of others, including corporate interests. She and her family live on a ranch in Washington State. She is a regular columnist for *Anabaptist World* and author of *The Land is Not Empty: Following Jesus in Dismantling the Doctrine of Discovery*.

Rev. Sarah Ann Bixler, MDiv, PhD (Princeton Theological Seminary), is assistant professor of formation and practical theology and associate dean of the seminary at Eastern Mennonite University in Harrisonburg, Virginia. Her scholarship addresses adolescent formation, education, Anabaptist theology and ecclesiology, and current issues in Mennonite contexts. A member of Mennonite Church USA, Sarah has worked for Mennonite institutions as a teacher, youth minister, writer, and conference administrator. She and her spouse, Benjamin Bixler, have three school-aged children, and together they are engaged in a holistic restoration of the historic Lincoln Homestead in Linville, Virginia.

Torah Bontrager (Bon-tray-grrrr), raised traditional Amish, grew up with no electricity and cars and speaks English as a second language. At age fifteen, she escaped in the middle of the night, and she later became, to her knowledge, the first Amish person to graduate from an Ivy League school, Columbia University. She is a sexual assault survivor, the author of *An Amish Girl in Manhattan: A True Crime Memoir*, the host of the podcast Amish Entrepreneur Show, and the founder of the 501(c)(3) nonsectarian nonprofit The Amish Heritage Foundation (www.AmishHeritage.org). Among other initiatives, AHF is attempting to overturn Wisconsin v. Yoder, the landmark 1972 Supreme Court case that ruled that a religion's rights outweigh the right of an Amish child to receive an education beyond the eighth grade. Torah's story has been featured on MTV, Forbes. com, and HuffPost, among other outlets.

Bryan Born, MTh, DTh (University of South Africa), was born and raised in Abbotsford, British Columbia. Prior to taking on the role of Columbia Bible College president in 2012, he served as director of the intercultural studies (missions) program for eight years. Previously, he and his wife, Teresa, spent twelve years ministering in Botswana with African Initiated Churches where they were involved in discipleship, biblical training, and HIV/AIDS-related ministries. His passion is to follow the way of Jesus and to encourage people to experience reconciliation with God, life transformation, and a sense of purpose and hope.

Steph Chandler Burns, MTS (Conrad Grebel University College, Waterloo, Ontario), works as a pastor. Steph is bisexual, queer, non-binary, and very opinionated. You can often find Steph on Twitter, live-tweeting about church meetings and events. Steph has published theological reflections on being queer and Mennonite and enjoys thinking about the ways that queerness reveals parts of the divine. When not engaging with church, Steph can be found playing board games or getting new tattoos. Steph lives with a partner, Greg, and two cats in Kitchener, Ontario, on the Haldimand Tract, the traditional territory of the Haudenosaunee, Anishinaabe, and Attawandaron First Peoples.

Jenny Castro is director of programs at the Martinez Street Women's Center in San Antonio, Texas. She has a BA in English and has enjoyed a meandering yet fulfilling career finding paid work in a variety of contexts, including community and women's health, public education, international relief and development, communications, and women's advocacy. Jenny is passionate about justice, truth, and their connection. She is a fierce mother of three remarkable children and has been married to Jake for two decades. She loves camping, authentic conversation, and a good cup of coffee.

Jennifer Delanty began attending Seattle Mennonite Church with her four children in 1999. She currently chairs the congregation's Spiritual Leadership Team. Jennifer's home and church are situated on the unceded lands of the Duwamish, a vibrant Indigenous people unrecognized by the US government, who have resided for millennia in what is currently known as the Puget Sound region of the State of Washington.

Joanne Gallardo, MDiv (Anabaptist Mennonite Biblical Seminary), is conference minister for Indiana-Michigan Mennonite Conference of Mennonite Church USA in Goshen, Indiana. Previously, she worked as a mental health professional in several cities across the mid-Atlantic. In addition to church work, Joanne has spent part of her career working in mental health. Joanne is interested in intersectional feminism, LGBTQ+ equality, preaching, writing, and taking things one day at a time.

Brenda Gerber is a mother of two children, who loves truth, justice, and words. Brenda believes words have the power to shift and transform our lives. She grew up in a large Conservative Mennonite farm family and experienced firsthand the trauma of incest and hidden generational pain. This deeply affected and stunted her emotional growth. It took hard work to go to the root of these realities. Writing has become both a vent and a way of transforming pain into hope. Brenda lives with her husband and their two children in Ontario, Canada.

Elsie Goerzen has been the coordinator of the End Abuse Program run by Mennonite Central Committee British Columbia for over eleven years. She has previously worked as a registered nurse, a child abuse prevention facilitator, a parenting educator, and for nineteen years was coordinator of Sardis DoorWay, a support program for single mothers with preschool age children in Chilliwack. Elsie has been married to Walt for over half a century, and they have two sons, two daughters-in-law, and five grandchildren. Walt and Elsie enjoy gardening, reading, and spending time with family in British Columbia, Canada. They have been members of Sardis Community Church since 1975.

Amanda K Gross was born and raised in the heart of Atlanta, Georgia, by white Mennonite parents. She is a mixed media fiber artist and anti-racist organizer currently living and working in Pittsburgh, Pennsylvania. After studying conflict transformation and restorative justice from Eastern Mennonite University's Center for Justice and Peacebuilding, she organized her 2,000 closest friends to yarn bomb the Andy Warhol Bridge with the goal of bridging Pittsburgh's segregated communities and demonstrating community control of public space. In her recent role as program director of the American Friends Service Committee Pittsburgh Office, she supported youth in undoing institutional racism in their school systems. It was through hearing their powerful stories that Amanda realized that white ladies are everywhere, prompting her to organize with other status quo and passing white women to fight against institutional racism. This affinity organizing work involves facilitating White Women's Groups, writing regularly on the Mistress Syndrome blog (www.mistresssyndrome.com), and having coffee with lots and lots of white ladies. Her local anti-racist organizing is grounded in anti-racist analyses and maintains accountability through a dynamic relationship with Felicia Savage Friedman and her Certified YogaRoots On Location Anti-Racist Raja Yoga Teacher School. In her spare time, Amanda is working on a book on the topic of healing from Post-Traumatic Mistress Syndrome.

Jeanette Harder, PhD, MSW (University of Texas at Arlington), is a social work professor at Goshen College in Goshen, Indiana, and the director of the new collaborative MSW program at Goshen College and Bluffton University. She is also the author of *For the Sake of a Child: Love, Safety, And Abuse in Plain Communities* (Ridgeway) and *Let the Children Come: Preparing Faith Communities to End Child Abuse and Neglect* (Herald).

Lydia Neufeld Harder, PhD (Toronto School of Theology), is retired from her formal work as theologian and pastor, but she continues to reflect on Mennonite theology and practice, particularly on the way power has functioned within the church and scholarly communities. She has taught sessionally, presented at numerous academic conferences, and worked as a pastor in the Mennonite Church. Her most recent book, *The Challenge Is in the Naming*, chronicles her theological journey by placing earlier published essays into the personal, social, and church contexts in which they were written. Lydia and her husband, Gary, live in Toronto, Ontario, where they attend the Toronto United Mennonite Church. Their three children and their spouses and their nine grandchildren and one great grandchild give them ample reason to travel and to keep in touch with the challenges of the next generations.

Jerry Holsopple, PhD (European Graduate School), is an artist, photographer and renowned videographer who teaches photography and digital media-related courses. Jerry was the artist in residence at The Henry Luce III Center for the Arts and Religion at Wesley Theological Seminary during the fall of 2015. He created a major project, 7×7: Laments for an Age of Sexualized Power. Jerry spent the 2009–2010 academic year as a Fulbright scholar at LCC International University in Lithuania. Jerry is the recipient of more than a dozen awards in recognition of his video, public service announcements, and websites. *Journey toward Forgiveness*, a documentary that he produced, originally aired on ABC in December of 2001 and was aired again in 2003 and 2008 on the Hallmark Channel. Jerry's photographic work has periodically been on exhibit, and two series, "On the Way" and "Art of the Call," are permanently installed. While much of Jerry's work focuses on the visual, he also enjoys writing songs and playing acoustic stringed instruments such as guitars, mandolins, and bouzoukis. He lives in Virginia.

Julia Kasdorf, PhD (New York University), is a poet, essayist, and editor. She is the author of numerous volumes of poetry and has taught at Pennsylvania State University, the University of Pittsburgh, and New York University.

Sylvia Klauser, MDiv, PhD (University of Edinburgh), is a theologian, ethicist, and an ACPE Certified Educator. She received her bachelor and graduate training at Mennonite institutions in Switzerland and the USA. She is the manager of spiritual care and bereavement services at Children's Hospital Colorado in Denver, Colorado. Sylvia moved from her native Germany in order to join her spouse, Susan, a retired US federal immigration judge and Unitarian-Universalist minister.

Ruth E. Krall, PhD (Southern California School of Theology at Claremont) is professor emerita of religion, nursing, and psychology and program director emerita of peace, justice and conflict studies at Goshen College, Indiana. With her academic discipline in applied theology, she specializes in the area of gender-based violence. She is particularly interested in understanding all who work as healers in situations of personal violence. Ruth is retired and lives in Arizona.

David Martin, MDiv (Associated Mennonite Biblical Seminaries), now retired, held the position of executive minister of Mennonite Church Eastern Canada for fifteen years. Before that he served as a pastor in various Mennonite congregations for twenty-five years. David is an avid curler and fitness enthusiast and in his free time can often be found at the gym, on a walking trail, or at the curling rink. He lives in Waterloo, Ontario.

Keturah C. Martin is the pen name of a single mom of four awesome children who was raised in a Conservative Mennonite setting. She is a survivor of thirty-three years of abuses of every nature by more than thirteen perpetrators and many church leaders. She has emerged as a surviving victor from the abuses and extreme domestic violence through the miraculous preservation and healing touch of Jesus Christ. Keturah has been called by God to propagate hope, help, and healing for all survivors of abuse. She is also an advocate and works full-time with survivors of human trafficking. She believes that there is nothing too hard for Jesus to heal and completely restore from the ashes of human suffering.

Peter Niemeyer served as a Mennonite pastor for more than seventeen years and currently attends Toronto United Mennonite Church and works in various faith-based social justice initiatives.

Kimberly L. Penner, PhD (Toronto School of Theology), is a full-time pastor at Stirling Avenue Mennonite Church and a sessional instructor. She has taught Christian ethics at Conrad Grebel University College and ethics at Victoria College in the University of Toronto. She specializes in feminist liberative theological ethics, sexuality and embodiment, Mennonite peace theology, and institutional ethics. Kim lives with her partner, Dylan, children, Jackson and Ethan, and their two cats in Kitchener, Ontario, Canada.

Lisa Schirch, PhD (George Mason University), is Starmann Chair in Peace Studies at the University of Notre Dame in South Bend, Indiana. She also directs the social media, technology, and peacebuilding program for the Toda Peace Institute. She is a former Fulbright Fellow in East and West Africa, the author of eleven books, and a frequent public speaker at high-level policy events around the world.

Kimberly D. Schmidt, PhD (Binghamton University), is professor of history and director of the Washington Community Scholars' Center. Her publications include *Magpie's Blanket*, a Women Writing the West WILLA Literary Awards Finalist in the historical fiction category, and *Strangers at Home: Amish and Mennonite Women in History*. Kimberly divides her research interests between Amish and Mennonite women's social history and women's histories of the Southern Cheyenne. She teaches local multicultural history in Washington, DC, and is particularly interested in accessing the histories of social movements and poor people's experiences through various visual and performing arts media. She has lived in the Washington area since 1989 and has two children.

Sylvia Shirk, DMin (San Francisco Theological Seminary), has been an ordained pastor in Mennonite Church USA since 1996. She completed her doctoral degree with a concentration in international feminist theology in 2010. Throughout her career as a campus minister, congregational pastor, and conference oversight minister, she has shared in the journey of persons who suffered the consequences of sexual abuse. She lives in Portland, Oregon, where she works as a district pastor and is an interpreter of French and Haitian Creole. She finds that cross-cultural partnerships enrich her understandings and transform her ministry.

Bradley G. Siebert, PhD (University of Arizona), is an assistant professor of English at Washburn University in Topeka, Kansas. He is married to Kay (Preheim) Siebert, and they have three grown daughters, Aimee, Megan, and Jill. In his work, Bradley specializes in composition and rhetoric studies, researching religious rhetoric in the discursive and communitarian discernment practices of Anabaptists and in the discursive implications of Gordon D. Kaufman's constructive theology. From 1996 to 1998, Bradley edited *Kansas English* for the Kansas Association of Teachers of English. From 1998 to 2012, Bradley wrote the monthly column, Views from the Pew, for the *Mennonite Weekly Review*.

Regina Shands Stoltzfus, PhD (Chicago Theological Seminary), currently teaches at Goshen College in the peace, justice, and conflict studies (PJCS) and Bible, religion, and philosophy (BRP) departments, where her courses include Race, Class, and Ethnic Relations; Personal Violence and Healing; Spiritual Path of the Peacemaker; and Transforming Conflict and Violence. Regina is cofounder of the Roots of Justice Anti-Oppression program (formerly Damascus Road) and continues as a core trainer with Roots of Justice. She has worked in peace education with Ohio Conference of the Mennonite Church, Mennonite Central Committee, and Mennonite Mission Network.

Catherine Thiel Lee, MDiv (Regent College), is a hospice chaplain in North Carolina at Transitions Lifecare and serves part-time as children's and youth pastor at Chapel Hill Mennonite

Fellowship. She has worked with refugee claimants in Vancouver, British Columbia, and on the board of a rural community garden. She loves big cities, small farms, poetry, Lindy Hop, and the Marvel Cinematic Universe. Catherine lives, plays, and looks after a scrappy garden in Chapel Hill, North Carolina, with her husband and two sons.

Rev. SWANA TANGIZA TENDA (Sidonie), MA (Université Protestante du Congo), is an ordained minister in the Mennonite Community of Congo (CMCO). Her master's thesis topic and subsequent ministry focus on married life, women, and youth. SWANA is president of the Association of Protestant Women Theologians of Congo (ATPCO) and of the Association of Mennonite Women Theologians of Congo (ATMCO). She is a member and editor of the Circle of Concerned African Women Theologians, a chaplain at the Christian University of Kinshasa (UCKIN) secondary school, and the assistant pastor to her spouse, Reverand Pastor Falanga Gitulo Leonard at the 27thCMCO La Colombe de Macampagne congregation of Kinshasa. A teacher since 1975, SWANA's passion is editorial work.

Johannes van der Meer studied theology in Amsterdam, Berlin, and Jerusalem. He graduated from the Amsterdam Mennonite Theological Seminary. He worked as a minister in several Mennonite congregations in the Netherlands for over forty years, in both rural and city settings, including twenty years in Amsterdam. After his retirement, he continues to preach on invitation, counsel, and teach courses on Jewish and Talmudic literature and Rabbinical Torah-exegesis. Johannes lives with his wife, Rosalie Steinmann, and their children in Akkrum, Netherlands.

Elizabeth (Liz) Wenger (1946–2022) was an artist and poet from Goshen, Indiana. She created many pieces of art using the medium of needlepoint, had exhibitions of her work in both the United States and Canada, and published three volumes of poetry.

Ingrid Bettina Wolfear was born into the Blackfoot Nation, where all of her larger family and community were survivors of

Residential School. She was in survivor mode from before the time she was born with blood memory as her backbone. She was a single parent to three children born within twenty-five months, until she met her husband of ten years. She and her husband live with their school-age daughter on Sagamok Anishnawbek Nation in Ojibway territory. Healing continues for all.

Bibliography

Adler, Garfield. *Die Tauf- und Kirchenfrage in Leben und Lehre des Samuel Heinrich Fröhlich, VDM, von Brugg 1803–1857.* Basler und Berner Studien zur historischen und systematischen Theologie. Pieterlen and Bern, Switzerland: Peter Lang International, 1980.

Adorno, Theodor W. *Negative Dialectics.* Translated by E.B. Ashton. New York: Continuum, 1973.

Albrecht, Elizabeth Soto. *Family Violence: Reclaiming a Theology of Nonviolence.* Maryknoll, NY: Orbis, 2008.

Altaras, Cameron. "Can Sex with a Pastor be an Affair?" *Canadian Mennonite* 19, Issue 17 (August 26, 2015). Online: https://canadianmennonite.org/reader/5407.

Altaras, Cameron. "Naming Mennonite Harvey Weinsteins: When Resilience Requires Community." *The Mennonite.* March 2018.

Altaras, Cameron. "Sex with a Pastor is Never an Affair." *2015 SNAP (Survivors' Network of those Abused by Priests) Annual Conference.* Arlington, VA: August 2, 2015. Online: https://www.youtube.com/watch?v=32iVyVVta2s&t=13s.

The Amish Heritage Foundation (AHF). Online: https://www.amishheritage.org.

Arendt, Hannah. *The Human Condition.* 2nd ed. Chicago: The University of Chicago Press, 1958.

Arendt, Hannah. *On Violence.* New York: Harcourt, Brace & World. Inc., 1969.

Association for the Treatment of Sexual Abusers. Online: https://www.atsa.com.

Augustine, Sarah. "My commissioning." Doctrine of Discovery series. February 27, 2015. Online: http://mennoniteusa.org/featured-blogs/doctrine-of-discovery-series-my-commissioning/.

Augustine, Sarah. "Negotiating Christian and Indigenous Identities: The Story of Laughing Warrior Girl." In *All You Need is Love: Honoring the Diversity of Women's Voices in Theology*, edited by Jennifer Castro, 105–115. Elkhart, Indiana: Women in Leadership Project, Mennonite Church USA, 2016.

Augustine, Sarah, John Diefenbaker-Krall, Robert Miller, and Steven Newcomb, "Statement on the Doctrine of Discovery and its Enduring Impact on Indigenous Peoples." *World Council of Churches.* February 17, 2012. Online: https://www.oikoumene.org/en/resources/documents/executive-committee/2012-02/statement-on-the-doctrine-of-discovery-and-its-enduring-impact-on-indigenous-peoples.

Baker, Connie, A. *Traumatized by Religious Abuse: Courage, Hope, and Freedom for Survivors.* Eugene, OR: Luminare Press, 2019.

Bancroft, Lundy. *Why Does He Do That? Inside the Minds of Angry and Controlling Men.* New York: Berkley, 2002.

Baril, Karine. "Sexual Abuse in the Childhood of Perpetrators." *Institut National de Santé Publique du Québec.* Last modified November 2012. Online: https://www.inspq.qc.ca/en/sexual-assault/fact-sheets/sexual-abuse-childhood-perpetrators/.

Beachy, Kirsten Eve, ed. *Tongue Screws and Testimonies: Poems, Stories and Essays Inspired by the "Martyrs Mirror."* Scottdale, PA: Herald Press, 2010.

Beard, Mary. "Women in Power," *London Review of Books,* 39 no. 6 (2017).

Beck, Richard. *Stranger God: Meeting Jesus in Disguise.* Minneapolis, MN: Fortress Press, 2017.

Blackburn, Pete. "Five Maryland Prep Football Players Charged with Rape after Alleged Hazing Ritual with Broomstick." *CBS Sports.* November 8, 2018. Online: https://www.cbssports.com/general/news/five-maryland-prep-football-players-charged-with-rape-after-alleged-hazing-ritual-with-broomstick/.

Berry, Malinda Elizabeth. "Shalom Political Theology: A New Type of Mennonite Peace Theology for a New Era of Discipleship." *The Conrad Grebel Review* 34, no 1 (Winter 2016): 49–73.

Beyler, Clayton Vern. "Meaning and Relevance of the Devotional Covering: A Study in the Interpretation of I Corinthians 11:2–16." Master's thesis. Louisville: Southern Baptist Theological Seminary, 1954.

Billig, Michael. "A Few anthropologists' Lessons about the Amish Studies." *Real Amish Podcast.* From the Disrupting History Conference, September 28–29, 2018. Online: https://www.amishheritage.org/podcast.

Bixler, Sarah Ann. "Can I Get a Witness? Transforming the Common Shock of Patriarchy." In *I've Got the Power: Naming and Reclaiming Power as a Force for Good,* edited by Jenny Castro, 9–25. Elkhart, IN: Women in Leadership Project, Mennonite Church USA, 2018.

Blume, E. Sue. *Secret Survivors: Uncovering Incest and its Aftereffects in Women.* New York: Ballentine, 1990.

Bode, Sabine. *Die vergessene Generation: Die Kriegskinder brechen ihr Schweigen.* Stuttgart: Verlag Klett-Cotta, 2015.

Bode, Sabine. *Kriegsenkel: Die Erben der vergessenen Generation.* Stuttgart: Verlag Klett-Cotta, 2017.

Bontrager, Torah. *An Amish Girl in Manhattan.* New York: Know-T, 2019.

Bowler, Kate. *Blessed: A History of the American Prosperity Gospel.* New York, NY: Oxford Press, 2013.

Bowler, Kate. "Death, the Prosperity Gospel and Me." Opinion. *New York Times.* February 14, 2016. Section SR, 1.

Boyes-Watson, Carolyn. "Looking at the Past of Restorative Justice." In *Routledge International Handbook of Restorative Justice,* edited by Theo Gavrielides, 7–20. London: Routledge, 2018.

Brown v. Canada (AG). 2017 ONSC 251 [Sixties Scoop Class Action] para.7 [4].

Brueggemann, Walter. *The Prophetic Imagination.* Philadelphia: Fortress Press, 1978.

Bruenig, Emily. "What Do We Owe Her Now?" *The Washington Post,* September 19, 2018. Online: https://www.washington-post.com/graphics/2018/opinions/arlington-texas/.

Brunk, H. A. *History of Mennonites in Virginia 1727–1900.* Harrisonburg, VA: H.A. Brunk, 1959.

Buhner, Stephen Harrod. *The Fasting Path: The Way to Spiritual, Physical, and Emotional Enlightenment.* New York: Avery/Penguin, 2003.

Burkholder, Carolyn. *No More Silence.* Self-published, 2012.

Burkholder, J. Lawrence. *Mennonite Ethics: From Isolation to Engagement.* Edited by Lauren Friesen. Victoria, BC: Friesen, 2018.

Carne, Patrick J. *The Betrayal Bond.* Deerfield Beach, FL: Health Communications, 1997.

Caruth, Cathy. *Listening to Trauma: Conversations with Leaders in the Theory and Treatment of Catastrophic Experience.* Baltimore, MD: John Hopkins University Press, 2014.

Cassel, Anje Ackerman. "I, Anje." *Survivors Standing Tall.* January 31, 2018. Online: https://www.survivorsstandingtall.org/single-post/2018/01/28/The-Heart's-Unreaped-Secrets.

Chandler Burns, Steph. "Nonbinary Identity in Ruth and the Restructuring of Power." In *I've Got the Power: Naming and Reclaiming Power as a Source for Good,* edited by Jenny Castro, 95–106. Elkhart: Women in Leadership Project, Mennonite Church USA, 2018.

"Christian Fundamentals (Mennonite Church, 1921)." *Global Anabaptist Mennonite Encyclopedia Online.* Mennonite Church, June 18, 2018. Online: https://gameo.org/index.php?title=Christian_Fundamentals_(Mennonite_Church,_1921).

Clayworth, Jason, and Rodney White. "1965 Amish school photo started rural revolution." *USA Today,* May 12, 2015. Online: https://www.usatoday.com/story/news/nation/2015/05/12/amish-lost-schools-iowa/27204767/.

Clohessy, David. "Clergy Sex Abuse: Why a National All-Faiths Inquiry is Needed." *Religion News Service,* November 15, 2018.

Coffman, S.F. "Mennonite Dress Customs in Ontario." *Mennonite Historical Bulletin,* January 1955.

Cohen, Stanley. *States of Denial: Knowing about Atrocities and Suffering.* Cambridge, UK: Polity Press, 2001.

Collins, Patricia Hill. *Black Feminist Thought: Knowledge, Consciousness, and the Politics of Empowerment.* New York: Routledge, 2000.

"Columbia University at a Glance." Office of Public Affairs, Columbia University. Online: http://www.columbia.edu/cu/pr/special/cuglance.html.

Confession of Faith in a Mennonite Perspective. Scottdale, PA: Herald Press, 1995.

Cranford, Sharon, and Dwight Roth. *Kinship Concealed: Amish-Mennonite & African-American Family Connection.* Morgantown, PA: Masthof Press, 2017.

Crenshaw, Kimberlé. "Mapping the Margins: Intersectionality, Identity Politics, and Violence against Women of Color." *Stanford Law Review* 43, no. 1242 (1990–1991): 1241–1299.

Crenshaw, Kimberlé. *On Intersectionality: The Essential Writings of Kimberlé Crenshaw.* New York, NY: The New Press, 2019.

Crossley, Alison Dahl, and Shelley J. Correll, "Leader Messaging and Attitudes toward Sexual Violence." *Socius* (November 12, 2018).

Daniels, Carol Rose GoldenEagle. *Bearskin Diary.* Gibsons, BC: Nightwood Editions, 2015.

Davies, Susan E., and Eleanor H. Haney, eds. *Redefining Sexual Ethics: A Sourcebook of Essays, Stories, and Poems.* Cleveland, OH: The Pilgrim Press, 1991.

Detweiler, Richard C. *The Christian Woman's Head-Veiling: A Study of 1 Corinthians 11:2–16.* Lancaster, PA: The Christian Education Board of the Lancaster Mennonite Conference, 1972.

Detweiler, Richard C. "The Historical Background, Development, and Symbolism of the Woman's Head-Covering as Practiced in the Mennonite Church." Unpublished paper, Princeton Theological Seminary, 1966.

Dhamoon, Rita Kaur. "Considerations on Mainstreaming Intersectionality." *Political Research Quarterly* 64, no. 1 (2011): 240–43.

Douglas, Diana. "Are Private Schools Immoral?" *The Atlantic.* December 14, 2017. Online: https://www.theatlantic.com/education/archive/2017/12/progressives-are-undermining-public-schools/548084/.

Douglas, Kelly Brown. *Stand Your Ground: Black Bodies and the Justice of God.* Maryknoll, NY: Orbis, 2015.

Douglas, Kelly Brown. "When the Subjugated Come to the Center." *Journal of Religious Thought* 52, no. 2 (1996): 37–43.

Dueck, Alvin, and Thomas Parsons. "Ethics, Alterity, and Psychotherapy." *Pastoral Psychology* 55, no. 3 (2007): 271–82.

Durkheim, Emile. *The Elementary Forms of the Religious Life*. London: Allen and Unwin, 1957; c. 1915.

Epp, Marlene. "The Memory of Violence: Soviet and East European Mennonite Refugees and Rape in the Second World War." *Journal of Women's History* 9, no. 1 (Spring 1997): 58–87.

Epp, Marlene. *Mennonite Women in Canada: A History*. Winnipeg, MB: University of Manitoba Press, 2008.

Epp, Marlene. "The Semiotics of Zwieback: Feast and Famine in the Narratives of Mennonite Refugee Women." In *Sisters or Strangers? Immigrant, Ethnic and Racialized Women in Canadian History*, edited by Marlene Epp, Frances Swyripa, and Franca Iacovetta, 416–31. Toronto: University of Toronto Press, 2004.

"Erben Bekommen Weit Mehr als Bisher Angenommen." *Deutsches Wirtschaftsinstitut. Frankfurter Allgemeine*. May 7, 2017.

Everhart, Ruth. *The #MeToo Reckoning: Facing the Church's Complicity in Sexual Abuse and Misconduct*. Downers Grove, IL: Intervarsity Press, 2020.

FaithTrust Institute. Online: www.faithtrustinstitute.org.

Federici, Silvia. *Caliban and the Witch*. New York: Autonomedia, 2004.

Fiorenza, Elisabeth Schüssler. *Congress of Wo/men: Religion, Gender, and Kyriarchal Power*. Cambridge, MA: Dog Ear, 2016.

Firestone, Tirzah. *The Receiving: Reclaiming Jewish Women's Wisdom*. San Francisco: Harper Collins, 2004.

Firestone, Tirzah. *Wounds into Wisdom: Healing Intergenerational Jewish Trauma*. Rhinebeck, NY: Monkfish, 2019.

"Forbearance in the Midst of Differences." *Mennonite Church USA*. Online: https://www.mennoniteusa.org/resource-portal/resource/forbearance-in-the-midst-of-differences-2015/.

Fortune, Marie. *Domestic Violence and Its Aftermath; New perspectives on crime and justice, Occasional Papers*. Mennonite Central Committee (United States) Office of Criminal Justice: Akron, PA. August, 1989.

Fortune, Marie. *Is Nothing Sacred? When Sex Invades the Pastoral Relationship*. San Francisco: Harper & Row, 1989.

Fortune, Marie. *Responding to Clergy Misconduct: A Handbook*. Seattle: FaithTrust Institute, 2009.

Fortune, Marie. *Sexual Violence: The Sin Revisited*. Cleveland: Pilgrim Press, 2005.

Fortune, Marie. *Sexual Violence: The Unmentionable Sin*. Cleveland: Pilgrim Press, 1983.

Foucault, Michel. *Archaeology of Knowledge and the Discourse on Language*. Translated by A.M. Sheridan Smith. New York: Vintage, 1972.

Foucault, Michel. *The History of Sexuality*, vol. 1. Translated by Robert Hurley. New York: Vintage, 1980.

Fournier, Suzanne, and Ernie Crey. *Stolen From our Embrace*. Vancouver: Douglas & McIntyre, 1997.

Freyd, Jennifer J. *Betrayal Trauma: The Legacy of Forgetting Childhood Abuse*. Cambridge, MA: Harvard University Press, 1996.

Friedmann, Robert. "Gelassenheit." *Global Anabaptist Mennonite Encyclopedia Online*. December 31, 2018. Online: https://gameo.org/index.php?title=Gelassenheit&oldid=162946.

Friedman, Steven Morgan. "A Brief History of the University of Pennsylvania." *Penn University Archives & Records Center*. Online: https://archives.upenn.edu/exhibits/penn-history/brief-history.

General Assembly of the State of North Carolina and the Session of 1830–1831. Raleigh: 1831.

Gilligan, Carol and Richards, David A.J. *Darkness Now Visible: Patriarchy's Resurgence and Feminist Resistance*. Cambridge, UK: Cambridge University Press, 2018.

Gingerich, Melvin. *Mennonite Attire through Four Centuries. Publications of the Pennsylvania German Society 4*. Breinigsville, PA: The Pennsylvania German Society, 1970.

Goering, Melvin. "Dying to be Pure: The Martyr Story." *Mennonite Life* 47, no. 4 (December 1992): 9–15.

Goossen, Benjamin W. "Book Review: Martyrs Mirror: A Social History." *Mennonite World Review* February 27, 2017. Online: https://anabaptistworld.org/book-review-martyrs-mirror-a-social-history/.

Goossen, Benjamin W. *Chosen Nation: Mennonites and Germany in a Global Era*. Princeton, NJ: Princeton University Press, 2017.

Goossen, Benjamin W. "Mennonite Fascism." *Anabaptist Historians*. April 27, 2017. Online: https://anabaptisthistorians.org/2017/04/27/mennonite-fascism/.

Goossen, Benjamin W. "Mennonite War Crimes Testimony at Nuremburg." *Anabaptist Historians*. December 7, 2019. Online: https://anabaptisthistorians.org/2019/12/07/mennonite-war-crimes-testimony-at-nuremberg/.

Goossen, Rachel Waltner. "'Defanging the Beast': Mennonite Responses to John Howard Yoder's Sexual Abuse." *The Mennonite Quarterly Review* 89, no. 1 (Jan 2015): 7–80.

Graber, Barbra. "A Timeline of What Happened in Harrisonburg in 2016: My View." *Survivors Standing Tall*. February 17, 2017. Online: https://www.survivorsstandingtall.org/single-post/2017/09/02/A-Timeline-of-What-Happened-in-Harrisonburg-My-View.

Graybill, Beth, and Linda B. Arthur. "The Social Control of Women's Bodies in Two Mennonite Communities." In *Religion, Dress and the Body*, edited by Linda B. Arthur, 9–29. New York: Berg, 2000.

Halifax, Joan. *Standing at the Edge: Finding Freedom where Fear and Courage Meet*. New York: Flatiron, 2018.

Hamilton, Marci. *God vs. the Gavel: The Perils of Extreme Religious Liberty*. 2nd ed. Cambridge, UK: Cambridge University Press, 2014.

Hamilton, Marci A. *Justice Denied: What America Must Do to Protect Its Children*. Cambridge, UK: Cambridge University Press, 2012.

Hammerschlag, Carl A. *The Dancing Healers: A Doctor's Journey of Healing with Native Americans*. San Francisco: Harper San Francisco, 1988.

Hanson, Erin. "The Sixties Scoop & Aboriginal Child Welfare." Indigenous Foundations. Online: https://indigenousfoundations.arts.ubc.ca/sixties_scoop/.

Harder, Lydia Neufeld. *Obedience, Suspicion, and the Gospel of Mark: A Mennonite Feminist Exploration of Biblical Authority*. Waterloo, ON: Wilfred Laurier University Press, 1998.

Harris, Maria. Australia Truth and Justice Commission. *The Irish Catholic*. Online: http://www.irishcatholic.ie/article/synod-briefs.

Harrison, Beverly Wildung. *Making the Connections: Essays in Feminist Social Ethics*, edited by Carol S. Robb. Boston, MA: Beacon Press, 1985.

Hart, Chloe Grace, Alison Dahl Crossley, and Shelley J. Correll. "Leader Messaging and Attitudes toward Sexual Violence." *Socius* 4 (November 12, 2018). Online: https://doi.org/10.1177/2378023118808617.

Hartman, Jerry. *The Doctrine of Discovery: In the Name of Christ.* Dismantling the Doctrine of Discovery Coalition, 2015. Online: https://dofdmenno.org/movie/.

Hartzler, Rachel Nafziger. *No Strings Attached: Boundary Lines in Pleasant Places: A History of Warren Street/Pleasant Oaks Mennonite Church.* Eugene, OR: Resource Publications, 2013.

Heaney, Katie. "Almost No One Is Falsely Accused of Rape." *The Cut.* October 5, 2018.

Heggen, Carolyn Holderread. *Sexual Abuse in Christian Homes and Churches.* Scottdale, PA: Herald Press, 1993.

Herman, Judith L. *Father-Daughter Incest.* Cambridge: Harvard University Press, 1981/2000.

Herman, Judith L. *Trauma and Recovery: The Aftermath of Violence from Domestic Abuse to Political Terror.* New York: Basic Books, 1997/2015.

Hermans, William. *Einstein and the Poet: In Search of the Cosmic Man.* Brookline Village, MA: Branden Press, 1983.

Hess, Cynthia. *Sites of Violence, Sites of Grace: Christian Nonviolence and the Traumatized Self.* Plymouth, United Kingdom: Lexington, 2009.

Heyward, Carter. *The Redemption of God: A Theology of Mutual Relation.* Lanham, MD: University Press of America, 1980.

"History & Vision," *Pink Menno.* http.//www.pinkmenno.org/history-vision/.

Hoover, Allen, and Jeanette Harder. *For the Sake of a Child: Love, Safety, and Abuse in Plain Communities.* Stoneboro, PA: Ridgeway, 2019.

Hopkins, Julie. "The Epiphany of the Dove: Healing and Prophecy in Mark's Gospel (New Approaches in Women's Studies)." In *Biblical Interpretation: The Meanings of Scripture – Past and Present,* edited by John M. Court, 285–309. London: T & T Clark International, 2003.

Horton, Anne L., and Judith A. Williamson, eds. *Abuse and Religion: When Praying Isn't Enough*. Boston: Lexington/D.C Heath, 1989.

Hostetler, John A. *Amish Society*. 4th ed. Baltimore, MD: The Johns Hopkins University Press, 1993.

Houser, Gordon and Hannah Heinzekehr. "Church acknowledges reports of abusive relationship with Hartman." *The Mennonite*, March 24, 2016. Online: https://themennonite.org/daily-news/church-acknowledges-reports-abusive-relationship-hartman/.

Huber, Tim. "Conference to License Gay Pastor." *Mennonite World Review*, January 6, 2014, 1, 14.

Huber, Tim. "Lancaster Conference to Leave Denomination." *Mennonite World Review*, December 7, 2015.

Human Rights Watch. "LGBT Rights." Online: https://www.hrw.org/topic/lgbt-rights.

Hurst, Brenda Martin. *The Articulation of Mennonite Beliefs about Sexuality, 1890–1930*. PhD dissertation. Richmond, VA: Union Theological Seminary, 2003.

Hymnal: A Worship Book. Elgin, IL: Brethren Press, 1992.

"Impact of the 'Doctrine of Discovery' on Indigenous Peoples." *United Nations Department of Economic and Social Affairs*. June 1, 2012. https://www.un.org/en/development/desa/newsletter/desanews/dialogue/2012/06/3801.html.

An Inclusive Language Lectionary. Louisville: John Knox Press, 1990.

Into Account. "About: Into Account." Online: https://intoaccount.org/about/.

Isasi-Díaz, Ada María. *En La Lucha—In the Struggle: Elaborating a Mujerista Theology*. Minneapolis: Fortress, 2004.

Jacobson, Matthew Frye. *Whiteness of a Different Color: European Immigrants and the Alchemy of Race.* Cambridge, MA: Harvard University Press, 1998.

Janoff-Bultmann, Ronnie. *Shattered Assumptions: Towards a New Psychology of Trauma.* New York: Free Press/Macmillan International, 1992.

Jantz, Harold. "Women and community sort fall-out from sexual abuse." *Christian Week,* October 5, 1993.

Jenkins, Philip. *Jesus Wars: How Four Patriarchs, Three Queens, and Two Emperors Decided What Christians Would Believe for the Next 1,500 Years.* New York: HarperCollins, 2010.

Ji-Sun Kim, Grace, and Susan M. Shaw. *Intersectional Theology: An Introductory Guide.* Minneapolis: Fortress, 2018.

Johnson-Weiner, Karen M. *The Lives of Amish Women.* Baltimore: Johns Hopkins University Press, 2020.

Johnston, Patrick. *Native Children and the Welfare System.* Toronto: James Lorimer and the Canadian Council on Social Development, 1983.

Juhnke, James C. "Martyr We Remember Most." *Mennonite World Review,* November 14, 2011. Online: https://www.mennoworld.org/archived/2011/11/14/martyr-we-remember-most/.

Juhnke, James C. "Rightly Remembering a Martyr Heritage." *Mennonite Life* 58, no. 3 (September 2003). Online: https://mla.bethelks.edu/ml-archive/2003Sept/juhnke.php.

Kahl, Brigitte. *Galatians Re-Imagined: Reading with the Eyes of the Vanquished.* Minneapolis, MN: Fortress, 2010.

Kasdorf, Julia. *Eve's Striptease* Pittsburgh: University of Pittsburgh Press, 1998.

Kasdorf, Julia Spicher. "Mightier than the Sword: Martyrs Mirror in the New World," *The Conrad Grebel Review* 31, no. 1 (Winter 2013): 44–70.

Kauffman, Daniel, ed. *Doctrines of the Bible: A Brief Discussion of the Teachings of God's Word.* 2nd ed. Scottdale, PA: Mennonite Publishing House, 1929.

Kauffman, Daniel. *Manual of Bible Doctrines: Setting Forth the General Principles of the Plan of Salvation, Explaining the Symbolical Meaning and Practical Use of the Ordinances Instituted by Christ and His Apostles, and Pointing out Specifically Some of the Restrictions Which the New Testament Scriptures Enjoined upon Believers.* Elkhart, IN: Mennonite Publishing, 1898.

Kauffman, Jeffrey, ed. *Loss of the Assumptive World: A Theory of Traumatic Loss.* New York: Routledge, 2002.

Kelly, John. "'Guns' Running: A Distinctive Sculpture from D.C.'s Dark Days is on the Move Again." *The Washington Post*, September 11, 2017. Online: https://www.washingtonpost.com/local/guns-running-a-distinctive-sculpture-from-dcs-dark-days-is-on-the-move-again/2017/09/11/38b027a2-96fa-11e7-87fc-c3f7ee4035c9_story.html?noredirect=on&utm_term=.a6f463120786.

Kerr, Michael, E. *Bowen Theory's Secrets: Revealing the Hidden Life of Families.* New York and London: Norton and Company, 2019.

Khazan, Olga. "Can Game Theory Help to Prevent Rape?" *The Atlantic.* September 17, 2015.

Klassen, Pamela E. *Going by the Moon and the Stars: Stories of Two Russian Mennonite Women.* Waterloo, ON: Wilfrid Laurier University Press, 1994.

Klassen, William, and Hans-Juergen Goertz. "Discipleship." *Global Anabaptist Mennonite Encyclopedia Online.* 2019. Online: http://gameo.org/index.php?title=Discipleship&oldid=103766.

Koontz, Gayle Gerber. "Introduction." In *Peace Theology and Violence against Women,* edited by Elizabeth G. Yoder, 1–4. Elkhart, IN: Institute of Mennonite Studies, 1992.

Kralik, Alexandra. "We Finally Understand that Gender isn't Binary. Sex isn't Either." *SLATE* November 13, 2018. Online: https://slate.com/technology/2018/11/sex-binary-gender-neither-exist.html.

Krall, Ruth E. *Clergy and Religious Leader Abuse of the Laity: Religious and Spiritual Consequences.* Self-published, 2017. Online: https://ruthkrall.com/downloadable-books/religious-and-spiritual-consequences/.

Krall, Ruth E. *Soul Betrayal: Spiritual and Religious Trauma.* Self-published, 2016. Online: https://ruthkrall.com/downloadable-books/soul-betrayal-spiritual-and-religious-trauma/.

Kraybill, Donald B. "Mennonite Woman's Veiling: The Rise and Fall of a Sacred Symbol." *Mennonite Quarterly Review* 61, no. 3 (1987): 298–320.

Krehbiel, Stephanie. "Our Rock is the Truth." *Into Account.* October 24, 2018. Online: https://intoaccount.org/2018/10/24/our-rock-is-the-truth/.

Krehbiel, Stephanie. "Staying Alive: How Martyrdom Made Me a Warrior." In *Tongue Screws and Testimonies: Poems, Stories and Essays Inspired by the "Martyrs Mirror,"* edited by Kirsten Eve Beachy, 133–44. Scottdale, PA: Herald, 2010.

Krehbiel, Stephanie. "Who Defines Celibacy? Why Mennonite Central Committee's 'Lifestyle' Policy Enables Sexual Harassment." *Into Account.* May 2, 2018. Online: https://intoaccount.org/2018/05/02/who-defines-celibacy-why-mennonite-central-committees-lifestyle-policy-enables-sexual-harassment/.

Lamott, Anne. *Bird by Bird: Some Instructions on Writing and Life.* New York: Anchor, 1994.

Lapide, Pinchas. *Er predigte in ihren Synagogen/Jüdische Evangelienausleg.* Gütersloher Verlaghaus Gerd Mohn, Gütersloh, 1980.

Lebacqz, Karen and Ronald G. Barton, *Sex in the Parish*. Louisville: Westminster/John Knox, 1991.

Lederach, John Paul. *Preparing for Peace: Conflict Transformation across Cultures*. Syracuse, NY: Syracuse University Press, 1995.

Leichty, Joseph. "Staying Mennonite: Why Martyrs Still Matter." *Mennonite Life* 62, no.1 (Spring 2007). Online: https://mla. bethelks.edu/ml-archive/2007spring/liechty.php].

Leotta, Allison. "I Was a Sex-Crimes Prosecutor. Here's Why 'He Said, She Said' Is a Myth." *Time Magazine*. October 3, 2018. Online: https://time.com/5413814/he-said-she-said-kavanaugh-ford-mitchell/.

Levine, Peter A. *Trauma and Memory: Brain and Body in a Search for the Living Past*. Berkeley, CA: North Atlantic, 2015.

Linder, Douglas. "Yoder v. Wisconsin: The Amish Challenge Compulsory Education Laws." *University of Missouri-Kansas City School of Law*. Online: https://law2.umkc.edu/faculty/projects/ftrials/conlaw/YoderStory.html.

Litz, Brett.T., Nathan Stein, Eileen Delaney, Leslie Lebowitz, William P. Nash, Caroline Silva, and Shira Maguen. "Moral Injury and Moral Repair in War Veterans: A Preliminary Model and Intervention Strategy." *Clinical Psychology Review*, 29 (2009): 695–706.

Loewen, Harris J. "New Earth, Heavens New." *Assembly Songs— A Hymnal Supplement: Hymns Both New and Old*. Scottdale, PA: Faith and Life, 1983.

London, Ross. "A New Paradigm Arises." In *A Restorative Justice Reader,* edited by Gerry Johnstone. 2nd ed. Gerry Johnstone. New York: Routledge, 2013.

Luthy, David. *Dirk Willems: His Noble Deed Lives On*. Aylmer, ON: Pathway, 2011.

Martin, Darvin L. *A Clash of Cultures: Native Americans and Colonization in Lancaster County* Morgantown, PA: Masthof, 2008.

Martin, Harold S. *The Scriptural Headveiling.* Carollton, OH: Amish Mennonite Publications, 1981.

Mast, C. Z. *Mast Family History.* Scottdale, PA: Mennonite Publishing House, 1911.

McCrummen, Stephanie, Beth Reinhard, and Alice Crites. "Woman Says Roy Moore initiated sexual encounter when she was 14, he was 32." *Washington Post*, November 9, 2017.

Melcher, Ruth Elizabeth. *Borne on the Danube: A Danube Swabian Story.* Boulder, CO: Barky, 2002.

"Membership Guidelines." *Mennonite Church USA.* Online: https://mennoniteusa.org/wp-content/uploads/2015/03/MembershipGuidelines_2013_July.pdf.

Mendelsohn, Michaela; Judith Lewis Herman, Emily Schatzoa, Melissa Coco, Dya Kallivayalil, and Jocelyn Levitan. *The Trauma Recovery Group: A Guide for Practitioners.* New York: Guilford, 2011.

Mennonite Central Committee. "Abuse: Response and prevention: A guide for church leaders." 2012. https://mcc.org/media/resources/1134.

"Mennonite Confession of Faith, 1963." *Global Anabaptist Mennonite Encyclopedia Online.* http://gameo.org/index.php?title=Mennonite_Confession_of_Faith,_1963&oldid=100737.

Meyer, Stephen Grant. *As Long as they Don't Move Next Door: Segregation and Racial Conflict in American Neighborhoods.* Lanham, MD: Rowman and Littlefield, 1999.

M.G. "Save the Apology, We Need Accountability: Spoken Word by M.G," *Our Stories Untold.* July 25, 2016. Online: http://www.ourstoriesuntold.com/m-g-s-spoken-word-taking-a-stand-against-rape/.

M.G. "We Can Do Better: How my Report of Rape at a Christian School Made Things Worse." *Our Stories Untold*. July 25, 2016. Online: http://www.ourstoriesuntold.com/we-can-do-better/.

Miller, Alice. *Breaking Down the Wall of Silence: The Liberating Experience of Facing Painful Truth*. New York, NY: Penguin/Dutton, 1991.

Miller, Melissa. *Family Violence: The Compassionate Church Responds*. Scottdale, PA: Herald, 1994.

Miller, Robert J. *Native America, Discovered and Conquered: Thomas Jefferson, Lewis and Clark, and Manifest Destiny*. Lincoln, NE: University of Nebraska Press, 2008.

Minutes of the 64th Session of the Conference of Mennonites in Canada. In *the 1966 Yearbook*. Winnipeg, MB (July 6–10, 1966), 1.

Mitchell, Robert D. "From the Ground Up: Space, Place, and Diversity in Frontier Studies." In *Diversity & Accommodation: Essays on the Cultural Composition of the Virginia Frontier*, edited by Michael J. Puglisi, 23–58. Knoxville: The University of Tennessee Press, 1997.

Muller, Wayne. *Legacy of the Heart: The Spiritual Advantages of a Painful Childhood*. New York, NY: Simon and Schuster Touchstone, 1993.

Nason-Clark, Nancy. *The Battered Wife: How Christians Confront Family Violence*. Louisville, KY: Westminster John Knox, 1997.

Nepo, Mark. *The One Life We're Given: Finding the Wisdom that Waits in Your Heart*. New York: Atria, 2016.

Newsom, Carol A., and Sharon H. Ringe. *The Women's Bible Commentary*. Louisville: Westminster, 1992.

Niebuhr, Reinhold. *The Nature and Destiny of Man: A Christian Interpretation*. New York: Charles Scribner's Sons, 1964.

Nussbaum, Martha. *Anger and Forgiveness: Resentment, Generosity, Justice.* New York: Oxford University Press, 2016.

Nyce, Dorothy Yoder. "Head Covering." *Global Anabaptist Mennonite Encyclopedia Online,* 1989. Online: http://gameo.org/index.php?title=Prayer_Veil&oldid=143665.

O'Donnell, Karen, and Katie Cross, eds. *Feminist Trauma Theologies: Body, Scripture and Church in Critical Perspective.* London: SCM Press, 2020.

"On the Status of the Membership Guidelines." *Mennonite Church USA.* Online: http://www.mennoniteusa.org/wp-content/uploads/2015/07/ResolutionOnStatusofMembershiPGuidelines_2015Jul02.

Oudshoorn, Judah; Lorraine Stutzman Amstutz and Michelle Jackett. *The Little Book of Restorative Justice for Sexual Abuse: Hope through Trauma.* New York: Good Books, 2015.

Our Stories Untold. "About: Our Stories Untold." Online: http://www.ourstoriesuntold.com/about/.

Oyer, John S. "Suffering." *Global Anabaptist Mennonite Encyclopedia Online.* Online: https://gameo.org/index.php?title=Suffering&oldid=162896.

Painter, Nell Irvin. "Nell Irvin Painter on Soul Murder and Slavery." *Africans in America. PBS.* Online: http://www.pbs.org/wgbh/aia/part4/4i3084.html.

Painter, Nell Irvin. "Soul Murder and Slavery." The Fifteenth Annual Charles Edmondson Historical Lecture, Baylor University. Waco, Texas, April 5–6, 1993.

Paris, Susanne Sartor. "The Bible on Steroids: The Effect of Androcentrism on the Lectionary." *New Theology Review* 15, no. 1 (February 2002): 21–31.

Peachey, Linda Gehman. "Naming the Pain, Seeking the Light: The Mennonite Church's Response to Sexual Abuse." *Mennonite Quarterly Review* 89, no. 1 (January 2015): 111–28.

Penner, Carol. "Content to Suffer: An Exploration of Mennonite Theology from the Context of Violence against Women." In *Peace Theology and Violence against Women*, edited by Elizabeth G. Yoder, 99–111. Elkhart, IN: Institute of Mennonite Studies, 1992.

Penner, Carol. "How Inclusive Is the Inclusive Church?" In *At Peace and Unafraid: Public Order, Security, and the Wisdom of the Cross*, eds. Duane K. Friesen and Gerald W. Schlabach, 195–210. Scottdale, PA: Herald, 2005.

Penner, Carol. "Jesus and the Stories of our Lives." In *Liberating the Politics of Jesus: Renewing Peace Theology Through the Wisdom of Women*, edited by Elizabeth Soto Albrecht and Darryl W. Stephens, 33–52. New York: Bloomsbury / T&T Clark, 2020.

Penner, Carol. *LeadingInWorship* (blog). Online: https://www.leadinginworship.com.

Penner, Carol. "Mennonite Silences and Feminist Voices: Peace Theology and Violence against Women." PhD diss., University of St. Michael's College, 1999.

Penner, Carol. "Mennonite Women Doing Theology: A Methodological Reflection on Twenty-five Years of Conferences." In *Recovering from the Anabaptist Vision: New Essays in Anabaptist Identity and Theological Method*, edited by Laura Schmidt Roberts, Paul Martens and Myron Penner, 53–76. New York: Bloomsbury / T & T Clark, 2020.

Penner, Carol. "Violence Against Women in the Mennonite Brethren Church: Abuse Policies Are Not Enough." *Direction* 45, no. 2 (Fall 2016): 192–208.

Penner, Kimberly L. "Erotic Peacemaking: Toward a Feminist Mennonite Theo-ethics of Embodiment and Sexuality." PhD diss., University of St. Michael's College, 2017.

Penner, Kimberly L. "Mennonite Peace Theology and Violence against Women." *Conrad Grebel Review* 35, no. 3 (2017): 280–92.

Poling, James N. *The Abuse of Power: A Theological Problem.* Nashville: Abingdon, 1991.

Power, Garrett. "Apartheid Baltimore Style: The Residential Segregation Ordinances of 1910–1913." *Maryland Law Review* 42, no. 2 (1983): 289–328.

Pranis, Kay. "Peacemaking Circles." In *A Restorative Justice Reader*, edited by Gerry Johnstone, 117–21. 2nd ed. New York: Routledge, 2013.

Preheim, Rich. "Mennonites apologize for history of sex abuse following theologian John Howard Yoder Scandal." *The Washington Post.* July 7, 2015. Online: https://www.washingtonpost.com/national/religion/mennonites-apologize-for-history-of-sex-abuse-following-theologian-john-howard-yoder-scandal/2015/07/07/9fdb2092-24b7-11e5-b621-b55e495e9b78_story.html.

Proctor-Smith, Marjorie. "Lectionaries—Principles and Problems: Alternative Perspectives." *Studia Liturgica* 22 (1992): 84–99.

Proctor-Smith, Marjorie. *Praying with Our Eyes Open: Engendering Feminist Liturgical Prayer.* Nashville: Abingdon, 1995.

Rambo, Shelly. *Resurrecting Wounds: Living in the Afterlife of Trauma.* Waco, TX: Baylor University Press, 2017.

Ramer, Megan. "Letter to the Pastoral Leadership Team of the Pacific Northwest Mennonite Conference." Unpublished letter. January 30, 2019.

Reaves, Jayme R., and David Toombs. "#MeToo Jesus: Naming Jesus as a Victim of Sexual Abuse." *International Journal of Public Theology* 13 (2019): 387–412.

Rebell, Michael A. *Flunking Democracy: Schools, Courts, and Civic Participation.* Chicago: University of Chicago Press, 2018.

Redekop, Benjamin W., and Calvin W. Redekop, eds. *Power, Authority, and the Anabaptist Tradition.* Baltimore: Johns Hopkins University Press, 2001.

Reimer, Margaret Loewen. "Kristen Uncovers Her Aboriginal Heritage." *Mennonite Reporter*, September 20, 1993, 5.

RFI. "Top Catholic Church Official Says Files on Pedophile Priests Were Destroyed." *France Médias Monde*. February 23, 2019.

Robbennolt, Jennifer K. "Apologies and Medical Error." *Clinical Orthopedics and Related Research* 467, no. 2 (2009): 376–82.

Robinson, Leah. *Embodied Peacebuilding: Reconciliation as Practical Theology*. Bern, Switzerland: Peter Lang, 2015.

Rogalsky, Dave. "A Voice from Outside the Gate," *Canadian Mennonite* 21, no. 7, (March 22, 2017).

Rosenbloom, Dena, and Mary Beth Williams. *Life After Trauma*. 2nd ed. New York: Guilford, 2010.

Roth, John D. trans. and ed. *Letters of the Amish Division: A Sourcebook*. 2nd ed. Goshen, IN: Mennonite Historical Society, 2002.

Roth, John D. "Mennonites and Land." *The Mennonite*. February 1, 2014. Online: https://themennonite.org/opinion/mennonites-land/.

Rudy-Froese, Allan. "Preaching." Course at Conrad Grebel University College. Waterloo, June 2017.

Ruether, Rosemary Radford. *Sexism and God-Talk: Toward a Feminist Theology*. Boston: Beacon, 1983.

Russell, Letty M. "Inclusive Language and Power." *Religious Education* 80, no. 4 (Fall 1985): 582–602.

Russell, Shari. "Still Questioning: The Theft of Indigenous Children." *Intotemak* (Fall/Winter, 2016): 28–31.

Ruth, John L. *The Earth Is the Lord's: A Narrative History of the Lancaster Mennonite Conference*. Studies in Anabaptist and Mennonite History, no. 39. Scottdale, PA: Herald, 2001.

Rutter, Peter. *Sex in the Forbidden Zone: When Men in Power Abuse Women's Trust*. Los Angeles: Jeremy P. Tarcher, 1989.

Salter, Anna. *Predators: Pedophiles, Rapists, and Other Sex Offenders*. New York: Basic Books, 2003.

Sammis, John Henry. "Trust and Obey." English lyrics. Online: https://www.hymnal.net/en/hymn/h/582.

Saussy, Carroll. *God Images and Self Esteem: Empowering Women in a Patriarchal Society*. Louisville, KY: Westminster/John Knox, 1991.

Schirch, Lisa. "Afterword: To the Next Generation of Pacifist Theologians." In *John Howard Yoder: Radical Theologian*, edited by J. Denny Weaver. Eugene, OR: Wipf and Stock, 2014.

Schirch, Lisa. "Sexual Abuse in Mennonite Contexts." *The Mennonite*. September 7, 2016.

Schirch, Lisa. "Toward Mennonite Sexual Integrity." *Mennonite World Review*. March 23, 2015.

Schrag, Paul. "MC USA Won't Recognize Colorado Pastor's Licensing." *Mennonite World Review*, July 7, 2014. 1, 13.

Schrag, Paul. "Membership Rules Divide Delegates: Effort to Pass U.S. Guidelines Fails; Two-Year Delay Gets Approved." *Mennonite Weekly Review*. July 29, 1999. 1–2.

Schrag, Paul. "Mennonite Church USA Formed as Delegates Approve Membership Rules." *Mennonite Weekly Review*. July 12, 2001.

Schrag, Paul. "What Works for Denominations Now?" *Mennonite World Review*, December 19, 2015. 12.

"Sexual Violence." *Center for Disease Control and Prevention*. January 17, 2020. Online: https://www.cdc.gov/violenceprevention/sexualviolence/fastfact.html. Sheppard, Phillis Isabella. *Self, Culture, and Others in Womanist Practical Theology*. New York: Palgrave Macmillan, 2011.

Showalter, Shirley Hershey. "Mennonite Bonnet and Covering Stories: Part One." *Magical Memoir Moments* (blog). February 19, 2014. Online: https://www.shirleyshowalter.com/mennonite-bonnet-and-covering-stories-part-one/.

Smith, Elizabeth J. *Bearing Fruit in Due Season: Feminist Hermeneutics and the Bible in Worship*. Collegeville, MN: Liturgical Press, 1999.

Snyder, C. Arnold, and Hecht, Linda A. Huebert, eds. *Profiles of Anabaptist Women: Sixteenth-Century Reforming Pioneers*. Studies in Women and Religion 3. Waterloo, ON: Wilfrid Laurier University Press, 1996.

Sojourners. "100 Sermons." Online: https://sojo.net/100sermons.

STAR Level I Participant Manual. Harrisonburg: Eastern Mennonite University, 2009.

"Statistics." *National Coalition against Domestic Violence*. Online: https://ncadv.org/statistics.

Stella, Rachel. "Dark Side to Amish Religious Freedom?" *Mennonite World Review*. August 13, 2018. Online: https://mennoworld.org/2018/08/13/news/dark-side-to-amish-religious-freedom.

Stenson, Esther. "Veiled and Free." *The Mennonite*. April 6, 2010. Online: https://themennonite.org/feature/veiled-free/.

Stoltzfus, Louise. *Quiet Shouts: Stories of Lancaster Mennonite Women Leaders*. Scottdale, PA: Herald, 1999.

Strochlic, Nina. "An Unlikely Feud Between Beekeepers and Mennonites Simmers in Mexico," *National Geographic*. April 12, 2019. Online: https://api.nationalgeographic.com/distribution/public/amp/environment/2019/04/unlikely-feud-beekeepers-mennonites-simmers-mexico.

Sugrue, Thomas J. *Sweet Land of Liberty: The Forgotten Struggle for Civil Rights in the North*. New York: Random House, 2008.

Swana Falaga, Sidonie, "La vie sexuelle chez les Pende hier et aujourd'hui: cas des Pende du territoire de Gungu, Province de Bandundu, RDC." [Sexual life of the Pende Yesterday and Today: The Case of the Pende of the Territory of Gungu, Bandundu Province]. Master's Thesis. Universite Protestante de Kinshasa, 1995.

Swana Falaga, Sidonie. "Marriage is words—and affectionate practices: Lessons from Congo on enhancing sex in marriage." Translated by Sylvia Shirk Charles. *Vision* 9, no 2 (Fall 2008): 82–86.

Takao Ozawa v. United States, 260 U.S. 178 (1922).

Thieleman J. van, Jan Luiken, and Pieter Jansz. *The Bloody Theater: or, Martyrs Mirror of the Defenseless Christians Who Baptized Only Upon Confession of Faith, and who Suffered and Died for the Testimony of Jesus, Their Savior, from the Time of Christ to the Year A.D. 1660.* Scottdale, PA: Herald, 1987.

Thompson, John B. *Studies in the Theory of Ideology.* Cambridge: Polity, 1984.

Trible, Phyllis. *Texts of Terror: Literary Feminist Readings of Biblical Narratives.* Philadelphia: Fortress, 1984.

Trothen, Tracey J. *Shattering the Illusion: Child Sexual Abuse and Canadian Religious Institutions.* Waterloo, ON: Wilfrid Laurier University Press, 2012.

Truth and Reconciliation Commission of Canada. Online: https://www.trc-ca.

Tuck, Eve, and K. Wayne Yang, "Decolonization Is Not A Metaphor." *Decolonization: Indigeneity, Education & Society* 1, no.1 (2012): 1–40.

"UN Issues First Report on Human Rights of Gay and Lesbian People." *UN News.* December 15, 2011. Online: https://news.un.org/en/story/2011/12/398432-un-issues-first-report-human-rights-gay-and-lesbian-people.

United Nations General Assembly, Resolution 48-10. December 20, 1993. "Declaration on the Elimination of Violence Against Women."

"Urgency. Accountability. Transparency: Lessons from Maple Leaf Foods SVP Randy Huffman." *NEWS@IVEY.* November 26, 2014.

Van der Kolk, Bessel. *The Body Keeps the Score: Brain, Mind, and Body in the Healing of Trauma*. New York: Penguin, 2014.

Van der Kolk, Bessel, Alexander C. McFarlane, and Lars Weisaeth. *Traumatic Stress: The Effects of Overwhelming Experiences on Mind, Body and Society*. New York, NY: Guilford, 1996.

van Uden, Dodo, "Weg van de Tora." Part VII, 104–107. Amsterdam, NL: Algemene Doopsgezinde Sociëteit, 2019.

Volf, Miroslav. *The End of Memory: Remembering Rightly in a Violent World*. Grand Rapids: Eerdmans, 2006.

Walker, Alice. *In Search of Our Mothers Gardens: Womanist Prose*. San Diego: Harcourt, Brace, Jovanovich, 1983.

Walker, Connie. *Missing and Murdered: Finding Cleo*. CBC Radio. Podcast Audio. April 2, 2018. Online: https://www.cbc.ca/radio/findingcleo.

"The Walking Purchase." *Official Website of the Delaware Tribe of Indians*. Online: http://delawaretribe.org/blog/2013/06/27/the-walking-purchase/.

Waite, Gary K. *Eradicating the Devil's Minions: Anabaptist Witches in Reformation Europe*. Toronto: University of Toronto Press, 2007.

Weaver, Laura H. "Writing about the Covering and Plain Clothes as a Mennonite 'Family' Possession." *Mennonite Life* 49 (December 1994): 4–7.

Weaver-Zercher, David L. *Martyrs Mirror: A Social History*. Baltimore: Johns Hopkins University Press, 2016.

Weber, Max. *From Max Weber: Essays in Sociology*. Edited by S. M. Miller. New York: Thomas Y. Crowell Co., 1963. *Een keuze uit het werk van Max Weber* (A selection from the work of Max Weber), translated into Dutch from German original by G.R. de Bruin. Deventer, NL: Van Loghum Slaterus, 1975.

Weingarten, Kaethe. *Common Shock: Witnessing Violence Every Day: How We Are Harmed, How We Can Heal*. New York: Dutton, 2003.

Wenger, Elizabeth. *Foretaste: Poems*. Goshen, IN: Pinchpenny, 1972.

Wenger, Elizabeth. *Heal on Monday: 31 Poems with Line Drawings*. Goshen, IN: Pinchpenny, 1974.

Wenger, John Christian. *The Prayer Veil in Scripture and History: The New Testament Symbol of Women as the Glory of the Race*. Scottdale, PA: Herald, 1977.

Wenger, John C., and Elmer S. Yoder. "Prayer Veil." *Global Anabaptist Mennonite Encyclopedia Online*. Online: http://gameo.org/index.php?title=Prayer_Veil&oldid=143665.

Wenger, John Christian. *Separated unto God: A Plea for Christian Simplicity of Life and for a Scriptural Nonconformity to the World*. Scottdale, PA: Mennonite Publishing House, 1951.

West, Traci C. *Disruptive Christian Ethics: When Racism and Women's Lives Matter*. Louisville: Westminster John Knox, 2006.

White, Josh. "Vienna Presbyterian Church Seeks Forgiveness, Redemption in Wake of Abuse Scandal," *Washington Post*. April 2, 2011.

Wiebe, Katie Funk. "Me Tarzan, Son of Menno—You Jane, Mennonite Mama." *Journal of Mennonite Studies* 17 (1999): 9–21.

Wiesel, Elie. *The Night Trilogy: Night, Dawn, Day*. New York: Hill and Wang, 2008.

Williams, Delores. *Sisters in the Wilderness: The Challenge of Womanist God-talk*. Maryknoll, NY: Orbis, 1993.

Williams, Delores S. "Womanist Theology: Black Women's Voices." *Christianity in Crisis* 47, no. 3 (March 1987): 66–70.

Winter, Miriam Therese. *WomanWisdom: A Feminist Lectionary and Psalter: Women of the Hebrew Scriptures*. New York: Crossroad, 1991.

Winter, Miriam Therese. *WomanWord: A Feminist Lectionary and Psalter: Women of the New Testament.* New York: Crossroad, 1990.

Wisconsin v. Yoder. 406 U.S. 205 (1972).

Wood, Karenne. *The Virginia Indian Heritage Trail.* Charlottesville: Virginia Council on Indians, Virginia Foundation for the Humanities and Public Policy, 2007.

Yantzi, Mark. *Sexual Offending and Restoration.* Scottdale, PA: Herald, 1998.

Yoder, Carolyn. *Little Book of Trauma Healing.* Intercourse, PA: Good Books, 2005.

Yoder, Elizabeth G., ed. *Peace Theology and Violence against Women.* Elkhart, IN: Institute of Mennonite Studies, 1992.

Zehr, Howard. *Little Book of Restorative Justice.* Intercourse, PA: Good Books, 2002.

Zijpp, Nanne van der, Harold S. Bender and Richard D. Thiessen. "Martyrs' Mirror." *Global Anabaptist Mennonite Encyclopedia Online.* Online: https://gameo.org/index.php?title=Martyrs%27_Mirror&oldid=163291.

Made in the USA
Middletown, DE
04 September 2022

73166221R00268